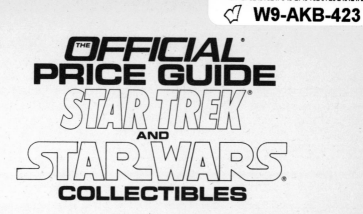

THE OFFICIAL
PRICE GUIDE
STAR TREK
AND
STAR WARS
COLLECTIBLES

THE OFFICIAL PRICE GUIDE
STAR TREK AND STAR WARS COLLECTIBLES
THIRD EDITION

SUE CORNWELL AND MIKE KOTT

HOUSE OF COLLECTIBLES
NEW YORK

Important Notice. All of the information, including valuations, in this book has been compiled from the most reliable sources, and every effort has been made to eliminate errors and questionable data. Nevertheless, the possibility of error, in a work of such immense scope, always exists. The publisher will not be held responsible for losses which may occur in the purchase, sale, or other transaction of items because of information contained herein. Readers who feel they have discovered errors are invited to *write* and inform us, so they may be corrected in subsequent editions. Those seeking further information on the topics covered in this book are advised to refer to the complete line of *Official Price Guides* published by the House of Collectibles.

© 1991 Random House, Inc.

This is a registered trademark of Random House, Inc.

All rights reserved under International and Pan-American Copyright Conventions.

Published by: House of Collectibles
201 East 50th Street
New York, New York 10022

Distributed by Ballantine Books, a division of Random House, Inc., New York, and simultaneously in Canada by Random House of Canada Limited, Toronto.

Text design by Holly Johnson

Part title pages designed by Philip Draggan

Manufactured in the United States of America

Library of Congress Catalog Card Number: 84-644977

ISBN: 0-876-37831-9

Third Edition: September 1991

10 9 8 7 6

TABLE OF CONTENTS

STAR WARS

ACKNOWLEDGMENTS

We wish to express our sincere thanks to all those people who have contributed to this book in the past and, in particular, to those listed below who helped make this edition possible.

Audrey K. Anderson, St. Paul, MN; Linda, Roger, and Jeremy Baird, Salinas, CA; Robin Bowden, AZ; Richard M. Brown, Detroit, MI; Jim Butterbaugh, Albuquerque, NM; Betsy Caprio, Culver City, CA; John Chintala, Exeter, PA; Ben H. Cooper, Hyndman, PA; Megan E. Dargen, Tacoma, WA; Victor A. Darrin, Yuba City, CA; Robert Daugherty, Barstow, CA; Jody Davies, Oneonta, NY; Bob Douglas, Canada; Juliet Gourd, Winfield, IL; Matthew Gross, Portland, OR; Jeff Grossman, Larchmont, NY; Melanie Guttierez, New Orleans, LA: Chuck and Carol Ann Hale, Mountain View, CA: Eddie Van Der Heijden, The Netherlands; Cindy Helferstay, Torrance, CA; Laurie Hock, Kanas City, KS; Kevin Hollaway, Sunnyvale, TX; Anthony Innarelli, Lilburn, GA; Thill Jean-Luc, Luxembourg; Jay Jengo, Colonia, NJ; Lynn Jones, Lincoln, NE; Mitchell Katz, Oceanside, NY; Lauren Kenney, Horsham, PA; Kenneth W. Kraft, Orlando, FL; Jeff Kula, Uhrichsville, OH; Laura Kyro, St. Louis, MO; John Lane, Sacramento, CA; Robert W. Likes, Chubbuck, ID; Alisa Loeper, Calhen, CO; Sharon Lowachee, Canada; Shirley S. Maiewski, Hatfield, MA; Michael D. Maynard, USAF, Korea; Benjamin Meyers, Bronx, NY; Matt Morgan, Milwaukee, WI; Thomas C. Nelson, Davisville, WV; Juan Onaz; Frank Owens, Winfield, KS; Vera Reeves, Fenton, MO; Vic Roberts, Canada; Danilo Rose; Matt Roth, Manhattan, KS; Charles Russell, England; James A. Simmonds, England; John H. Spruhan, Chicago, IL; Michael Weinstock, Great Neck, NY; R. David Wells, Lexington, KY; Suzie Wolin, Phoenix, AZ.

Special thanks to Steve and KathE Walker of *Datazine* for their help with the fanzine sections of this book.

BECOME A CONTRIBUTOR!

EXPERIENCED COLLECTORS—Lend us the benefit of your knowledge to improve, update, and expand this book. By doing so, you are helping your fellow collectors and ensuring that the hobby keeps growing. If you know of items not in this book or have new information on items already included, send a full outline plus your return address and phone number to: Sue Cornwell, P.O. Box 1516, Longwood, FL 32750 (no phone calls, please). If your contribution is accepted, your name will appear on the contribution page as a participating member of our editorial team.

OVERVIEW

MARKET REVIEW

There is no longer any doubt that *Star Trek* and *Star Wars* collecting is a legitimate field of investing. Gone are the days when a collector was made fun of for his collection of *Star Trek* toys. Gone also are the days of finding *Star Wars* action figures on sale in the toy store for 99 cents. Such is the awareness of the collectibility of these items that some of them barely see time on the store shelf at the intended retail price. Case in point are the "Star Trek: The Next Generation" alien action figures. In many instances, these figures were picked out of the cases in the stockroom by knowledgeable collectors or even store employees without ever being offered to the general public. Indeed, more and more items are being manufactured with the collector in mind. Limited issue coins, ceramics, figurines, and books all acknowledge the legitimacy of the field. Considering that *The Empire Strikes Back* just celebrated its 10th anniversary and 1991 marks the 25th year of *Star Trek*, this trend seems sure to continue. This longevity has a definite effect on the market. First, because of the constant influx of new fans into the field and, secondly, because the long-time fans of the series are reaching a stage in life of financial security, with more money to devote to their hobby. The future also seems secure. Despite *Star Trek V*'s weak performance in the theaters, *Star Trek VI* is firmly in the planning stages with a proposed release date of 1991 (to correspond with the 25th anniversary). Even if this were to be the last original *Star Trek* movie, "Star Trek: The Next Generation" is poised to take over. Indeed, after its fourth year, "Next Generation" has more episodes than the original show. And collectors were ready this time. While many original "Star Trek" items languished in discount stores for years, "Next Generation" merchandise was rising in price before it was even out of production.

Lucasfilms' renowned secrecy makes predicting *Star Wars*' future more difficult. Lucas has announced that the long-awaited fourth *Star Wars* movie will be made for 1997, *Star Wars*' 20th anniversary. However, rumors are rampant, even within the film industry, that the movie will be made sooner. In any event, the anticipation certainly has not hurt the collectors' market. Not only are values continuing to rise on the old *Star Wars* items but there is increased interest on the part of manufacturers to make new and reissued products. Also, the opening of the Star Tours attractions at the Disney theme parks and the associated merchandising has added an entirely new dimension to the field.

Which items are likely to be of particular interest to collectors in the future? From the original "Star Trek" series, dolls, especially the 8″ Mego figures, are very strong. While many of the expensive toy items have leveled off somewhat, these dolls, in particular the rarer alien figures, are still rising in price despite the fact that they are already very expensive. The *Star Trek V* figurines, a limited series, have increased in value and seem likely to go higher. From "Star Trek: The Next Generation," all of the action figures and toys made by Galoob are potentially excellent collectibles. Galoob lost interest in its "Star Trek" line early on and never produced enough to meet demand. Plates from both series have increased in value dramatically since they went out of production, the second series of original TV episode plates in particular. Also, the Picard and Data "Next Generation" plates, the only two made by Ernst from their planned eight plate series, look like good collectible possibilities because such a low number (about 4,000 of each) were produced.

In *Star Wars*, the continuing trend is in the area of small action figures and action figure-related toys. Figures in earlier *Star Wars* and *Empire Strikes Back* packaging, and the last series of figures that they made fewer of, are of particular interest. This is such a strong field, however, that any figure and even complete unpackaged figures are in demand by collectors. Large dolls are also still rising in value, though not to the extent of the small figures. As with *Star Trek*, the now out-of-production *Star Wars* plate series has increased dramatically in price.

General trends stress condition more and more. Original packaging is also of increasing importance. Serious collectors are stressing these two areas. In short, if you follow a few common sense guidelines, the wise collector can enjoy his/her hobby while building a sound investment for the future.

STAR TREK: FROM THE BEGINNING

When thinking about *Star Trek*, most of us can picture clearly what we know to be the form and substance of the TV series. We tend to forget the chameleon character of the program and how it metamorphosed continuously from its inception until its cancellation. We picture Dr. McCoy hovering solicitously over Captain Kirk's shoulder and Mr. Spock lifting his eyebrow in silent contempt while the Captain smiles benignly at his two friends and comrades. We forget, or perhaps were not even aware, that the interaction of these personalities and many other "regular" features did not originally exist. In fact, in the first show filmed (but not the first to be seen on TV), the captain was played by Jeffery Hunter, not William Shatner, and the captain's name was Christopher Pike.

In 1964, Gene Roddenberry, an experienced and already successful screenwriter, developed a 16-page synopsis of an idea for a science-fiction TV series called "Star Trek." For those fans who would like to read the second version of this outline, it is printed in the book, *The Making of Star Trek*. Very few of the names we associate with the series were in either of these drafts; for example, the starship was called the *S.S. Yorktown* instead of the *Enterprise*.

When the synopsis was presented to Metro-Goldwyn-Mayer, the producers seemed intrigued, but did not follow up with any offer. When the Desilu Company was approached, it contracted with Gene Roddenberry to develop and produce television pilots based on the synopsis during the following three years. This agreement was reached only a month after Roddenberry had completed the outline.

The vice-president for Desilu, Oscar Katz, offered the series to CBS first, but it was NBC that provided payment to Roddenberry and the go-ahead to write three story outlines. From these outlines, the network chose the story "The Cage" as the series pilot. The story outline, dated June 29, 1964, can be found in full, printed in *The Making of Star Trek*. The title was later changed to "The Menagerie."

The first pilot was filmed during late November and December of that same year, although some of the special optical effects were filmed as early as September.

The greatest challenge for the producers was devising special effects that were not phony looking. Since the most important effect was the starship, much effort was expended towards the design of a realistic one. The final design was a combination of several different styles. The Howard A. Anderson Company, which specialized in optical effects, contracted to make the models. Twenty technicians were assigned to this difficult project.

Three miniature models were constructed—the first being a wooden scale model only four inches long, the second a more detailed work three feet long, and the third a fourteen-foot model. The largest piece required hundreds of hours of work. Made mostly from sheet plastic, the nacelles were tooled from hardwood. Today, this model is displayed in the Air and Space Museum of the Smithsonian. In this model, the dome was larger and rounder than the ship that eventually became familiar to Trek fans. There are several other differences, particularly with the nacelles.

The largest of the models was placed on a pipe which led down to a pedestal on a tripod mount. This device allowed the model to be turned or tilted during the filming. For the scenes where the *Enterprise* is seen zooming through space, both the model and camera were in motion to create the effect of great speed. It is uncertain as to how many of these models were eventually constructed or what their sizes were.

During this period, there were few of the special effects that we are so familiar with today. The technology available to today's producers offers great freedom in creating spectacular sights and sounds. But these techniques were not available for the producers of "Star Trek." Besides production costs, the deadlines for a TV series limited their options as compared to a full-length movie film.

Another special effect that required great care and innovation was the transporter. Difficulty arose from the need to produce something spectacular, but affordable, week after week. After much experimentation, they devised a method where they photographed the actors on the transporter platform, stopped the camera while they stepped off, then shot the empty platform. By placing a duplicated negative print of the footage, they could create a matte of the subject. This matte allowed the actors to be dissolved out of the scene. Later, the glitter effect was added.

In February 1965, the complete pilot was submitted to NBC. The network turned the work down, but commissioned a second pilot to be filmed. Many characters in the original script were cut; NBC requested that Mr. Spock also be dropped from the series, but Gene Roddenberry insisted that he remain.

At this time, first draft scripts for three different stories were written. Roddenberry wrote two of these: "The Omega Glory" and "Mudd's Women." Novelist and screenwriter Samuel Peeples wrote the third one, "Where No Man Has Gone Before." When the three rough drafts were submitted in June 1965, NBC chose the third script even though this particular story line involved more expense and presented a greater challenge in production. Since Jeffery Hunter was unavailable for the shooting of this second pilot, another actor had to be found for the part. William Shatner had already proven himself an able actor with many impressive credits, and he was offered the role.

James Doohan joined the staff in this episode because of his ability to recreate different accents. Roddenberry was captivated by his Scottish brogue, since he had not completely formulated the personality of the Chief Engineer prior to Doohan's reading.

Sulu also appeared in this early Trek show, but had a part that required only two lines. In this episode, the ship's doctor was a Dr. Piper played by actor Paul Fix. At this point, the relationship between the doctor and the captain was of no importance, although the first pilot had a Dr. Boyce who was supportive of the emotional stress faced by the Captain.

Many other changes occurred. The costumes were redesigned, Spock's makeup was modified to give him a more exotic appearance, and many of the props were revamped. Animation was used to provide special effects for glowing eyes, phaser blasts, and showers of light and energy releases.

The second version was submitted to NBC in January 1966; a month and a half later, NBC accepted "Star Trek" as a series. The original version of this show has never been televised. Although the story line and the action are basically the same, the variations are sufficient to be noticeable.

Modifications continued, with most of the major cast changes being made during the first season. Dr. McCoy, Lieutenant Uhura, and Yeoman Janice Rand were added to the cast. But the last of the eight major characters, Mr. Checkov, didn't join the show until the beginning of the second season.

"Star Trek" appeared on TV from September 1966 through the 1969 season. The show inspired little enthusiasm from the media and received mixed reviews. Some thought it to be a show strictly for children. In fact, many of its viewers were in their teens or early twenties. Because of the weak ratings, NBC announced its intention to cancel the series. The "Star Trek" fans responded with vehement protests— thousands of letters deluged the NBC offices with pleas that the series be continued. In an unprecedented move, NBC reversed its former decision and continued the show for another season. Unfortunately, the series was moved to a time slot unfavorable for its particular audience—Friday night. Since most of its viewers were young, many of them were on dates or at the movies on Friday evenings. Even so, the series garnered more and more devoted fans, though the Nielsen ratings indicated that it lacked popularity. At this time, the first of the Star Trek fanzines emerged, further increasing the number of followers (see "Fanzine" section).

During its first season, "Star Trek" was nominated for five Emmy awards: as the best dramatic series, for the best dramatic actor (Leonard Nimoy), special photographic effects, special mechanical effects, and film and sound editing. Despite these honors, NBC again contemplated cancelling the series during its second season. Again, fans organized an impressive writing campaign. The fans were fearful that the show would either be cancelled or converted into a kiddie format. Fans even wrote up a guideline "How to Write Effective Letters to Save Star Trek," targeting the people and agencies to send these letters to. Apparently, this convinced NBC to continue with the series—the network announced that 115,893 letters had been received from "Star Trek" fans.

At the start of the third season, there were rumors that the series would be moved to a time slot geared to its audience, but at the last moment it was announced that the series would be stuck in the 10 to 11 PM slot on Friday. This was worse than the second season.

Over the three seasons, a change of producers evolved. For the first 12 episodes, creator/writer Gene Roddenberry, as producer, was closely involved with all aspects of the show. At that point, Roddenberry became executive producer, with Gene L. Coon taking the reins of producer. Although the two conferred often, Roddenberry's direct participation had come to an end.

During the second season, John Meredyth Lucas followed Coon as the producer. Again, in the third season, a new producer was chosen—Fred Freiberger. Although no one will deny that some outstanding episodes were made in the last season, many fans felt that the important ingredients that had made the series worthwhile were missing in some of the shows. Most of the criticism was directed at situations in which Mr. Spock uncharacteristically showed excessive emotion. When he is forced to laugh in "Plato's Stepchildren," plays in a jam session in "The Way to Eden," and conspires against the Captain in "The Turnabout Intruder," it goes against his persona so obviously that the fans resented the lack of continuity.

On June 3, 1969, the last network episode, "The Turnabout Intruder," was shown. But fans adamantly refused to let their favorite series disappear unforgotten. The number of fanzines grew; they supplied an outpouring of poetry, original stories, artwork, trivia questions, and suppositions about the actors and characters.

At first, NBC syndicated "Star Trek" only to its affiliate stations all over the United States. But eventually, they prepared a promotional package, touting the enthusiastic public response from its fans. By 1978, "Star Trek" was one of the most successful syndications in TV history. It had been translated into 42 languages, appearing in 51 countries. The series was being shown 300 times per day across the world. Within the United States alone, the show had 134 different outlets.

Syndication led to a continual increase in the number of followers. Fan clubs, fanzines, and collectible objects increased to meet the need. By 1978, there were 371 fan clubs, 431 fanzines, innumerable collectibles, and some 30 annual conventions.

From 1972 to 1974, an animated version of "Star Trek" was shown on Saturday mornings as part of the usual kiddie cartoons. There were 22 of these. Although the voices were those of the original actors, the animation was stilted and uninspiring. But it did garner more fans for the series.

THE STAR TREK MOVIES

Since 1972, when the first *Star Trek* convention drew 3,000 people, rumors circulated that the series would be brought back to TV as a new production, with the original cast. Tentative announcements from Paramount from time to time that production preparations were under way encouraged the fans to keep hoping. During the mid 1970s, Paramount was working with Gene Roddenberry on a feature film for television. Even though the sets were built and the story outline completed, they had a good reason to change their plans.

After the overwhelming success of *Star Wars*, Paramount decided that the day of the big-budget science-fiction film had arrived. A decade after the cancellation of the TV series in 1969, *Star Trek: The Motion Picture* was released.

The original cast was present with several new faces added. Not only were those familiar faces older, but the time and budget for a full-length film gave the producers, writers, and director a much greater range of freedom to make *Star Trek* different in many respects. Also, the innovative work on special effects, pioneered by George Lucas in *Star Wars*, opened up an entirely new way of adding excitement that was previously unavailable.

During the TV series, fans had been accustomed to seeing minor changes in the appearance of the *Enterprise*, the props, and quite often the characters. But for the movies, an entirely new ship was built. In was eight feet long, four feet wide, and weighed 70 pounds. The ship was built around an aluminum frame that allowed it to be supported in five different places. The ability to change the points of support meant that the *Enterprise* could be filmed from any angle. As much detail as possible was added—individual plates were visible on the outer surface and there were miniature lights inside.

The set for the bridge was changed. The chairs were restyled and the instrument panels were more complicated and larger. A security station and an electronic map of the ship were new features.

All the areas familiar to *Star Trek* fans—sick bay, the engineering areas, the recreation deck, the officers' quarters, the hallways, and the transporter—were also transformed. All were made larger, more elaborate in detail, and much more technical in appearance. Even the costumes were changed—not only were the standard uniforms redesigned, but a larger variety of outfits were used. One-piece fatigues, specialized uniforms, and working uniforms gave the crew a more realistic appearance.

Unfortunately, the reviews were not outstanding and there was some dissatisfaction on the part of the audience: the dramatic characterization and the warm interactions between the major characters that were so vital to the TV series seemed to be missing in the motion picture. There seemed to be too much emphasis on special effects, fast-paced action, and breath-taking scenes. Despite these flaws, the first film earned over $175 million. And when the sequel was released, the fans flocked to see *Star Trek II: The Wrath of Khan* in the hope that the old charm and essence of the TV series had been recaptured. In the second film, their hopes were realized.

Filming for *The Wrath of Khan* began in November 1981. Again, there were thoughts of producing a film for television that might possibly be released in theaters at a later time.

Harve Bennett, a talented and experienced TV producer, was offered the executive producer's position. He was the one responsible for developing the story line. After watching all 79 episodes of the TV series, he not only zeroed in on what ingredients were missing in the first film, but became fascinated with further developing a particular episode, "Space Seed," into the major plot. The episode was about Khan, the diabolical, genetic superman who was out to destroy Captain Kirk and was a worthy adversary to oppose the crew of the *Enterprise*. The only problem was that Khan had been played by Ricardo Montalban and it was thought that his role in the popular TV series "Fantasy Island" would prevent him from being in the film. Fortunately, this was not the case. Montalban loved the part of Khan and wanted to play it again in the movie. To have someone else play Khan was never considered—fans know the characters in all the episodes too well for that to be acceptable.

Nicholas Meyer was named the director. He also realized the life and death questions that were lacking in the first film and incorporated the idealistic, humanistic striving, the loyalty, and deep friendships that made fans care about the *Enterprise* and her crew. He was more concerned with portraying a story about human beings, struggling with their conflicts—internal and external—and facing the consequences of their actions, not a story about whizzing spaceships and extravagant space battles.

The plot centers around the three major characters—Kirk, Spock, and Dr. McCoy—just as the TV series did. They are faced with a frightening, powerful, and evil foe.

Only 43 days were allotted for shooting. The set was closed to anyone not involved in producing the film. The security was as tight as possible. All cast and production members were sworn to secrecy; no one divulged the plot. All members were required to wear I.D. badges with their photos. In spite of these precautions, props were stolen from the set continuously. Cast members found that they had to be careful about putting down even their I.D. badges—or they were stolen, too.

Halfway through the filming, rumors leaked out that the character Spock would die. A wave of protest erupted from fans. Although Leonard Nimoy had no say-so as to what would happen to Spock in the film, some of the anger from the fans was directed at him. In an attempt to alleviate his unenviable position, director Nick Meyer concocted a list of the different possible ways that the film could end (some in which Spock would not die). Rumors about the multiple endings dissipated the strident clamorings.

Since all of *Star Trek II* was filmed inside Paramount studios, the designers had a menagerie of sets to create: the bridges for three different spaceships, a space station, a desert, an Eden cave, and various planetary settings. This task fell to Joe Jennings, Designer, Mike Minor, Art Director, and Lee Cole, Graphics Designer.

Their first chore was to redesign the bridge of the *Enterprise*. There were several problems with the bridge used in the first movie. The first bridge was constructed of one piece that limited the mobility of the camera, and the characters were often crowded into a very confining area. These problems were resolved by taking all of the 11 sections apart. This allowed the camera to move in close or to be placed in a number of locations. With the maneuverability of the camera, the bridge appears larger and the shots are much more interesting and poignant.

In the first film, the monitors on the bridge were 8mm and 16mm film loops. This caused two problems: the projectors that were used to run them were too noisy (all of the dialogue had to be dubbed in later), and very dim light was necessary when filming in order for the objects on the monitors to show up at all. Also, the monitors had to be filmed from a straight-on position, so the camera was limited in its movement. The result was a dreary, uninteresting bridge in the first movie.

For the second film, all the film loops were transferred to videotape. When video images are filmed by a motion picture camera, they appear to be vibrating, and a special technique was utilized to overcome this obstacle. Not only did this allow for more lighting and camera movement, but the videotapes eliminated the need to re-play an entire film loop every time there was a retake.

The bridge of the *Enterprise* was revamped into three different versions. In one scene, it was the *Enterprise* bridge; in another scene, it was the bridge of its sister ship, the *U.S.S. Reliant*; and in the beginning of the show, it appeared as the simulator room at Starfleet Academy.

The *Enterprise* bridge was partially converted to the *Reliant* bridge by placing partitions in front of an elevator and a console. In the scene where Khan blows up the bridge of the *Reliant*, the designers created partitions for these sections made of paper, balsa wood, and gel. Paper decals and blinking lights behind gave the fragile frames the appearance of realism. These flimsy sections blew up quite convincingly during the scene.

More was seen of the *Enterprise* during the second movie, and more attention was given to creating the illusion of a busy, bustling ship. For the first time, the audience saw the torpedo room and the inner rooms of the sick bay. Kirk's quarters were redesigned to look less sterile and more lived-in with a nautical type of decor. The same set was used for Mr. Spock's quarters but with a spiritual appearance, almost austere. Both of these sets were styled to match the well-known personality traits of these two characters.

The most difficult sets were the desert planet and the Eden cave. For the desert, they built 60-foot sand dunes that dropped off at a 45-degree angle. Frames were constructed, then packed with fuller's earth. This was covered with a sand substance that was blown about with large fans. During the filming on the desert set, the production crew wore goggles, surgical masks, and protective clothing. Also on this set, they had to create Khan's living quarters, which had to be used as an interior and an exterior set. Khan's quarters were decorated with objects that would have been available after the "Space Seed" episode.

Constructing the Eden set posed a puzzling situation. In the show, the Eden cave is a subterranean paradise, a product of Dr. Marcus' "Project Genesis." A huge bubble-like structure was made to look like an onyx stone. It was designed so it could be composited with large matte paintings.

Throughout the filming, Dr. Richard Green of NASA's Jet Propulsion Laboratory, who aided Harve Bennett with the science logistics for the story line, continued to provide guidance. He reviewed all aspects of the show—the script, the designs, and the actual production—in order to make sure that everything corresponded to current scientific thought.

For the special effects, director Nick Meyer chose to use the top-notch experts at Industrial Light and Magic Company (ILM), first set up by George Lucas to produce the effects for *Star Wars*. All of the space battles, take-offs, and other spectacular scenes, which totaled 150, were done by ILM.

Normally, special effects are created after the live action has been filmed. But because of *Star Trek*'s tight schedule, both were done at the same time by working from duplicate story boards. When necessary, ILM's camera crew would go down to Paramount Studios in Hollywood (from their San Francisco location) to film background plates of the various sets. This footage was composited with the special effects.

With a budget one-third that of the first *Star Trek* movie, *The Wrath of Khan* recreated once again the magic of the legendary TV series—and more; it added a tantalizing vista with spectacular effects never possible more than a decade ago.

Star Trek III: The Search for Spock began almost as a comedy of errors. Harve Bennett, the writer/producer of *Star Trek III*, wanted to use Leonard Nimoy as director for the new film but was given the erroneous impression that Leonard's prior contract from *The Wrath of Khan* precluded him from working on *Star Trek III*; that he, in fact would be "dead." During a casual conversation, Harve mentioned to Leonard that he would have loved to have had him take a shot at directing the new film, but it was a shame that the contract stated he couldn't. Leonard didn't know what Harve was talking about, so Harve sent for a copy of the contract. No such mention was found. Harve then offered Leonard the job of director, and he accepted.

Leonard's extensive background in films and on stage more than qualified him for the task. Fans were also delighted with the prospect of having Leonard direct. Here, at last, we would have a director completely familiar with the "feel" of the original series. There was an additional bonus having Leonard direct. He knew the cast. This allowed for a kind of "shorthand" in direction because Leonard already knew the skills and range of the actors. Because of this, the film was brought in ahead of schedule and within the budget.

One difficulty with the new film concerned replacing actress Kirstie Alley, who played Lt. Saavik, with newcomer Robin Curtis. Fans generally felt that though Robin did a good job in a difficult situation, Kirstie would have been a stronger screen presence.

The use of one word—remember—just before Spock's death in *The Wrath of Khan*, successfully links the two films together and allows for the regeneration of a new Spock via the Genesis effect. Nimoy has expressed on several occasions the great personal emotional pain he felt during the filming of his death scene. He said it was very difficult for him to do and he was very happy to be reborn.

Christopher Lloyd's performance as the Klingon commander Kruge was particularly outstanding.

Several new ships were introduced in this film, including: the *Grissom* research ship, the hybrid *Klingon-Romulan Bird of Prey* scout ship, the transwarp-drive *Excelsior*, and the *Merchantman*.

During the filming of *Star Trek III*, a great fire struck the Paramount lot, destroying the famous "New York street" that had been used in countless films for decades. Science-fiction fans will remember it from the George Pal production of *War of the Worlds*. There was great fear that the fire could spread to Stage 15, where many of the complex *Star Trek* sets were housed. Yet even with fire-burning, filming continued and the day's shooting was completed successfully.

Special effects were once again handled capably by the team at ILM who, this time around, produced the most convincing planetary explosion seen since *When Worlds Collide*.

Though *The Search for Spock* is loaded with special effects, the story centers around the characters as Kirk fights to save, but loses, his son, at the same time trying to prevent the capture of the Genesis process and deal with an unstable planet, an equally unstable McCoy, his hijacking of the *Enterprise*, the possible regeneration of his closest friend Spock, the destruction of the *Enterprise*, and a very angry Federation. The film ends with the destruction of the *Enterprise*, and the saving of a re-generated Spock—but at what cost—and we must remember Saavik's haunting words . . . "And what is yet to come."

Strangely, there was almost no merchandising associated with this film, and the fans were left hungry for toys and other merchandise. It is possible that the toy companies, badly burned by *Star Trek: The Motion Picture*, didn't want to take the risk. The FASA Company did produce a successful line of games linked to the later films. For collectors, it meant turning their attention back to the TV toys that had been produced in great variety. These still have very strong investment potential, particularly since at about this time the Mego Corporation went out of business.

As effective as *Star Trek II* and *III* had been in attempting to recapture the feel of the "Star Trek" TV series, it wasn't until *Star Trek IV: The Voyage Home* that the effort really succeeded. Here at last was the real humor and spirit of the original show. The terrific script was a co-effort of Harve Bennett and Leonard Nimoy. The story dealt directly with serious 20th-century problems but contained the most humor and warmth of any of the *Star Trek* films.

Leonard Nimoy was once again faced with the twin burden of being both actor and director in the same film. And once again he brought the picture in on time.

Star Trek IV saw the return of Mark Leonard as Ambassador Sarek (Spock's father), Jane Wyatt as Amanda (Spock's mother), and Grace Lee Whitney as Yeoman Rand. The film also featured actress Catherine Hicks, whose performance as marine biologist Gillian Taylor helped make the film a success.

The film's only weak spot occurs in the beginning when yet another probe-spaceship comes from deep space to threaten Earth. This overused plot device immediately makes one think of *Nomad* from the TV series and *Voyager* from *Star Trek: The Motion Picture*. However, once past this weak point, the picture soars.

Unlike the other *Star Trek* films, which were shot entirely at the studio, *Star Trek IV* went on location in San Francisco, San Diego, and Monterey, California. Leonard, while continuing from the trilogy, wanted to give this film a completely different look.

A brilliant team of artists created the world's first free-swimming model of a whale. This four-foot model allowed greater freedom in shooting the underwater shots. The small whale was so well designed that the water pump designed to propel it forward wasn't needed; the swimming motion so perfectly copied the real thing that it swam by itself. The pump was used only when the whale had to dive or surface.

Where it was necessary to have larger whale models, the film crew used the astronaut training tank at McDonnell Douglas. One of the models was thirty feet long. When the small model was filmed at high speed and the film played back at normal speed, the whale looked real. When a human had to be in the same shot with a whale, larger life-size sections (models) were used.

One of the more difficult scenes was shot just after the Klingon *Bird of Prey* crash-lands in San Francisco Bay after a harrowing time-travel sequence. If you drive in the front gate at Paramount, directly ahead of you is a huge, painted sky. At the foot of this is the sunken parking lot that was flooded (after first removing the cars, of course) to create the aftermath of the crash. Wave and wind machines combined to produce a terrible and convincing storm. Added to this was a giant mechanical whale.

Another complex matte shot was filmed on the runway at Oakland Airport. This is the brief scene of the starbase at San Francisco with the Golden Gate Bridge in the background.

Still another complex sequence was created for the time-travel dream in which the actors' faces seem to float up from a fog and change before our eyes to other people. These effects were created by a company called Cyberware in Monterey, California. By using a slit-scan technique and computers, they can create a styrofoam duplicate of a person's face in a few hours. The heads were then lit to create dreamlike color and photographed, all with computers. It took a total of two weeks to complete this effect.

To create the new *Enterprise* used at the end of the film, it was necessary to repair the old model (destroyed in *The Search for Spock*). The model had been painted with a coating of rubber cement and spray-painted black with pieces of foil to give it a ripped and torn look. This all had to be removed and the ship repainted with the new numbers added. The old bridge had a bit of reworking done to it for the final bridge shot.

In *Star Trek IV*, each of the original cast had their moment on-screen without it feeling forced. In all, this was a warm, wonderful film, very well received by both fans and the general public.

With the trilogy begun in *Star Trek II* finished, *Star Trek V: The Final Frontier* had to begin anew. Not only did it not have a familiar storyline to anchor it, but it also had a new director. As per contractual agreements, William Shatner was to direct *Star Treks V* and *VI* to balance out the opportunity given to Leonard Nimoy. In addition to directing and, of course, acting in *Star Trek V*, Mr. Shatner made a major contribution to writing the script and initially was to be responsible for much of the editing, though in the end he did much less of this than originally intended. Although the film does have its avid supporters, for the most part both fans and the general public found the film disappointing. The plot, essentially the search for God, is weak, the special effects not borrowed from earlier films are not of the quality of the previous films, and in many instances the performances of the actors seem forced. Considering his large role in the production of the film, the natural tendency is to blame Mr. Shatner for its faults and, in truth, he must bear much of the responsibility. In all fairness, however, there were some circumstances beyond his control and certainly no one can say he did not work hard on the film or give it an honest effort.

Since *Star Trek V* was his first theatrical directing effort, it's not surprising that Shatner might be caught somewhat off guard by the pitfalls of budget and time. The film had to be continually trimmed in both scope and content to fit into these limitations, making the grandiose plot less and less workable.

Even worse for a science-fiction film in this day and age were the inferior special effects. ILM, which had done all of the previous films, was unable to do *Star Trek V*. A company called Associates & Ferren were chosen to do the effects for the film with disappointing results. Perhaps they would have been acceptable in the days of the original TV series, but for a major theatrical production presented to an audience used to seeing better, they just didn't work.

All of the original actors were present, with each having at least a small opportunity to be featured on-screen. The extremely physical roles played in the film, however, made the more mature members of the crew seem juvenile. This plus the strained pace of the movie, made many of the well-intentioned jokes and gags fall a little flat.

Even with all its problems, the film did have its high points, notably Laurence Luckinbill as Sybok, Spock's half-brother. *Star Trek* has been far too long-lived for either the fans or the studio to give up on it because of one less than perfect outing. As of this writing, *Star Trek VI* is planned for release in 1991, *Star Trek*'s 25th anniversary, and it's a certainty that all previous successes and failures will be taken into account to make the best film possible for the occasion.

STAR TREK: THE NEXT GENERATION

As much as *Star Trek V* did not live up to its expectations, "Star Trek: The Next Generation" has gone far beyond theirs. Riding the wave of success culminating in the recently released *Star Trek IV*, it was announced that a new "Star Trek" television series would begin airing in September of 1987. The series is set 75 years after the events of the original "Star Trek" with a new ship and new characters. Gene Roddenberry is executive producer with total control over the new series, something he never had with the *Star Trek* theatrical releases that are controlled by Paramount. Originally many of the original production personnel from the first TV series worked on the show as well. Entirely new sets were built for the new *Enterprise* (NCC-1701 D), which offered a roomier, more spacious feel than that of the original ship. New concepts were the holodeck, a recreational area utilizing the transporter effect to create desired places and/or scenarios and living quarters for families, since in this new era the emphasis is on long-term exploration rather than militarism. Interesting additions to the new crew are Data, an android, and Worf, a Klingon (Klingons now being part of the Federation). The model of the ship itself was built by ILM, which also did some of the initial special effects including the interesting "rubber band" warp effect. Though this and some other of the initial stock effects were done on film, most of what is seen on "Next Generation" is done on videotape. Though the live action portions of the episodes are done on standard 35mm film, only by using the video technology available today are the many complex effects that are needed to make a "Next Generation" episode believable able to be done in the time frame of a weekly TV series. This was a radical, new idea and one not very well received by the studio since it meant that completed episodes would exist only on videotape, thereby negating any chance of a theatrical release (something they had been considering for foreign markets). When it was pointed out that this method would also save them a great deal of money, however, they seemed to see the light. Another new approach to the series was that it would be offered in syndication instead of the standard method of selling to one of the major networks. This was a new idea at the time but has since gained popularity, due in part, at least, to the success of "Star Trek: The New Generation." The show premiered with a special two-hour pilot in a heightened atmosphere of expectation on the part of the fans. DeForest Kelley had a cameo role as a 137-year-old Dr. McCoy. The show was generally well received despite some dicotomy between supporters of "old" and "new" "Star Trek." The special effects worked very well on screen and the ensemble of characters showed promise of meshing together nicely. The one area that seemed to need improvement was in the quality of the writing. Often a story seemed to rehash a too familiar theme, and endings often left the audience hanging. The cause of these problems seemed to be that restrictions put on writers to keep strictly to the initial tenets of the show left little room for drama to develop. Luckily, the problem seemed to be diagnosed around the middle of the first season. Scripts suddenly seemed to get better and, in most people's opinions, have been improving ever since. Fewer and fewer people seemed to feel that the new show was an unwanted usurper of the old crew but was, indeed, genuine "Star Trek." Changes have taken place over the years since the show premiered. Denise Crosby (security officer Tasha Yar) left the series but reprised her role in the episode "Yesterday's Enterprise." Riker grew a beard. The uniforms changed (the old, one-piece, tight-fitting jumpsuits required too much dieting on the part of the cast members). Whoopi Goldberg joined the cast in the recurring role of Guinan. Gates McFadden was replaced in her role as doctor by Diana Muldare . . . who was replaced by Gates McFadden (again). And as of this writing, Wesley Crusher is due to depart for the academy (finally). "Next Generation" is, in fact, about to achieve a distinction the original "Star Trek" never achieved—a fourth television season.

THE CREATION OF STAR WARS

After six years, over 10 million dollars, and the work of hundreds of artists and technicians, George Lucas unleashed his spectacular film, *Star Wars*. In his early thirties, Lucas drew on his childhood love of Flash Gordon, fantastic science fiction, Westerns, mythology, and samurai movies to write and direct a movie that combines the excitement and adventure found in all of these forms. He created the type of film he wanted to see as a child—not based on science and logic, as many of the more recent science-fiction shows had been, but one based on sheer fantasy, a modern fairy tale where good confronts the forces of evil and wins. The story occurs in another galaxy far away from our own, and in a time long before our existence. This ploy allows Lucas to bring into being a unique universe where our laws of physics and aerodynamics could be ignored.

Following his tremendous success with *American Graffiti*, Lucas tried to buy the rights to produce a film based on the old TV series "Flash Gordon." When he was unable to do so, he decided he would write his own fantasy adventure. Despite his box-office success with his first major film, Universal studios turned down Lucas' proposal for a science-fiction film. But Twentieth Century Fox, which had been successful with its film *Planet of the Apes*, willingly backed him. After two years, Lucas produced a script he was happy with.

In casting, he chose fairly unknown actors—Mark Hamill and Harrison Ford had very little experience. But each possessed the qualities that Lucas had envisioned for these characters. Ford had an arrogant, roguish appearance that suited Han Solo, and Mark Hamill had the wistful look of a youth yearning for adventure that was essential for Luke Skywalker. Even though Lucas' close friend Cindy Williams wanted the role of Princess Leia, Carrie Fisher was chosen because she possessed the combination of regal beauty and combative toughness necessary for the part.

Although Lucas balked at the thought of working with a big-name actor, Twentieth Century Fox insisted that one be selected in order to increase the film's box office appeal. Talented veteran Alec Guinness was found to be an invaluable asset and quite easy to work with.

One of the first steps to translating ideas of a fantastic nature onto film is to have a visualizer transform them into pictures. Numerous artists worked with George Lucas, but Ralph McQuarrie was the main one. His chores included the designing of the characters, costumes, props, and scenery to suit Lucas' ideas. From rough charcoal sketches to completed, polished storyboards, McQuarrie provided the details of R2-D2, Threepio, the Jawas, the Death Star, and various landscapes of planets.

The visualizer creates a detailed sketch for every scene—showing the costumes, the comparative sizes of people and objects, and any special lighting. McQuarrie achieved Lucas' objective—a blend of the fantastic with the realism of a documentary.

The shooting began in the desert of Tunisia. Although Lucas was aiming for a documentary appearance, the lighting problems inherent in the desert led to artistic touches. Working on location caused a variety of problems, as is often the case. The continually bad weather slowed the shooting, and the chief makeup artist, Stuart Freeborn, had to be hospitalized from food poisoning by the time they returned to London for further shooting. This meant that he was unavailable during the shooting of Mos Eisley's bar—the humorous, raucous scene with the largest and strongest collection of aliens shown in the film. Later, parts of this were reshot on the Utah desert with the expertise of makeup artist Rick Baker, making for a much more satisfying scene.

There were other problems: making Banthas, the mammoth-like creatures ridden by the sand people, that looked realistic, and building a transporter for the Jawas that was large enough. A compromise ended with only the lower portion being built and the remainder painted on matte backdrops.

Intermingled with days of exhilaration and a sense of accomplishment were days of frustration and depression. *Star Wars* took much more time and much more money than Lucas had anticipated. He felt that, despite the years and millions of dollars, he was constantly having to compromise—accepting a scene that wasn't quite the way he wanted it, cutting corners whenever possible. Lucas' invovement with the film was total—seven days a week, long working hours, week after week with painstaking care and attention to all details. Unlike more mature directors, Lucas was accustomed to controlling all aspects of his films, and this cost him in time and energy.

Besides all these obstacles, there were the overwhelming challenges of superimposing the special effects onto the film. Lucas and his producer, Gary Kurtz, understood the importance of impressive but believable effects.

Lucas set up the Industrial Light and Magic Company (ILM) to produce the special effects for *Star Wars*. It was originally located in Los Angeles, but was moved to San Francisco in 1978 when *The Empire Strikes Back* was being shot. ILM continues to produce the special effects for various major films including the *Indiana Jones* trilogy and most of the *Star Trek* movies.

During the filming of *Star Wars*, the optical department worked 24 hours a day, six days a week. Although Lucas selected more mature members for the operations, the artists, engineers, technicians, model-makers, and cinematographers were, for the most part, unusually young. Their average age was below 30.

In order to achieve the stunning and exciting effects that Lucas was after, hundreds of hours were necessary, and these often resulted in only a few seconds for the film.

The most difficult challenge for special effects was the large space battle in *Star Wars* that takes up the last 20 minutes of the film. In order to acquire the authentic appearance of an aerial fight, Lucas and Kurtz videotaped a number of dogfights out of World War II movies. From these they selected portions and transformed them onto black and white 16mm film. This patched-together sequence was used as a guideline to their battle scene. This film was converted to storyboards, and the special effects people worked arduously to recreate the battle on film.

Special effects had to produce footage where there was an appearance of continuous motion, a number of ships banking and rolling, explosions, plus planets and stars in the background. The motion-control camera created the illusions of tremendous speed. ILM had four of these computer-controlled cameras but only two were used for *Star Wars*. The models are actually still during the filming. Instead, the cameras move at various speeds with numerous types of movements. The model can appear to bank, roll, and twist in innumerable styles and speeds.

A computer recorded each move so that any action could be duplicated if need be. The use of a lighted backdrop with a blue light and a red filter over the camera lens allowed for other objects or images to be superimposed onto the scene until everything was included.

Stop-motion animation was used extensively in *The Empire Strikes Back*, although only briefly in *Star Wars* for the chess game sequence. The movements of the Tauntaun and the AT-AT Walker portions were accomplished by this method. This technique was similar to that used in ordinary animation, except that each shot involves the model placed in a different pose.

Special effects also included the model-makers to design the different types of spaceships; the special creatures, such as Yoda and the Tauntaun; the matte painters who produced the realistic backgrounds; the designers and builders of the special equipment; and the programmers for the computer software.

The scenes where charts are shown on monitors or screens, such as when the Rebel pilots read the printouts of the Death Star, involved special effects people programming the machines to draw the diagrams. This technology allowed these to be produced much faster than if they had been done by hand. Still, months of work often resulted in only a few minutes of the film.

Certainly, the effects used in these films were revolutionary—new techniques that explored the possibilities available with our new advanced technology. Lucas was viewed as the pioneer in special effects.

The matching of a film with appropriate music that adds to the drama or humor offered an important challenge. Lucas chose the talented John Williams to write the score—an award-winning composer who had done the scores for all of Steven Spielberg's films, plus many other major pictures.

Lucas had already decided that he wanted an expansive score—one that had a sense of high adventure, strength, and soaring hope. Williams worked on the music for over a year, finally recording the 90-minute score in 14 different recording sessions with the London Symphony Orchestra. As Williams conducted the orchestra, the appropriate sequences of the film were shown on a screen behind the orchestra. This allowed him to match the speed of the music with the action and to know when to give the music extra emphasis. Of course, all this time and attention paid off; the *Star Wars* album, as well as several singles from it, became big hits.

The sound effects, recognized by fans as an integral and important aspect of the movie, were created by expert Ben Burtt. Most films average 200 sound effects; *Star Wars* has about 2,000. Burtt provided alien languages (most of which are really nonsense, but several are actually Peruvian Inca dialect), the animalistic sounds of a Wookie, and the eerie buzzing noise of a lightsaber. Most of these were a blend of sounds, so that each was realistic but unearthly.

Although there was no attempt at designing scientifically sound spaceships, there was great effort to make each and every one believable—as was true with all features in *Star Wars*. The strange silence of space so accurately portrayed in *2001* was abandoned for the more emotionally satisfying screeches of spaceships zooming past each other, the deadly hum of laser guns, and the resulting explosions. The audience's sense of what an aerial war should look and sound like were fulfilled.

Another aspect of *Star Wars* completely different from other science-fiction films was the usual appearance of a sterile, almost-perfect environment. In *Star Wars*, Lucas conjures up a universe that shows evidence of being recycled—Jawas collect and sell scrap metal, the Millennium Falcon shows signs of being patched and repaired. The choice of ships seems to be as varied as our vehicles are today. Ships are designed for specialized tasks—speed, maneuverability, power, transportation, or heavy armament.

Even when the majority of the work was finished, Lucas balked, wanting to reshoot some of it again. When Twentieth Century Fox said no to this request, Lucas and his editors cut and spliced the film together. The resulting show ran two hours.

The trilogy was completed by the release of *Return of the Jedi*. The elements that changed the way movies were made had begun with *Star Wars* and by the third film, Lucas had perfected his formula. The dazzling effects, the aura of space, and the realistic portrayal of healthy, robust heroes combined to make yet another blockbuster film.

Return of the Jedi was originally to be tilted *"Revenge" of the Jedi* and some early advertising paraphernalia, promotional items, and a few retail products with the title were released. Lucas and Twentieth Century felt, after getting into the filming, that the title connotated a negative image for the heroic warriors of the Jedi. The change was made to *Return of the Jedi*, creating some of the most interesting, and sought after, collectibles in movie memorabilia history.

Since *Return of the Jedi* ended the movie trilogy, Lucasfilm concentrated on the television medium for the continuation of the *Star Wars* saga. There have been two Ewok television movies (released theatrically in foreign markets) and two animated shows, "Ewoks" and "Droids."

There are two noticeable differences between *Star Wars* in this medium compared to how it was presented in the theatrical movies. The first one is production values. Television can't support the high costs for sets, makeup, and special effects that a major motion picture can, and the Ewok movies reflect this lower standard. Television-style animation, of course, is inherently cheaper to produce.

The second difference is that the television offerings seemed aimed at a distinctly different audience, a much younger one, than those that were attracted to the movies. The major characters of the Ewok films are young children and both the animated series were standard Saturday morning cartoons, the traditional kiddie slot. The majority of the original *Star Wars* audience felt understandably abandoned and it showed. The Ewok movies fell somewhat flat and the two cartoon shows were short lived.

Still, the fact that the television fare was made at all reflected the realization that there was still an eager audience for *Star Wars*. Recently, Lucas has relented and announced a date, 1997, the 20th anniversary of *Star Wars*, for the continuing of the saga. But there are the ever-present rumors, some by people in quite knowledgeable positions and, of course, the hope that *Star Wars* will return sooner.

CONVENTIONS

In the early '70s, before *Star Trek* conventions became separate entities, there had been a growing *Star Trek* following at comic and science-fiction conventions. In 1972, the first convention devoted entirely to *Star Trek* was held in New York City. It was an overwhelming success. The organizers at this first convention were a mixture of professional convention organizers and dedicated fans. The convention became an annual affair and grew steadily until, in 1974, a break occurred between the professional and fan organizers, each setting up their own convention. In the meantime, other individuals around the country, both fan and professional organizers, had been saying to themselves, "Hey, I can do that too!" The convention phenomenon has grown steadily; there is a convention virtually every weekend in some part of the country.

Today conventions are generally mixed media in nature, reflecting the diverse interests of today's fans. (Lucasfilm has permitted only one convention, the Tenth Anniversary Convention, to use the *Star Wars* name.) Actors and other personalities associated with *Star Trek*, "Star Trek: The Next Generation," and other TV shows and movies are present as guests at the larger conventions. In addition, "Star Trek" episodes and movies, as well as other films, are shown on 16mm film and/or video-tape, and there are usually other activities, trivia contests, costume contests and, of course, there is the dealers' room. The dealers' room at a large convention can be one of the best places to buy, sell, and trade collectibles. You can inspect the items firsthand, and prices are sometimes more flexible.

The hardest thing about going to a convention may be finding one! With very few exceptions, there are no annual shows held predictably at the same time each year. Though there are now professional organizations that put conventions on all over the country, neither these nor the many fan-run conventions keep any kind of regular schedule as a rule. If you have a local comic book or science-fiction bookstore, they can often supply you with information on upcoming local conventions. You may find small fan-run conventions disappointing, however, if you are looking for a large show with guests and an extensive dealers' room. Guest fees are very expensive, and large, out-of-town dealers can't meet expenses at a show with a small attendance. To find a large convention, the best sources are in the various national science-fiction-oriented magazines and *Official Fan Club* publications. These usually have listings and/or ads for upcoming conventions. It should be noted that the larger conventions are confined almost entirely to bigger cities that have the facilities and population needed to support such activity. So, if you don't live near a major city you may need to travel to a convention once you find one.

BUILDING A COLLECTION

Despite the fact that 1991 is *Star Trek*'s 25th anniversary, and that 1990 marked the 10th anniversary of *The Empire Strikes Back*, compared to other collectible fields where the objects may be years, decades, or even centuries old, *Star Trek* and *Star Wars* collecting is a relatively new field. In this short time, however, we have managed to form some general ideas about condition and value.

Because *Star Trek* and *Star Wars* cover such a wide variety of different types of items, we have been able to borrow many guidelines from other well-established collecting fields. A *Star Trek* book is still a book. A *Star Wars* toy, still a toy. We are fortunate also to live in an age when most people understand the concept of collectibility. We realize that an item may become valuable. Much was lost in past generations because, from their point of view, an old worn-out item was just that, not a potentially valuable collectible. Probably for this reason as much as any other, there are *Star Trek* and *Star Wars* items around in collectible condition.

For the beginning collector, it is best to arm yourself with as much knowledge as possible—about the shows and their productions, as well as the collectibles derived from them. Only through study and experience will you be able to avoid the major pitfall faced by all collectors: paying too much for an item. Everyone does it eventually, even the most expert collectors and dealers. Don't let this discourage you. Accept your mistakes, but try to gain the expertise to keep these to a minimum.

The beginner will find it wise to take his or her time in order to let their collecting take some direction before accumulating a number of items. As your collecting progresses, you'll find that certain items are out of place in your collection or that your interest in them has waned. But this varies from collector to collector. Some hobbyists will want to possess all the *Star Wars* items; others will find that they're interested in certain types of objects, such as the books or the models. Whether you build a general or specialized collection depends on you; both types of collections will be valuable. But if your budget limits you, you may find a specialized collection more suitable.

For the majority of items, dealers are the most viable source for older items. Don't ignore current items you may see, however, as too new to be collectible. Such is the nature of this field that a "Star Trek: The Next Generation" "Q" figure that was available in stores for under $5 only a few months ago is going for upwards of $75 today.

Though stores that specialize in *Star Trek* and *Star Wars* are relatively rare, quite often you will find a comic or science-fiction book shop that carries some items of interest. In addition, they may be able to point you to other dealers that carry more of a selection.

You can also locate dealers through magazines and fanzines. Subscriptions to these can be worthwhile. Not only are they fun to read, but they have ads from dealers and private collectors looking to buy or sell *Star Trek* and *Star Wars* objects.

You may want to study several issues of the same publication before you decide to order from a particular dealer. Although most dealers are honorable, you should be wary. Though few people are out to deliberately bilk you, it's easy for individuals and small or new companies unused to business practices to find themselves in over their head and be unable to meet their obligations to their customers. It's little consolation that they meant well when your money is gone, and you have nothing to show for it and no way to get your money back. If the same dealer has consistently advertised in the same publication over a period of time, you can surmise that he is probably reputable.

Read the ad carefully. If descriptions of the articles are vague, you might be better off phoning or writing to get any information you need. Most professional dealers and some individuals offer detailed lists or catalogs they can send you. Most require a nominal fee or at least a self-addressed, stamped envelope. Before ordering, make sure you know what their procedures involve. Will they give a refund if you are dissatisfied with an object and want to return it? You should buy only from dealers who give you that option. But prepare to be reasonable; returns should be sent back within three days, packaged carefully, and in the same condition as when you received them.

If you don't want to encounter any delays, a money order or (in the case of larger dealers) a credit card will expedite your order, since most dealers will not ship anything until your check clears the bank.

Instead of providing price lists, some dealers would rather you send a want list. Since most dealers don't know which pieces they will have available from one month to the next, many of them prefer taking want lists instead of running large ads listing their entire stock, or publishing their own catalogs. The want lists are particularly helpful to the more advanced collector who is looking for particular hard-to-find items.

Your want lists should include your name, address, and phone number, plus a full description of what pieces you want. Indicate what you want by name and any identification numbers or dates. If you are looking for a particular size, variation, or color, include this information also. The dealer will check his stock. If he has the piece or pieces, he'll inform you of his prices and terms of sale. Obviously, you should not list a large number of articles you're not seriously intending to purchase. This type of list will discourage the dealer from helping you or taking you seriously. It would be much better to list several pieces that you want and maybe several alternatives if these are not available.

If the dealer doesn't have any of the pieces that you want, he'll probably inform you that he has placed your list in his file. Then, if he receives a piece that is on your want list, he will contact you. As to whether he will keep the piece for you until he hears from you depends on whether or not you've been a long-standing customer of his. This really varies from dealer to dealer. Sometimes, the dealer will know of someone who has the piece for sale and can secure it for you. He may charge you a commission for such a sale, so be sure to find out beforehand. The more dealers you work with, the greater the chance you will have of finding the pieces you want.

When you find a dealer who provides satisfactory service, you can use him as your main source for collectibles. But as your collection grows, you may find it more and more difficult to find the rarer items. There are ways to expand your resources.

Private parties—either collectors or persons disposing of items no longer wanted—can be the source of great bargains, but the risks are much greater than other sources. Collectors must sometimes sell their collections quickly in order to raise cash for an emergency. They don't have time to wait for a good offer in such cases.

Private parties usually only have a few pieces to sell and generally aren't knowledgeable about them as collectibles and tend to misjudge condition. If they advertise through the mail, they may not include pertinent information, because they don't realize it is of importance. Flea markets and garage sales have the same drawback. It's easy to spend hours of time and miles of travel only to find a disappointing array of battered and incomplete articles. Also keep in mind that none of the above groups are likely to refund your money if you decide you are dissatisfied with the piece.

One of the best sources when buying are conventions. Both science-fiction and *Star Trek* conventions are enjoyable and stimulating for the collector. Conventions, especially larger ones, can be found through the usual advertising media; i.e., radio, TV, newspapers, etc. Also, be sure to check science-fiction publications that often have lists of upcoming conventions around the world.

Along with guest speakers, films, costume contests, and art shows, the dealers' room at a convention is one of the major activities. Dealers, many of whom subsist completely by selling their wares at such affairs, will have on display *Star Trek* and *Star Wars* items of every description.

The best advice is to proceed with caution. Often, beginners will be so excited about coming across a desirable item that they will pay whatever price is asked without scanning any other booths to see if it can be bought at a better price. Quite often, patience pays off. Remember: many of the major science-fiction dealers will be present. Many scarce items will show up at one or more of the dealers' tables. So use your judgment and take time to find the best deal.

There may come a time when you will want to or need to sell your collectibles— either a few pieces or an entire collection. Just as in buying, there are various avenues open to you, each with its advantages and disadvantages. Your circumstances and how many items you have to sell may dictate the method you choose. If you are forced to sell your items quickly because you need to raise cash in a hurry, you should anticipate a loss, though this is not always the case. Any time you have to sell a collectible of any type quickly, you dramatically decrease your chances of selling the item at a profit or breaking even. It takes time to sell a collectible—time to shop around for an eager buyer who is willing to pay close to book price or higher. To sell a collectible at a profit, you normally need to hold onto an article for awhile (to let it appreciate in value) and sell it at your leisure.

If you're in a great hurry to raise cash, selling to a dealer is the quickest method. If you have a large collection and you want to sell it all at once, it may be your only option. Individuals and smaller dealers rarely have the capital to be able to afford to buy extensive collections. Buying from the public is the best source of collectibles for dealers, but you will be disappointed if you expect to receive the full value for your articles. You may have to pay 80% to 100% of the market value for a piece, but a dealer couldn't do that and stay in business. He will rarely offer you more than 40% to 60% of book price. And you will rarely receive a better percentage from a dealer by trying to haggle with him, because he has usually figured out just how much he must make on his articles in order to pay his overhead and still make a small profit.

If there is a shop within traveling distance that carries science-fiction items, it may be worth your while to arrange a visit with the owner. Try to be there at a time when the shop is not too busy, so that he can give his full attention to your items. Pack each piece carefully—not only for protection, but to impress the dealer with the idea that you value your pieces. If he thinks you just want to get rid of them in a hurry, he'll assume he can buy them from you at a bargain. It's probably best not to appear to be overly eager or anxious about obtaining immediate cash for the same reason. With a large collection, you could take in just several pieces: then, if the dealer is interested in the entire collection and can afford it, he may be able to visit your home to give you an estimate of his buying price.

If you are trying to sell your items through the mail, make up a thorough list of the pieces you want to sell, giving special attention to condition. Be realistic. In the long run, it won't do you any good to overestimate the condition of your collectibles. If you have a price in mind that you'd like to receive, go ahead and mention that too. If the dealer feels it is too high, he can always make a counteroffer. If you agree on a price, pack your pieces carefully. Remember, the dealer is expecting them in the condition you described and won't feel abliged to pay you if they arrive damaged. If you can, send the package C.O.D. Few dealers will agree to this, however; after all, they've never seen these objects. They need time to take inventory and make sure they are as described. Your best shipping method is United Parcel Service. They automatically insure packages against damage or loss up to $100 and added insurance is available at a nominal fee. They also automatically keep records of all packages they deliver so there is no question that the dealer received your goods. If you must use the Post Office, be sure to send the package certified mail and request a return receipt. Insurance is also available if you ask for it, but collecting on a claim can be a very long process involving a lot of paperwork.

You'll have greater success for a satisfactory sale when you can take your time. Get estimates from a number of dealers—their offers can vary greatly. You never know if a dealer has a customer eager to purchase the exact pieces you have or whether he has only a few customers for these particular types of objects. There can be numerous reasons why one dealer will offer you a low price while another will offer you considerably more. One dealer might have exceeded his budget for buying from the public or be overstocked at the moment. Another might have a low inventory and be looking for something to fill his shelves. You can never know until you've taken the time to talk to them and receive an estimate. Their offers will reflect their particular business and their clientele.

If it irks you to receive only half of the book price for your items, you could place them with a dealer on consignment, though many dealers won't bother, especially with smaller items. This is a much slower method, but you will receive a higher price. If you don't mind waiting months for your pieces to sell, you can set the price yourself. Make sure you know the market value of your item before you agree on a selling price. If you agree to let a dealer sell an item for $50 when it is really worth

$75, he could easily sell it for the $75 and pocket the extra $25 without you ever being the wiser.

You should insist upon a written agreement that stipulates the selling price, how long you agree to leave it on consignment, the amount for his commission (which will probably be about 20%), and for how much he will insure your item from damage or theft. Your regular insurance will not cover your piece when it is in a dealer's shop.

If you are determined to obtain full book value for your items, there are a couple of options open to you. You can try advertising in a collector's or science-fiction publication with national distribution. By reaching a large, select readership, you will increase your chances for some excellent sales. But this can be time consuming, and you get what you pay for in that the publications with the higher readership charge the most for their advertising space. *Starlog* magazine, for example, charges $90 per column inch for space in their classified section.

You can choose to either state prices for each piece or offer to take mail bids. Either way, be sure to state your terms of sale clearly and fully. You will need to list enough information so that the readers can determine exactly which pieces and variations you have. List the names, any numbers or dates, the sizes, colors, and any trademarks. You will attract a greater response if your ad is easy to read, includes all necessary information, and looks professional. Many advertisements are poorly written because the advertiser was trying to save space (and thus, advertising money) or was just plain careless. You can try to conserve space and still present a professional-looking ad. If you have a number of pieces of the same size, group them under a heading indicating the size. The same method can be done with other important traits. If all of your pieces are in top condition, you can just state that once in the ad; but if most of your pieces are in top condition, with some in less than mint, you could place asterisks next to those works and state that the asterisks indicate pieces in less than mint condition. Experiment with what you will include in your ad; try writing it in several different ways. If you leave out some crucial information, such as your address (which has been done), you will have incurred the cost of an ad without the benefits.

Be sure to get the necessary ad information from the publisher. Magazines often have ad deadlines weeks prior to publication. Also be sure to find out in what form you are expected to present your ad. Most publications will lay out a classified advertisement for the customer, but more complex ads are expected to be delivered "copy ready."

You should begin receiving responses to your ad immediately upon the ad's appearance on the newsstand; assuming, of course, that the items you are selling are desirable and fairly priced. You'll get faster response if you also include a phone number, but be sure to keep a list of pertinent information near the phone to answer questions and, if you are only available by phone certain hours, state that in your ad.

As the checks arrive, deposit them in your bank account and allow ten days to make sure they clear before shipping any pieces off. It might be a good idea to put this stipulation in your ad. With money orders and drafts, you will not need to wait. Duplicate checks that arrive late or bids that didn't win should be returned immediately.

Some collectors sell their items by answering want ads in national collector publications. Usually, these ads are run by people who are looking for specific pieces. They quite often receive offers from people selling pieces at very low prices who are trying to dispose of their collections quickly and easily. But sometimes these advertisers are searching for scarce or rare pieces that they have been unable to find and are willing to pay well above book price for such items.

Finally, you might try buying a dealers' table at a *Star Trek* or science-fiction convention if there is going to be one in your area. This is another instance of getting what you pay for, however. The larger conventions, the ones that attract the most potential customers, generally have table prices in the $200 range, and the best table locations will already have been reserved by the professional dealers months or even years in advance. To be sure you even get a table, you should arrange to get your table as far ahead of the convention date as possible. Most convention organizers won't hold a table for you unless you pay in full, in advance. Be sure to find out when the set-up times for the dealers' room are. If possible, try to determine your table location in advance also, although this information often won't be available until set-up. Be prepared to transport your own merchandise to your table. Most conventions are held either at convention centers or large hotels and, as a rule, neither of these provide hand trucks; in the case of a hotel, a bellhop will usually take your items to your table—for a tip, of course. Try to arrange your items as attractively as possible, but keep in mind that small, easy to steal items should be kept in a spot where you can keep an eye on them. It is also a good idea to keep particularly valuable or fragile items out of reach of the customer. You can always hand them to a serious potential customer for inspection.

Make sure you're at your table well in advance of opening the room to the general public. Dealers are usually admitted to the room at least an hour before opening time. Be prepared. You should have change, pens for signing checks, and something to hand out with your address on it, in case the customer decides at a later date he wants an object he saw on your table.

If the convention is more than one day (most are two) and you want to return, you'll have to decide what to do with your merchandise overnight. Ask the convention organizer about overnight security. Arrangements vary from professional armed guards and off-duty police officers to none at all. If you are uncertain about the security, it is best to take your items with you. If this isn't practical, get as much as possible off your table and out of sight. Conventions usually (but not always) provide cover cloths for this purpose. It is still best to take, at least, your most valuable items with you. Remember, conventions are not liable for loss or theft, so it's all up to you.

COLLECTING AS AN INVESTMENT

Though there are a few brave souls who try, for most people it isn't practical to try to collect everything related to *Star Trek* and/or *Star Wars*. Or at least to concentrate on all areas to the same degree. There is simply too much of it. So, for most people, a time comes when they will have to decide in what direction they want their collections to grow. Some already have a starting point for one reason or another. Perhaps they still have a few toys left from their childhood or became interested through another hobby, such as comic book collecting.

The first and best criterion for collecting should be to pick the subjects that you find interesting, whatever they may be. This guarantees you the most satisfaction with your hobby. But strictly from the standpoint of investing, certain areas are strong and others weak.

One of the best indicators for a good potential investment is whether it fits into another collectible field. An item in this category is in demand by more than one group. More people competing for a limited number of collectibles can only cause the value to rise. They only made a certain number of 1976 Topps *Star Trek* gum cards. This set is very popular among *Star Trek* collectors. It is also very popular among non-sports card collectors who may know very little about *Star Trek* collecting in general. Other kinds of items that this rule applies to include action figures, books, toys, plates, comics, movie posters, and models, to name a few.

Another very important thing to consider, especially for the beginning collector, is ease of manufacture. For an item to become collectible, its numbers must be finite. This is definitely not to say that you shouldn't buy an item still being made. In fact, that's the best time to buy an article because it will never be cheaper. But certain items, usually the hard to make ones, are only likely to be made for a certain period of time.

Let's start with the kind of things that aren't very hard to make. At any convention you can see the attendees dressed in Tee shirts festooned with buttons, patches, and costume jewelry. They'll be carrying armloads of blueprints, stills, scripts, and posters. They've spent a considerable sum of money on all kinds of fun stuff that will never again be worth what they paid. Why? Most of these kinds of items are made by fans or dealers. They are inexpensive to make in small quantities and as long as they continue to sell, someone will continue to make them.

So what makes an article a safe investment? Toys are a good example. To make a plastic toy requires an expensive mold and skilled technicians. No fan is going to reproduce a die-cast TIE Bomber in his basement. At least not in quantity. Also, because of the competitive nature of the toy business, toy companies change their lines quite often. When a toy goes out of production, it almost never goes back in, especially, as in the case of *Star Trek* or *Star Wars* toys, where an expensive license from the studio is also involved. Some other examples are plates and other ceramics or glassware, coins, books, action figures, and models. It should be noted, however, that model manufacturers do *sometimes* reissue their products. Since they employ the same molds and the model is virtually identical, this can turn a collectible piece into just another model almost overnight.

Also, unfortunately, as prices rise on *Star Trek* and *Star Wars* collectibles, the enticement to counterfeit collectibles grows. Printed matter that employs a full-color printing process (not to be confused with a photograph, which can be done in small numbers), such as movie posters and book covers, used to be considered safe from reproduction because it requires the manufacturer to make a considerable number of each item. The cost is also considerable, though not up there with that of a toy. But if an item attains enough value, it becomes worthwhile. An example of this is what happened with the *"Revenge of the Jedi"* advance movie poster. When they changed the name of the movie to *"Return,"* the few *"Revenge"* posters that had already been made began to rise in value rapidly. When they were selling for about $100, suddenly there seemed to be a lot more of them around. Dealers, of course, soon realized what had happened and found minute differences that could tell the two apart. This was too late, however, for the many people who had paid $100 for a counterfeit poster.

Finally, we should mention original production items. Almost every collector would love to own an original prop, costume, script, or other piece of memorabilia from one of the movies or TV shows. In the early days, this was a realistic possibility, not only because these things were (though expensive) within the range of most people's finances, but also because they were there at all. A surprising number of people naively assume that when a *Star Trek* or *Star Wars* movie was over that these items were either sold or given away. This couldn't be further from the truth. In actuality, studios try very hard to keep items from getting out. It does happen occasionally, but the studios take a very dim view of this activity and recently have pursued it more aggressively; to the extent of having the offenders arrested. It is, after all, their property.

When you do see an item like this offered for sale, it's best to be more than a little skeptical. First of all, even if the article is genuine, it may be impossible to authenticate more recent ones, for the reasons mentioned above, and older ones simply by virtue of time. It has, after all, been 25 years since they last filmed an episode of the original "Star Trek" series.

Secondly, these kind of items are particularly susceptible to counterfeiting. Modern scripts are nothing more than photocopies, and one photocopy looks pretty much like every other photocopy. Costumes and props are all handmade anyway, so quality must be ruled out as a determining factor of authenticity. In fact, prop reproductions are generally better looking than the originals, most of which were not designed for close examination.

And finally, even if you are sure the object is authentic, unless it is either an extremely minor piece or in absolutely wretched condition, the asking price is likely to be astronomical, such is the demand for this type of item.

But don't be discouraged. For every pitfall to collecting, there are a dozen opportunities for the knowledgeable collector to profit from his investment while enjoying a fascinating hobby. Few "traditional" investments appreciate in value as quickly as *Star Trek* and *Star Wars* items, and it is probably within the top five of all collectible fields. In addition, because *Star Trek* and, to a limited extent, *Star Wars* items are still being produced, it is also an expanding field. Products are still being manufactured that in a year's time may be worth many times what you paid for them.

CONDITION AND CARE

More and more emphasis is being placed on the condition of items in the *Star Trek* and *Star Wars* collectible field. This is not to say that pieces in lesser condition are not valuable. On the contrary, as rarer items become harder to find, collectors are often happy just to obtain a particularly desirable piece. But values for items in exceptionaly nice shape are much higher, so much so that they will often sell for two or three times the amount of a piece in average condition.

To ensure that your collection obtains the best investment value, it is best to follow a few simple common sense rules. For starters, most serious collectors want their items to be as close as possible to the condition in which they came from the factory. Pieces should always be complete. Most collectors will accept applied decals or a lost instruction sheet, but few will buy an item with a missing part of a toy or game, missing page from a book, missing jigsaw puzzle piece, etc. Toys and games often came with a list of parts that can be helpful in determining if an item is complete. In the same vein, a worked craft kit, written-in puzzle book, or assembled model is usually not acceptable. If you wish to buy a current production model that you think may become collectible but still would like to assemble it, buy two, one to build and one to set aside. One of the most important factors and one of the most overlooked is the package. To collectors, condition refers not only to the item itself but to the box it originally came in. Many disappointed collectors have learned that their carefully cared for collection is only worth a fraction of what they thought it was because they didn't save the boxes. In the case of items blister packed on cardboard backings, an unopened one is much more desirable than even one where the backing has been saved. If you are determined to handle the item, do as in the case of the models and buy two.

An operating toy or game should be in its original working condition. This is rarely a problem when buying from another collector, since they usually don't play with the item themselves. Sometimes, however, you may run across an item that is broken but can be repaired, either by a professional or by yourself if you are talented at this sort of thing. If you do fix a piece, however, be aware that a careless repair job that mars the surface in some way may do more harm than good.

It is also possible to repair, or have repaired, paper items (books, comic books, posters, etc.). In fact, there is a growing industry in the comic book collectible field devoted to such repairs. It should be noted, however, that while in general these repairs increase the value of your collectibles, some collectors do not consider repaired paper goods to constitute "original condition," so when selling repaired paper items you should always make it clear to the buyer that a repair has been done.

Collectibles made of paper present other problems. Age and environmental conditions deteriorate paper items quickly, and while a torn or wrinkled item can be repaired, a brittle or faded one is usually beyond restoration. To avoid this, first of all, take special care to buy paper collectibles in good condition and once having purchased them take special precautions with their storage. Be sure they are kept away from sunlight, moisture, and dust. Magazines, books, and comics should be stored in plastic collectibles bags available from mail-order companies and comic book stores. These are made in several sizes to match different types of publications. Plastic kitchen bags should not be used, as these tend to adhere to the paper. If magazines and comics are to be stored upright on shelves or in boxes, use cardboard backing boards to keep them from sagging and getting damaged. The best kind are the special "acid-free" boards that don't contain certain chemicals used in some cardboards, which can deteriorate the paper in books.

Trading cards should be free from creases and dog ears, and ideally the pictures on the cards should be well centered. Gum stains on older cards are also undesirable. Trading card sets should not be wrapped with rubber bands, although you will often see dealers display sets this way. Over time, the rubber band can dent and discolor the top and bottom cards. Sleeves, albums, and loose-leaf pages are available to store individual cards, and boxes are available for sets.

Posters are best displayed either framed or, if this is too expensive, shrink-wrapped onto a cardboard poster board. Posters are best stored loosely rolled in cardboard tubes that will prevent them from being crushed. Lastly, never use any kind of adhesive tape on posters or any other kind of paper goods.

WHERE TO BUY

Though *Star Trek* and *Star Wars* collectibles are bought and sold through private transactions (i.e., personal ads, garage sales, etc.), probably 75% or more are exchanged through dealers. Dealers generally fall into three categories: convention dealers, stores, and mail-order companies. Though stores and mail-order companies do set up at conventions, there are many dealers whose entire business is conducted at the conventions. For this reason, conventions are one of the best places to find a good selection of merchandise. Conventions are not always conveniently available, however. Stores that could conceivably sell *Star Trek* and *Star Wars* items are available in most towns of any size. The best way to find them is to use your local yellow pages phone directory and look under categories such as "books," "games," and "toys." Dealers who advertise comics and/or science fiction items under these categories also often carry *Star Trek* or *Star Wars* items. A quick phone call and a few questions are all that is needed to find out. The final source of dealers, mail-order companies, is available to everyone no matter how remote your place of residence or limited your means of transportation. Though small mail-order companies exist, the following is a list of the better established ones that sell *Star Trek* and/or *Star Wars* items.

> **Intergalactic Trading Co., Inc.**
> P.O. Box 1516
> Longwood, FL 32750

> **Lincoln Enterprises (Star Trek only)**
> P.O. Box 69470
> Los Angeles, CA 90069

> **New Eye Studio**
> P.O. Box 632
> Willimantic, CT 06110

> **Star Land**
> P.O. Box 19413
> Denver, CO 80219

> **Star Tech**
> P.O. Box 456
> Dunlap, TN 37327

HOW TO USE THIS BOOK

The items in this book are divided into two major sections: *Star Trek* and *Star Wars* collectibles. Within each section, items are alphabetically listed in groups by type of item, such as button, poster, toy, etc. The Table of Contents lists each topic grouping. Within the group, each individual item is listed either alphabetically by its most common name or short descriptive term, chronologically by issuing date, or alphabetically by manufacturer, depending on which is the most logical, easy form of reference for the item. Thorough descriptions are given when possible in order to aid you in positively identifying your pieces. Manufacturer, color, size, date, and any other pertinent information is given when known.

Thousands of collectibles are listed with prices in this book. A price range is given for each article. The range shows the lowest and highest selling prices for a particular piece at the time this book was compiled. These prices are retail selling prices—what dealers sell these items for to the public. Prices were determined by averaging the prices of actual sales or sale offers from across the country. Sales at secondary sources, such as flea market and garage sales, which can be much higher or much lower, were not included in the averaging of prices.

These prices should be used as guidelines and not set laws. Just as in buying other articles, you can find differences in prices by shopping around. You will discover prices much higher and much lower than these averages, but these will be exceptions, not the rule. It is not unusual for very high or very low prices to be paid at auctions. Also, the prices dealers charge will vary depending on their volume of business, their overhead, and the type of customers they have. A dealer who pays high rent for an attractively situated shop may have to charge more to meet his high overhead; another dealer may have such a large number of customers that he can afford to make a smaller margin of profit on each piece, so his prices may be lower.

A 20% to 30% variation from these prices might indicate a changing trend for that particular piece, especially if you keep encountering prices consistently higher or lower. In fact, you should remain aware of any fluctuations in prices, as this may affect your strategy as to what you'll purchase, and when.

These prices are those at which dealers sell *Star Trek* and *Star Wars* collectibles to the public. Dealers will not buy them from you at these prices. In order to meet their overhead expenses and still make a profit, dealers buy at wholesale—which is about 40% to 60% of the retail price. This can vary, too, depending on the dealer's circumstances.

STAR TREK LISTINGS

ACTION AND COLLECTORS' FIGURES

This section is divided into three categories: large and small action figures, and collectors' figures. The first two categories are organized chronologically by original TV show, movies, and *Star Trek: The Next Generation*. Because avid interest on the part of collectors has caused the value of action figures to increase so dramatically, price ranges will be given for both packaged and unpackaged figures. Values listed for unpackaged dolls assume doll is otherwise complete.

Large Action Figures
Original Star Trek Action Figures

Mego Corp., 8″ tall, 1975. These were issued in three different series and values are based on scarcity of each series. A small hoard of first series dolls surfaced in Canada in 1985, keeping these values artificially low until the supply is depleted. All are fully costumed with movable joints and hand equipment. Figures came blister packed on display cards.

FIRST SERIES
Captain Kirk, with phaser, communicator, and belt, Packaged..................................$30–$45
  Unpackaged...$15–$25
Mr. Spock, with phaser, communicator, belt, and tricorder, Packaged.....................$30–$45
  Unpackaged...$15–$25
Dr. McCoy, with tricorder, Packaged...$80–$125
  Unpackaged...$50–$75
Mr. Scott, with phaser, communicator, and belt, Packaged.....................................$80–$125
  Unpackaged...$50–$75

Kirk action figures. Back: Mego 12″, Knickerbocker soft figure, Ernst porcelain. Front: ERTL ST III, Mego 8″, Mego 3¾″.

Cheron in package.

8″ Mego Romulan doll.

Lt. Uhura, with tricorder, Packaged ....$80–$125
    Unpackaged...$50–$75
Klingon, with phaser, communicator and belt, Packaged...$35–$60
    Unpackaged...$20–$30

SECOND SERIES

Cheron, black and white alien, Packaged ....$150–$200
    Unpackaged..$50–$75
Gorn, reptilian alien, with phaser, Packaged ....$150–$250
    Unpackaged...$75–$100
The Keeper, blue, barefooted alien in light-colored robe, Packaged ....$150–$200
    Unpackaged..$50–$75
Neptunian, green amphibian with webbed feet and hands, Packaged ....$150–$250
    Unpackaged..$50–$75

THIRD SERIES

Andorian, blue, antennaed alien, Packaged..$400–$700
    Unpackaged..$300–$350
Mugato, horned apelike alien, Packaged ....$300–$600
    Unpackaged..$200–$250
Romulan, gold helmet, with phaser, Packaged.......................................$500–$800
    Unpackaged..$300–$350
Talosian, yellow outfit, belt and boots, Packaged...................................$300–$500
    Unpackaged..$200–$250

Star Trek: The Motion Picture Figures

Mego Corp., 12″ tall, 1979. All are fully costumed with posable joints and hand equipment. Came boxed with clear plastic window. *Note:* The plastic used in the faces of this series of dolls has a tendency to discolor with long exposure to sunlight.
Capt. Kirk, with phaser and belt buckle, Packaged ....$70–$100
    Unpackaged..$40–$60
Mr. Spock, with phaser and belt buckle, Packaged ....$70–$100
    Unpackaged..$40–$60
Decker, with phaser and belt buckle, Packaged......................................$100–$150
    Unpackaged..$50–$75
Ilia, with white shoes and necklace, Packaged...$60–$90
    Unpackaged..$35–$55
Arcturian, fleshy head, beige uniform, Packaged ....$60–$90
    Unpackaged..$35–$55
Klingon, ridged head, uniform, Packaged..$100–$150
    Unpackaged..$50–$75

Star Trek Doll Collection

Ernst, 13″ tall, 1988. Collectors series of original TV dolls from Ernst. Porcelain head, arms, and feet. Soft bodies with cloth uniforms. All dolls came with to-scale accessories and metal doll stand. Packaged in white cardboard boxes with blue Star Trek logo and illustration of original TV Enterprise.

Kirk, with silver phaser...$150–$200
Spock, with black and gold communicator ....$150–$200
McCoy, with orange painted clear beaker...$125–$175
Scotty, with phaser and communicator...$125–$175
Sulu, with phaser and communicator..$75–$125
Chekov, with phaser and communicator ....$75–$125
Uhura, no accessories ....$75–$125

Knickerbocker Soft Posable Figures

1979, 13″ tall, plastic head, soft body in *Star Trek: The Motion Picture* uniform.
Came boxed in window box without plastic. Photo of Kirk, Spock, and movie Enter-
prise on box.
Kirk ....$25–$40
Spock..$25–$40

Small Action Figures
Star Trek: The Motion Picture
Mego Corp., 3¾″ tall, 1979, posable. Came blister packed on color cards.

FIRST SERIES
Kirk, Packaged...$25–$50
    Unpackaged...$10–$15
Spock, Packaged...$25–$50
    Unpackaged...$10–$15
Ilia, Packaged ....$15–$20
    Unpackaged..$5–$10
Decker, Packaged ....$20–$25
    Unpackaged..$8–$12
Dr. McCoy, Packaged...$30–$40
    Unpackaged...$15–$20
Scotty, Packaged...$20–$25
    Unpackaged..$8–$12

SECOND SERIES
Made primarily for overseas markets. Some were available in the United States
through Sears mail order but these did not come on cards.

Mego 3¾″ aliens. Left to right: Betelgeusian, Arcturian, Megarite, Rigellian, Klingon, Zaranite.

Arcturian, wrinkle-faced alien, Packaged .... $100–$150
  Unpackaged.. $50–$75
Betelgeusian, dark-skinned alien with black headpiece, Packaged .... $175–$250
  Unpackaged... $100–$150
Klingon (movie version), Packaged .... $100–$150
  Unpackaged.. $50–$75
Megarite, multilipped, black outfit, Packaged .... $150–$200
  Unpackaged... $75–$125
Rigellian, purple-skinned, white outfit, Packaged .... $100–$150
  Unpackaged.. $50–$75
Zaranite, silver mask, gray outfit, Packaged .... $125–$175
  Unpackaged... $75–$125

Star Trek III: The Search for Spock

ERTL, 3¾″ tall, 1984, fully posable. Came blister packed on color card, included hand equipment for each figure.
Captain Kirk, with communicator, Packaged .... $15–$25
  Unpackaged.. $10–$20
Mr. Spock, with phaser, Packaged .... $15–$25
  Unpackaged.. $10–$20
Mr. Scott, with phaser, Packaged .... $10–$20
  Unpackaged... $8–$15
Klingon, with pet, Packaged .... $10–$20
  Unpackaged... $8–$15

Star Trek: The Next Generation

Galoob, 3¾″, 1988, posable. Came blister packed on blue card. These figures were released in mixed cases with very unbalanced distribution. Prices reflect scarcity of figures. Galoob originally intended to release two additional figures, "Wesley Crusher" and a "Romulan." Though these are pictured on the packages of many Galoob *Next Generation* products, they were never produced.

ENTERPRISE CREW
Capt. Picard, Packaged .... $3–$6
  Unpackaged... —
Commander Riker, Packaged... $3–$5
  Unpackaged... —

Complete set of Next Generation aliens in package.

Star Trek V figures.

Lt. Data*, Packaged ....$15–$25
   Unpackaged..$5–$10
Lt. Commander La Forge, Packaged ....$3–$6
   Unpackaged...—
Lt. Worf, Packaged ....$3–$6
   Unpackaged...—
Lt. Yar, Packaged...$15–$25
   Unpackaged..$5–$10
*There are several variations on Data's face coloration, including speckled, blue or white. These sell for up to $100 depending on the variation and the preference of the individual collector. The white/blue variation is usually considered the rarest.

ALIENS
Antican, felinoid, gray outfit, Packaged ....$35–$65
   Unpackaged..$15–$25
Ferengi, striped vest, olive pants, Packaged ....$45–$75
   Unpackaged..$20–$30
"Q", black outfit, Packaged ....$45–$75
   Unpackaged..$20–$30
Selay, green reptilian, Packaged..$35–$65
   Unpackaged..$15–$25

Star Trek V Collectors' Figures (Galoob, 1989)

These are technically not action figures since they are unjointed, permanently posed statuettes. Approximately 7″ tall, came packaged in window boxes with color photos of character on side and color artwork backdrop for figure. Prices are for packaged figures only.
Captain James T. Kirk ....$40–$60
Dr. Leonard McCoy ....$40–$60
Klaa ....$40–$60
Mr. Spock...$40–$60
Sybok...$40–$60

ARTWORK

It would be improper to write a book about collectibles without mentioning original works of art. At the same time, it is impossible to catalog art because it is, by nature, unique. When considering Star Trek art as a collectible, it is, first of all, best to use the same criteria you would use for any other category: Does it appeal to you? This

Original painting that became cover of FASA Star Trek role-playing game.

might be both difficult and easy at the same time because Star Trek art is so diverse. The word art means a painting to most people, but this overlooks a vast assortment of skills and crafts. At a large Star Trek convention you can find sculptures, ceramics, jewelry, needlepoint, leatherwork, and much more that fits into the category of art.

When buying an item with an eye toward future collectibility, however, you may wish to consider a few things. Is the piece well made? Is the person who made it a good craftsman as well as a good artist? Does the piece have a unique quality? Does it fit in with your other collectibles? Is the artist well known in his or her field? Has the work ever been published, say as a book cover?

Some very well-known artists in the fantasy and science fiction art field have done artwork for published Star Trek items.

Prices range from a few cents for a fan-made craft item to several thousand dollars for a painting by a nationally known artist.

BADGES

In this section, the badges referred to are either the hard plastic pinback type or paper or card stock inserted into pliable plastic pinback badgeholders. Other items that might be considered badges are found in the "Buttons" and "Jewelry" sections. Badges are very easily reproduced. For this reason they rarely become valuable. Most have more than one manufacturer.

Star Fleet Divisional ID (original TV), light card stock, vertical format, personal data, six different divisional symbols available. All black or black and blue UFP symbol.................$1–$3
Star Trek: The Next Generation Hard Plastic, words embossed on holographic foil..$2–$5
United Starship Enterprise Boarding Pass, paper, space for name and contrasting color foil or photo. Signed by the character of choice ....$1–$3
Enterprise Badge, 3½" long, silver and blue, original TV ship, silkscreen on die-cut hard plastic...$1–$3
Star Fleet Command, 3½" × 2¼" paper stock, blue and white UFP symbol on black background, personal data on reverse ....$1–$3
Star Fleet ID Badges (original TV), hard plastic, gold, blue or red, engraved words and original TV symbol engraved or applied with contrasting plastic..$1–$3
Star Fleet ID Badges (Star Trek: The Motion Picture), hard plastic in white, orange, green, red, yellow or silver. Engraved words and command symbol..$1–$3

BLUEPRINTS

Though almost always referred to as "blueprints," a process used most commonly to reproduce architectural drawings, plans of the type listed in this section are usually

Star Trek blueprints. Two on bottom are only licensed blueprints.

printed in the standard offset manner. Most are fan produced and vary greatly in quality and detail. Except where noted, they come packed in printed envelopes or sometimes, in the case of one-sheet designs, merely rolled or folded. Plans packaged this way are easily reproduced and rarely become valuable as collectibles.

Alaska, one-sheet poster format, 20″ × 26″, intermediate Enterprise design .... $4–$6

Almeida Class Heavy Cruiser-Freighter, M. Morrissette, five sheets, 8″ × 22″ .... $4–$5

Animated Freighter Blueprint Set, Geoffrey Mandel, 12-sheet set .... $4–$6

Aurora, alien vessel from original TV show, set of two sheets, 16″ × 22″ .... $4–$6

Avenger Class, 1983, D.J. Nielsen, six-sheet set, Reliant from Star Trek II .... $8–$10

Bridge Blueprints, M. McMaster:

   1st edition, vertical cover format, blue ink .... $15–$20

   2nd edition, horizontal format, red and blue cover .... $10–$15

   3rd edition, black ink, horizontal format cover .... $10–$12

Caracal Class Command Cruiser, T. Guenther, shows interiors and exteriors, 12 sheets, 8½″ × 28″ .... $10–$15

Class F Shuttlecraft, Omega Prints, six sheets .... $6–$8

Decater, Starstation Aurora, one sheet, several different ships .... $3–$4

Detroyat Class Heavy Destroyer, M. Morrissette, general plans, six sheets, 10½″ × 28″ .... $5–$6

Dreadnought, Allie C. Peed III, ten sheets .... $10–$12

Drone Blueprints, four sheets, sensor carrying drone .... $5–$6

Durance Cargo Tug Class Starship, T. Guenther, exterior and cutaway views, five sheets, 8″ × 17″ .... $5–$6

DY 500, Starstation Aurora, one sheet .... $3–$4

Enterprise, pilot film version from original TV show, two-sheet set, shows detailed exterior .... $6–$8

Enterprise, regular season from original TV show, two-sheet set .... $6–$8

Enterprise Blueprints, Franz Joseph, rolled edition, a few were produced prior to professional production by Ballantine Books .... $75–$125

Enterprise Blueprints, professional edition, Franz Joseph, Ballantine Books, 1975, brown plastic pouch .... $30–$50

Enterprise Blueprints, from Star Trek—The Role Playing Game, boxed with book of descriptions, set of nine, 22″ × 33″, FASA .... $15–$25

Enterprise Construction Plans, A. Everhart, four sheets, shows deck plans for the construction in outer space of the Enterprise, 18″ × 24″ .... $6–$8

Enterprise Evolution, three 24″ × 36″ sheets, ten different ship variations .... $9–$11

Enterprise Exterior Profiles, 24″ × 60″, Starcraft Productions .... $6–$8

Enterprise Legacy, one-sheet poster format, shows evolution of Enterprise, 20″ × 26″ .... $4–$6

Excelsior, Starstation Aurora, eight sheets, white plastic pouch, blue cover sheet .... $9–$11

Federation Reference Series, Vol. 1, Star Fleet Printing Office, Technical Manual, booklet form...$4–$6

Federation Reference Series, Vol. 2, Star Fleet Printing Office, Technical Manual, booklet form...$4–$6

Federation Reference Series, Vol. 3, Star Fleet Printing Office, Technical Manual, booklet form...$4–$6

Federation Reference Series, Vol. 4, Star Fleet Printing Office, Technical Manual, booklet form...$4–$6

Federation Reference Series, Vol. 5, Star Fleet Printing Office, Technical Manual, booklet form...$4–$6

Federation Reference Series, Vol. 6, Star Fleet Printing Office, Technical Manual, booklet form...$4–$6

Federation Size Comparison Charts, special edition, two sheets, Starstation Aurora ..$6–$8

Federation Size Comparison Charts, Vol. II, two sheets, Starstation Aurora ....$6–$8

Federation Starship Profiles Chart, 24″ × 36″ poster format displays 45 starship silhouettes ....$4–$6

Galaxy Class Blueprints, five sheets..$6–$8

Galileo Shuttlecraft Plans, A. Everhart, two sheets, exterior and cutaway views, 18″ × 24″ ....$3–$4

Glenn Class Fleet Survey Vessel, four sheets...$5–$8

Gorn Blueprints, depicts exterior of the Gorn ship, two sheets, 8½″ × 14″...................$4–$6

Hornet Class Starship, fan produced, seven sheets...$10–$12

Katanga Class Klingon Vessel, exterior profile, Starcraft Productions ....$7–$9

Klingon Blueprints, M. McMaster, supplement detail sheet, exterior and interior, all levels and decks, set of eight, 13″ × 29″...$8–$10

Klingon D-7 Blueprints, from Star Trek—The Role Playing Game, boxed, with book of descriptions, set of six, 22″ × 33″, FASA...$11–$13

Klingon K'torr Blueprints, interior and exterior plans, nine sheets...........................$9–$10

Klingon Scout Vessel, from Star Trek III: The Search for Spock, six sheets ....$10–$12

Kobayashi Maru, David Nielsen, four sheets..$4–$6

Merchantman, from Star Trek III, five sheets ....$6–$9

Olympus Class Battle Dreadnought, 20″ × 26″, one-sheet poster design.....................$4–$6

Paladin Class Scout/Destroyer, 20″ × 26″, one-sheet poster design..............................$4–$6

Regula I Space Station, five sheets..$8–$10

Renner, four sheets ....$4–$6

Romulan Bird of Prey Cruiser, M. McMaster, five sheets......................................$6–$8

Romulan L-85 Battleship, from Star Trek: The Next Generation, one-sheet poster format, 20″ × 26″..$4–$6

Saladin Class Destroyer Scout, deck-by-deck plans, Jeffries tube plans, inside view of space warp propulsion unit, set of nine sheets, Starcraft Productions.....................................$8–$9

Size Comparison Chart, showing the exterior designs of all the ships of Star Trek, includes Romulan, Tholian, Klingon D-7, Enterprise...$3–$4

Space Station K-7, interior and exterior, six sheets ....$5–$7

Star Trek: The Motion Picture Blueprints, shows exterior detail only of the Enterprise bridge, Klingon ship and bridge, Vulcan shuttle, travel pod, and more, black plastic pouch with blue insert, out of print, Wallaby, 1980..$30–$50

Star Trek: The Motion Picture Blueprints, unauthorized reprint, comes in paper envelope ....$7–$12

Vadenda Class Freighter Plans, large 12-page blueprint set ....$10–$12

Warp Drive Blueprints, 1984 ....$2–$3

Weapons and Field Equipment, Vol. I, 1983, fan produced, five sheets, features phasers, communicator, and phaser rifle*..$8–$10

Weapons and Field Equipment, Vol. II, fan produced, five sheets*............................$8–$10

Weapons and Field Equipment, Vol. III, fan produced, five sheets* ....$8–$10

*These three were later compiled into book form as "Weapons Manual."

A selection of more collectible Star Trek books.

BOOKS

Adult Books

This section is generally organized alphabetically by title. Exceptions have been made, however, in cases where there are several titles in a particular series. These have been listed together under general title for ease of reference.

Note: *As it is used in the book industry, the term paperback here refers to the size (cover dimension, not thickness) book common to most paperback novels while "trade" paperback refers to an oversize paperback book.*

Bantam Novels

An early series of Star Trek novels. All have been reprinted since their original publication dates with different cover art. As prices indicate, some are much more common than others. Published in the United Kingdom, by Corgi.

Death's Angel, Kathleen Sky, 1981 ....$12–$15
    Reprint..$12–$15
Devil World, Gordon Eklund, 1979..$10–$12
    Reprint..$8–$10
Fate of the Phoenix, The, S. Marshak and M. Culbreath, 1979, sequel to Price of the Phoenix
....$4–$5
    Reprint..$4–$5
Galactic Whirlpool, The, David Gerrold, 1980...$4–$6
    Reprint..$4–$5
Mudd's Angels, J.A. Lawrence, 1978 ....$12–$15
    Reprint..$10–$12
Perry's Planet, J. Haldeman II, 1980 ....$8–$12
    Reprint..$6–$8
Planet of Judgement, Joe Haldeman, 1977 ....$4–$6
    Reprint..$4–$5
Price of the Phoenix, S. Marshak and M. Culbreath, 1977 ....$4–$5
    Reprint..$4–$5
Spock Messiah, Theodore Cogswell and Charles Spano, 1976 ....$4–$6
    Reprint..$4–$5
Spock Must Die, James Blish, 1970..$4–$6
    Reprint..$4–$5
Starless World, Gordon Eklund, 1978 ....$10–$12
    Reprint..$8–$10

Trek to Madworld, Stephen Golkin, 1979 ....$8–$12
    Reprint...$6–$8
Vulcan, Kathleen Sky, 1978 ....:...$12–$15
    Reprint...$10–$12
World Without End, Joe Haldeman, 1979 ....$8–$12
    Reprint...$6–$8

Best of Trek, The

A current series, now published by Signet (later ROC), based on *Trek*, a high-quality, fan-published magazine from the '70s. Each book is a collection of articles from different sources concerning Star Trek characters, actors, fan activities, etc. Though the publisher does not keep all books in print, to date none have stayed out of print long enough to give them serious collectible value. Dates shown are original Signet publication dates. Editors are Walter Irwin and G.B. Love.

   1 1978, **2** 1980, **3** 1981, **4** 1981, **5** 1982, **6** 1983, **7** 1984, **8** 1985, **9** 1985, **10** 1986, **11** 1986, **12** 1987, **13** 1988, **14** 1988, **15** 1990, **16** 1991 ....$3–$6
Best of Best of Trek, 1990, trade paperback ....$9–$11

Blish Novelizations

Adapations of the original TV episodes by James Blish. Published in the United States by Bantam and in the United Kingdom by Corgi. There were numerous printings and cover art often varied between editions. The final book, #12, was co-authored by J.A. Lawrence, James Blish's wife, because Mr. Blish died before the book could be completed. First printings and higher numbers (because there were fewer printed) tend to be more valuable.

   No. 1 January 1967, **No. 2** February 1968, **No. 3** April 1969, **No. 4** July 1971, **No. 5** February 1972, **No. 6** April 1972, **No. 7** July 1972, **No. 8** November 1972, **No. 9** August 1973, **No. 10** February 1974 ....$3–$6
   No. 11 April 1975 ....:...............................$5–$8
   No. 12 November 1977...$12–$20
Captain's Log: Star Trek V, The Final Frontier, Lisabeth Shatner, Pocket, 1989. A personal account of the making of the movie. Trade paperback...$9–$11
Chekov's Enterprise, Walter Koenig, Pocket, 1980. A personal journal of the making of Star Trek: The Motion Picture. Paperback..$25–$40
Encyclopedia of Trekkie Memorabilia, Chris Gentry and Sally Gibson Downs, Books Americana, 1988. Trade paperback ....$16–$18

Chekov's Enterprise.

Fotonovel #2 (U.S.). Venezuelan and Japanese edition.

Enterprise Officers' Manual, Geoffrey Mandel, fan produced, 8½″ × 11″, spiral bound ....
....$10–$12
Enterprise Officers' Manual (revised edition), Geoffrey Mandel, fan produced, 8½″ × 11″,
square bound ....$12–$15
Fotonovels, Bantam. Scene-by-scene color adapations of the original TV show. Series of 12.
Note: *This popular series of books has been translated into several languages by foreign publishing houses. Foreign language editions have approximately the same value as U.S. editions.*
No. 1 *City on the Edge of Forever*, Nov. 1977 ....$10–$15
No. 2 *Where No Man has Gone Before*, Nov. 1977 ....$10–$15
No. 3 *The Trouble with Tribbles*, Dec. 1977 ....$10–$15
No. 4 *A Taste of Armageddon*, Jan. 1978 ....$10–$12
No. 5 *Metamorphosis*, Feb. 1978 ....$10–$12
No. 6 *All Our Yesterdays*, March 1978 ....$10–$15
No. 7 *The Galileo 7*, May 1978..$12–$18
No. 8 *A Piece of the Action*, June 1978 ....$12–$18
No. 9 *Devil in the Dark*, July 1978 ....$15–$20
No. 10 *Day of the Dove*, Aug. 1978...$15–$20
No. 11 *The Deadly Years*, Sept. 1978..$15–$20
No. 12 *Amok Time*, Oct. 1978..$20–$30
I am Not Spock, Leonard Nimoy, autobiography of the Spock/Nimoy relationship.
Trade paperback, Celestial Arts, 1975...$35–$60
Regular paperback size, Del Rey, 1977 ....$15–$30

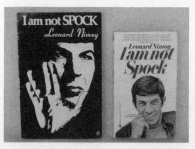

"I Am Not Spock" Celestial Arts and Del Rey editions.

The Making of Star Trek, first ed. (far left) and later editions.

Note: *Leonard Nimoy also did a series of poetry and photography books which, while not tech-nically Star Trek books, are still in demand as collectibles. They are as follows:*
　Will I Think of You, Celestial Arts (1st edition), *Will I Think of You,* Dell, *You and I,* Celes-tial Arts (1st edition), *You and I,* Avon, *Thank You for Your Love,* Blue Mountain, *Come Be with Me,* Blue Mountain, *These Words are for You,* Blue Mountain, *We are All Children Searching for Love,* Blue Mountain, ...$15–$25
　Warmed by Love, Blue Mountain, hardback, excerpts from other books ....$16–$20
Klingon Dictionary, Mark Okrand, Pocket, 1985. English/Klingon, Klingon/English. Paper-back ....$5–$7
Letters to Star Trek, Susan Sackett, Ballantine, 1977 ....$8–$12
Line Officers Requirements, 1978, fan produced, 1st printing in one book ....$16–$20
Line Officers Requirements, later editions divided into three separate books with some added information. Fan produced.
　Vol. I, 1987..$12–$14
　Vol. II, 1987..$14–$16
　Supplement, 1987..$9–$11
Make-Your-Own-Costume Book, Wallaby, 1979, Lynn Edelman Schnurnberger. Simplified costumes from Star Trek: The Motion Picture. Oversize hardback ....$15–$25
　Trade paperback...$10–$20
Making of Star Trek, The, Stephen Whitfield and Gene Roddenberry, Ballantine, 1968. His-tory of the making of the original TV series. 1st edition..$10–$25
　Later editions (changed to Del Rey, a division of Ballantine) ....$5–$10
Making of Star Trek: The Motion Picture, The, Susan Sackett with Gene Roddenberry, Wallaby, 1980. Trade paperback..$30–$40
　Hardcover..$40–$60

Hardcover book. *Mission to Horatius.*

Making of Star Trek II: The Wrath of Khan, The, Allan Asherman, Pocket, 1982. Trade paperback...$20–$35
Making of the Trek Conventions, The, Joan Winston. Photographs and behind-the-scenes descriptions. Hardcover, Doubleday, 1977 ....$20–$30
 Regular size paperback, Playboy Press, 1979 ....$10–$20
Meaning in Star Trek, Karen Blair. Explains Star Trek's popularity through Jungian psychology. Hardcover, Anima, 1977...$10–$12
 Regular size paperback, Warner Books, 1977 ....$8–$10
Mirror Friend, Mirror Foe, George Takei and R. Aspirin, Playboy Press, 1979. Original science fiction...$10–$15
Mission to Horatius, Western, 1968, Mack Reynolds. Hardback. First professional Star Trek novel..$20–$40
Monsters of Star Trek, The, D. Cohen, Pocket, 1980....................................$2–$5
Mr. Scott's Guide to the Enterprise, Shane Johnson, Simon and Schuster, 1987. Trade paperback...$10–$12
My Stars, M.C. Goodwin, Vulcan Books, 1980. Collection of comic strips about Star Trek and the Enterprise ....$10–$15
Official Star Trek Cooking Manual, The, Ann Piccard, Bantam, 1978 ....$40–$60
Official Star Trek Quiz Book, The, Mitchell Magilo, Pocket, 1985. Trade paperback
....$8–$15
Official Star Trek Trivia Book, The, Rafe Needleman, Pocket, 1980. Paperback.......$8–$12
 Hardcover..$10–$15
On the Good Ship Enterprise, Bjo Trimble, Donning, 1982. Humorous anecdotes from Star Trek fandom. Trade paperback ....$7–$9
Phaser Fight (Which Way Book No. 24), Barbara and Scott Siegel, Archway (Pocket), 1986
....$2–$4

Pocket Books Original Star Trek Novels

Pocket keeps virtually all books in this ongoing series in print at all times. Books are organized alphabetically by title for ease of reference. Pocket, however, organizes them by the order in which they were originally published and this number is included. First printings have raised lettering in the title, which is not used in subsequent printings. Because the books are always in print, first printings are generally not considered more valuable. Foreign language editions exist and have same approximate value.

A Flag Full of Stars, *No. 54*, Brad Ferguson, 1991 ....$4–$6
Abode of Life, The, *No. 6*, Lee Corey, 1982..$4–$5
Battlestations, *No. 31*, Diane Carey, 1986 ....$4–$5

Star Trek series books. Top: Pocket Star Trek Next Generation and Classic Star Trek novels. Bottom: "Best of" books.

Black Fire, *No. 8*, Sonni Cooper, 1982...$4–$5
Bloodthirst, *No. 37*, J.M. Dillard, 1987..$4–$5
Chain of Attack, *No. 32*, Gene DeWeese, 1987..$4–$5
Corona, *No. 15*, Greg Bear, 1984 ....$4–$5
Covenant of the Crown, *No. 4*, Howard Weinstein, 1981 ....$4–$5
Crisis on Centaurus, *No. 28*, Brad Furguson, 1986 ....$4–$5
Cry of the Onlies, *No. 46*, Judy Klass, 1989...$4–$5
Deep Domain, *No. 33*, Howard Weinstein, 1987 ....$4–$5
Demons, *No. 30*, J.M. Dillard, 1986 ....$4–$5
Doctor's Orders, *No. 50*, Diane Duane, 1990...$4–$5
Double, Double, *No. 45*, Michael Jan Friedman, 1989 ....$4–$5
Dreadnought, *No. 29*, Diane Carey, 1986 ....$4–$5
Dreams of the Raven, *No. 34*, Carmen Carter, 1987 ....$4–$5
Dwellers in the Crucible, *No. 25*, Margaret W. Bonanno, 1985 ....$4–$5
Enemy Unseen, *No. 51*, V.E. Mitchell, 1991..$4–$6
Entropy Effect, *No. 2*, Vonda McIntyre, 1981 ....$4–$5
Final Reflection, *No. 16*, John M. Ford, 1984 ....$4–$5
Ghost Walker, *No. 53*, Barbara Hambly, 1991..$4–$6
Home is the Hunter, *No. 52*, Dana Kramer-Rolls, 1991.......................................$4–$6
How Much for Just the Planet, *No. 36*, John M. Ford, 1987 ....$4–$5
IDIC Epidemic, The, *No. 38*, Jean Lorrah, 1988...$4–$5
Ishmael, *No. 23*, Barbara Hambly, 1985...$4–$5
Killing Time, *No. 24*, Della Van Hise, 1985. First printing (raised title lettering on cover), contained passages objectionable to Paramount that are absent in subsequent printings
....$8–$12
    All other printings ....$4–$5
Klingon Gambit, The, *No. 3*, Robert Vardeman, 1981...$4–$5
Kobayashi Maru, *No. 47*, Julia Ecklar, 1989 ....$4–$5
Mindshadow, *No. 27*, J.M. Dillard, 1986..$4–$5
Mutiny on the Enterprise, *No. 12*, Robert Vardeman, 1983..................................$4–$5
My Enemy, My Ally, *No. 18*, Diane Duane, 1984 ....$4–$5
Pandora Principle, *No. 49*, Carolyn Clowes, 1990 ....$4–$5
Pawns and Symbols, *No. 26*, Majliss Larson, 1985 ....$4–$5
Prometheus Design, The, *No. 5*, S. Marshak and M. Culbreath, 1982 ....$4–$5
Renegade, *No. 55*, Gene DeWeese, 1991 ....$4–$6
Romulan Way, *No. 35*, D. Duane and P. Norwood, 1987......................................$4–$5
Rules of Engagement, *No. 48*, Peter Norwood, 1990..$4–$5
Shadow Lord, *No. 22*, Laurence Yep, 1985...$4–$5
Star Trek: The Motion Picture, *No. 1*, G. Roddenberry, 1979................................$4–$5
Star Trek II: The Wrath of Khan, *No. 7*, V. McIntyre, 1982 ....$4–$5
Star Trek III: The Search for Spock, *No. 17*, V. McIntyre, 1984.............................$4–$5
Tears of the Singer, *No. 19*, Melinda Snodgrass, 1984...$4–$5
Three Minute Universe, The, *No. 41*, Barbara Paul, 1988 ....$4–$5
Time For Yesterday, *No. 39*, A.C. Crispin, 1988 ....$4–$5
Timetrap, *No. 40*, David Dvorkin, 1988 ....$4–$5
Trellisane Confrontation, The, *No. 14*, David Dvorkin, 1984 ....$4–$5
Triangle, *No. 9*, S. Marshak and M. Culbreath, 1983...$4–$5
Uhura's Song, *No. 21*, Janet Kagan, 1985 ....$4–$5
Vulcan Academy Murders, The, *No. 20*, Jean Lorrah, 1984.................................$4–$5
Vulcan's Glory, *No. 44*, D.C. Fontana, 1989..$4–$5
Web of the Romulans, *No. 10*, M.S. Murdock, 1983 ....$4–$5
Wounded Sky, The, *No. 13*, Diane Duane, 1983 ....$4–$5
Yesterday's Son, *No. 11*, A.C. Crispin, 1983 ....$4–$5

Pocket Giant Novels

Giant Novels are not included in the numbering system Pocket uses for its other original Star Trek novels. The first three movie novelizations were included with the regular novels. The fourth and fifth movies were done as Giant Novels.

Note: *Many Star Trek original novels (including the movie novelizations) have been done as hardback book club editions, each $10–$15.*

Enterprise, The First Adventure, V. McIntyre, 1986...$4–$6
Final Frontier, Diane Carey, 1988 ....$4–$6
Spock's World, 1988 (also done in hardback) ....$4–$6
Star Trek IV: The Voyage Home, V. McIntyre, 1986...$4–$6
Star Trek V: The Final Frontier, J.M. Killard, 1989...$4–$6
Strangers from the Sky, Margaret Bonanno, 1987...$4–$6

Pocket Star Trek: The Next Generation Novels

Pocket is using a similar system for numbering this series to the one they use on the original Star Trek series.

A Call to Darkness, *No. 9*, Michael Jan Friedman, 1989 ....$4–$5
A Rock and a Hard Place, *No. 10*, Peter David, 1990.......................................$4–$5
Captain's Honor, *No. 8*, David and Daniel Dvorkin, 1989 ....$4–$5
Children of Hamlin, The, *No. 13*, Carmen Carter, 1988...................................$4–$5
Encounter at Farpoint, David, Gerrold, 1987. Novelization of the pilot episode of the series (done separately from the novel series)..$4–$5
Ghost Ship, *No. 1*, Diane Carey, 1988...$4–$5
Gulliver's Fugitives, *No. 11*, Keith Sharee, 1990 ....$4–$5
Masks, *No. 7*, John Vornholt, 1989..$4–$5
Peacekeepers, The, *No. 2*, Gene DeWeese, 1988 ....$4–$5
Power Hungry, *No. 6*, Howard Weinstein, 1989...$4–$5
Strike Zone, *No. 5*, Peter David, 1989 ....$4–$5
Survivors, *No. 4*, Jean Lorrah, 1989...$4–$5
Vendetta, *No. 17*, Peter David, 1991 ....$4–$6

Pocket Star Trek: The Next Generation Giant Novel

Similar format as the Star Trek original Giant Novels.

Metamorphosis, Jean Lorrah, 1990..$4–$6
Shatner: Where No Man has Gone Before, Ace, W. Shatner, S. Marshak, and M. Culbreath, 1979. Biography, paperback ....$40–$60
Ships of Star Fleet, Calon Riel, 1988. Fan produced. Horizontal format with 11 fold-out pages in back..$24–$26
Six Science-Fiction Plays, Pocket, 1976, Roger Elwood (editor). Anthology which includes script for "City on the Edge of Forever" episode. Paperback ....$25–$40
Spaceflight Chronology, Star Trek, Wallaby, 1980, Stan and Fred Goldstein. Trade paperback ....$25–$45
Spock's World, Pocket, 1988, Diane Duane. Special hardback edition (later done as Pocket Giant novel) ....$16–$18

Original (left) and reprints (right) of Medical Reference and Technical Manual.

Star Fleet Medical Reference, 1977, Eileen Palestine (editor). Trade paperback size. Fan edition (white cover)..$50–$75
> Ballantine edition (blue cover, originally came shrink-wrapped with silver cover sheet) ....$25–$40

Star Fleet Technical Manual, Ballantine. Franz Joseph. Original edition, 1975. Trade paperback with red cover in black binder...$35–$85
> 20th Anniversary reprint, 1986. Trade paperback with black cover, no binder ....$10–$12

Star Fleet Uniform Recognition Manual, Shane Johnson, 1985. Fan produced ....$12–$14

Starlog Science Fiction Trivia, Signet, 1986. Paperback....................................$3–$6

Startoons, Playboy Press, 1979, Joan Winston. Comic strips compiled into paperback form ....$10–$15

Star Trek Annuals

BBC Productions (Western Publishing), British, 1970 to present. Comics and articles in oversize hardcover editions.
> **1970–1972**..$35–$50
> **1973–1975**..$25–$35
> **1976–1980**..$20–$25
> **1981–1983**..$15–$20
> **1984–1990**...$8–$15

Star Trek Catalog, Grosset & Dunlap, Gerry Turnball, 1979. Trade paperback size ...$7–$10
> Regular paperback size ....$4–$6

Star Trek Compendium, Allan Asherman, trade paperback. Original edition, Wallaby, 1981, blue cover..$10–$15
> British (Star) edition, 1983, purple cover ....$10–$15
> 1st U.S. revision, Pocket, 1986, red cover..$10–$15
> 2nd U.S. revision, Pocket, 1989, black cover...$10–$15

Star Trek Concordance, Ballantine, Bjo Trimble, 1976. Trade paperback with index wheel on cover. Cross-referenced information directory. *Note:* The fan version of this book, two volumes in offset print format, had considerable collector value until recently. Counterfeiting has made this publication virtually worthless. ....$60–$100

Star Trek: Good News in Modern Images, Sheed, Andrews, and McNeel, 1976. Betsy Caprio. Hardback ....$35–$60
> Paperback ....$25–$50

Star Trek Intergalactic Puzzles, Bantam, James Razzi, 1977. Trade paperback, silver cover ....$12–$15

Star Trek Interview Book, Pocket, Allan Asherman, 1988. Trade paperback ....$7–$9

Star Trek Log Books

All by Alan Dean Foster, Ballantine (later Del Rey). These are novelizations of the Star Trek animated series. Original editions of one through eight had cover art from the series. Nine and ten, and subsequent printings of the other numbers, had solid-

Log One. Original and current editions.

color covers with pictures of the Enterprise. One through six contain several episodes in each volume and have remained in print. Seven through ten have one story per book and are currently out of print.

Log One 1974, **Log Two** 1974, **Log Three** 1975, **Log Four** 1975, **Log Five** 1975, **Log Six** 1976...$3–10

Log Seven 1976, **Log Eight** 1977..$10–$15

Log Nine 1977...$15–$25

Log Ten 1978...$25–$35

Star Trek Maps, Bantam, 1980. Two 29″ × 40″ two-sided color star maps plus 32-page technical booklet. Packaged in color card stock envelope...$125–$200

Star Trek Puzzle Manual, Bantam, J. Razzi. Black cover with artwork of Enterprise (both formats). Trade paperback, 1976 ....$12–$15

Regular paperback size, 1977 ....$8–$10

Star Trek Quiz Book, Signet, 1977, B. Andrew with B. Dunning. Later titled *Trekkie Quiz Book* ....$10–$12

Star Trek Readers

Dutton. These were hardback compilations of the Star Trek original episode adaptations by James Blish. They were done in both regular and book club editions, which are not as thick and use slightly coarser paper stock.

Vol. I 1970, 21 episodes ....$15–$25

Vol. II 1972, 19 episodes..$15–$25

Vol. III 1973, 19 episodes ....$20–$30

Vol. IV 1974, 12 episodes plus "Spock Must Die"..$20–$30

Star Trek: The Lost Years, Pocket, 1989, J.M. Dillard. Hardcover novel ....$17–$19

Star Trek, TV and Movie Tie-ins, 1979, Creative Education and Publishing, James A. Lely. Hardback...$15–$25

Star Trek: The Motion Picture, Futura (British), 1979, G. Roddenberry (novelization). Same as Pocket's American edition except for color photo section..$6–$10

Star Trek: The Motion Picture, G. Roddenberry, 1979. Pocket special autographed hardcover edition with slip-case. Limited to 500 copies...$50–$75

Star Trek: The Motion Picture, Marvel Comics, 1979. Issues 1 and 2 of the comics in paperback form...$3–$5

Star Trek: The Motion Picture Peel-Off Graphics Book, Wallaby, 1979, Lee Cole. Peel-off stickers and designs from the movie..$30–$40

Star Trek: The Motion Picture Photostory, Pocket, 1980, Richard J. Anobile. Color throughout...$12–$20

Star Trek II: The Wrath of Khan Photostory, Pocket (Methuen U.K.), 1982. Black and white..$5–$10

Star Trek Readers.

Star Trek II Biographies, Wanderer, 1982, William Rotsler. Trade paperback............$5–$10
Star Trek II Distress Call, Wanderer, 1982, William Rotsler. Trade paperback. A plot-your-own-adventure story ....$5–$10
Star Trek II Short Stories, Wanderer, 1982, William Rotsler. Trade paperback..........$5–$10
Star Trek III Movie Trivia, Wanderer, 1984, William Rotsler. Shrink-wrapped with pen ....$5–$10
Star Trek III: The Search for Spock More Movie Trivia, Wanderer, 1984. Comes with pen to reveal answers..$5–$10
Star Trek III Short Stories, Wanderer, 1984, William Rotsler. Five stories, trade paperback ....$5–$10
Star Trek III: The Search for Spock Storybook, Simon & Schuster, 1984, Lawrence Weinberg. Oversize hardback and trade paperback formats. Includes color photos.......$6–$10
Star Trek III The Vulcan Treasure, Wanderer (Ravette in U.K.), 1984, William Rotsler. Plot-your-own-adventure story..$5–$10
Star Trek IV: The Voyage Home, (photo story book), Wanderer, 1986. Text and color photos ....$5–$7
Star Trek: Voyage to Adventure, "Which-Way Book No. 15," Archway (Simon & Schuster), 1984, Michael J. Dodge. Plot-your-own-adventure story. Carousel (British) edition has different cover art ....$2–$4
Star Wars, Star Trek, and the 21st-Century Christians, Bible Voice, 1978, Winkie Pratney ....$10–$15
Strange and Amazing Facts About Star Trek, Simon & Schuster, 1986, Daniel Cohen ....$2–$4
Tek War, Ace (Putnam), 1989, William Shatner. Original science-fiction novel. Hardback ....$17–$19
TNG-1, fan produced, 1989, Larry Nemecek. Star Trek: The Next Generation concordance and episode guide...$11–$13
Trek or Treat, Ballantine, 1977, T. Flanagan and E. Ehrhardt. Humorous captioned photo book. Horizontal format...$3–$5
Trekkie Quiz Book (*See* Star Trek Quiz Book)
Trivia Mania, Star Trek, Zebra Books, 1985, Xavier Einstein....................................$5–$10
Trouble with Tribbles, Ballantine, 1973, David Gerrold. Making of the episode ......$10–$15
Who was That Monolith I Saw You With?, Heritage, 1976, Michael Goodwin. Trade paperback. Cartoon strip compilation...$10–$15
World of Star Trek, David Gerrold. Ballantine (later editions Del Rey), 1973. Regular paperback format ....$6–$10
     Bluejay, 1984. Trade paperback, up-dated version ....$9–$11
Worlds of the Federation, Pocket, 1989, Shane Johnson. Trade paperback ....$11–$13
Writer's Guide, Lincoln Enterprises. Offset press format. Pamphlet originally used as a guideline for potential writers...$4–$6

Children's Books

Coloring Books

Cliredon Press, 1985. Star Trek Play Pad ....$3–$5
Parkes Run Publishing, 1978. "The Uncharted World" ....$5–$8
Saalfield Publishing, 1975. Two different. Each ....$5–$10
Wanderer
     Star Trek Activity Book, 1986...$3–$5
     Star Trek Adventure Coloring Book, 1986...$3–$5
     Star Trek Alien Coloring Book, 1986..$3–$5
     Star Trek Giant Coloring Book No. 1, Star Trek: The Motion Picture, 1979 ....$3–$8
     Star Trek Giant Coloring Book No. 2, Star Trek: The Motion Picture, 1979 ....$3–$8
     Star Trek Puzzle Coloring Book, 1986...$3–$5
Western, 1978. Published by Western's Whitman division. Books had original TV artwork covers.
     A Blast of Activities ....$3–$8
     A Launch Into Fun..$3–$8

Children's books. *The Prisoner of Vega, Truth Machine.*

Far-Out Fun...$3–$8
Futuristic Fun...$3–$8
Planet Ecnal's Dilemma...$3–$8
Rescue at Raylo ....$3–$8
    Books were reissued in abridged form in 1979 by Merrigold, also a division of Western, with *Star Trek: The Motion Picture* covers. Prices are the same.
Jeopardy at Jutterdon (Whitman), 1979...$3–$8

Game Books

Star Trek Action Toy Book, Random House, 1976, James Razzi............................$10–$20
Star Trek Make-a-Game-Book, Wanderer, 1979, Bruce and Greg Nash...................$10–$20
Star Trek: The Motion Picture Bridge Punch-Out Book, Wanderer, 1979 ....$10–$20
Star Trek: The Motion Picture U.S.S. Enterprise Punch-Out Book, 1979.............$15–$25
Star Trek: The Next Generation Starship Enterprise Make A Model, Chatham River Press
(Simon and Schuster in Great Britain), 1990 ....$6–$10

Hardbacks

Random House, 1977. Both these books were done with both regular glossy bindings and Gibralter Library binding, which is rougher in texture. Price is the same.
Prisoner of Vega, S. Lerner and C. Cerf...$20–$30
The Truth Machine, C. Cerf and S. Lerner ....$20–$30

Pop-Up Books

Giant in the Universe, Random House, 1977...$20–$40
Star Trek: The Motion Picture, Wanderer, 1980, Tor Lokvig and Chuck Murphy ...$15–$35
Trillions of Trilligs, Random House, 1977..$20–$40

Star Trek pop-up books.

Bumper stickers.

BUMPER STICKERS AND AUTO ACCESSORIES

Bumper Stickers

The bumper stickers listed here have all had some sort of legal sanction from Paramount. There are many more unlicensed ones; more than would be practical to list. Bumper stickers are generally silkscreened onto paper, vinyl, or mylar (a shiny surfaced foil) and, though very popular, tend to have little collectors' value due to ease of reproduction. List is organized by manufacturer.

Aviva

1979. This series of stickers, made at the time of *Star Trek: The Motion Picture*, were two or three colors, printed on vinyl.

Beam Me Up Mr. Spock	$2–$3
Dr. McCoy Doesn't Make House Calls	$2–$3
Federation Vehicle: Official Use Only	$2–$3
I am a Trekkie	$2–$3
Live Long and Prosper	$2–$3
Star Trek: The Motion Picture	$2–$3

Lincoln Enterprises

All black lettering on colored background.

Bring Back the Enterprise	$1–$2
Don't Tailgate, This is a Klingon War Cruiser	$1–$2
Government Vehicle, Vulcan Embassy	$1–$2
The Human Adventure is Just Beginning	$1–$2
I am a Carbon Unit	$1–$2
I Grok Spock	$1–$2
Jaws is a Klingon Minnow (with picture)	$1–$2
Live Long and Prosper	$1–$2
Mr. Spock for President	$1–$2
Mr. Spock, Phone Home	$1–$2
Star Trek Lives	$1–$2
Support the Right to Arm Klingons	$1–$2
Vote Yes on Star Trek	$1–$2
We Want Star Trek III	$1–$2
Smile (picture) if You Like Star Trek	$1–$2
Trekker on Board	$1–$2

Mid-priced button machine with parts, cut circles, and finished buttons.

Don't Tailgate—This is a Ferengi War Cruiser...$1–$2
Star Trek The Next Generation—The 24th Century is Just Beginning...................$1–$2
I am Fully Functional—Data...$1–$2
Support Your Local Android—Data...$1–$2

Miscellaneous Auto Accessories

Starpool, Inc., 1982, Starpool. Waving figures for car windows. Kirk or Spock. Each
....$15–$25
License Plates, fan made. Enterprise over red planet.....................................$2–$5
    Blue Enterprise on white plate...$2–$5

BUTTONS

The primary thing to consider when collecting buttons is the ease of manufacture. Button-making machines are available to the hobbyist for about $20. In addition, there are companies that will produce relatively small quantities of buttons for a

Licensed (left) and unlicensed buttons (right).

modest price. Word buttons are particularly easy. They can be hand-lettered or run off cheaply at any local Quickprint. As for picture buttons, it is easy and perfectly legal to cut any picture out of a magazine and incorporate it into a button. For this reason, we are only including those button series which had sheets printed in large quantities for the specific purpose of making buttons or licensed promotional buttons. It is arguable whether certain other buttons may have collectors' value, especially those from conventions, but because they could be so easily duplicated, it is unlikely they would ever become very valuable. "Button" here is used to refer to items printed directly onto a metal pinback surface or printed onto paper affixed to a pinback. For enamel, cloisonne, or epoxy surfaced pins, sometimes referred to as buttons, see "Jewelry."

Aviva

Star Trek: The Motion Picture, 1979. Color licensed buttons, 2¼". All have logo in addition to picture.

Group Shot, on the bridge ....$2–$3
Kirk, in gray uniform ....$2–$3
Kirk, standing, blue background ....$2–$3
Kirk, Spock, and McCoy ....$2–$3
Spock in uniform ....$2–$3
Spock, in Vulcan attire ....$2–$3

Button-Up

1½" licensed color buttons from the original TV series, 1984.

Captain Kirk, close-up of head ....$1–$2
Enterprise ....$1–$2
Group Shot, Dr. McCoy, Lt. Uhura, and Chekov..$1–$2
Group Shot, Captain Kirk, Dr. McCoy, and Mr. Spock ....$1–$2
Kirk and Dr. McCoy, head shots ....$1–$2
Kirk and Mr. Spock, close-up from "Errand of Mercy" ....$1–$2
Lt. Sulu, close-up of head ....$1–$2
Starships, the Enterprise and Constellation..$1–$2

Button-Up

1½" licensed color buttons from *Star Trek III: The Search for Spock*, 1984. All have logo in addition to photo.

Captain Kirk, close-up of head ....$1–$2
Captain Kirk, head and shoulders shot..$1–$2
Commander Chekov, close-up of head..$1–$2
Commander Sulu, close-up of head..$1–$2
Commander Uhura, holding a phaser ....$1–$2
Dr. McCoy ....$1–$2
David Marcus, head and shoulers shot...$1–$2
Kruge, Klingon, close-up of head...$1–$2
Lt. Saavik, close-up of head ....$1–$2
Logo from Star Trek III ....$1–$2
Spock, in Vulcan garb ....$1–$2

Image Products

Star Trek: The Wrath of Khan, 3" buttons, 1982. Color, logo and photo, licensed.

Enterprise ....$2–$3
Group Shot ....$2–$3
Khan ....$2–$3
Kirk ....$2–$3
Spock ....$2–$3

Langley & Associates

An early manufacturer of licensed merchandise, now out of business, 1976, 2¼″, color.

Captain Kirk, Close-up of head ....$1–$2
  In dress uniform ....$1–$2
  In "Trouble with Tribbles" ....$1–$2
  Ready to beam down ....$1–$2
  With communicator ....$1–$2
  Hand reaching out through cell bars ....$1–$2
Captain Pike, the original commander of the Enterprise ....$1–$2
Dr. McCoy, close-up of face ....$1–$2
Dr. McCoy, looking puzzled ....$1–$2
Dr. McCoy, speaking ....$1–$2
Enterprise, Captioned "Star Trek" ....$1–$2
  Looming over planet ....$1–$2
  Rear view ....$1–$2
  Shooting phasers ....$1–$2
  With red planet ....$1–$2
Khan, original character ....$1–$2
Klingon Ship, overhead shot ....$1–$2
Lt. Uhura, with headset on ....$1–$2
Lt. Uhura, leaning on communication equipment ....$1–$2
Mr. Chekov, Flanked by crew ....$1–$2
  In a deep frown ....$1–$2
  On the bridge ....$1–$2
  Smiling ....$1–$2
Mr. Scott, close-up of head ....$1–$2
Mr. Spock, As Science Officer ....$1–$2
  Close-up profile ....$1–$2
  Laughing ....$1–$2
  Looking logical ....$1–$2
  Smiling ....$1–$2
  Talking on the bridge ....$1–$2
  Tight close-up of head ....$1–$2
  With beard ....$1–$2
Mr. Sulu, the navigator ....$1–$2
Mr. Sulu, close-up shot of head ....$1–$2
Mr. Sulu, looking up ....$1–$2
Nurse Chapel, close-up shot ....$1–$2
Yeoman Rand, with plaited hair ....$1–$2

Paramount and Pocket Books

Promotional Button, Paramount, 1989. Star Trek V: The Final Frontier. Blue rectangular with logo. ....$2–$3
Promotional Button, Pocket. Pictures Spock, "Star Trek: The Only Logical Books to Read" ....$1–$2

Star Trek Galore

Manufacturer of unlicensed merchandise, now out of business. These color buttons variously came in 2¼″, 2½″, and 3″ sizes, 1976.

Captain Kirk, in full dress uniform ....$1–$2
Chekov and Sulu, on bridge ....$1–$2
The Crew of the Enterprise, on the bridge ....$1–$2
Enterprise, firing phasers ....$1–$2
Galileo, the Enterprise's mini transport ....$1–$2
Kirk, Spock, and McCoy, on the bridge ....$1–$2
Kirk, with hand on chin ....$1–$2
Kirk, in "Trouble with Tribbles" ....$1–$2

Scotty, looking worried ....$1–$2
Scotty, portrait type ....$1–$2
Spock, Aiming phaser ....$1–$2
   Giving hand signal ....$1–$2
   In rare display of emotion ....$1–$2
   Making point ....$1–$2
   With beard...$1–$2
   With child Vulcan ....$1–$2
   With harp...$1–$2
   With three-dimensional chess game ....$1–$2
Uhura, the Enterprise's Communication Officer ....$1–$2
Spock, from animated series ....$1–$2
Kirk, glitter button, black background...$1–$2
McCoy, glitter button, black background.....................................$1–$2

Taco Bell

Promotional, 1984. *Star Trek III: The Search for Spock*, 3″, blue and yellow.
Beam Home with the Enterprise Crew ....$2–$3
Beam Home with T'Lar ....$2–$3
Beam Home with Spock ....$2–$3
Beam Home with Kruge ....$2–$3

Universal Studios

Promotional Button, 1989. Color photo of Enterprise with words "Paramount Pictures Star Trek Adventure" underneath...$3–$5

CALENDARS

Calendars from Ballantine and the first Pocket calendar came boxed. Prices here assume boxes for these are still present. Writing in calendars or otherwise defacing them reduces value considerably. Calendars are organized chronologically.

1973, Lincoln Enterprises, color TV pictures ....$10–$15
1974, Lincoln Enterprises, animated pictures ....$10–$15
1976–1978, Lincoln Enterprises, three-year calendar, color TV photos....................$10–$12
1976, Ballantine Books, photos from the TV series, color, Kirk and Spock on cover, light blue border, boxed ....$25–$45
1977, Ballantine Books, original TV color photos, Kirk and Spock on cover with black border, boxed...$20–$30
1977, Franco, cloth hanging, in envelope...................................$30–$50
1978, Ballantine Books, color original TV photos, Kirk, Spock, McCoy with blue border on cover, boxed ....$20–$30

Star Trek calendars.

1979, Ballantine Books, color original TV photos, Spock with silver border on cover, boxed ....$20–$30
1980, Pocket Books, color photos from Star Trek: The Motion Picture. Enterprise and main characters on cover. Last year for boxed calendars (future calendars came shrink-wrapped) ....$10–$20
1980, Wallaby, The Official U.S.S. Enterprise Officer's Date Book. Spiral bound 5½″ × 8″ desk calendar...$8–$15
1980, Blue Montain Press, nature art and poems by Leonard Nimoy, Nimoy on cover ....$10–$15
1981, Pocket Books, color photos from Star Trek: The Motion Picture, Enterprise in space dock on cover...$15–$25
1981, Blue Mountain Press, Leonard Nimoy Calendar. Art and poetry, spiral bound ....$10–$15
1982, Pocket Books, color photos from Star Trek: The Motion Picture, Enterprise, Kirk, and Spock on cover...$15–$25
1983, Pocket Books, color photos from Star Trek II: The Wrath of Khan. Enterprise approaching Regula I space station on cover...$10–$15
1984, Pocket Books (Timescape), color photos from original TV show. Kirk and Spock on cover...$10–$15
1985, Pocket Books, color photos from Star Trek III: The Search for Spock. Enterprise approaching space dock on cover..$10–$15
1985, Datazine, Hysterical Calendar, cartoons and dates pertinent to Star Trek.............$8–$9
1986, Pocket Books, color photos of characters from the movies. Group shot on cover........... ....$10–$15
1986, Datazine, Hysterical Calendar, cartoons and dates pertinent to Star Trek.............$5–$6
1987, Pocket Books, color photos from original TV show. Kirk, Spock, McCoy, and Uhura on cover...$10–$15
1987, Datazine, Hysterical Calendar, cartoons. Kirk and Spock from original TV show on cover..$5–$6
1988, Pocket Books, color photos from the original TV series and from the first four movies ....$8–$12
1988, Datazine, Star Trek Hysterical Calendar, cartoons...$5–$6
1989, Pocket Books, Star Trek Celebration Calendar, color photos from original TV series. Kirk, Spock, and Scotty on cover..$8–$10
1989, Pocket Books, Star Trek: The Next Generation Calendar, color photos from the first season of the Next Generation. Group shot on cover...$8–$10
1989, Datazine, Trek Classic Hysterical Calendar, cartoons pertaining to Star Trek IV: The Voyage Home...$5–$6
1989, Datazine, Trek Next Generation Hysterical Calendar, Next Generation cartoons ....$5–$6
1990, Pocket Books, Star Trek V: The Final Frontier Calendar, color photos from Star Trek V. Group shot on cover..$10–$12
1990, Pocket Books, Star Trek: The Next Generation Calendar, color photos from the Next Generation. Next Generation Enterprise on cover...$10–$12
1990, Datazine, Trek Classic Hysterical Calendar, cartoons...$5–$6
1990, Datazine, Next Generation Hysterical Calendar, cartoons from the Next Generation ....$5–$6
1991, Pocket Books, Star Trek Classic Calendar, color photos from all five movies....$8–$10
1991, Pocket Books, Star Trek: The Next Generation Calendar, color photos from the third season..$8–$10

CELS AND STORYBOARDS

Cels are the transparencies on which the action parts of an animated film are printed. Storyboards are the preliminary sketches made for an animated story. There are hundreds of storyboards and thousands of cels for each half hour of an animated Star Trek episode. Until fairly recently, the value of cels as original art had gone largely unrecognized by the general public. This has changed dramatically and the price of cels has skyrocketed. Although Filmation, the company whch made the Star Trek

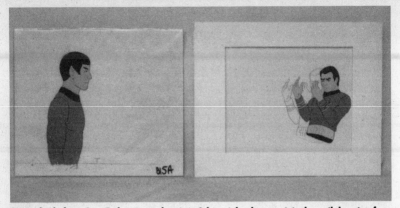

Original cels from Star Trek animated series. Cel on right shows original pencil drawing for cel.

animated episodes, is better known for being prolific than for the quality of their artwork, due to the subject matter, Star Trek must be considered one of their more select products. Desirable features in cels are complete well-centered figures and, of course, main characters and groups. Authentic cels seldom have backgrounds since one backdrop could serve for many "action" sequences. An original storyboard should sell for between $50–$100, a good quality original cel for $75–$200.

Filmation

1977. A series of 14 cel reproductions from the Star Trek animated series. These came in 14″ × 18″ mats and included a seal of authenticity.

1A The Crew of the Enterprise	$35–$75
5 Yesteryear	$35–$75
6 More Tribbles, More Troubles	$35–$75
9 The Ambergris Element	$35–$75
11 Jihad, composite of aliens	$35–$75
12 Spock, the boy atop L'Chaya	$35–$75
14 The Time Trap	$35–$75
15 The Enterprise and the Aqua Shuttle	$35–$75
16 Beyond the Farthest Star	$35–$75
20 Kulkukan and the Enterprise	$35–$75
22 Time Warp	$35–$75
23 About to Battle a Klingon	$35–$75
25 The Counter Clock Incident	$35–$75
00 Title Scene from Star Trek	$35–$75

Lincoln Enterprises

1983. 4″ × 8″ copies of character cels on acetate.

Chapel	$2–$3
Enterprise	$2–$3
Kirk	$2–$3
Lt. Arex	$2–$3
Lt. M'Hress	$2–$3
McCoy	$2–$3
Scotty	$2–$3
Spock	$2–$3
Sulu	$2–$3
Uhura	$2–$3

Paramount

1989. Reproductions of original animation cels with backgrounds. Value reflects issue price.

S96A Spock and Kirk, waist-up ....$200–$250
S96B McCoy, waist-up on planet...$200–$250
S96C Spock, waist-up action pose...$200–$250
S96D Scotty, holding tricorder...$200–$250
S96E McCoy and Kirk, with machinery ....$200–$250
S96F Spock and Kirk, in transporter ....$200–$250
S96G Arex and Scott..$200–$250
S96H Alien and Crew Member...$200–$250
S96I Kirk, holding communicator ....$200–$250
S96J Sulu, waist-up...$200–$250
S96K Sulu, machinery in background ....$200–$250
S96L Scott, waist-up..$200–$250
S96M Kirk and McCoy, with hypo ....$200–$250
S96N Spock, with machinery...$200–$250
S96O Spock, waist-up..$200–$250
S96P McCoy, behind window..$200–$250
S96Q Kirk, waist-up action pose..$200–$250
S96R Kirk, waist-up..$200–$250
S96S Spock, with two aliens...$200–$250
S96T Chapel and Kirk..$200–$250
S96U Kirk, full-figure..$200–$250
S96V Kirk and Spock, on planet ....$200–$250
S96W Scott, on bridge ....$200–$250
S96X Kirk and Spock, on bridge..$200–$250

CERAMICS

Decanters

Full-Figure Spock Liquor Decanter, Grenadier, 1979, 13″ tall Spock standing, gold metallic glaze. Some came with dark blue satin display box. Probably never held liquor. Rare
....$700–$1,000
Spock Bust Liquor Decanter, Grenadier, 1979, 10″ tall, came in window display box, originally held Cielo liquor. Decanters still containing liquor and those with boxes are more collectible...$50–$100
Note: *Some Spock bust decanters display white insignia patches instead of the orange that is correct for the character, but neither design seems more prevalent.*

Grenadier Spock decanters.

Dolls

(*See* "Action and Collectors' Figures")

Plates

To date, three series of Star Trek Collectors' Plates have been issued. Original paintings for all three series were by artist Susie Morton for Hamilton, the company responsible for the plates' design. Physical manufacture of the plates was done by the Ernst Co. All plates were numbered and often, though not always, came with a Certificate of Authenticity. The plates were generally advertised as having a limited number of firing days. This, however, is largely a merchandising ploy. Standard business factors played a much more important role in the duration of the plates' production. They are nevertheless very popular and their value has escalated accordingly.

First Series, original TV series character plates. Released one at a time starting in 1985 and continued production through 1989, 8½" diameter. Blue borders with "The Voyages of the Starship Enterprise" and "To Boldly Go Where No Man Has Gone Before."

Beam Us Down Scotty, group portrait on transporter	$60–$75
Chekov	$60–$75
Kirk	$60–$75
McCoy	$60–$75
Scotty	$60–$75
Spock	$60–$75
Sulu	$60–$75
Uhura	$60–$75

Enterprise Collector's Plate, 1987–89, Hamilton/Ernst. Artist Susie Morton. 10¼" diameter. Depicts Enterprise with heads of seven major characters around lower edge of plate. Gold edging with embossed words "U.S.S. Enterprise NCC 1701" at top and character names below. Produced after the last plate in the first series was released. There were two versions—an unsigned and a signed edition which had reproduction signatures of the seven actors plus Susie Morton and Gene Roddenberry around the back rim. Although advertised as a "special" edition, there is a good possibility that more signed than unsigned plates exist. Both versions are numbered on the back ....$75–$125

Second Series, episode scenes from the original TV series, 1987–89. This series was released much more rapidly and ceased production sooner than the first series. Hamilton did extensive research and customer surveys to determine not only which episodes but which scenes from the episodes were most popular. This and the fact that this colorful series is generally

Enterprise plate.

Examples of three Star Trek plate series. Character Spock plate, Trouble with Tribbles episode plate, and Data Next Generation plate.

considered more attractive than the first series has made it the more desirable of the two. Plates are 8½″ in diameter, embossed gold edging with small Enterprises, and words "Star Trek" and "The Commemorative Collection." Numbered on reverse.

Amok Time, Kirk and Spock fighting with Lirpas..$75–$150
City on the Edge of Forever, Kirk, Spock, and McCoy in front of Mission.........$150–$300
Devil in the Dark, Spock mind-melding with Horta ....$100–$200
Journey to Babel, Kirk, Sarek, and Telerite at party...$75–$150
Menagerie, Pike and Vina in front of Rigel castle..$75–$150
Mirror, Mirror, group scene in Alternate Universe..$100–$200
Piece of the Action, Kirk and Spock in gangster dress ....$75–$150
Trouble with Tribbles, Kirk buried in Tribbles..$75–$150

Third Series, 1989–90, Star Trek: The Next Generation Portrait Plates. Silver embossed edging with words "Star Trek: The Next Generation." Numbered on back.

Picard ....$200–$300
Data..$150–$250

Note: *Ernst lost the license to do plates after the first two in this planned series of eight were finished. Only about 4,000 of each were made compared to approximately 40,000 each of the first series.*

Mugs

Hamilton/Ernst, 1986–89, same designs as first series plates, originally sold only in sets of eight. Reissued by Hamilton in 1991.

Ernst character mugs.

Disappearing original crew mug.

Beam Us Down Scotty..$8–$12
Chekov ....$8–$12
Kirk ....$8–$12
McCoy...$8–$12
Scotty ....$8–$12
Spock...$8–$12
Sulu ....$8–$12
Uhura..$8–$12
Set of eight ....$60–$90

Star Trek Magic Mugs, heat-sensitive design allows figures in mug illustration to "disappear" when hot beverage is added, leaving background visible. Images return as mug cools.

Star Trek Crew (original TV) Magic Mug, 1989, blue and black drawing of Kirk, Spock, and McCoy in transporter on front, Star Trek logo on back.............................$11–$13
Star Trek Enterprise Magic Mug, Image Design Concepts, Inc., 1990. Depicts Enterprise on starfield. Klingon Bird of Prey "uncloaks" when hot beverage is added..................$11–$13

Star Trek Next Generation Magic Mugs, 1990, Image Design Concepts, Inc. Mugs feature logo and illustration of character on transporter pad on front, and signature of actor on back.

Dr. Crusher..$11–$13
Wesley Crusher ....$11–$13
Lt. Commander Data..$11–$13
Lt. Geordi LaForge ....$11–$13
Capt. Picard...$11–$13
Commander Riker ....$11–$13
Counselor Troi ....$11–$13
Lt. Worf ....$11–$13

Official Star Trek Fan Club Mug, 20th anniversary and fan club logos ....$8–$15
Star Trek II: The Wrath of Khan, 1982, Image Products, 6″ tall, character's features molded into mug front, logo back, blue glaze lining.

Khan...$175–$250
Kirk ....$75–$125
Spock..$75–$125

UFP Mug, several versions by different manufacturers. Blue and silver United Federation of Planets design on black or gray mug ....$8–$12

Steins

Ernst, 1986, 6¼″ tall, sepia tone, individually numbered.

Kirk ....$25–$40
Spock...$25–$40

CERTIFICATES AND DIPLOMAS

Though these are popular novelty items, their ease of reproduction makes it unlikely they will ever attain much collector value.

April Publications

All of the following are 8½″ × 11″ on heavy paper stock, often with gold borders.

Deltan Oath of Celibacy	$2–$4
Doctorate of Space Medicine	$2–$4
Federation Birth Certificate	$2–$4
Klingon Academy Diploma	$2–$4
Klingon Captain	$2–$4
Only Vulcan Spoken Here	$2–$4
Phaser Marksman Certificate	$2–$4
Spock's Death Certificate	$2–$4
Star Fleet Academy Diploma	$2–$4
Star Fleet Admiral	$2–$4
Star Fleet Officer's Club	$2–$4
Star Fleet Operations Officer	$2–$4
Starship Captain's Certification	$2–$4
Tribble Pedigree	$2–$4
U.S.S. Enterprise Crew Member	$2–$4
Vulcan Academy of Science	$2–$4
Vulcan Birth Certificate	$2–$4
Vulcan Kolianar Discipline	$2–$4
Vulcan Land Deed	$2–$4
Vulcan Master	$2–$4
Vulcan Marriage License	$2–$4
Vulcan Officer's Club	$2–$4

Lincoln Enterprises

Deluxe Flight Deck Certificate, Enterprise superimposed on background, on parchmentlike paper, two-color ribbon, insignia sticker, signed by Captain Kirk and Gene Roddenberry .... $2–$3
Flight Deck Certificate, blue picture of Enterprise superimposed on background, signed by Captain Kirk and Gene Roddenberry .... $1–$3

T-K Graphics

Both of the following are 8″ × 10″ with foil seals.

Star Fleet Academy	$2–$4
Vulcan Science Academy	$2–$4

CLOTHING AND ACCESSORIES

Belts and Belt Pouches

Belt, Star Trek: The Motion Picture, stretch cloth with woven-in Star Trek logo .... $10–$15
Belt, 1989, Rarities Mint, reversible brown/black leather belt with silver U.S.S. Enterprise (picture of original TV ship and Star Trek logo) in gold-plated buckle .... $40–$45
Belt Pouches, T-K Graphics, 6″ × 9″ vinyl, snap closure, with silkscreened designs.

Enterprise schematic	$5–$10
Star Fleet Academy (UFP Janus Head design)	$5–$10
Star Fleet Headquarters Tactical Operation Center	$5–$10
U.S.S. Enterprise/NCC 1701	$5–$10
UFP Diplomatic Service	$5–$10
Vulcan Science Academy	$5–$10
Imperial Klingon Fleet	$5–$10

Vulcan ear hat.

Caps

All caps listed below are baseball type. Caps with embroidered patches in this section were designed specifically for hats (although all were also sold separately).

Star Trek III, Lincoln Enterprises, embroidered patch...$10–$12
Star Trek IV, corduroy, embroidered with logo, Official Star Trek Fan Club, 1986...$12–$15
Star Trek V, 1989, black and white cap with silver and red logo embroidered on hat
....$10–$20
Star Trek 20th Anniversary, 1986, Lincoln Enterprises, embroidered patch.............$10–$15
U.S.S. Enterprise, Thinking Cap Co., embroidered patch with command star ....$8–$10
United Federation of Planets, Thinking Cap Co., embroidered movie UFP patch ......$8–$10
Vulcan Ear Hat, Thinking Cap Co., rubber pointed ears attached (also came with embroidered "Spock Lives" patch)...$8–$12
Star Trek II: The Wrath of Khan, Thinking Cap Co., silkscreened.........................$10–$15
Star Trek Crew, 1989, Paramount Special Effects, black cap with old TV logo in white embroidered lettering, "Crew" below in smaller letters..$15–$20

Checkbook Covers

All checkbook covers were produced by T-K Graphics. They are vinyl, fit standard checkbooks, and have silkscreened designs.

Star Fleet Academy...$4–$8
Star Fleet Headquarters Tactical Operations Center ....$4–$8
UFP Diplomatic Service ....$4–$8
U.S.S. Enterprise/NCC 1701 ....$4–$8
Vulcan Science Academy ....$4–$8

Iron-On Transfers

These are primarily used for tee shirts. In recent years, silkscreened shirts have become much more popular.

AMT, color, original TV, offered in promotion with model kits.
    Assortment of small transfers, insignias, U.S.S. Enterprise, How's Your Tribble, and Vulcan Power with hand ....$2–$4
    Keep on Trekkin' (Enterprise) ....$2–$4
    Klingon Power (Klingon Ship) ....$2–$4
    Star Trek Lives..$2–$4
General Mills, 1979, Star Trek: The Motion Picture. Promotional. Set of five: Kirk and Logo; Spock and Logo; Kirk, Spock, and Logo; Enterprise and Logo; Blank (make own design). Price per set..$5–$10
Lincoln Enterprises, poor quality color photo reproductions. All from original TV show.
    Enterprise firing phasers ....$1–$2
    Kirk in dress uniform...$1–$2
    Kirk with phaser...$1–$2

Kirk and Spock from "Patterns of Force" ....$1–$2
Kirk and Spock from "Spock's Brain" ....$1–$2
Kirk and Spock looking down ....$1–$2
Kirk and Spock with phaser...$1–$2
Kirk, Spock, and McCoy from "Patterns of Force" ....$1–$2
Spock with lyre ....$1–$2
Spock (Vulcan salute) ....$1–$2
Star Trek III: The Search for Spock logo ....$1–$2
Miscellaneous Fan Produced, black only.
"Pet me, I'm a Tribble" ....$1–$2
"Keep on Trekkin' " with character stepping out...$1–$2
Outrageous Put-Ons
TV Enterprise being fired upon by Klingon ship ....$1–$2
Pacific Transfer, 1982.
Wrath of Khan logo ....$1–$2
Kirk from Wrath of Khan ....$1–$2
Spock from Wrath of Khan...$1–$2
Khan from Wrath of Khan ....$1–$2
Star Trek: The Motion Picture, 1979. Sold primarily on shirts.
Enterprise and logo ....$1–$2
Glitter Enterprise and logo...$1–$2
Enterprise, Kirk, Spock, and logo..$1–$2
Kirk, Enterprise, and logo..$1–$2
Ilia and Enterprise..$1–$2

Jackets

D.D. Bean & Sons, Star Trek: The Motion Picture, 1979, lightweight, silver first movie insignia design ....$75–$100
D.D. Bean & Sons, Star Trek: The Motion Picture, 1979, deluxe L.E.D. jacket, UFP patch on front. Back movie title logo over Enterprise outline embellished with red flashing L.E.D.s ....$100–$125
Great Lakes, 1974, light blue with black collar and cuffs and two white accent stripes on arms. Leatherette old TV science emblem. Promotional item sold through AMT ....$35–$50
Great Lakes, 1974, silver with embroidered old UFP design ....$35–$50
Lincoln Enterprises
Star Trek III: The Search for Spock lightweight black jacket with white trim. Embroidered Star Trek III patch on front with "U.S.S. Enterprise" on back........................$25–$30
Also came in white or blue satinique...$50–$60
Star Trek IV: The Voyage Home crew jacket, white satin trimmed in navy. Back has fully embroidered Star Trek IV logo design showing Enterprise, Golden Gate Bridge, and whales ....$125–$150

AMT promotional jacket.

Star Trek IV: The Voyage Home windbreaker, lightweight, white, black or navy with patch depicting Bird of Prey over Golden Gate Bridge and whales. U.S.S. Enterprise on back ....$30–$35
Also came in white, black, navy, gray or red satinique ....$50–$60
(Similar windbreakers and jackets came with patch showing Enterprise over whales)
Twentieth anniversary windbreaker, lightweight black, white or navy with patch showing Enterprise and words "Star Trek—20th Anniversary," "U.S.S. Enterprise" on back ....$30–$35
Also came in white, black, navy, gray, and red satinique...$50–$60

Official Star Trek Fan Club
Star Trek IV jacket, 1986, silver satin with two-color Star Trek IV logo on back....$40–$50

Paramount Special Effects
Star Trek: The Next Generation jean jacket, 1989, airbrushed Enterprise and Star Trek logo on front. "U.S.S. Enterprise" down arm...$180–$200
Star Trek: The Next Generation satin jacket, 1989, silver with insignia logo on front and large insignia on back (also came in navy)...$90–$100
Star Trek V denim jacket, 1989, embroidered logo strip over front pocket.............$75–$80

Pajamas

Nazareth Mills, 1979. Two-piece toddler's pajamas. Star Trek: The Motion Picture. Four different: Kirk, Enterprise, Enterprise and Planet, Spock. Price each ....$20–$30
Pajama Corporation of America, Star Trek: The Motion Picture. 1979. Children's sizes. Two-piece. Four different: Kirk in spacesuit, Spock and planet, Spock in spacesuit and Enterprise, Enterprise. Price each...$25–$35
Paramount Special Effects, Star Trek: The Next Generation, 1989, Children's sizes, two-piece, green, red or blue. Black yoke with silver uniform insignia...............................$15–$20

Socks

John Batts Co., 1979, original TV. Kirk or Spock iron-on on white. Character plus logo ....$10–$15
Charleston Hosiery, 1979, white with iron-ons of Star Trek: The Motion Picture characters, Kirk, Spock, Kirk and Spock, Decker or Ilia ....$10–$15
Carolina Casuals, 1989, original TV letter logo embroidered in white on black sock .$8–$10
Paramount Special Effects, 1989, Star Trek: The Next Generation logo with insignia embroidered on white sock...$8–$10

Sweat Shirts

Star Trek (original TV), Novel Teez (Canadian), 1986, silkscreened color picture of Spock doing Vulcan salute. "Live long and Prosper" ....$15–$20
Star Trek (original TV), Novel Teez (Canadian), 1986, silkscreened color picture of Kirk and Enterprise, "Scotty, Beam Me Up . . . There's No Intelligent Life on Earth!" ....$15–$20
Star Trek IV, Novel Teez (Canadian), 1986, silkscreened color picture of Spock and McCoy, "Damn it, Spock . . . Keep Your Volcanic Space Farts to Yourself"..............................$15–$20
Star Trek IV, Novel Teez (Canadian), 1986, silkscreened color picture of Spock and Kirk driving car. "Spock, If You Don't Like the Way I Drive . . . Get Off the Sidewalk!" ..$15–$20
Star Trek IV, Novel Teez (Canadian), 1986, silver, red, and blue puffy logo on front ....$15–$20
Star Trek, 1989, Paramount Special Effects, white movie letter logo (Star Trek) embroidered on black shirt..$20–$25
Star Trek V, 1989, Great Southern, color silkscreened picture of Klaa with letter logo on front, Klingon Bird of Prey, and words "Keep on Trekking" on back. Black shirt ....$20–$25
Star Trek: The Next Generation, Great Southern, 1989, Next Generation ship and logo on front. Call letter energy burst design on back, color, silkscreen....................................$20–$25
Star Trek: The Next Generation, Paramount Special Effects, 1989, logo with insignia on white or blue ....$20–$25

Star Trek Next Generation tee shirt.

Tee Shirts

Because of the current trend in the tee shirt industry toward inexpensive silk-screened tee shirts, available in relatively small quantities, unlicensed Star Trek shirts have become very common. The shirts listed here are all either promotional or licensed items. While some of the unlicensed products are very attractive, it is unlikely they will ever become collectible.

Boston Star Trek Convention, 1976, blue seated Spock silhouette.............................$8–$10

Star Trek: The Cruise, 1987, Lincoln Enterprises. Drawing of the Enterprise with various vacation activities going on around it...$10–$15

Trek Cruise '87, official convention shirt. Drawing of *S.S. Emerald Seas* with Enterprise-style saucer section and nacelles. "I Have Gone Where No Fan Has Gone Before" ....$10–$15

Star Trek Lives, Lincoln Enterprises, original TV ship plus words, silkscreened ....$6–$8

NBC Star Trek TV Promo Art, Lincoln Enterprises, early, on tank top, color..............$6–$8

Bloom County, Lin-Tex, 1986, silkscreened characters in Star Trek phase with caption "Ahead Warp Zillion"..$10–$15

Funky Winkerbean, Datazine, 1986, character silkscreened with "Beam Me Up Scotty" ....$10–$15

Star Trek IV, Official Star Trek Fan Club, 1986, logo on black shirt............................$8–$10

The Next Generation, Paramount, 1986, silkscreened, silver letters on black. Came in early promo kit..$10–$20

20th Anniversary Logo, early version, Paramount, 1986...$10–$20

20th Anniversary Logo, late version, Official Star Trek Fan Club, 1986...................$10–$15

25th Anniversary Design, Lincoln Enterprises. Insignia design with "25" in center and Enterprise flying around design. Full color...$10–$15

Star Trek: The Aliens, collage shirt, 1989, Paramount Special Effects. Color drawing of several original TV aliens silkscreened on black shirt...$15–$20

Star Trek: The Aliens, Gorn shirt, 1989, Paramount Special Effects. Color silkscreened drawing of Gorn from original TV show on white shirt ....$15–$20

She Lives, 1987, Lincoln Enterprises. Color picture of NCC–1701–A Enterprise with words ....$15–$18

The Ultimate Voyagers, 1987, Lincoln Enterprises. Color picture of NCC–1701–A Enterprise, whale, and words ....$15–$18

Star Trek V: The Final Frontier, group design, 1989, Great Southern, color silkscreen of crew plus logo on front. Picture of Enterprise and "Crew" on back............................$10–$15

Star Trek V: The Final Frontier, Klingon design, 1989, Great Southern. Color silkscreen of Klaa and logo on front. Klingon Bird of Prey and "Keep on Trekkin' " on back ....$10–$15

Star Trek V: The Final Frontier, promotional shirt (originally designed for sale at theaters), 1989, Great Southern. Color silkscreen of logo and ship on front. Logo on back........$10–$15

Star Trek: The Next Generation, 1987, Lincoln Enterprises. Picture of Next Generation Enterprise and puff logo. White on navy ....$15–$20

Star Trek: The Next Generation, United Federation of Planets design, 1987, Lincoln Enterprises. Navy and while puff Next Generation UFP design on beige shirt....................$15–$20

United Federation of Paramount, 1987, Lincoln Enterprises. Next Generation Enterprise flying around Paramount's trademark mountain, words underneath............................$15–$20
Star Trek: The Next Generation, 1989, Great Southern, Next Generation Enterprise and logo on front. Starfield back, silkscreened ....$15–$20
Star Trek: The Next Generation, 1989, Great Southern, Next Generation Enterprise and logo on front. Call letters in energy burst design on back, silkscreened ....$15–$20

Miscellaneous

Credit Cards, Visa and MasterCard have issued Star Trek credit cards with color pictures of the original and Next Generation Enterprises. Value of a valid card depends on the holder's credit limit. Defunct card ....$2–$5
Hat, 1976. Two kinds.
    Orange and brown knit with K-7 space station patch on front...................................$10–$15
    Ski hat with patch that says "Star Trek/U.S.S. Enterprise" and shows ship ....$10–$15
Shirt, Huk-A-Poo Clothing. Original TV Kirk, Spock, and Enterprise.........................$10–$15
Shorts and Top Sets, Dawnelle, 1979. Star Trek: The Motion Picture. Tank top. Three different: Kirk and Spock, Spock, Enterprise and Crew. Price each......................................$20–$25
Sleep Shirt, 1989, Paramount Special Effects. Original TV letter logo in white on black material with word "Crew" below ....$25–$30
Tie, Lee, brown, maroon or navy with original TV Enterprise and Star Trek logo. Each ....$15–$25
Underwear, Nazareth Mills, 1979, Star Trek: The Motion Picture, tee shirt and underwear set, boy's..$2–$5
Wallet, Larami. Original Star Trek TV Enterprise...$15–$25
Wallet, Larami, 1979. Star Trek: The Motion Picture. Enterprise or Kirk, Spock, and Enterprise..$10–$15

COINS AND MEDALLIONS

Hanover Mint Star Trek Medallions, First Series, 1974, serial numbers stamped on edge of coin. Came with detachable rim for necklace chain. 1½″ diameter. Front pictured Kirk and Spock in front of alien background. Reverse pictures original TV Enterprise.
    Bronze ....$50–$100
    Gold Plating over silver ....$150–$200
    Silver ....$200–$500
Hanover Mint Star Trek Medallions, Second Series, same as originals, but with serial numbers omitted. Bronze only ....$30–$50
Hanover Mint Star Trek Medallions, Third Series, rougher strikes, featured hole for chain cast as part of coin, serial numbers on rim. Bronze only ....$20–$40

Above: Hanover mint (second series), Lincoln tenth and twentieth Anniversary medallions. Left: Set of one-ounce gold coins in case.

Star Trek III: The Search for Spock Commemorative Medallion, Lincoln Enterprises, lightweight metal. Front: Kirk and Spock with title around faces. Reverse: Enterprise and planet. 1½″ diameter. Came with coin rim and chain ....$10–$15

Star Trek IV: The Voyage Home/Challenger Commemorative Medallion, 1986, Lincoln Enterprises. Front shows Enterprise over Golden Gate Bridge and whales. Reverse shows Challenger and text. Numbered at bottom, 2½″ with molded bezel for neck ribbon (ribbon came with coin)

    Bronze ....$20–$25
    Gold plated..$60–$65
    Gold and silver plated ....$80–$85
    Pewter ....$20–$25

Tenth Anniversary Commemorative Medallion, Lincoln Enterprises. Front shows Kirk, Spock, McCoy, and Scotty in profile with dates 1966–1976. Reverse: Enterprise orbiting planet. 1½″, copper color..$6–$8

Twentieth Anniversary Commemorative Medallion, Lincoln Enterprises, 1½″. Kirk and Spock on front. Enterprise and dates 1966–1986 on reverse ....$10–$15

Vulcan Nickel, Huckleberry Designs, large wooden nickel, drawing of Spock on face, legends "In Spock We Trust" and "Leonard Nimoy Wouldn't Lie" on reverse. 1972 (reissued in 1975) ....$5–$10

Rarities Mint Star Trek Coins, 1989, front shows character in original TV uniform in frosted relief on mirrored background. All coins have common reverse design of original TV Enterprise over Star Trek logo and metal content. Number appears around edge of coin. Numbers are deceiving, as they may be higher than the number of coins that exist. At the end of a minting, unsold coins are melted.

    1 ounce solid silver coins, came in plastic holder inside velveteen box
        Chekov ....$50–$75
        Kirk ....$50–$75
        McCoy..$50–$75
        Scotty ....$50–$75
        Spock ....$50–$75
        Sulu ....$50–$75
        Uhura...$50–$75
        Set of seven..$400–$600

    ¼ ounce gold-plated silver, came as keychain or necklace in velveteen box, Spock only ....$35–$45

    ¹⁄₁₀ ounce silver, came as necklace inside velveteen box
        Kirk ....$15–$25
        McCoy..$15–$25
        Spock...$15–$25

    ¼ ounce gold, came in plastic container in velveteen box
        Chekov ....$300–$400
        Kirk ....$300–$400
        McCoy...$300–$400
        Scotty ....$300–$400
        Spock...$300–$400
        Sulu ....$300–$400
        Uhura...$300–$400
        Set of seven...$2,100–$2,800

    1 ounce gold, a special order item from the Rarities Mint. These were made only in sets which came in special embossed leather display books. Probably no more than 15 sets were ever produced.
        Individual coin ....$1,500–$3,000
        Set of seven...$15,000–$25,000

COMICS

The listing is chronological by publisher. Values listed are per book and for books in near mint condition. Books in less than near mint condition are worth less.

Examples of Star Trek #1 comics from different series.

Gold Key Comics, 1967–1979

This series featured original stories based on the *Star Trek* characters. Most of the series was drawn by an artist who had never watched Star Trek!

No. 1 (photo cover)..$50–$100
No. 2–5..$30–$60
No. 6–9 (last photo cover) ....$25–$40
No. 10–20..$15–$25
No. 21–40..$10–$15
No. 41–59...$5–$10
No. 60–61 (last issue) ....$10–$20

Dan Curtis Giveaways, 1974

Full-color, 3″ × 6″, 24-page reprints of Gold Key stories.
No. 2 Star Trek, Enterprise Mutiny...$5–$10
No. 6 Star Trek, Dark Traveler...$5–$10

The Enterprise Logs, 1976–1977

Published by Golden Press. Each of these reprints eight of the above Gold Key comics. A warehouse fire destroyed much of the print run on these.
No. 1 (reprints 1–8 comics) ....$15–$25
No. 2 (reprints 9–17 comics) ....$15–$25
No. 3 (reprints 18–26 comics) ....$20–$30
No. 4 (reprints No. 27, 28, 30–34, 36, 38 comics) ....$20–$30

Enterprise Logs (Gold Key Comics compilations).

Dynabrite Comics, 1978–1979

Full-color, 48-page, cardboard covered reprints of Gold Key stories.

No. 11357 Star Trek, No. 33 and 41 ....$5–$10
No. 11358 Star Trek, No. 34 and 36 ....$5–$10

Marvel Comics, 1980–1982

Starts with adaptation of *Star Trek: The Motion Picture* and then continues with original stories.

No. 1..$3–$5
No. 2–7...$2–$4
No. 8–17...$3–$5
No. 18 (last issue) ....$6–$10
Marvel Super Special No. 15, magazine size, adapts complete movie
   $1.50 cover price...$5–$10
   $2.00 cover price (scarce)..$10–$20

DC Comics

1984–1988

This series had original stories based on the movie crew of the Enterprise with flashbacks and references to characters from the TV show.

No. 1 (Sutton art begins)...$5–$10
No. 2–10...$3–$6
No. 11–18, 20–33...$2–$4
No. 19 (written by Walter Keonig) ....$4–$6
No. 34–55...$1–$2
No. 56 (last issue) ....$3–$6
Annual No. 1–3..$2–$4
Who's Who in Star Trek No. 1, 2 ....$5–$10

Star Trek Movie Specials, 1984–1989

No. 1 Adapts Star Trek III ....$4–$8
No. 2 Adapts Star Trek IV ....$3–$4
No. 1 Adapts Star Trek V ....$3–$4

1989–Present

Original stories based on the *Star Trek* movie crew.

No. 1..$3–$5
No. 2–9...$1.50–$3
Annual No. 1 ....$2.50–$5

Star Trek: The Next Generation Mini-Series, 1988

This was a six-issue mini-series based on the "Next Generation" TV show.

No. 1..$5–$8
No. 2–6...$4–$8

Star Trek: The Next Generation, 1989–Present

Original stories based on "Next Generation" characters.

No. 1..$3–$5
No. 2–9...$1.50–$3
Annual No. 1 ....$2.50–$5

Parodies

There have been several parodies of Star Trek in other comics and magazines. An issue of *Mad* magazine or *Cracked* with a Star Trek parody is worth between $5 and $10 (*see* "Magazines"). Individual comics such as *Elf Trek* or *Imagi-Mation* with Star Trek parodies are worth between $2 and $5.

CONVENTION PROGRAM BOOKS

In the early days of Star Trek conventions, it was common practice to produce souvenir program books. Rising production costs have discouraged them in recent years. As with most printed collectibles these days, quality paper and especially color covers and/or interior photos tend to make the item harder to reproduce and therefore more valuable.

Books often came in a convention "package," a printed plastic convention bag which sometimes contained other items—badges, pocket programs, stickers, etc. These types of items generally have minimal collectors' value, usually no more than $1 or $2.

1972 International Star Trek Convention Program Book, small-size black cover with picture of Enterprise, black and white pictures inside...$15–$30
1973 International Star Trek Convention Program Book, second New York convention, Doohan, Takei guests, color cover...$10–$15
1974 International Star Trek Convention Program Book, New York, full color, Spock cover, Kelly, Koenig, Nichols, and Takei guests, full of photos, 48 pages ....$5–$10
1974 New York Star Trek Convention Program, smaller format, color cover...........$5–$10
1975 International Star Trek Convention Program Book, New York, full-color cover of Spock, Kirk, and McCoy, Shatner, Doohan, and Koenig guests, 24 pages, 8½″ × 11″ ....$3–$6
1975 New York Star Trek Convention Program, similar to 1974 ....$3–$6
1975 Miamicon I Convention Program Book, Miami, cover by Jack Kirby, art by Adams, Kirby, and Bode, Jimmy Doohan guest, 36 pages, 8½″ × 11″ ....$3–$6
1975 International Star Trek Convention Program Book, Philadelphia, color Spock cover, pictures inside ....$3–$6
1975 Trekcon I Program Book, West Palm Beach, Beck cover, Takei, Kelly Freas, and Noel Neill guests, 32 pages ....$3–$6
1976 Bicentennial Ten Convention Program Book, New York, Shatner, Kelly, Doohan, Nichols, Takei, Koenig, and Grace Lee Whitney guests, 8½″ × 11″ ....$3–$6

Convention program books.

1976 Boston Star Trek Convention Program Book, full-color wraparound cover, Doohan, Kelly, Koenig, Nichols, and Takei guests, 48 pages...$3–$6
1976 Omnicon Program Book, Kelly guest, program guides for Star Trek, Outer Limits, UN-CLE, etc. ....$8–$12
1977 Space-Con Four Program Book, Los Angeles, color wraparound cover, Shatner, Kelly, Whitney, and Harlan Ellison, 48 pages..$2–$4
1978 Odyssey One Convention Program Book, Milwaukee, full color covers, Takei and Koenig guests, 12 pages...$2–$4
1978 Space-Con Seven Program Book, Los Angeles, Shatner, Takei, Nichols, and Ellison guests, 30 pages ....$2–$4
1979 Star-Con Program Book, Dallas, Grace Lee Whitney guest, 48 pages ....$2–$4
1982 Ultimate Fantasy Program Book, Houston, billed as "The Star Trek con of all time"
....$5–$6

COSTUMES AND COSTUME PATTERNS

Costumes and uniforms have always been popular items with collectors and fans who often wear them at conventions. Though there have never been many mass-produced, professionally made uniforms, patterns are readily available and very popular. Original costumes are, of course, rare. Collectors have long ago obtained those still existing from the original show and Paramount is careful not to let those from the movies and the "Next Generation" out into general circulation. An actual costume's value would vary considerably based on which "Star Trek" episode or movie it came from, who wore it, what the condition of the item was, and the collector's personal taste. Any original item would, of course, be very expensive and a collector would be wise to research its authenticity before the purchase.

Note: *See "Patches" and "Jewelry" sections for costume accessories.*

Original Television Show

Star Fleet Uniforms, this company produced uniforms under a limited license during the '70s. Virtually all sales were to the fan market.

Star Trek (original) TV shirt, knit material, authentic reproduction. Adult sizes only. Gold, blue, and red available ....$30–$50

Left: Collegeville and Ben Cooper Star Trek costumes.
Right: Rubies men's TV costume shirt.

Collegeville Halloween Costume, 1967, lightweight material, tie-on jumpsuit with drawing of Enterprise and "Star Trek" in felt/sparkle design on front and plastic character mask. Children's sizes. Came window boxed

Kirk ....$20–$40
Spock..$20–$40

Ben Cooper, Halloween costume, 1973, one-piece jumpsuit, picture of Spock and Enterprise. Plastic mask, came boxed as "Super Hero" costume ....$15–$35

Ben Cooper, Halloween costume, 1975, one-piece jumpsuit picturing character and Enterprise, and plastic mask. Children's sizes, came window boxed

Kirk ....$15–$25
Klingon ....$15–$25
Spock..$15–$25

Rubies, original TV uniforms, 1990, adult size in gold, blue, and red with silkscreened insignia. Better quality than average children's boxed costume

Men's shirt ....$25–$30
Women's dress ....$30–$35

Vulcan Ears, Franco, 1974, came bagged with header depicting line drawing of Spock ....
....$5–$10

Lincoln Enterprises

Men's uniform shirt pattern, 1976, several sizes included ....$4–$6
Women's uniform pattern, 1976, several sizes included ....$5–$7

Star Trek: The Motion Picture

Aviva, Spock ears, 1979, children's size. Came blister packed on header with color photo of Spock..$10–$20

Collegeville, Halloween costume, 1979, one-piece outfit depicting characters and logo. Children's sizes, came window boxed

Klingon ....$15–$30
Ilia ....$15–$30
Kirk ....$15–$30
Spock..$15–$30

Pocket Star Trek: The Motion Picture Make-Your-Own-Costume Book, 1979, simplified patterns. See "Books."

Star Trek II: The Wrath of Khan

Collegeville, Halloween costume, 1982, one-piece outfit depicting characters, Enterprise, and Star Trek II logo. Children's sizes, came window boxed

Kirk ....$15–$25
Spock..$15–$25

Don Post, Spock ears, 1982, came bagged on header with color Star Trek II logo........$7–$12

Lincoln Enterprises, patterns, 1983. Several sizes in each pattern

Men's jacket ....$7–$10
Women's jacket...$7–$10
Recreational jumpsuit ....$7–$10
Trousers..$5–$8
Turtleneck undershirt ....$4–$7

20th Anniversary Vulcan Ears, promotional giveaway from Ballantine Books. Came bagged with 20th Anniversary sticker..$5–$8

Star Trek: The Next Generation

Ben Cooper, Halloween costume, 1988. Packaged on hangers.

Ferengi ....$10–$20
Klingon ....$10–$20

Lincoln Enterprises, patterns, 1988, several sizes included in each

Men's jumpsuit (original low collar version) ....$10–$15
Women's jumpsuit (original low collar version) ....$10–$15

Simplicity pattern and finished product.

Men's skant ....$8–$12
Women's skant ....$8–$12
Lincoln Enterprises, patterns, 1990, several sizes included in each
Men's third season top (with collar) ....$7–$8
Women's third season top ....$7–$8
Pants...$5–$6
Lincoln Enterprises, visor, 1989, plastic, as worn by Geordi LaForge in the series...$12–$15
Simplicity, patterns, 1989, patterns for original low collar-style jumpsuits. Came packaged in
typical pattern envelope with color photo on cover. Several sizes in each
Men's jumpsuit, man and woman in outfits on cover..$6–$8
Women's jumpsuit, man and woman in outfits on cover...$6–$8
Children's, two children on cover...$6–$8

DECALS AND STICKERS

Decals, Lincoln Enterprises
Sheet No. 1, three different insignia designs, two-color, water mount.........................$1–$2
Sheet No. 2, decals of the Enterprise, the Klingon Fighter, Galileo ....$1–$2
Sheet No. 3, decals of a communicator, a phaser, and 3-D chess game.........................$1–$2
Sheet No. 4, decals of NCC-1701 in various sizes...$1–$2
Sheet No. 5, decals of eight different Star Trek monsters...$1–$2
Sheet No. 6, 7, four different stars from the series on each. Price each........................$1–$2
Decal, Star Fleet Academy, words, fan produced...$2–$4

Left: Star Trek stamp album and two of the stamp packets.
Right: Star Trek: The Motion Picture "Instant Stained Glass" decals.

Decal, Star Trek V: The Final Frontier, silver and red logo, Enterprise on starfield, promotional item ....$3–$5

Decal, Vulcan Science Academy, words only ....$2–$4

Federation Seal Sticker, Lincoln Enterprises, blue on white, Star Fleet Academy ...$1–$1.50

Puffy Sticker Sets, Aviva, 1979, Star Trek: The Motion Picture, three sets, features characters and ships. Each ....$3–$8

Star Trek Stamp Album, Celebrity Stamps, 1979. Set includes album and six different stamp packets

Set No. 1 (U.S.S. Enterprise)..$6–$10

Set No. 2 (Captain Kirk)...$6–$10

Set No. 3 (Mr. Spock) ....$6–$10

Set No. 4 (Klingons and Romulans)..$6–$10

Set No. 5 (Aliens of the Galaxy) ....$6–$10

Set No. 6 (Creatures of the Galaxy) ....$6–$10

Complete set ....$50–$100

Star Trek: The Motion Picture, Aviva, 1979, instant stained glass stickers, reusable.

Admiral Kirk..$1–$4

Enterprise ....$1–$4

Spock...$1–$4

Spock giving Vulcan salute...$1–$4

Spock with Science symbol ....$1–$4

The Vulcan salute...$1–$4

Sticker, Lincoln Enterprises. Command insignia, black on gold foil ....$1–$4

Sticker, Pocket, promotional, 1986, blue and yellow "Star Trek 20th Anniversary, the only logical books to read!"..$1–$2

Sticker Books, Canadian, 1975. "The Siege." Story plus stickers ....$10–$15

T-K Graphics Stickers, this company has done an extensive line of offset-printed, pressure-sensitive labels from Star Trek and other sources ....$.25–$1

Twentieth Anniversary Sticker, Paramount, promotional ....$.25–$.50

United Federation of Planets Sticker, Lincoln Enterprises. Next Generation design ....$1–$1.50

Vending Capsule Decals, Paramount, 1979, set of four, color peel-back stickers of Spock, Kirk, Kirk and Spock, and the Enterprise, McDonald's promotion ....$6–$12

Walls Ice Cream Stickers, New Zealand, 1982, set of six ....$10–$15

Note: *See "Trading Cards and Stickers" section for additional sticker sets.*

FAN CLUBS

Though impromptu fan clubs of all sizes have existed ever since the original TV series first appeared on the air, the more recent trend has been toward a more organized, cohesive form of fandom. Today, in addition to the many small "just for fun" type of clubs, there are two that deserve particular note.

First is the Official Star Trek Fan Club. This club is authorized and supported by Paramount. Its primary function is to keep fans informed through its professionally done news magazine which offers articles and photos on both the old and new Star Treks in addition to letters, a convention list, articles on fandom, etc.

> **Official Star Trek Fan Club**
> **P.O. Box 111000**
> **Aurora, CO 80011**

The second one is actually a loose confederation of many smaller clubs or "ships," called Star Fleet. Star Fleet's function is more of a social nature. In addition to meeting to discuss Star Trek and club affairs, most branches organize trips to conventions, make costumes, have parties, etc. They also have a bi-monthly newsletter. Their headquarters address is as follows:

Official Fan Club magazine.

Star Fleet
P.O. Box 430
Burnsville, NC 28714

One other organization, though *not* a club, deserves special mention. This is the Star Trek Welcommittee. This organization, which has been around nearly as long as Star Trek, is a resource organization designed to help and inform fans. If you have a question about Star Trek or Star Trek fandom, these are the people to contact. Please note, however, that this is an entirely nonprofit organization and if you write them you must send along a self-addressed, stamped envelope.

Star Trek Welcommittee
P.O. Box 12
Saranac, MI 48881

FANZINES

Fanzines are fan-written magazines containing stories, poetry, artwork, and letters of comment. Star Trek fanzines had their genesis in the mid-seventies. Fans of the "Star Trek" TV series composed their collective ideas and adventures for the Enterprise crew into small publications which were generally passed among fellow fans at conventions. Typical print runs for the earliest fanzines were less than a hundred copies. Although fanzines can still be found at conventions today, most fanzines are now sold through the mail and have print runs of up to a thousand copies.

Early fanzines were produced on mimeograph machines and as such were available in a rainbow of ink colors and almost always on scrap or low-quality paper. They were often bound by hand using copper brads which could be removed to form a sort of scrapbook. With the advent of Xerographic machines, which facilitated larger print runs, stapled and bound fanzines became more commonplace. For the most part, mimeographed fanzines are now a thing of the past. Current fanzines are usually offset printed with card stock covers.

Cover art for modern fanzines has taken on great improvements. They range from simple borders on fanzines like *Echoes of the Empire* to the full-color portraits on *Mind Meld*. Zineds (a short term for Fanzine editors and publishers) have become aware that great cover art can actually help the sale of their zines. Awards and friendly competition for the services of popular cover artists is very intense. In the last couple of years, fanzine editors have incorporated full-color 4″ × 5″ photographic prints of artwork into fanzine covers to inexpensively enhance the look and appearance of their fanzines.

The general improvement and advancement of fanzine production has perhaps been helped more with the advent of desk-top publishing. Instead of border tape and rub-off lettering, zined's now use sophisticated computer systems equipped with easy-to-use page layout and graphic enhancements. By printing their originals using laser printers, zined's are able to improve their originals, which are duplicated using Xerographic copiers. Since most of the publications are produced on office copiers or at small print shops, they are still considered nonprofit ventures.

Due to the small print runs, most fanzines may seem relatively expensive when compared to professional publications. Fanzines are available directly from the publishers for an average price of $10 per 100 pages. Different types of binding and cover stock can affect the overall price as well as whether you purchase the fanzine from the original publisher. Often zineds will try to control the mark-up of their fanzines by printing the suggested price in the zine. Older fanzines can be found at conventions and through fanzine auctions listed in *Datazine*.

There are basically five types of Star Trek fanzines. Action/Adventure (AA), Mixed Media (MM), Adult (Adult or K/S for Kirk/Spock relationships), Love/Romance (LR), and Informational (I). Fanzines with a love/romance theme are sometimes referred to as "Mary Sue" stories; typically the heroine of the story is the only one who can save the Enterprise, be Captain Kirk's or Mr. Spock's only *true* love, and/or save the galaxy from total destruction. Fanzines with adult themes cover the entire spectrum from gentle romance to hard-core sex. Some contain explicit Kirk/Spock love stories or detailed hurt/comfort themes. Most fanzine editors of sexually explicit fanzines will require that you send an age statement before they will allow you to purchase their fanzines. Zines of an adult nature command the highest prices and seem to hold the greatest investment value over time, although certain older action/adventure fanzines still sell for relatively high prices. Mixed media fanzines contain non-Star Trek stories or "mixed" stories, where the characters of Star Trek meet up with the characters of another TV show or movie. Since the airing of "Star Trek: The Next Generation," many mixed stories revolve around the original crew meeting up with the new crew.

One might ask, what makes a fanzine collectible? It is really up to the individual reader. If a fanzine has a particular story in it that really appeals to you, then you would probably want to keep the zine for your collection. Some fanzines, however, have earned certain honors because they have broken new ground or appealed to a large number of fans. There are numerous fanzine awards given to fanzines and their editors that are awarded by readers. Among the most highly praised and well thought of are the FanQ and Surak awards. If a fanzine has received either of those awards, you can count on it being one of the better fanzines in its category. Because fanzines have provided a means of creative outlet for many budding writers over the years, many professional writers' earliest works are featured in fanzines. Due to the freedom of subject matter, many pro writers continue to publish works of fiction for the fanzine market. It is remarkable that the small press market has continued to thrive and explore uncharted horizons similar to the TV show that inspired its creation.

Below are some of the currently available fanzines. However, due to their limited press runs, some may be sold out.

Currently Available Fanzines

All are listed by title, content, and publisher of fanzine.

Abode of Strife, Adult, Bill Hupe..$16.50
Act Five, K/S, MKASHEF Ent..$15
Alexi, K/S, MKASHEF Ent..$18
All Our Yesterdays No. 4, LR, Dolly Weissberg..$16
Alternaties, Adult, K/S, Bill Hupe...$10
As I Do Thee, K/S, MKASHEF Ent...$20
Azimuth to Zenith, AA, Mary Case...$15
Before the Glory, K/S, Kathleen Resch..$18
Beside Myself, Adult, Merry Men Press..$18
Beyond Antaries, Adult, Bill Hupe..$6
Beyond the Farthest Star, Adult, Bill Hupe...$10.25
Complete Kershu Fighter, AA, Poison Pen...$10
Crucible for Courage, AA, Bill Hupe..$15
Day of Vengeance, K/S, Kathleen Resch..$15
Daystrom Project, AA, Bill Hupe...$14
Empire Books, AA, Empire Books..$5
The Enterprise Review, AA, Dolly Weissberg...$16
Elysia, AA, Bill Hupe...$10
Eridani, AA, Bill Hupe...$8.50
Fetish, K/S, Merry Men..$20
Final Frontier, K/S, Sandra Gent..$18.50
First Time, K/S, Merry Men...$20
Formazine, A Light Stimulant, LR, Linda Chanack.......................................$9
Games of Love and Duty, LR, Poison Pen...$14
The Garden Spot, AA, Bill Hupe..$4.75
A Gathering of Blacque, K/S, MKASHEF..$14
Genesis Aftermath, AA, Bill Hupe...$5
Hailing Frequencies, AA, LR, Natash Mohr...$10.65
Hellguard Social Register 1, AA, Bill Hupe..$15.50
Idylls, AA, LR, Bill Hupe...$10
In a Different Reality, AA, Bill Hupe...$7.75
In the Wilderness, K/S, Rosemary Wild..$22
Interlude, LR, Bill Hupe...$9
In Triplicate, K/S, MKASHEF..$12
Just This Once, AA, Bill Hupe..$5
Kefrendar, AA, Bill Hupe...$13
Laff Trek, MM, Bill Hupe..$8.50
Lifeboat, AA, Bev Zuk..$16.50
Lore, AA, Bill Hupe..$6.50
The Marriage, LR, Dolly Weissberg..$22
Masiform D, AA, Poison Pen..$6.50
Matter/Antimatter, K/S, Sandra Gent...$20
McCoy Gets the Last Word, AA, Nancy Borden...$6.50
NCC–1701D, I, Natasha Mohr...$6
The Neofan's Guide to Fandom, I, Joan Verba..$1
A Next Generation Compendium, I, FOTP..$5
No Peaceful Roads Lead Home, LR, Poison Pen.......................................$11.50
Nu Ormenel Collected No. 5, AA, Poison Pen..$3.50
One Way Mirror, LR, Poison Pen...$8.50
Orion, AA, Bill Hupe...$16
Pit of Archeron, AA, Bill Hupe..$7.50
Portraits, LR, Merry Men..$20
The Price of Freedom, K/S, Kathleen Resch..$20
Rendevous, AA, Mary Case..$15
Renegades, AA, Mary Case..$15
Ring of Deceit, AA, Empire Books...$7
Scattered Stars, K/S, Merry Men...$20

The Search for Patrick Stewart—The Bibliography, I, Helen Bookman.............................$3
The Search for Patrick Stewart—The Collection, I, Helen Bookman $20
Sensor Readings, AA, Bill Hupe $5
Shades of Grey, K/S, MKASHEF..$20
Ship's Log, MM, Lee Pennell...$16.50
Spock, AA, LR, Bill Hupe...$8.50
Spockanalia, AA, Poison Pen $22
Spunk, Adult, Bill Hupe $8.50
Squired Again, AA, LR, Mary Case $15
Star Art, Art, Dolly Weissberg $6
Starbound 2, AA, LR, FONN $12
Starlines, AA, Bill Hupe $5.75
Third Verdict, AA, Bev Zuk...$9
Thoroughbreds, MM, Rowena Warner $21
T'HY'LA, K/S, Kathleen Resch $18
Timeshift, AA, Florence Butler $7.75
Transwarp, AA, Bill Hupe $7.50
Trojan Angel, AA, Bill Hupe $15
The Uhura Papers, AA, Jan Walker $10
Ultimate Mary Sue, MM, Bill Hupe $8
Vaeya, AA, Lee Pennell...$12.50
A Very Special Short Leave, AA, LR, D. Weissberg $16
The Voice, Adult, Rosemary Wild $12.50
Vulcan's Lyre, I, Kelly Cline...$8.95
Where Do We Go from Here?, AA, Lee Pennell $12.50

Note: *Information on currently available fanzines can be found in a publication titled:* Datazine, *P.O. Box 24590, Denver, CO 80224.* Datazine *has a* TV Guide-*type format and lists zine contents and prices bi-monthly. It is available by subscription.*

Out of Print Fanzines

Accumulated Leave, AA, Yeoman Press ....$12–$15
Alternate Universe, No. 1–2, AA, Shirley Maiewski ....$18–$20
Archives, AA, Yeoman Press..$12–$15
As I Do Thee, K/S, series by A. Gelfand ....$18–$20
Babel, AA, Laura and Margaret Basta ....$40–$60
Berengaria, AA, V. Kirlin ....$10–$12
Bloodstone, Adult, C. Frisbie ....$40–$60
Broken Images, K/S, V. Clark..$40–$60
Castaways, The, AA, V. Kirlin...$15–$18
Cheap Thrills, K/S, Carol Hunterton ....$18–$20
Contact, No. 1–4, Adult, Bev Volker and Nancy Kippax ....$50–$60
Contact, No. 5, 6, Adult, Bev Volker and Nancy Kippax ....$25–$30
Companion, K/S, series by Carol Hunterton..$25–$30
Courts of Honor, Adult, Syn Ferguson ....$30–$40
Daring Attempt, K/S, series by W. Rathbone...$15–$18
Delta Triad, AA, series by Melinda Reynolds ....$18–$20
Diamonds and Rust, LR, Cheryl Rice ....$15–$18
Displaced, LR, series by L. Welling ....$10–$15
Don't Tell It to the Captain, AA, M. Lamski ....$15–$20
Duet, K/S, edited by D. Dabinett..$35–$40
Echoes of the Empire, Adult, series by J. Thompson...$18–$20
Epilogue, AA, Jean Lorrah...$12–$15
Eridani Triad, No. 1–5, AA, Judith Brownlee...$10–$12
Fesarius Series, AA, T.J. Burnside...$16–$18
Full Moon Rising, LR, Jean Lorrah..$8–$10
Furaha, AA, Virginia Walker..$12–$15
Grup, Adult, series by Carrie Brennan ....$35–$45
Handful of Snowflakes, AA, M.L. Steve Barnes ....$12–$15
Honorable Sacrifice, Adult, B. Zuk ....$15–$18
In a Different Reality, AA, M. Krause ....$15–$18

It Takes Time on Impulse, Adult, H. Stallings ....$15–$20
Interphase!, AA, series by Connie Faddis..$35–$40
Kraith Collected Series, AA, Carol Lynn ....$30–$35
Masiform-D, AA, Devra Langsam..$12–$15
Menagerie, AA, Sharon Ferraro and Paula Smith ....$8–$10
Mirrors of Mind and Flesh, K/S, Gayle Feyrer..$18–$20
Mixed Metaphors, AA, D. Barry ....$18–$20
Naked Times, K/S, series by Pon Farr Press ....$15–$20
Night of the Twin Moons, LR, Jean Lorrah..$8–$10
Nome Series, K/S, V. Clark and B. Storey ....$30–$35
Nu Ormenel, Adult, series by F. Marder..$18–$20
Nuage, AA/LR, series by K. Bates..$12–$15
Obsession, LR, M. Lowe and K. Scarrett..$12–$15
Odyssey, AA/LR, series by Ingrid Cross ....$15–$18
OSC'Zine, Adult, T'Kuhtian..$18–$20
One Way Mirror, LR, Barbara Wenk ....$35–$40
Out of Bounds, K/S, series by P. Rose and L. Shell ....$30–$35
Penumbra, AA, M. Arvizu..$12–$15
Perfect Object, Adult, Yeoman Press ....$12–$15
Pledge, LR, C. Davis ....$12–$15
Precessional, AA, Laurie Huff..$15–$18
Price and the Prize, K/S, Gayle Feyrer..$30–$35
R & R, No. 1–5, Adult, Yeoman Press ....$12–$15
Sahaj, AA, series by Leslie Lilker ....$35–$40
Sensuous Vulcan, Adult, D.T. Steiner..$45–$50
Showcase, No. 1, LR, Sharon Emily ....$20–$25
Sol Plus, AA, Jackie Bielowicz..$10–$12
Spock Enslaved, Adult, D.T. Steiner..$40–$45
Spockinalia, No. 1–5, AA, Devra Langsam..$20–$15
Stardate Unknown, No. 1–5, AA, Gerry Downes..$20–$25
Sun and Shadow, Adult, C. Frisbie..$18–$20
T'Hy'La, Adult, series by Kathleen Resch ....$18–$20
Tales of Feldman, AA, series by Mindy Glazer ....$18–$20
Thrust, K/S, C. Frisbie..$45–$50
T-Negative, AA, Ruth Berman ....$5–$8
Vault of Tomorrow, AA/LR, series by Marion McChesney..$22–$25
Warped Space, AA, T'Kuhtian Press ....$10–$15
Weight, The, AA/Adult, Leslie Fish..$25–$30

FILM AND VIDEO

Films

All of the original "Star Trek" episodes and all five movies do, of course, exist on film of various sizes, but this is more and more a field for very specialized collectors. Since video cassettes have become popular, the number of individuals willing to deal with finicky projectors and bulky film libraries has dwindled considerably. In addition, since the studios did not intend for these films to be sold to the public, private collecting, especially of more recent films, exists in a sort of twilight zone of legality. Still, there is much to be said for the quality of film over that of video tape, and many people still prefer this medium. For collecting purposes, the only really practical form of Star Trek film is 16mm. This pretty much limits the field to the original TV show. The movies were done either in 35 or 70mm, and the projection equipment for this size film just isn't designed for home use. "Star Trek: The Next Generation" episodes are not done on film at all but stored on professional-quality video tape. If you are determined to buy a Star Trek film, then be sure to watch it before you buy. Not only should the film be complete and free from jumps caused by

Original episode and animated videotapes.

splices and stretched sprocket, but original Star Trek film is coming of an age where it tends to turn red if not treated and stored properly. A good quality film should cost anywhere between $100 and $300, depending primarily on the desirability of the episode.

Video Discs, RCA

The first four movies and several episodes of the original TV series exist in this format. Episode discs each contain two shows.
Movie or Episode Disc ....$25–$35

Video Tape

Paramount Home Video.
  All are available on VHS or Beta. Packaging generally has color photo of subject on slipcase.
Original Star Trek Episodes, several double episode tapes were released in 1982. Currently all episodes are available in single format
  1982 double episode tapes ....$20–$30
  Single episode ....$12–$15
  The Cage (original pilot), No. 1...$20–$30
  The Cage (all-color version), No. 99 ....$20–$30
  Menagerie, two-part episode...$20–$30
Star Trek Animated Episodes, the entire series is available on 11 tapes, each containing two episodes. Per tape...$12–$15
Star Trek Movies
  Star Trek: The Motion Picture ....$15–$20
  Star Trek II: The Wrath of Khan..$15–$20
  Star Trek III: The Search for Spock..$15–$20
  Star Trek IV: The Voyage Home ....$15–$20
  Star Trek V: The Final Frontier ....$15–$20

GAMES AND ACCESSORIES

This section is divided by manufacturer, i.e. FASA Corp., Task Force Games, and others. All additions and accessories for these games are listed in this section.

Cititel Miniatures

This company made a series of 25mm pewter gaming pieces based on *Star Trek: The Motion Picture*.
Pewter Sets, 1979. Andoreans, Deltans, Enterprise Crew, Ilia and Janice Rand, Klingons, McCoy, Scotty and Chekov, Security Guards, Spock, Sulu and Decker, Uhura and Chapel. Price per set...$5–$10

FASA

Star Trek Role-Playing Game and Accessories

In this game, the players assume the personalities of the characters from "Star Trek" and react to situations as the character would.

Star Trek: The Role-Playing Game, 2001 (Deluxe Limited Edition), this game contains the Star Trek Basic Set (2004) and the Star Trek III Combat Game (2006), plus a set of three adventures and deck plans for the Constitution cruiser and the Klingon D–7 battle cruiser ....$40–$50

    Special autographed edition, signed by James Doohan or Walter Koenig.............$75–$100

    Enterprise deck plans, to game 2001 ....$15–$20

    Klingon deck plans, to game 2001 ....$10–$15

Star Trek: The Role-Playing Game, Second Deluxe Edition, no deck plans for ships ....$25–$30

Star Trek: The Role-Playing Game, 2004 (Basic Set), the complete rules to role playing are contained in three easy-to-read books outlining the Star Trek universe and how to begin adventuring...$15–$17

The Klingons: A Sourcebook and Character Generation Supplement, 2002, this add-on module for the Role-Playing Game allows you to play the part of a Klingon. Included is a description of Klingon history and culture

    Books..$12–$15

    Boxed set..$15–$25

The Romulans: A Sourcebook and Character Generation Supplement, 2005, this add-on module for the Role-Playing Game allows you to play the part of a Romulan. Included is a description of Romulan history and culture ....$10–$12

The Orions: A Sourcebook and Character Generation Supplement, 2008, includes a "Book of Common Knowledge" and a "Book of Deep Knowledge"...............................$12–$15

Trader Captains and Merchant Princes, 2203, this rules supplement provides all the charts and rules needed for creating traders, merchants, con-men, and rogues of space. A complete system for economics in the Star Trek universe is also included ....$12–$15

    More recent, two-book version..$11–$12

Ship Construction Manual, 2204, this rules supplement contains all the information and tables necessary for building your own starship. Also included is the starship combat efficiency system for rating your ship in combat.

    First edition ....$12–$15

    All other editions ....$10–$12

FASA gaming material.

Star Trek III: Movie Update and Sourcebook, 2214, allows players to bring their games up to the time period of the movies. Includes information necessary for adding new ships and personnel to games...$10–$12

Star Trek II: Starship Combat Game, 2003, predecessor to Star Trek III game. Only released for a short time...$15–$20

Starship Combat Game, 2003, generic version of movie update games. Boxed ....$18–$20

The Triangle, 2007, setting for a Star Trek campaign. Comes with full-color map and two books about the Triangle area..$10–$12

The Federation, 2011, complete sourcebook of the United Federation of Planets......$10–$12

Star Fleet Intelligence Manual, 2014, brings spies and secret operatives into the game ....$10–$12

Star Trek Adventure Books, these add new scenarios to the Role-Playing Game

Witness for the Defense, 2202 ....$7–$8

Denial of Destiny, 2205 ....$8–$10

Termination, 1456–2206 ....$8–$10

Demand of Honor, 2207 ....$8–$10

The Orion Ruse, 2208..$7–$8

Margin of Profit, 2209 ....$7–$8

The Outcasts, 2210 ....$8–$10

A Matter of Priorities, 2211 ....$7–$8

A Dommsday Like Any Other, 2212 ....$7–$8

The Mines of Selka, 2213 ....$7–$8

Triangle Campaign, 2215..$8–$10

Graduation Exercise, 2216...$7–$8

Where Has All the Glory Gone, 2217 ....$7–$8

Return to Axanar, 2218..$7–$8

Decision at Midnight, 2219 ....$7–$8

Imbalance of Power, 2220..$11–$12

Old Soldiers Never Die/The Romulan War, 2221 ....$11–$12

A Conflict of Interest/Klingon Intelligence Briefing, 2222....................................$11–$12

Dixie Gambit, 2223..$7–$8

The White Flame, 2225, a starship combat scenario pack ....$7–$8

The Strider Incident/Regula I deck plans, 2226 ....$11–$12

Deck plans alone..$7–$9

Ship Recognition Manuals, these books contain all the game statistics for the Role-Playing and the Starship Combat Games. Each book contains 40 ships with a variety of variants and brief descriptions of performance and history.

The Klingons, 2301..$7–$8

The Federation, 2302 ....$7–$8

The Romulans, 2303 ....$7–$8

PLAYING AIDS

Playing aids are used to add to the enjoyment of your games. None of the items are required to play, but each will certainly increase the appeal of your games.

Starship Combat Hex Grid, 2801, contains three 22″ × 33″ starfield maps for use with 2006 ....$3–$5

Gamemaster's Kit, 2802, three-panel gamemaster's screen displaying all important tables and charts; 16-page book containing all charts and tables needed by players and gamemasters ....$6–$8

Tricorder/Sensors Interactive Display, 2803, this play aid allows players to use a tricorder for scans and scientific readings. The unit is a hand-held simulated tricorder with display windows ....$10–$12

Starship Miniatures

⅓₉₀₀ scale lead. Come in several pieces which need glue for assembly. Blister packed on color headers.

U.S.S. Enterprise (new), 2501 ....$4–$5

U.S.S. Reliant (cruiser), 2502..$4–$5

Klingon D–7 (battlecruiser), 2503 ....$4–$5

Romulan Bird of Prey (cruiser), 2504..$4–$5

U.S.S. Enterprise (old), 2505 ....$4–$5
Regula I Space Laboratory, 2506 ....$4–$5
U.S.S. Larson (destroyer), 2507 ....$4–$5
Klingon D–10 (cruiser), 2508 ....$4–$5
Klingon D–18 (destroyer), 2509 ....$4–$5
Gorn MA–12 (cruiser), 2511 ....$4–$5
Orion Blockade Runner, 2512..$4–$5
Klingon L–9 (frigate), 2513...$4–$5
U.S.S. Loknar (frigate), 2514...$4–$5
Romulan Winged Defender (cruiser), 2515 ....$4–$5
U.S.S. Chandley (Frigate), 2516...$4–$5
U.S.S. Excelsior (battleship, Star Trek III), 2517 ....$10–$12
Klingon L–42 Bird of Prey (Frigate, Star Trek III), 2518 ....$4–$5
U.S.S. Grissom (research vessel, Star Trek III), 2519 ....$4–$5
Deep Space Freighter, 2520..$4–$5
Romulan Graceful Flyer (scout), 2521 ....$4–$5
Orion Wanderer, 2522 ....$4–$5
Kobayashi Maru (freighter), 2523..$4–$5
Romulan Gallant Wing (cruiser), 2524...$4–$5
Gorn BH–2 (Battleship), 2525..$9–$12
U.S.S. Baker (Destroyer), 2526..$4–$5
Romulan Nova (battleship), 2527 ....$11–$12
Romulan Bright One (destroyer), 2528...$4–$5
Klingon L–24 (battleship), 2529...$11–$12
Klingon D–2 (Missile Destroyer), 2530 ....$4–$5
Romulan Whitewind (cruiser), 2531 ....$4–$5
U.S.S. Northampton (frigate), 2532...$4–$5
U.S.S. Remora (escort), 2533 ....$4–$5
U.S.S. Andor (missile cruiser), 2534..$4–$5

Star Trek II: The Wrath of Khan

25mm lead miniature figures. Came blister packed on color headers.
James T. Kirk, 2601 ....$2–$4
1st Officer Spock, 2602..$2–$4
Dr. McCoy, 2603..$2–$4
Lt. Saavik, 2604 ....$2–$4
Scotty, 2605 ....$2–$4
Lt. Uhura, 2606 ....$2–$4
Sulu, 2607...$2–$4
Chekov, 1608...$2–$4
Khan, 2609..$2–$4
David Marcus, 2610 ....$2–$4
Joachim, 2611 ....$2–$4
Carol Marcus, 2610..$2–$4
Capt. Terrell, 2613 ....$2–$4
Khan (Ceti Alpha V), 2614..$2–$4
Klingon Officer, 2615...$2–$4
Klingon Soldier, 1, 2616...$2–$4
Klingon Soldier 2, 2617 ....$2–$4
Boxed Sets, each set contains one ship and eight crew member figures.
Enterprise and crew, 3001 ....$15–$25
Reliant and Khan's crew, 3002 ....$15–$25
Regula and scientists, 3003...$15–$25
Klingon D–7 and crew, 3004...$15–$25

Star Trek Microadventure Games

Small boxed games with short playing times and simple rules.
Star Trek III: The Search for Spock, 5001 ....$6–$10
Star Trek III: Starship Duel 1, 5002 ....$6–$10

Star Trek III: Struggle for the Throne, 5004 ....$6–$10
Star Trek III: Starship Duel 2, 5005 ....$6–$10

Star Trek: The Next Generation

Star Trek: The Next Generation Officer's Manual, this book was issued and then withdrawn at the request of Paramount. Unauthorized reprints of this book do exist. Reprints have poorly printed covers.
   Original FASA copy ....$30–$50
   Reprint...$10–$15
Star Trek: The Next Generation First-Year Sourcebook...........................$10–$12

Task Force Games

Star Fleet Battles

These are true war games with combat between individual ships or whole fleets. All the items listed in this section are for use with the game.
Introduction to Star Fleet Battles, 3000, basic introduction to the game ....$5–$6
Star Fleet Battles, 5001, starting set for game. Includes 108-page Volume I Commander's Rulebook, 32-page SSD and chart booklet, 216 die-cut counters and a large map. Boxed
....$20–$25
Star Fleet Battles Volume II, 5008, adds changes to game. Commander's Rulebook Volume II plus SSD booklet and playing pieces. Boxed ....$20–$25
Star Fleet Battles Volume III, 5009, more changes to game. Includes Commander's Rulebook Volume III plus SSD booklet and playing pieces. Boxed ....$20–$25
Star Fleet Battles Supplements, game expansions include playing pieces and rules.
   No. 1 Fighters and Shuttles, 3003..$9–$10
   No. 2 X-Ships, 3013 ....$9–$10
   No. 3 Fast Patrol Ships ....$9–$10
Star Fleet Battles Reinforcements, 3014, additional playing pieces...............$6–$7
Star Fleet Battles Rules Update 1, 3015, update pages for Star Fleet Battles and Supplement No. 1..$5–$6
Federation and Empire, 5006, creates the Galactic War that brought about Star Fleet Battles. A larger scale game. Includes two large maps, 1,080 playing pieces, eight charts, and a rules scenario booklet ....$35–$40
Federation and Empire Deluxe, 5006...$40–$50
Federation and Empire Deluxe Fleet Pack, 3203..$12–$15
Federation and Empire Deluxe Folio Pack, 3204 ....$5–$6

Captain's Logs

Each features a story, over 20 scenarios, and new rules for playing Star Fleet Battles.
No. 1, 3004..$5–$6
No. 2, 3008..$5–$6
No. 3, 3010..$5–$6
No. 4, 3012..$5–$6

Commander's SSD Books

Each contains 48 SSDs per book.
No. 1, 3005, Federation, Andromedan, Orions, and Kzinti...............................$5–$6
No. 2, 3006, Klingon, Lyran, Hydran, and Wyn..$5–$6
No. 3, 3007, Romulan, Tholian, and Gorn ....$5–$6
No. 4, 3009, tugs, star bases, battle stations, and freighters.........................$5–$6
No. 5, 3016, Q-ships, booms and saucers, special and variant ships ....$5–$6
No. 6, 3018, police ships, light tugs, survey cruisers, and space control ships.................$5–$6
No. 7, 3020, Tholian, Gorn, Federation, Kzinti, and Hydran ships....................$5–$6
No. 8, 3021, Klingon, Lyran, Orion, and Romulan ships...................................$5–$6
No. 9, 3023, New Commander's SSD for all races...$5–$6

Starline 2200 Miniatures

1/3900 scale plastic or lead miniatures.

Starline 2200 Hex Sheets, 7000, four 18″ × 24″ maps ....$6–$10

The Federation

Federation Dreadnought, 7010 ....$4–$5
Federation Heavy Cruiser, 7011 ....$4–$5
Federation New Light Cruiser, 7012 ....$4–$5
Federation Light Cruiser, 7013 ....$4–$5
Federation Destroyer, 7014...$4–$5
Federation Scout, 7015 ....$4–$5
Federation Tug, 7016 ....$4–$5
Federation Frigate (2), 7017 ....$4–$5
Federation Carrier, 7020 ....$6–$8
Federation Starbase, 7025...$6–$8

The Klingons

Klingon B–10 Battleship, 7040 ....$6–$8
Klingon C–8 Dreadnought, 7042..$6–$8
Klingon D–7 Battlecruiser, 7043 ....$4–$5
Klingon D–5 Cruiser, 7044...$4–$5
Klingon F–5 Frigate (2), 7046 ....$4–$5
Klingon Tug (carrier), 7051 ....$6–$8
Klingon PFs (6), 7053...$5–$6

The Romulans

Romulan Condor, 7060..$4–$6
Romulan Warbird (2), 7064 ....$4–$6
Romulan Sparrowhawk, 7071..$4–$6
Romulan Skyhawk and Seahawk, 7073...$4–$6

The Gorns

Gorn Dreadnought, 7080 ....$4–$6
Gorn Heavy Cruiser, 7081 ....$4–$6
Gorn Light Cruiser, 7082..$4–$6
Gorn Destroyer (2), 7084..$4–$6

The Kzintis

Kzinti Space Control Ship, 7100 ....$4–$6
Kzinti Carrier, 7101 ....$4–$6
Kzinti Escort Carrier, 7103 ....$4–$6
Kzinti Strike Cruiser, 7104 ....$4–$6
Kzinti Frigate (2), 7107 ....$4–$6
Kzinti Tug, 7108 ....$4–$6
Kzinti PFs (6), 7110..$4–$6

The Lyrans

Lyran Lion Dreadnought, 7120...$4–$5
Lyran Cruiser, 7122 ....$4–$5
Lyran War Cruiser, 7123 ....$4–$5
Lyran Destroyer (2), 7124...$4–$5
Lyran PFs (6), 7126 ....$4–$5

The Hydrans

Hydran Paladin DN, 7140..$4–$5
Hydran Ranger, 7141 ....$4–$5
Hydran Horseman, 7142..$4–$5
Hydran Lancer (2), 7143..$4–$5
Hydran Hunter/Scout (2), 7144 ....$4–$5
Hydran PFs (6), 7147...$4–$5

The Tholians

Tholian Dreadnought, 7160...$4–$5
Tholian Cruiser (2), 7161..$4–$5
Tholian Patrol Cruiser (2), 7164...$4–$5
Neo-Tholian Dreadnought, 7172...$4–$5
Neo-Tholian Cruiser (2), 7174..$4–$5

The Orions
    Orion Heavy Cruiser, 7181 ....$5–$6
    Orion Salvage Cruiser, 7182..$5–$6
    Orion Raider (2), 7183...$5–$6
    Orion Slaver (2), 7184...$5–$6
The Andromedans
    Andromedan Intruder, 7221...$5–$6
    Andromedan Satellite Ships (3), 7222 ....$5–$6
    Andromedan Conquistador and Python, 7223..$5–$6
The Interstellar Concordium
    ISC Dreadnought, 7250 ....$5–$6
    ISC Star Cruiser, 7252 ....$5–$6
    ISC Destroyer and Frigate, 7256 ....$5–$6
All Races
    Small Freighter (2), 7200...$4–$5
    Battle Station, 7211...$4–$5
Starline 2220 Starships, 7300, boxed set. Includes one each of Federation Heavy Cruiser,
Klingon D–7 Battlecruiser, Klingon F–5 Frigate, Gorn Destroyer, and Romulan Warbird
....$10–$13

Gamescience

Star Fleet Battle Manual, starship combat game.
    Booklet..$10–$12
    Deluxe boxed set, includes eight plastic ships ....$25–$30
Ships, $1/3788$-scale plastic gaming pieces with stands. Ships each came in white, clear, glow-in-
the-dark green, and glow-in-the-dark blue to represent different states in the game.
    Cruiser, 10504 ....$2–$4
    Destroyer, 10505 ....$2–$4
    Scout, 10506 ....$2–$4
    Dreadnought, 10507..$2–$4
    Tug, 10508 ....$2–$4

Other Games
Arcade Game

Sega, 1980. Star Trek: The Motion Picture. Standing or sitting versions made for commercial
use ....$800–$2,500

**Star Trek: The Motion
Picture board game
by Milton Bradley.**

Left to right. Star Trek: The Adventure Game, Enterprise Encounter, and Star Trek III.

Board Games

(Boxed)

Hasbro, 1974. Fold-out board, game pieces, and spinners. Box art shows animated characters on blue background...$25–$40

Ideal, 1966. Includes board, four game cards, and numerous playing pieces. Color box art shows Kirk, Spock, and Uhura on bridge..$40–$65

Milton Bradley, 1979, Star Trek: The Motion Picture. Includes board, play cards, markers, and playing pieces...$15–$25

Palitoy (British), Star Trek Game. Box has blue cover with Kirk and Spock.............$25–$35

West End Games, 1985. Three different boxed games designed for the adult player. Each game includes map(s), rules, counters, cards, and other gaming pieces.

　Enterprise Encounter, red box with color photo of Kirk, Spock, and Scotty from original TV show ....$15–$20

　Star Trek: The Adventure Game, box art shows Kirk and Spock with Enterprise and Klingon ship in background...$15–$20

　Star Trek III, three solitaire games in one. Blue box with color art of movie Enterprise ....$15–$20

Cartridge Games

For home game systems.

General Consumer Electronics, 1982. Star Trek: The Motion Picture game for their Vectrex system ....$5–$10

Microvision (Milton Bradley), 1979. Star Trek Phaser Strike. Cartridge for hand-held game ....$10–$20

Sega, 1983. Home version of Sega's commercial arcade game.....................................$10–$20

Computer Games

Many unofficial Star Trek-based computer programs exist. The ones listed below from Simon and Schuster are licensed. All exist in formats for several types of PCs. They come packaged in hardback book format with color cover art.

First Contact...$25–$35

The Kobayashi Alternative ....$35–$45

The Promethean Prophecy...$20–$30

The Rebel Universe..$35–$45

Transinium Challenge ....$45–$55

Star Trek II playing cards.

Crossword Puzzle

Running Press, 1976. In the form of large color poster. Puzzle is shaped like Enterprise. Comes in envelope with color artwork ....$6–$10

Photon Balls

Lincoln Enterprises. Played like darts except with styrofoam balls thrown at cloth "board." Targets are drawings of ships...$15–$20

Pinball Games

Bally, 1979. Commercial electronic pinball game with Star Trek: The Motion Picture theme. Available in two different playing surfaces ....$400–$800
Azrak-Hamway, original TV. 12″ plastic toy pinball game. Two versions, Kirk or Spock ....$40–$75

Playing Cards

Aviva, 1979. Star Trek: The Motion Picture. Standard deck with drawing of Enterprise on back. Came blister packed on cardboard header with rainbow logo ....$15–$20
Movie Players, 1982. Star Trek II: The Wrath of Khan. In addition to suit and number, each card has a color picture of a character on the face. Comes boxed. Back of card and box art is color movie logo. First printing accidently omitted "II" from logo.
  First printing ....$15–$20
  Second printing...$10–$15

Trivia Game

Western Publishing, 1985. Trivial Pursuit-type game. Two versions. Complete game has trivia cards, game board, and dice. Smaller version is cards only. Both come boxed with color photos from original TV show.
  Complete game ....$35–$50
  Cards only ....$25–$40

The Golden Star Trek trivia games.

GREETING CARDS

California Dreamers

These were 5″ × 7″ cards with envelopes featuring color photos from the original TV series.

First Series, 1985

Chekov Screaming, "Inhuman Cossacks! Pigs! They've destroyed everything. You'll never be 29 again. Happy Birthday" ....$1–$2

Spock Giving Vulcan Salute, "You were born on this day. It is therefore quite logical to wish you a Happy Birthday . . . Live long and prosper"..$1–$2

Kirk and Spock, "Fire all phasers . . . Fire all photon torpedos . . . What the heck. It's your Birthday!" ....$1–$2

Spock Wearing Visor, "Just because one is logical . . . does not mean one cannot be cool. You're cool. Happy Birthday" ....$1–$2

McCoy Checking Instrument, "I've run every test, checked every medical reference in the galaxy, and damn it. I can't find a cure for what you've got . . . Old Age . . . Happy Birthday" ....$1–$2

Scotty, "Three dilithium crystals, a tablespoon of kironide, a pinch of antimatter, and just a dash of phaser . . . I'm going to make you a birthday cake that will light up the universe . . . Happy Birthday"..$1–$2

Spock, "Readings indicate an unparalleled cosmic phenomena occurred on this day. It was in a time so ancient, the year cannot be ascertained by ship's computers . . . I guess we'll just have to look at the cake and count all those candles! Happy Birthday"......................................$1–$2

Kirk Talking Into Communicator, "The landing party is expendable. The ship is not. If we're not back by 0500, contact Star Fleet Command, get the Enterprise out of here, and whatever you do . . . Have a good time on your Birthday!" ....$1–$2

McCoy (injured) "Listen to me. I'm a doctor. I know . . . Birthdays are hell!" ....$1–$2

Spock Looking at Bridge Instruments, "History banks indicate that inhabitants of 20th-century Earth would oftentimes undergo a strange suicidelike ritual on many of their post-30th birthdays . . . Death by chocolate. Happy Birthday."..$1–$2

Spock with Harp, "I fail to understand the inexplicable human need to so primitively celebrate the anniversary of one's birth. Nevertheless, I offer you the words of Surak, the most revered of all Vulcan philosophers. 'Krut Toba Grig-Toba Grig.' If you party, party BIG!! Happy Birthday"..$1–$2

Spock in Environment Suit, "The heat here is extreme. Far beyond normal ranges . . . How many candles were on that cake, anyway? Happy Birthday"..$1–$2

Spock Holding Cat, "There are 3 billion worlds in the known universe, with a combined population of approximately 6,307,000,000,000 composed of carbon- and noncarbon-based life forms . . . But there's only 1 of you. Happy Birthday" ....$1–$2

Kirk as Romulan Talking into Communicator, "This is Captain James T. Kirk of the Starship Enterprise. Our mission is a peaceful one. We mean no harm . . . Sure the check's in the mail and you're 29. Happy Birthday"..$1–$2

Spock Seated, "It is not logical. It makes no sense . . . It must be Love!" ....$1–$2

Spock Smiling, "You make me smile!"...$1–$2

Enterprise, "Space is not the final frontier . . . You are!"...$1–$2

Kirk, McCoy, and Uhura, "Phasers charged and ready. Photon torpedos fully armed . . . Here comes Monday!"...$1–$2

Plant on Bridge Screen, "To boldly go where no man has gone before . . . or woman either. Congratulations" ....$1–$2

Gorn Attacking Kirk, "Beam me up, Scotty . . . It's been one of those days" ....$1–$2

Kirk with the Providers from "Gamesters of Triskelion", "Who am I? Where am I? Why do I have on these strange clothes . . . Why do I have such strange friends?"..................$1–$2

Kirk, Spock, and McCoy from "Piece of the Action," "You've got to dress for success!" ....$1–$2

Kirk with Bow and Arrow, "I was going to shoot you with a phaser . . . But it seemed so unromantic"..$1–$2

Kirk with Arms Folded, "There's an amusing little custom we have on earth . . . Report to my quarters and I'll explain!" ....$1–$2
Kirk Looking Disgusted, "Sometimes I just want to say to hell with Star Fleet, to hell with regulations and responsibility, to hell with everything . . . Except you!" ....$1–$2

Second Series, 1986

Kirk and Spock in Force Field, "Time is a dimension, like height, width or depth, therefore we're getting shorter, fatter, denser, and older! Happy Birthday!" ....$1–$2
Spock, "Forgive me if I'm lengthy, however, mathematics is an extremely precise science . . . You're a 9.99999999999999" ....$1–$2
Smiling Group, "A group of us got together to do something special for your birthday . . . We're having you sent into space. Happy Birthday" ....$1–$2
Kirk, Spock, and McCoy (in bushes), "Analysis concludes that this is both the correct time and correct place . . . Throw down the blanket and let's party . . . Happy Birthday" ....$1–$2
Kirk and Spock, "You are correct, Captain, I see them. On our right as well as our left . . . Gray hair. Happy Birthday" ....$1–$2
Kirk, "The universe is a big place . . . How did two great people like us ever find each other?" ....$1–$2
Spock, "It is one of the most painful of all biological phenomena . . . I've got you under my skin" ....$1–$2
Kirk and Chekov on Bridge, "Damage control reports we've taken a direct hit. Power out on decks 1, 2, and 3. Life support systems functioning on auxiliary power . . . Has anybody got an aspirin? Get well soon" ....$1–$2
Kirk in Pain, "This syndrome is like that of the madness associated with severe cases of Rigelian fever. Actually, it's something quite different . . . Love" ....$1–$2
Spock, "Regrettably, the laws of gravity are absolute . . . Birthdays are a drag. Happy Birthday" ....$1–$2

Third Series, 1987

Kirk Talking to Tellarite at Party, "Call me . . . We'll do lunch!" ....$1–$2
Spock, "The thing most rare in the universe . . . A friend as good as you" ....$1–$2
Spock Holding Head, "The level of pain is quite extraordinary . . . I hate being so far away on your birthday" ....$1–$2
Kirk Talking into Communicator, "I've just ordered the ship's computers to provide me with your complete psychological profile . . . You're warped, factor-10. I like that in a person" ....$1–$2
Kirk and Spock, "You are now and shall always be . . . My best friend. Happy Birthday" ....$1–$2
Spock, "My conclusion is that you are a magnificently superior being. My method of analysis was simple . . . It takes one to know one! Happy Birthday" ....$1–$2
Kirk at Swordpoint, "Keep your shields up!" ....$1–$2
Spock Wearing Headpiece, "Batteries may fail . . . But Rock and Roll will never die!" ....
....$1–$2
Spock, "Logic dictates that you recently had a birthday. Correctly applied, logic is seldom wrong . . . Sometimes late, but never wrong. Sorry I missed your birthday. Hope you had a good one" ....$1–$2
Kirk and Spock in Chains, "Thought about in a logical fashion, current circumstances are not as desperate as they seem . . . Of course, who can think logically at a time like this. Hang in there!" ....$1–$2
Kirk, Spock, and Uhura on Bridge, "Incoming message is extremely primitive . . . But very sincere. Happy birthday to you" (with musical notes) ....$1–$2
Spock, "It would be illogical to assume that this card is your birthday present . . . So much for logic! Happy Birthday" ....$1–$2
Kirk, Spock, and McCoy at Party, "Star Fleet Command has created living conditions for us in space identical to those which we experience on Earth . . . Underpaid, Overworked, Underloved" ....$1–$2
Spock Reading Tricorder, "I must conclude that we are in a dimension where the laws of known physics do not apply . . . You're much too young to be that old! Happy Birthday" ....
....$1–$2

Chekov, "Captain, there's an unidentified object appearing on the screen. It's blocking our path . . . Another Birthday!" ....$1–$2
Kirk and Spock, "Captain, sensors indicate that subspace interference has prevented our transmission from arriving at the intended time . . . Sorry I was late! Happy Birthday"..$1–$2
Kirk and Crewman in Sickbay, "Twenty years in the fleet and I've never seen anything like it . . . 45 pieces of double fudge chocolate birthday cake! Happy Birthday!" ....$1–$2
McCoy, "Don't quote regulations to me and don't give me any of that 'logic stuff' . . . Just go out there . . . And have a Happy Birthday" ....$1–$2
Spock, "These tools are extremely antiquated . . . Just like you! Happy Birthday"..........$1–$2
Uhura, "What I'm picking up is barely understandable. Primitive music forms. Simplistic language patterns. Assorted and wildly off-key noises. I'm not sure what it is but it sounds as if they're trying to sing . . . Happy Birthday to you" ....$1–$2
Kirk and Spock, "Thought about in a logical fashion, current circumstances are not as desperate as they seem . . . Of course, who can think logically at a time like this. Hang in there!" ....$1–$2

Cambridge, 1979

Star Trek: The Motion Picture.
Crew with Enterprise Overhead..$1–$2
Enterprise (front view) ....$1–$2
Enterprise (head on)..$1–$2
Enterprise (side view) ....$1–$2
Kirk and Spock with Enterprise Overhead..$1–$2
Kirk with Wrist Communicator..$1–$2
Kirk, Spock, and McCoy on Bridge..$1–$2
Spock at Science Station...$1–$2

Hallmark

Cartoon of Kirk, Spock, and McCoy as Birds, "Your mission, Graduate, is to boldly go where no man has gone before . . . Bet you're proud as a peacock"...................................$1–$2
Spock Doing Vulcan Salute, "Congratulations" ....$1–$2
Halloween Card, cartoon of Spock and Enterprise. "Trekker treat!" ....$1–$2

Random House, 1976

Cards featured color photos from original TV series and came in assorted sizes. Larger ones had punch-out features.
McCoy and Kirk, caption, "Happy Birthday from one big shot . . .," inside caption ". . . to another." This includes a three-piece, punch-out blue phaser. ....$2–$3
Kirk with Open Communicator, inside caption, "Let's Communicate." This includes a two-piece, punch-out blue communicator ....$2–$3

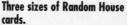

Three sizes of Random House cards.

U.S.S. Enterprise Over a Planet, caption "The world's a better place because of you"..........
....$2–$3
U.S.S. Enterprise Entering Orbit Around an Orange Planet (rear view), caption "I'm sending you something from outer space . . ." This includes a four-piece punch-out of the U.S.S. Enterprise ....$2–$3
Lt. Uhura, caption "I hear it's your Birthday," inside caption "Open all hailing frequencies!"
....$2–$3
Kirk Holding a Rose, caption "The Captain and I both wish you a very Happy Birthday"
....$2–$3
Spock Putting Hand on a Red Door (from the episode "A Taste of Armageddon"), inside caption "Let's keep in touch!"..$2–$3
Kirk, caption "This is your Captain speaking . . ." inside caption ". . . Have a far-out Birthday!"...$2–$3
Spock in Dress Uniform, caption "It is illogical not to wish a Happy Birthday to someone so charming" ....$2–$3
Spock in Yellow Triangle, caption "Know what I like about you" (in orange circle).....$2–$3
Kirk, Spock, Scott, Uhura, and McCoy in Five Individual Squares, caption "Happy Birthday to a great human being!" ....$2–$3
Spock Inside a Yellow Circle, inside an orange circle, inside a pink circle, caption "Sorry I blew it . . ."..$2–$3
Spock Giving Vulcan Salute, and has an eye shield, caption "Having a Birthday?"......$2–$3
Kirk Resting Head on Arm on a Small Viewer, inside two blue circles on a purple background (open card), "Courage!" ....$2–$3
U.S.S. Enterprise Orbiting an Orange Planet, caption "One of the nicest earthlings in the universe . . .," inside caption ". . . just opened this card! Happy Birthday".............$2–$3
Kirk, caption "Star light, star bright, first star I see tonight . . . I wished on star for your birthday" ....$2–$3
Kirk, on the front with medals and caption "Congratulations" ....$2–$3
Kirk, standing on a planet looking towards Earth with caption "There's so Much Space Between Us . . ."...$2–$3
McCoy and Kirk, on the Front with caption "Don't Worry—You'll Feel Better Soon"
....$2–$3
McCoy, Scott, Chekov, and Uhura, on front with caption "Happy Birthday"...............$2–$3
Scott, Spock, Kirk, McCoy, Uhura, and Chekov, on front with inside caption "Happy Birthday From the Whole Spaced-Out Crew"..$2–$3
Spock Listening to Headset, captioned "I Must Be Hard of Hearing" ....$2–$3
Uhura and Kirk on Bridge, caption "Off Course," inside caption "Hope You're Back on the Right Trek Soon" ....$2–$3
U.S.S. Enterprise on the front, caption "For Your Birthday I'd Like to Take You on a Trip to Venus" ....$2–$3

Strand Enterprises

All-Occasion Notecards, Leonard Nimoy for Actors and Other Animals, 1979.............$2–$3

HOUSEHOLD WARES

Assorted Items

Bandages, Adam Joseph, 1979, plastic, adhesive, silver, pink, and blue box with etching of Dr. McCoy, Mr. Spock, and the Enterprise, 30 assorted sizes. Package of 10.....................$5–$15
Bank, approximately 12″, plastic, Kirk, 1975, Play Pal ....$50–$75
Bank, approximately 12″, plastic, Spock, 1975, Play Pal...$50–$75
Bulletin Board, Whiting (Milton Bradley), die-cut board and four pens, 1979, Star Trek: The Motion Picture ....$10–$15
Chair, Decorion, beanbag, Star Trek: The Motion Picture, group drawing, assorted colors
....$50–$75
Chair, Director's, white metal with blue cloth Star Trek IV logo on backrest; Official Star Trek Fan Club, 1986..$45–$55
Chair, inflatable, Star Trek: The Motion Picture, Spock, 1979 ....$25–$50

Bean bag chair.

Clock

Clock-Wise, 1989, color photo of movie Enterprise orbiting planet, rectangular.....$45–$55
Digital travel alarm with TV command symbol in upper left corner, Lincoln Enterprises
....$25–$30
Zeon Character Clocks (British), twin bell alarm clock. Face shows Kirk and Spock with
Enterprise overhead. Red, white, and blue ....$35–$50
Picture of Kirk, Spock, and McCoy from TV series on face, no date or manufacturer, prob-
ably unlicensed ....$20–$30
White wall clock with red 20th anniversary logo on face. Official Star Trek Fan Club, 1986
....$25–$30
Comb and Brush Set, oval brush with color transfer, 6″ × 3″, blue with clear plastic box.
Gabil, 1977...$25–$35
Enterprise Statuette, 1990, Manon. 2″ tall, clear cut crystal on mirror base.............$85–$95
First Aid Kit, Aviva, 1979, pictures scenes from Star Trek: The Motion Picture, adhesive
bandages and tape...$15–$20
Flashlight, Azrak-Hamway, TV show, small phaser shaped, battery operated, 1976 ..$10–$15
Flashlight, "Star Trek" in Star Trek: The Motion Picture logo, 1979, small, blue, promotional
....$5–$10
Flashlight, Larami, 1979. Small hand flashlight, came blister packed with battery on header
card with color photos from Star Trek: The Motion Picture ....$10–$15
Freezicles, molds and concentrate, three kinds in set, busts of Kirk, Spock, and McCoy, color
box art ....$40–$60
Lamp, Enterprise, Prestigeline. Aluminum, hanging, globe lightbulbs at front of lower section
and nacelles...$150–$300
Lighter, 1988. White plastic, "Paramount Pictures Star Trek Adventure," promotional..$2–$3
Light Switch Cover, 1985, American Tack and Hardware. Color plastic shows scenes with
ships, two different..$10–$15
Note: *Prices given on the following lunch boxes include thermos. Missing thermoses devalue
the kit by about 50%.*

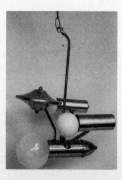

Enterprise lamp by Prestigeline.

Lunch Box

Aladdin, TV show, rectangular plastic, 1978 ....$40–$60

King-Seeley Thermos Co., from Star Trek: The Motion Picture, shows Kirk on one side, Spock and McCoy on the other, thermos captioned "Star Trek," 1979 ....$25–$45

Aladdin, Enterprise on the side with scenes from the TV show, Hump Backed, 1968 ....$500–$1,000

Thermos, 1988. Blue plastic with color photo decal of Star Trek: The Next Generation cast with Enterprise in background. Comes with blue plastic thermos with silkscreened Enterprise and logo..$15–$25

Thermos, 1990. Plastic box with photo deal of Wesley, Picard, and Data with Enterprise in background..$10–$15

Magnet, rectangular refrigerator magnet with cartoon of Scotty with his feet up............$2–$5

Mailbox, Paramount Special Effects Merchandise, Inc., blue with original TV Enterprise on side. Designed to be personalized..$40–$60

Matches, D.D. Bean & Sons, Star Trek: The Motion Picture, seven different variations on merchandise offers inside..$2–$4

Matches, D.D. Bean & Sons, Star Trek II: The Wrath of Khan, 1982, white with red print of movie logo on front and cap offer on back..$1–$2

Mirror, 1966. 2″ × 3″ metal. Black and white photo of crew on back............................$2–$4

Mirror, Kirk and Spock, or Spock, two sizes, 1977..$20–$50

Needlepoint Kit, Arista, design imprinted on No. 10 mesh canvas, black and white yarn portrait of Spock, captioned "Live Long and Prosper," 14″ × 18″, 1980..........................$30–$40

Needlepoint Kit, Arista, design imprinted on No. 10 mesh canvas, Captain Kirk on white background...$30–$40

Pennant, Image Products, 1982. Star Trek II: The Wrath of Khan. Black with movie logo, picture of Enterprise and words "U.S.S. Enterprise" in silver. 12″ × 30″ triangle ....$8–$15

Pennant, Image Products, 1982. Star Trek II logo, picture of Spock in Vulcan robes and words "Spock Lives." Black, yellow, and red on white. 12″ × 30″ triangular..........................$8–$15

Pennant, 1988, promotional. "Paramount Pictures Star Trek Adventure, Universal Studios Tour." Enterprise and planet. Multicolor, odd shape, approximately 9″ × 21½″ ....$5–$10

Space Ship Mobile, Mokato, six small silver plastic ships. "Enterprise" but with third nacelle. Difference was probably to avoid licensing. Long black window box ....$15–$25

Towelettes, Adam Joseph, 1979. Star Trek: The Motion Picture. Pink and silver box of 20 ....$5–$10

Throw Rugs, fake fur, four different, crew, action collage, crew with space scene, and Enterprise. Price each ....$40–$75

Tote Bags, Star Trek: The Motion Picture, Aviva, 1979, blue canvas

Kirk ....$20–$35

Spock...$20–$35

Enterprise ....$20–$35

Tote Bags, Sears, 1975, black and gray zippered. Approximately 12″.

Kirk ....$30–$40

Left: Enterprise tote bag. Right: Wallpaper.

Spock..$30–$40
Enterprise..$30–$40
Tote Bag, white canvas with carrying strap, decal on front reads "Star Fleet Space Shuttle" with original TV series uniform insignia, ca. 1976 ....$10–$15
Tote Bag, red with white letter "Star Trek to the Bahamas." TWA promotional ....$10–$15
Tray, Aviva, 1979. Metal, lap tray with legs, picture of Mr. Spock, length 17½".......$15–$25
Wallpaper, Imperial Wallcoverings. Light blue background with K-7 space station, original TV Enterprise, and other ships. Per roll ....$50–$75
Waste Basket, Chein, Star Trek: The Motion Picture, 1979. Front features the standard motion picture "rainbow" painting, back shows standard photograph of the Enterprise surrounded by smaller pictures. Metal, 13" high..$20–$40
Waste Paper Basket, 1977, Chein, black, pictures of the Enterprise and statistics, metal ....$50–$100

Cloth Goods
Beach Towels

Enterprise Design, 1976..$25–$30
Spock Design, 1976 ....$15–$25
Kirk and Spock, 1976 ....$15–$25
Kirk, Spock, and McCoy, in front of Rigel castle.....................................$25–$30
Star Trek: The Next Generation, pink background with Enterprise and words "The Legend Continues"...$25–$35

Bed Linens

Pacific Mills, 1975, original TV Enterprise and characters in action scenes
    Sheets (twin) ....$25–$35
    Pillow cases..$10–$15
Canon, 1979, Star Trek: The Motion Picture, scenes from the first movie.
    Sheets (twin) ....$20–$30
    Pillow cases..$5–$10
Aberdeen, comforter, 1986, original TV Enterprise, characters and scenes. Twin and full sizes ....$75–$100
Aberdeen, pillow sham, 1986, ships from the movies ....$10–$15

Draperies

Pacific Mills, 1975, original TV Enterprise and characters, assorted sizes..................$25–$40
Canon, 1979, Star Trek: The Motion Picture, scenes from the first movie, assorted sizes ....$20–$35
Aberdeen, 1986, ships from the movies, assorted sizes ....$25–$50

Miscellaneous

Shower Curtain, 1986, J.C. Penney. Black vinyl with movie Enterprise and Klingon ship orbiting planet ....$25–$50
Sleeping Bag, Alp Industries, says "Star Trek" and "U.S.S. Enterprise" with artwork of group on bridge, 1978 ....$60–$125
Sleeping Bag, Alp Industries, pictures the Enterprise with action poses of Kirk, Spock, and McCoy...$60–$125

Kitchen

Bowl, plastic, cereal, Star Trek: The Motion Picture, Deka, 1979....................................$5–$8
Bowl, plastic, soup, Star Trek: The Motion Picture, Deka, 1979.....................................$5–$8
Candy, Fleer, 1988. "Star Trek." 1¾" × 3", illustrated with cartoon................................$1–$2
Coasters, Ritepoint. White plastic with Star Trek and Star Fleet emblem......................$2–$3

Glasses

Coca-Cola, set of three with pictures on front and description on the back: one with Kirk, Spock, and McCoy; second with Decker and Ilia; third with the Enterprise. Coca-Cola never found a franchise to distribute these; a few stores carried them. Height 5½", 1979, per set ....$25–$30

Dr. Pepper, set of four drinking glasses with pictures on front and paragraphs on back describing picture: Captain James T. Kirk, Dr. Leonard McCoy, Mr. Spock, and the U.S.S. Enterprise. Height 6¼", 1976. Per set...$50–$75

Dr. Pepper, set of four, same glass style and subject matter as above, different artwork and date (1978), less common than the first set ....$75–$100

Taco Bell, four glasses based on Star Trek III: "Spock Lives," "Enterprise Destroyed," "Lord Kruge," "Fal-tor-pan," 1984. Set ....$10–$15

Marshmallow Dispenser, Star Trek V, Kraft, 1989. Gray and blue plastic with color Star Trek V decal, plastic fork, spoon, and belt hook included in kit ....$10–$25

Mug, porcelain, 20th anniversary and fan club logos, Official Star Trek Fan Club, 1986 ....$8–$12

Mug and Bowl, plastic, Star Trek: The Motion Picture, Deka, 1979. Photos of major characters, artwork of the Enterprise ....$8–$15

Mug and Bowl, Deka, 1975, 10-oz. mug and 20-oz. bowl with pictures of major characters and ships, sold as set...$15–$30

Mugs, Image Products, Wrath of Khan, plastic photo mugs, Kirk, Spock, Khan, and Enterprise
Each...$5–$10
Set..$30–$50

Shotglass, 1988. "Star Trek Adventure" on insignia design. 2½" tall.........................$10–$15

Spoons, collectors' spoons, Kirk, Spock, McCoy or Scotty, 4¼". Price each..............$20–$30

Spoon, 1988. Pewter. "Star Trek Adventure" on insignia on handle. Picture of Enterprise and word on bowl. Came in clear plastic box ....$10–$15

Tumblers

Plastic, 6 oz. and 11 oz., Star Trek: The Motion Picture, Deka, 1979, photos of character and artwork Enterprise, each ....$2–$5

Plastic, 1979, Star Trek: The Motion Picture, three-color artwork of characters and Enterprise. Coca-Cola promotion, four different. Kirk, Spock, McCoy or Decker, and Ilia, price each ....$1–$5

Star Trek IV, 1986, plastic, four different, Kirk, Spock, Bird of Prey, and group, Coca-Cola promotion
Each..$1–$2
Set ....$5–$10

Difference in art between 1976 (left) and 1978 (right) McCoy Dr. Pepper glasses.

Original series Star Trek: The Motion Picture plastic ware by Deka.

Star Trek V, 1989, red plastic with insignia and logo in black and gold, Paramount promotion ....$1–$2

Icee/K-Mart, 1987. Star Trek: The Next Generation, five different. Picard, Riker, Tasha, Dr. and Wesley Crusher, or Troi and Data. Price each. ....$1–$2

Note: *See "Ceramics" for decorative collectors' plates, mugs, etc.*

Liquor Decanters, Glass

Saurian Brandy Bottle, George Dickel commemorative, used on TV show as brandy bottle, curved neck, real leather base and strap

    Nipper size ....$15–$25

    Fifth size ....$40–$55

    Quart size ....$40–$85

Dickel Anniversary Special, approximately 2′ tall, given only to employees of distillery, 1 gal. Very rare...$200–$400

Note: *See "Ceramics" for other decanters.*

Party Goods

Cake Decorator, Tuttle, TV show, with scenes of the Enterprise on centerpiece, 1976

    10-piece set ....$5–$10

    22-piece set ....$10–$15

Paper Products, Tuttle, 1976, white background with Kirk, Spock, Dr. McCoy, and Enterprise printed in red, white, and blue

    Plates (7″ or 9″ package of eight) ....$3–$5

    Cups, pack of eight ....$2–$4

    Tablecloth (two sizes) ....$2–$4

    Beverage napkins, pack of eight..$2–$4

Dickel Saurian brandy bottles (Dickel Whiskey).

Tuttlecraft tablecloth and napkins.

Dinner napkins, pack of eight ....$2–$4
Set ....$15–$30

JEWELRY

Belt Buckles

Indiana Metal

Circular, embossed Enterprise and Saturn, painted or bronze tone, introduction to TV series impressed on back, some have "U.S.S. Enterprise" and "Star Trek" ....$6–$10
Enterprise, on triangular enameled background ....$15–$20

Lee Belts

Enterprise, orbiting planet, oval, 1976...$6–$10
TV show, metal, Kirk and Spock, the Enterprise, or Spock alone, 1976.........................$6–$10
Mr. Spock, round brass, some with enamel trim, 2″, 1976..$4–$6
Rectangular, brass, Kirk and Spock, enamel trim, 1979..$4–$6
Roughly Rectangular, Enterprise, "Star Trek: NCC-1701," 2″, brass, some with enamel trim
....$5–$10

Lincoln Enterprises

Kirk and Spock, looking to the left, the Enterprise and "Star Trek" are at the top, bronze, not dated, 2″ × 3″ ....$10–$12
Star Trek, The Final Frontier, brass trim, Movie Enterprise, 1985 ....$25–$30
   As above, with gold trim on black background...$60–$65
Star Trek III: The Search for Spock, with a picture of the Enterprise, limited edition, number on back and synopsis of story, 1984 ....$20–$25
U.S.S. Enterprise Commemorative, sterling silver with gold trim ....$175–$200
   As above, bronze with gold trim...$25–$30
Command Insignia, round, flat, gold plate, several sizes..$5–$8

Miscellaneous

Star Trek Commemorative, Buckles and Belts Co., 1990, oval pewter with Enterprise and "Star Trek," limited to 1,000 pieces ....$25–$40
Rectangular, Tiffany Studio. Original TV Enterprise in center. "Star Trek Lives," "U.S.S. Enterprise," and "To Boldly Go (etc.)" around ship...$10–$12
Painted, embossed Enterprise and lettering "Star Trek" ....$6–$10
Oval-shaped, Tiffany Studio, with four flat corners, Kirk and Spock in center with "Star Trek" on top, brass, ...$10–$15
Oblong-shaped, embossing, relief of Kirk and Spock in center circle, silver or gold finish
....$6–$10

Cloisonne Pins

(also includes enamel and poly) Star Trek: The Motion Picture

Aviva: 1979

Vulcan Salute, poly ....$5–$10
Spock, poly ....$5–$10
Enterprise, poly ....$5–$10
Uniform Insignia, poly ....$5–$10
McCoy, poly ....$5–$10
Kirk, poly ....$5–$10
Kirk, enamel...$3–$4
McCoy, enamel...$3–$4
Tie Clasp
    Circular with Vulcan salute, gold with hand and lettering in black ....$3–$4
    Circular with Mr. Spock, printing "Live Long and Prosper," gold and black...............$3–$4
    Outline of the Enterprise, gold with black outlines ....$3–$4
    Uniform insignia from the original TV series, gold ....$3–$4

Hollywood Commemorative Pin Co.

Colorful, high quality, military clutchback.
Enterprise Cutout, 1985 ....$6–$7
Enterprise and Logo, on blue background, 1985 ....$6–$7
Enterprise, on red background (large), 1985...$8–$9
Enterprise, on red background (small), 1985..$6–$7
Enterprise Crew, cutouts, 1986
    Spock..$8–$9
    Kirk ....$8–$9
    McCoy ....$8–$9
    Scotty ....$8–$9
    Chekov ....$8–$9
    Uhura..$8–$9
    Sulu ....$8–$9
Insignia Cutout, movie, small, blue, burgundy, green, orange, red, white, or yellow, 1985
....$6–$7
Insignia Cutout, large, 1986..$8–$9
Insignia Cutout, TV, 1986, 1991
    Command, black, white, red or blue on gold...$6–$7
    Science ....$6–$7
    Engineering ....$6–$7
Insignia and Logo, 1985
    Blue background ....$6–$10
    White background..$6–$10
Klingon Admiral, 1985 ....$6–$7
Klingon Captain, 1985 ....$6–$7
Klingon Symbol, 1985..$6–$7
Klingon Symbol, large, 1986...$8–$9
Live Long and Prosper, words and Vulcan salute on blue background, 1985.............$8–$12
    As above, red background ....$8–$12
    As above, burgundy background ....$8–$12
    As above, smaller, blue background ....$6–$10
Rank Insignias, 1986
    Admiral ....$6–$7
    Captain ....$8–$9
    Commodore...$8–$9
    Fleet Admiral ....$8–$9
Romulan Symbol, 1985...$6–$7
Romulan Symbol, cutout, 1985..$10–$15
Star Fleet Division Insignias, 1986
    Colonial Operations ....$8–$9

Communications ....$8–$9
Engineering ....$8–$9
Headquarters ....$8–$9
Intelligence..$8–$9
Marines ....$8–$9
Material ....$8–$9
Medical ....$8–$9
Merchant Marines ....$8–$9
Military ....$8–$9
Personnel...$8–$9
Security ....$8–$9
UFP Symbol, large cutout, 1985...$8–$9
UFP Symbol, small cutout, 1985 ....$8–$10
Twentieth Anniversary Pin, early logo, white and blue, blue and yellow, or red, white, and
blue versions, 1986 ....$10–$15
Twentieth Anniversary Pin, special 20th anniversary logo, large, 1986. ....$15–$20
Twentieth Anniversary Pin, "To Boldly Go . . .," 1986 ....$10–$15
Twentieth Anniversary "WOW Pin," 1986 ....$10–$15
Star Trek Lives, red, 1988...$8–$9
Star Trek Forever, blue, 1988..$8–$9
Vulcan Salute, gold, 1988...$4–$5
Spock: Live Long and Prosper, 1988 ....$8–$9
Phaser, 1989 (original TV) ....$8–$9
Communicator, 1989...$8–$9
Star Trek V: Final Frontier Pins
Star Fleet Insignia, red and white, 1989 ....$6–$7
Star Trek V logo over insignia, 1989...$8–$9
Star Trek V, small Enterprise, 1989 ....$8–$9
Star Trek V, large Enterprise, 1989 ....$10–$11
Star Trek V, small Galileo, 1989..$7–$8
Star Trek V, large Galileo, 1989 ....$9–$10
Star Trek V, Galileo logo, 1989 ....$5–$6
Star Trek V, The Final Frontier logo..$6–$7
Star Trek: Next Generation Pins
Next Generation communicator, full size, 1989 ....$15–$16
   As above, smaller size, 1988...$10–$11
U.S.S. Enterprise, NCC-1701-D, 1988...$8–$9
Caution Force Field, 1989 ....$6–$7
Caution Antimatter, 1989 ....$6–$7
Borg symbol, 1989...$8–$9
Make It So, 1989..$6–$7
Fully Functional, 1989 ....$6–$7
Next Generation Federation symbol, 1988 ....$6–$7
Next Generation crew, 1989–1990, 1989 ....$8–$9
Next Generation cast and crew, 1989–1990, 1990 ....$6–$8
Next Generation Star Fleet Command, 1989..................................$8–$9

Cloisonne Twentieth Anniversary pins. Bottom right is Lincoln Enterprises. All others are Hollywood pins.

Ferengi symbol, large, 1988..$6–$7
  As above, small, 1988...$4–$5
Romulan Bird of Prey symbol, 1989 ....$12–$13
Next Generation logo, blue, 1988.....................................$5–$6
Next Generation logo, red, 1988......................................$5–$6
Star Fleet Command Operations, green, 1989....................$5–$6
  As above, red, 1989 ....$5–$6
  As above, yellow, 1989...$5–$6
Starbase 74, 1989..$6–$7

Lincoln Enterprises, 1986–1990

Enterprise Cutout ....$6–$8
Enterprise and Statue of Liberty.....................................$6–$8
Klingon Bird of Prey..$6–$8
Peace in Our Galaxy (IDIC) ....$6–$8
Star Trek, Gateway to a New Beginning ....$6–$8
Star Trek: The Final Frontier ....$6–$8
Star Trek: The Motion Picture, movie poster design........$6–$8
Star Trek III: The Search for Spock, commemorative.......$6–$8
Star Trek III, movie poster design...................................$6–$8
Twentieth Anniversary Pin ....$6–$8
United Federation of Planets Symbol, movie, Star Trek IV ......$6–$8
  Movie poster art...$6–$8
  White poster art...$6–$8
  Cutout design ....$6–$8
  Logo and whales..$6–$8
Whales..$6–$8
Ferengi Ship Pin...$7–$9
Next Generation Enterprise Pin, blue ....$7–$9
  As above, white and black..$7–$9
  As above, white, black, and orange...................................$7–$9
She Lives, Enterprise in Orbit ....$7–$9
Next Generation UFP Symbol, red and black...................$7–$9
Next Generation Logo, rainbow......................................$7–$9
  As above, blue, silver, and white......................................$7–$9
Next Generation Communicator Pin, with logo................$7–$9

Miscellaneous Cloisonne Pins

Uniform Insignia, Command, Science or Engineering from original TV series, gold or silver with black, inlaid, as pendant, tie clasp or earrings.....................$4–$6
United Federation of Planets Emblem Tie Clasp, circular, blue, black, and silver, same emblem as appears on Star Fleet Technical Manual, Janus head with star map in the middle........
....$4–$6
United Federation of Planets Emblem Pendant, same as above ....$4–$6
Mirror, Mirror Pin...$7–$8

Coin Necklaces

(See "Coins and Medallions")

Command Insignia Jewelry

Command Insignia Necklace, from Star Trek: The Motion Picture, painted or plated gold, Lincoln Enterprises
  Large necklace ....$5–$8
  Small necklace ....$4–$6
Command Insignia Pin, same as above
  Large pin...$5–$8
  Small pin...$4–$6

Command Insignia Pin, brushed brass, came blister packed on color card, Don Post Studios
....$10–$15
Command Insignia Pin, gold plated, Lincoln Enterprises ....$4–$6
Command Insignia Charm, original TV style, with 18″ chain, Lincoln Enterprises.....$4–$6
   As above, sterling silver...$15–$20
   As above, 14K gold ....$90–$95
   As above, 14K gold and diamonds..$275–$300
Command Insignia Earrings, pierced, dangling or clip-on, Lincoln Enterprises ......$10–$12
   As above, sterling silver...$30–$35
   As above, gold ....$125–$150
   As above, gold and diamond ....$575–$600
Command Insignia Ring, adjustable, Lincoln Enterprises
   22K gold plated...$6–$8
   Sterling silver...$7–$10
Insignia Wire Charm, Lincoln Enterprises, with 18″ chain...$5–$6
   As above, earrings, pierced (wire) or clip-on ....$10–$12

Enterprise Ship Jewelry

This has always been a popular item for the fan market. All of the following are
metal from various manufacturers.
Original TV Charm, approximately 1½″, gold or silver plate, with or without chain ....
....$10–$15
Original TV Charm, approximately ¾″, gold or silver plate, with or without chain .....$6–$8
Original TV Ring, approximately 1½″, silver plate on adjustable ring......................$10–$15
Original TV Earrings, approximately ¾″, gold or silver plate, pierced or clip-on ....$10–$15
Movie Charm, approximately 1¾″, gold or silver plate, with or without chain.........$10–$15
Movie Charm, approximately 1″, gold or silver plate, with or without chain ....$8–$10
Movie Earrings, approximately 1″, gold or silver plate, pierced or clip-on ....$15–$20
Star Trek: Next Generation Charm, approximately 1″, gold or silver plate, with or without
chain..$8–$10
Next Generation Earrings, approximately 1″, gold or silver plate, pierced or clip-on
....$15–$20
Identification Bracelet, from Star Trek: The Motion Picture, General Mills premium, gold or
silver, children's...$2–$3

Lincoln Enterprises

Lincoln Enterprises has made a line of Enterprise jewelry as precious metals. These
are as follows:
Movie Enterprise 14K Gold
   Charm..$125
   Charm with diamonds...$300
   Earrings..$250
   Earrings with diamonds $600

IDIC and Enterprise jewelry.

Next Generation Enterprise 14K Gold
Charm...$125
Charm with diamonds...$300
Earrings...$250
Earrings with diamonds $600

IDICs

The IDIC, which stands for Infinite Diversity in Infinite Combinations, is a Vulcan symbol that was used in one original television episode and has been used somewhat in the movies. It consists of a gold circle with a superimposed silver triangle and a clear stone at the apex. All are metal. Several manufacturers.

Necklaces, assorted sizes ranging from ½″ to 2″ ....$5–$12
    As above, 14K gold, Lincoln Enterprises......................................$80–$85
Earrings, gold and silver plate, pierced or clip-on ....$10–$20
    As above, 14K gold, pierced, Lincoln Enterprises $150
Pin, gold and silver plate...$6–$10
    As above, 14K gold, Lincoln Enterprises......................................$80–$85
Ring, gold and silver plate, men's and women's styles available, adjustable...............$10–$20

Keychains
Aviva, 1979

Square lucite slabs with two-sided translucent pictures, 1½″.
Enterprise, with an oval blue background...$2–$3
Kirk and Spock with Enterprise, large, red and lavender planets, black background...$2–$3
Spock, "Live Long and Prosper," printed in semicircle, red, black, and lavender...........$2–$3
Mr. Spock Bust, with his uniform insignia, white and gray..............................$2–$3
Spock with Arms Behind His Back, "Star Trek: The Motion Picture" printed up the side
....$2–$3
Mr. Spock Giving Vulcan Salute, circular black background................................$2–$3

Button Up

Beam Me Up, Scotty, on yellow background, 1980....................................$2–$3

California Dreamers, 1987

Color photos from original TV series in 1½″ × 2″ plastic holders.
Chekov, "I Hate Mondays" ....$2–$4
Kirk, "Beam Me Up, Scotty"..$2–$4
Kirk, "The Captain"..$2–$4
Kirk, Spock, and McCoy, "Fire All Phaser Weapons" ....$2–$4
Kirk, Spock, and Uhura, "Keep Your Shields Up" ....$2–$4
Kirk, Spock, and Uhura, "Seek Out Strange New Worlds" ....$2–$4
Spock
    "Hang in There"...$2–$4
    "I Need Space" ....$2–$4
    "Spock for President" ....$2–$4
    "Live Long and Prosper"..$2–$4
    "Superior Being" ....$2–$4

Miscellaneous Keychains

Keychain, Star Fleet Headquarters, insignia from movies, gold-plated metal, 1¼″ ......$5–$10
Enterprise, all brass, metal cast, oval...$6–$8
Enterprise, "Star Trek" and "Starship Enterprise" on navy background....................$10–$15
Insignia and "Star Trek Adventure," on brass oval ....$5–$10
Spock, gold-plated silver, Rarities Mint. Reverse shows original TV Enterprise ....$30–$50
Keychain Viewer, various Star Trek TV film clips, Lincoln Enterprises ....$2–$3

Medallions
(See "Coins and Medallions")

Miscellaneous Jewelry

Pewter Medallion, 1989, blue silkscreen design on front surrounded by laurel leaf pattern. Numbered on reverse. Comes with blue neck ribbon. Three designs:
    Old TV UFP design ....$10–$12
    Next Generation TV UFP design..$10–$12
    UFP Star Fleet Academy with insignia design..............................$10–$12
Money Clip, Rarities Mint, 1989, gold-plated silver. Spock giving Vulcan salute. "Live Long and Prosper"..$35–$45

Necklaces and Pendants

Khan's Pendant, 1982, Don Post Studio, insignia in broken circle, bronze dipped in acid to "age" piece. Came blister packed on color cardboard header....................$20–$30
Mount Seleya Symbol Necklace, Lincoln Enterprises, 1985 ....$6–$8
Enterprise Orbiting on Pewter Medallion, Goodtime Jewelry ....$4–$6
Enterprise Orbiting Ringed Planet, American Miss................................$10–$15
Logo, American Miss ....$10–$15
Phaser Pendant, gold or silver, flat on back side, Star Trek Galore...............$3–$5
Spock or Kirk and Spock on TV Insignia, pewter, Goodtime Jewelry, poor quality....$4–$6
Spock on a Chain, lightweight, gold plated, American Miss ....$3–$5
Vulcan Salute, flat gold, stamped metal...$3–$5
Sparkle Necklace, pendant, circular, black background with silver movie command insignia. Gold or silver beveled frame ....$3–$4
Sparkle Necklace, pendant, circular, black background with silver outline of the Enterprise, rests on gold or silver beveled frame ....$3–$4
Sparkle Necklace, pendant, circular, black background with silver outline of the United Federation of Planets emblem, rests on silver beveled frame ....$3–$4
Try Trekking Pendant, quartz crystal, changes color with your mood, Lincoln Enterprises ....$4–$5
United Federation of Planets Security Badge, from Star Trek IV, hinged, two-piece, Lincoln Enterprises..$12–$18

Uniform Insignia

Star Trek: The Motion Picture, Don Post, 1982, star insignia in circle. Bronze, came blister packed on cardboard header ....$10–$15
Star Trek: The Motion Picture, Lincoln Enterprises. (*See* Command Insignia Pins)
Star Trek II–V Movie Insignia, Don Post, 1982, circle design superimposed on bar, bronze, came blister packed on color cardboard header...$20–$30
Star Trek II–V Movie Insignia, Lincoln Enterprises, same as Don Post version, lighter weight, plated and painted metal, two sizes
    Large ....$12–$15
    Small ....$8–$10
Star Trek: The Next Generation Communicator Insignia, metal, painted, and plated ....$12–$15
Uniform Belt Buckles, from Star Trek II–V, brushed bronze or gold-plated metal. Approximately 2½" diameter, several manufacturers...$15–$20

Uniform Rank Insignia

These were very popular for costuming. Early examples were of painted cast fiberglass and very fragile. Those that still exist are only worth $1–$2. The following are all plated and painted metal with assorted manufacturers.
Star Trek II–V
    Lieutenant J.G..$5–$7
    Lieutenant ....$5–$7

Uniform rank insignia.

Lieutenant Commander (several varieties) ....$6–$12
Commander ....$6–$12
Captain ....$6–$12
Commodore ....$6–$12
Admiral ....$6–$12
Fleet Admiral ....$6–$12
Star Trek: The Next Generation, collar pips, plain gold, silver or "hollow." Plated and painted. Individuals ....$2–$3
Captain, four on bar base, Lincoln ....$7–$10
Uniform Sleeve Pips, Star Trek II–V, round and oblong, ridged metal, unpainted or gold plated. Numerous manufacturers ....$2–$4
Uniform Shoulder Strap Back Pin, Star Trek II–V, eight-sided ridged metal pin. Unpainted or gold plated ....$3–$5

Watches

Bradley Time Co.
Mr. Spock appears on the dial from Star Trek: The Motion Picture ....$40–$55
Enterprise from Star Trek: The Motion Picture. Starburst behind ....$40–$55
Rectangular face, LCD display, Enterprise on blue face with Kirk and Spock (TV) below ....$50–$75
Collins Industrial, 1982, LED game watch, came boxed with Star Trek II art ....$15–$25
Lewco, 1986, Spock and Enterprise in relief on band, digital, 20th anniversary packaging ....$15–$25
Lincoln Enterprises, picture of Enterprise and the words "Star Trek" on the face, men's or ladies' ....$25–$30
Rarities Mint, 1989, limited edition gold-plated silver, shows original TV Enterprise. Came in padded brown plastic display box. Men's and women's styles ....$100–$200
Service Time, 1989, painted faces
Original TV Enterprise on front with gold Star Trek below. Black plastic band .....$40–$50
As above, only ¾ front view ....$40–$50
As above, only movie Enterprise with Klingon Bird of Prey in background ....$40–$50
As above, only original Enterprise in rear view orbiting planet ....$40–$50
Watch, pictures Kirk, Spock, and McCoy from TV series, men's or women's styles, no date or manufacturer, probably unlicensed ....$10–$20
Pocket Watch, same as above ....$10–$20

MAGAZINES

Accent West, March, 1983. "Bar Trek" cover ....$3–$5
Aerospace Education, Dec. 1977, Star Trek issue ....$3–$5

All About Star Trek Fan Clubs, Ego Enterprises, New York, NY, Dec. 1976, series of five fanzines with complete membership information plus biographies, portraits, episodes, and conventions

No. 1...$8–$12

No. 2–6...$4–$8

American Cinematographer, ASC Holding Corp., Hollywood, CA, Vol. 61, No. 2, Feb. 1980, issue devoted to a look behind the scenes of Star Trek: The Motion Picture .....$15–$25

Vol. 63, No. 10, Oct. 1982, "Special Effects for Star Trek II".....................................$4–$8

Vol. 65, No. 8, issue on Star Trek III...$5–$6

Vol. 67, No. 12, Dec. 1986, cover and article on Star Trek IV ....$5–$6

Bananas, No. 33, Kirk and Spock on cover, preview of Star Trek I, 1979 ....$4–$6

Best of Starlog

No. 1...$5–$10

No. 2...$5–$10

No. 3, Spock on cover..$5–$10

Byte, The Small Systems Journal Computer Magazine, No. 7, Vol. 9, July 1984, cover shows a sophisticated computer system with Mr. Spock appearing on the screen............$3–$5

Castle of Frankenstein

No. 11, 1967, Star Trek issue, Spock on cover...$12–$20

No. 14, 1969, Kirk and Spock cover ....$10–$15

Cinefantasque, F.S. Clark Publishers

Vol. 12, No. 5 and 6, July/August 1982, Star Trek II and The Revenge of the Jedi

....$15–$25

Vol. 17, No. 2, cover and article on Star Trek's 20th anniversary................................$5–$6

Cinefex, Dan Shay Publishing...$15–$20

No. 1, March 1980, "Into V'ger Mau with Douglas Trumball," director of special effects of Star Trek, beautiful color illustrations ....$15–$20

No. 2, August 1980, "Star Trekking at Apogee"...$10–$15

No. 18, "Last Voyage of Starship Enterprise"...$10–$15

No. 29, 1987, "Humpback to the Future"..$10–$15

No. 37, Feb. 1989, "Special Effects: The Next Generation"...$10–$15

Cue, Dec. 1975, Star Trek TV cover, "Can 1999 Match Trek" ....$5–$8

Cinemagic, No. 6, Spring 1976, Spock TV cover ....$5–$10

Communicator, The, No. 4/5, Fall 1975, Star Trek cover ....$3–$5

Cracked

No. 127, Sept. 1975, Star Trek article ....$5–$8

No. 169, July 1980, "Star Trek—The Moving Picture"...$5–$8

No. 228, July 1987, Star Trek II parody ....$5–$8

No. 232, Feb. 1987, "Star Trek: The Next De-generation"..$5–$8

Summer 1988, "Star Trek—The Last Hurrah"...$4–$6

Crawdaddy, Dec. 1976, Shatner cover...$5–$10

Dynamite

No. 10, Star Trek article..$3–$5

No. 65, Star Trek: The Motion Picture ....$3–$5

Electric Company, The

Dec. 1979/Jan. 1980, "The Outer Space Creatures of Star Trek, What Are They Like?" Cover and article..$3–$5

June 1982, "Star Trek Rides Again" ....$3–$5

Enterprise, HJS Publications

No. 1, April 1984 ....$5–$6

No. 2, July 1984 ....$4–$5

No. 3...$4–$5

No. 4–13..$4–$5

Enterprise Spotlight 2, New Media Publishing, memory book ....$4–$5

Enterprise Incident, Star Trek Federation of Fans

Issue 1 ....$20–$30

Issue 2 ....$15–$20

Issue 3 ....$15–$20

Issue 4–6 ....$10–$15

Issues 7–8..$10–$15

Enterprise Incident, issued by New Media Publishing, mass produced, lower production values

Issue 9 ....$5–$10
Issue 10–12 ....$5–$10
Issue 13–17 ....$3–$5
Issue 18–27 ....$3–$5
Issue 28 up, name changes to *SF Movieland*, No. 36 last issue ....$2–$3
Summer Special between issues 12 and 13 ....$5–$10
Collectors Edition No. 1, reprints No. 1 and 2 ....$6–$8
Collectors Edition No. 2, reprints No. 3 and 4 ....$5–$6
Collectors Edition No. 3, reprint No. 5...$4–$5
Collectors Edition No. 4, reprint No. 6...$4–$5
Collectors Edition No. 5, reprint No. 7...$4–$5
Collectors Edition No. 6, reprint No. 8...$4–$5
Spotlight on Leonard Nimoy ....$4–$5
Spotlight on interview of Star Trek personalities ....$4–$5
Spotlight on technical side...$5–$6
Spotlight on William Shatner...$4–$5

Famous Films, Blake Publishing Company

Vol. 1, No. 3, Aug. 1973, "Star Trek: Interview with Susan Sackett" ....$4–$6
Vol. 1, No. 5, Dec. 1978, "Spock Speaks," with cover of Leonard Nimoy ....$5–$10
Vol. 2, No. 4, Sept. 1979, Star Trek: The Motion Picture "Robert Wise: A Comprehensive Interview" ....$4–$6
Vol. 2, No. 8, Feb. 1980, "Designing Star Trek," "Star Trek: The Costumes".............$4–$6
Vol. 2, No. 9, March 1980, "Star Trek: The Costumes," part two of designer Bob Fletcher's interview ....$4–$6
Vol. 7, No. 3, May 1984, Star Trek III..$4–$6
Vol. 7, No. 4, July 1984, Star Trek III ....$4–$6
Vol. 7, No. 5, Sept. 1984, James Doohan interview ....$4–$6

Famous Monsters

No. 145, July 1978, Star Trek article ....$5–$8
No. 187, Star Trek III cover and article...$5–$8

Fantasy Enterprises, New Media Publishing, 1985 ....$4–$5

Fantasy Image No. 2, March 1985, Spock and Enterprise cover ....$5–$10

Future, Starlog Press

No. 4, Aug. 1978, preview of "Star Trek: The Movie"....................................$3–$4
No. 14, Nov. 1979, "Re-designing Star Trek"...$3–$4
No. 15, Dec. 1979, "Star Trek's New Faces" ....$3–$4
No. 16, Feb. 1980, "Star Trek Takes Off"...$3–$4
No. 17, March 1980, "Designing the 23rd Century"...$3–$4

Games, Jan. 1985, Star Trek article ....$3–$5

Globe (newspaper), Nov. 1987, Nimoy cover...$3–$4

Hollywood Studio Magazine, D. Denny Publisher, Vol. 12, No. 5, June 1968, "New 15 Million Star Trek Movie"...$5–$7

Journal of Popular Film and Television, Vol. 12, No. 2, Summer 1984, Spock cover ....$5–$10

Mad Magazine

Super Special No. 30, satire on Star Trek..$5–$10
Super Special No. 64, satire on Star Trek II..$5–$10
No. 186, Oct. 1976, "The Star Trek Musical"...$5–$10
No. 216, July 1980, Star Trek: The Motion Picture parody ....$5–$10
No. 236, Jan. 1983, Star Trek II parody ....$5–$10
No. 251, Dec. 1984, satire on Star Trek III ....$5–$10
No. 271, June 1987, satire on Star Trek IV ....$5–$10

Mediascene Preview, Supergraphics

No. 6, Feb. 1980, "Star Trek: The Motion Picture—The Enterprise encounters a most powerful obstacle, its own reputation"...$6–$10
Vol. 1, No. 31, Dec/Jan. 1978, "Backstage on the Star Trek Set".................$4–$6

Media Spotlight, J. Schuster Publishers

Issue 1, Summer 1975, issue devoted to Star Trek, the TV show, star biographies, and commentaries...$8–$10

Issue 2, Fall 1976, "Star Trek Lives Again," another issue on the TV show with a photo article on Mr. Spock...$6–$8

Issue 3, March 1977, "The Roddenberry Tapes," "The Spirit of Star Trek" ....$6–$8

Issue 4, May 1977, Spock on the cover plus articles on "Fandom, Nichelle Nichols," and robots..$6–$8

Issue 5, Oct. 1977, "Kirk the Exorcist"...$6–$8

Megastars Poster Magazine, magazine contains information on Star Trek III and a large Spock poster...$3–$5

Monster Magazine

Vol. 2, No. 7, April 1976, Star Trek article..$3–$5

Vol. 2, No. 8, May 1976, Star Trek article...$3–$5

Monsterland No. 16, Feb. 1987, Nimoy and Doohan article...$4–$8

Monsters of the Movie, Magazine Management, Inc., Vol. 9, Summer 1975, "An Interview with Leonard Nimoy"..$5–$7

Monster Times, newspaper format

No. 2, 1974, Star Trek cover..$10–$15

No. 45, Jan. 1976, Shatner cover ....$7–$10

No. 46, March 1976, Kirk and Spock cover..$5–$8

Muppet Magazine, Summer 1984, Star Trek III article..$3–$7

National Enquirer

Jan. 1987, Nimoy cover..$3–$5

Jan. 1988, Shatner cover..$3–$5

Newsweek, Dec. 22, 1986, Spock cover and Star Trek IV article ....$5–$10

Officers of the Bridge, one shot, 1976, blue cover with red UFP banner. Includes Kelly Freas portfolio...$10–$15

Parade Magazine, Dec. 10, 1978, Star Trek: The Motion Picture, issue with color cover ....$5–$8

People

July 1982, Kirstie Alley Star Trek II cover ....$5–$10

Aug. 1987, Next Generation preview article ....$4–$8

Preview, Summer 1985, Star Trek article..$3–$5

Questar, William Wilson Publishing, No. 5, Nov. 1979, Questar preview: "An Advance Look at the Crew of the New Enterprise" ....$5–$7

Science and Fantasy Film Classics, R. Fenton, Publisher, No. 3, July 1978, features Star Trek: the computers, technology, characters...$4–$8

Science Fiction Horror and Fantasy, Vol. 1, No. 1, Nov. 1979, Star Trek: The Motion Picture cover...$5–$8

Science Fiction Blockbusters, Vol. 1, No. 3, Fall 1984, Star Trek article.......................$3–$5

Science Fiction Now, 1978, Star Trek article ....$3–$5

Sci-Fi Monthly, Sportscene Publishers, Ltd., a British publication in poster format, high quality color photography

Issue 1, date unknown, the Star Trek story, Spock's boyhood ....$4–$6

Issue 2, more in the story of Spock's life, the Enterprise blueprints, an interview with Spock's creator...$4–$6

Issue 3, Star Trek's evil empires—Klingons and Romulans ....$4–$6

Issue 4, Enterprise bridge blueprints...$4–$6

Issue 6, Star Trek alien poster, Enterprise crew, Part 2 ....$4–$6

Sesame Street, 321 Contact, Star Trek: The Motion Picture cover..................................$3–$5

Sick, June 1980, Enterprise cover, Star Trek parody ....$4–$8

Space Odyssey, April 1977, Star Trek cover...$4–$8

Space Trek, Vol. 2, No. 1, Spring 1979, Star Trek article ....$3–$5

Space Wars, July 1978, "Star Trip" (X-rated)..$5–$10

Spectrum 30, Feb. 1977, Uhura cover, Star Trek cons...$4–$8

Star (newspaper), Nov. 1979, Star Trek: The Motion Picture cover ....$5–$8

Star Battles, Vol. 2, No. 2, Summer 1979, Star Trek article ....$3–$5

Starblaster Special

Aug. 1986, Star Trek article...$3–$5

Oct. 1986, Star Trek article..$3–$5

Starblazer Special, Vol. 1, No. 7, Summer 1986, Star Trek article ....$3–$5

Starburst, Starburst Magazines, Ltd., British publication, similar to *Starlog*, first published in 1978

Vol. 1, No. 1, "The Writers of Star Trek," "Star Wars Buccaneers of Space," "The Making of Star Wars" ....$10–$15

Vol. 1, No. 10, June 1979, "The Star Trek Interviews, Part 1" ....$8–$12

Vol. 1, No. 11, July 1979, "The Star Trek Interviews, Part 2" ....$8–$12

Vol. 2, No. 5, a preview of "Star Trek: The Motion Picture"......................................$4–$6

Vol. 2, No. 7, a review of "Star Trek: The Motion Picture"..$4–$6

Vol. 5, No. 1, Star Trek interview with the producer, Star Wars Double Bill, Star Trek II ....$4–$6

No. 79, Kirk and Spock (original TV cover), Mar. 1985 ....$4–$6

No. 106, Scotty (movie) cover, June 1987 ....$4–$6

No. 133, Star Trek V cover, Oct. 1989...$4–$6

Stardate, primarily a gaming magazine, some issues were devoted to the Star Trek Role Playing Game

No. 1, 1984..$5–$6

No. 2, 1984..$3–$5

Vol. 3, No. 1, 1987 ....$3–$4

Star Force

Vol. 2, No. 1, Feb. 1981, Star Trek article ....$3–$5

Vol. 2, No. 2, April 1981, Star Trek article..$3–$5

Starlog, O'Quinn Studios, Inc., New York, NY, features regular columns about Star Trek and its fandom, issues with cover stories and special features have added collector value

No. 1, Star Trek episode ....$10–$20

No. 2, interview with Roddenberry ....$6–$10

No. 3, convention news..$6–$10

No. 9, interview with Shatner ....$10–$15

No. 14, Star Trek Spock..$4–$7

No. 24, 3rd anniversary, Shatner and Nimoy..$6–$8

No. 25, Star Trek: The Motion Picture ....$5–$7

No. 30, Star Trek movie preview, Chekov's Enterprise ....$5–$7

No. 83, June 1984, Star Trek III, the new Mr. Saavik, Ann Crispin's Trek novel, poster of alien...$5–$7

No. 84, July 1984, Leonard Nimoy directs Star Trek III...$5–$7

No. 114, Jan. 1987, Spock cover, TV series news...$5–$7

No. 124, Nov. 1987, Next Generation crew cover ....$5–$7

No. 126, Jan. 1988, LaForge, Troi, Data cover ....$5–$7

No. 130, May 1988, Yar cover..$5–$7

No. 138, Jan. 1989, Worf cover ....$5–$7

No. 139, Feb. 1989, Next Generation crew cover ....$5–$7

No. 144, July 1989, Kirk cover, Star Trek V article..$5–$7

No. 147, Oct. 1989, Data cover ....$5–$7

Star Trek Files Magazines, New Media Publishing. These are square bound magazines with color covers. Magazines vary greatly in quality. Numbering system is inconsistent. Values reflect issue price of magazine. It is unlikely they will ever have collector value due to poor interior production values.

No. 1, 1985, Where No Man Has Gone Before...$10–$15

Reprint Part 1, 1985 ....$6–$8

Reprint Part 2, 1985 ....$6–$8

The Early Voyages, 1985 ....$6–$8

Reprint Part 1, 1985 ....$6–$8

Reprint Part 2, 1985 ....$6–$8

No. 2, Time Passages, 1985..$6–$8

No. 3, A Taste of Paradise, 1985 ....$6–$8

No. 4, On the Edge of Forever, 1985...$6–$8

No. 5, Mission Year Two, 1986 ....$10–$12

No. 6, Journey to Eternity, 1986..$6–$8

No. 7, The Deadly Years, 1986...$6–$8

No. 8, Return to Tomorrow, 1986..$6–$8

No. 9, Assignment Earth, 1986...$6–$8

No. 10, Enterprise Incident, 1986..$6–$8

No. 11, Tholian Web, 1986..$6–$8
No. 12, Whom Gods Destroy, 1986...$6–$8
No. 13, All Our Yesterdays, 1986..$6–$8
No. 15, The Animated Voyages Begin ....$6–$8
No. 16, The Animated Voyages End ....$6–$8
Star Trek: The Motion Picture ....$6–$8
Star Trek: The Motion Picture, Vol. 1 ....$6–$8
Star Trek: The Motion Picture, Vol. 2 ....$6–$8
Star Trek II: The Wrath of Khan..$6–$8
Star Trek III: The Search for Spock...$6–$8
Star Trek IV: The Voyage Home, Vol. 1 ....$6–$8
Star Trek IV: The Voyage Home, Vol. 2 ....$6–$8
Star Trek: 20th Anniversary Tribute ....$8–$10
Complete Guide to Star Trek
    Vol. 1 ....$6–$8
    Vol. 2 ....$6–$8
    Vol. 3 ....$6–$8
    Vol. 4 ....$6–$8
    Vol. 5 ....$6–$8
Enterprise Command Book...$14–$16
Star Trek Encyclopedia ....$19–$21
Enterprise Incidents, Vol. 1..$4–$6
Enterprise Incidents, Vol. 2..$4–$6
Enterprise Incidents 1989 Tributes ....$16–$18
Federation and Empire..$17–$19
Interviews Aboard the Enterprise ....$18–$20
Lost Years ....$12–$14
Monsters and Aliens, Vol. 1 ....$6–$8
Monsters and Aliens, Vol. 2 ....$6–$8
Star Trek, Year One...$12–$14
Star Trek, Year Two ....$12–$14
Star Trek, Year Three ....$12–$14
Captain Kirk..$6–$8
Spock...$6–$8
McCoy..$6–$8
Scotty ....$6–$8
Chekov...$6–$8
Uhura...$6–$8
Sulu ....$6–$8
Crew File Finale...$6–$8
Harry Mudd...$6–$8
Vulcans..$6–$8
Romulans...$6–$8
Klingons ....$6–$8
Spock and Vulcans...$6–$8
The Captains Before Kirk ....$6–$8
Character Guide, Vol. 1 A-D ....$6–$8
Character Guide, Vol. 2 M-R ....$6–$8
Character Guide, Vol. 3 S-Z...$6–$8
Star Trek Comics, Vol. 1 ....$6–$8
Star Trek Comics, Vol. 2...$6–$8
Reflections of the 60s ....$14–$16
Special Effects ....$4–$6
Starship Enterprise ....$14–$16
Super Villians ....$6–$8
Tech Files—Star Trek Devices $7–9
Tribute Book, Vol. 1...$12–$14
Tribute Book, Vol. 2...$12–$14
Star Trek That Almost Was...$5–$7
Star Trek That Never Was...$5–$7
Star Trek Universe ....$17–$19

Time Travel ....$6–$8
Undiscovered Star Trek
   Vol. 1 ....$6–$8
   Vol. 2 ....$6–$8
   Vol. 3 ....$6–$8
   Vol. 4 ....$6–$8
   Vol. 5 ....$6–$8
   Vol. 6 ....$6–$8
   Dagger of the Mind ....$6–$8
   Villains, Vol. 1 ....$9–$11
   Villains, Vol. 2 ....$9–$11
   Villains, Vol. 3 ....$9–$11
   Star Trek: The Next Generation Background Briefing ....$14–$16
   Next Generation Complete Guide ....$19–$20
   Creating the Next Generation ....$16–$18
   Guide to the Next Generation ....$16–$18
   Making of the Next Generation, Part 1 ....$16–$18
   Making of the Next Generation, Part 2 ....$16–$18
   Untold Tales of the Next Generation ....$16–$18

Starlog Poster Magazine, Vol. 2, 1984, contains ten 16″ × 21″ color posters, includes poster of Enterprise in Mutara Nebula with Reliant in background ....$10–$15

Star Trek II: The Wrath of Khan Official Movie Magazine, Starlog, 1982 ....$5–$10

Star Trek II: The Search for Spock, Official Movie Magazine, Starlog, 1984, "Final Voyage of the Starship Enterprise," making of the movie, "Nimoy Directs, Shatner Stars, Kirk Risks Everything for His Vulcan Friend" ....$5–$10

Star Trek III: The Search for Spock Poster Magazine, Starlog, 1984, contains ten color posters from the movie ....$5–$10

Star Trek IV: The Voyage Home Official Movie Magazine, Starlog, 1986 ....$5–$10

Star Trek IV: The Voyage Home Official Poster Magazine, Starlog, 1986, contains ten posters ....$5–$10

Star Trek IV: The Voyage Home Official Movie Special, Starlog, 1986, articles plus ten posters ....$5–$10

Star Trek V: The Final Frontier Official Movie Magazine, Starlog, 1989 ....$4–$6

Star Trek: The Next Generation Official Magazine Series, Starlog.
   No. 1, 1987, four posters ....$10–$15
   No. 2, 1987 ....$10–$15
   No. 3, 1987 ....$8–$12
   No. 4, 1988 ....$8–$12
   No. 5, 1989 ....$8–$12
   No. 6, 1989 ....$6–$10
   No. 7, 1989 ....$6–$10

Top: Next Generation Starlog magazines. Bottom: Starlog/Star Trek movie magazines.

No. 8, 1989...$6–$10
No. 9, 1989...$5–$8
No. 10, 1989...$5–$8
No. 11, 1990, eight posters ....$5–$8
No. 12, 1990...$5–$8
No. 13, 1990...$5–$6
No. 14, 1990...$5–$6
No. 15, 1991...$5–$6
No. 16, 1991...$5–$6

Super Visual, magazine and complete visual guide of Star Trek, Vol. 1–3, a Japanese publication of high-quality color styles of different television stories.....................................$25–$50

Tomorrow (newspaper), No. 1, 1980, Star Trek cover...$3–$5

Trek, G.B. Love and W. Irwing, Houston, TX, a fanzine turned prozine, dedicated to Star Trek information—about the show and the gaining momentum of fans—published from 1974–81, a series of 19

No. 1..$40–$50
No. 2–3...$10–$50
No. 4, rare..$20–$25
No. 5–19...$8–$15
Special Issue No. 1, Feb. 1977 ....$8–$12
Special Issue No. 2, Nov. 1978..$8–$12

TV Gold, Jan. 1987, "Star Trek is Flying Again" ....$4–$7

TV Guide, issues with cover stories have higher collectible value

March 4, 1967, Star Trek cover..$35–$50
July 15, 1967, Nichelle Nichols...$10–$15
Nov. 18, 1967, Star Trek cover...$30–$40
June 22, 1968, William Shatner..$10–$15
Aug. 24, 1968, Star Trek cover...$25–$35
Oct. 14, 1976, Star Trek article...$10–$15
March 25, 1972, Trek conventions ....$15–$20
Aug. 1978, UFO Report, "Beaming Aboard the Star Trek Movie," Enterprise shown on cover..$5–$10

TV Showpeople, Vol. 1, No. 2, June 1975, Star Trek article.............................$3–$5

Twilight Zone, Aug. 1984, Star Trek III, Valdris cover ....$4–$7

US Magazine

Dec. 1979, Spock, Star Trek: The Motion Picture cover..............................$4–$8
Jan. 1980, Star Trek: The Motion Picture cover...$4–$8
June 1982, Star Trek article...$3–$5

Videogaming, June 1983, article on computer of Star Trek, Spock on cover ....$5–$7

Video Viewing, Oct. 1987, Star Trek IV cover...$3–$5

World of Horror, No. 4, British, Star Trek article ....$3–$5

MODEL KITS

Models, in general, are excellent collectibles but only in original condition. An assembled model, even a rare one, is worth only a fraction of an unbuilt one. AMT, the original manufacturer of Star Trek models in this country, is no longer in business. ERTL, however, purchased AMT and has used AMT's original molds to reissue some of the original models and has added some new ones to the line.

For this chapter, "models" will be considered as kits to be assembled. See "Toys and Crafts," "Games and Accessories," "Pewter Figurines," etc., for other replicas.

Note: *Model collectors often put too much emphasis on whether a kit is still shrink-wrapped, assuming this denotes original condition. Shrink-wrapping machines are common and kits can easily be opened and rewrapped. Until the plastic is removed, it is impossible to examine the contents of the kit.*

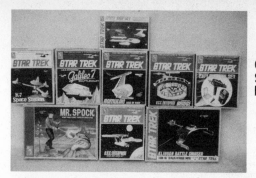

Original AMT Star Trek models. Spock and Klingon on bottom are large box versions.

Original TV Series
AMT/ERTL

AMT originally released its Star Trek model series in large 14½" × 10" boxes. Later editions of all models were in the smaller 8½" × 10" box.

Enterprise (large box, with lights), AMT, 1966, very early versions had vertical box art soon replaced by horizontal format used throughout large box series..............................$175–$300

Enterprise (large box, no lights), AMT, same box art as lighted version (side panel describing model differentiates lighted and unlighted versions)................................$100–$150

Enterprise (small box), AMT, 1968, same box art as large version............................$25–$50

Enterprise (small box), ERTL, 1983, same box art as AMT but with "ERTL" printed under AMT logo on side panels...$15–$20

Enterprise, ERTL, 1989, current box art, but still 8½" × 10"....................................$8–$10

Exploration Set (large box), AMT, 1974, featured undersized communicator, tricorder, and pistol phaser ....$100–$150

Exploration Set (small box), AMT, same box art as large box version, no ERTL reissue........ ....$75–$100

Galileo (large box), AMT, 1974, artwork of shuttlecraft...$50–$75

Galileo (small box), AMT, same box art as large version..$50–$75

K-7 Space Station, AMT, 1976, small box only, no ERTL reissue............................$75–$100

Klingon Ship (large box with lights), AMT, 1966, horizontal box art, description of lights on side panel ....$250–$400

Klingon Ship (large box, no lights), AMT, 1968, same basic box art as lighted version ....$100–$150

AMT Enterprise (original) box evolution. Model remained same size.

Klingon Ship (small box), AMT, same basic box art ....$50–$75
Romulan Bird of Prey, AMT, 1975, small box only, no ERTL reissue....................$75–$100
Mr. Spock (large box), AMT, 1966, Spock phasering a serpent ....$100–$150
Mr. Spock (small box), AMT, 1968, same box art as large version, no ERTL reissue ....
....$75–$100
U.S.S. Enterprise Command Bridge, AMT, 1975, diorama of originalTV bridge, no large
box version...$50–$75
Space Ship Set, AMT, 1976, included small replicas of Enterprise, Klingon Cruiser, and
Romulan Bird of Prey, box 6″ × 9¼″ ....$20–$30
Space Ship Set, ERTL, 1983, same box art and size as AMT version but with "ERTL" under
AMT on side panel ....$6–$10
Space Ship Set, ERTL, 1989, current box art...$5–$7
Note: *AMT had another ship in this series, called Interplanetary U.F.O. Technically, it was not*
a Star Trek ship but is of some interest to collectors.

Aurora

Enterprise, 1966, same model and box art as AMT version. Made for British market.............
....$75–$100
Mr. Spock, 1972, same model and box art as AMT version, made for British market..............
....$50–$75

Estes

Manufacturers of flying model rockets. Model was fired from stand and then para-
chuted down. Came packaged in plastic with full-color cover sheet and header.
Enterprise, 1975 ....$15–$25
Klingon Cruiser, 1975..$25–$40

Medori

Enterprise, 1969, Japanese model had propeller added to ship. Kirk and Spock on box art.....
....$75–$150

Star Trek: The Next Generation

ERTL

Adversaries Set, 1989, includes three ships: Ferengi Marauder, Klingon Bird of Prey, and
Romulan Warbird. Ships are to scale, 12″ × 17½″ box ....$12–$16
Enterprise, 1989, 18″ model, detachable saucer section, 12″ × 17½″ box ....$12–$16
U.S.S. Enterprise Three-Piece Set, 1989, original TV, movie, and Next Generation Enter-
prise. To scale, 12″ × 17½″ box...$12–$16
U.S.S. Enterprise Three-Piece Set, special 25th anniversary chrome edition ....$25–$30

Next Generation models.

Enterprise models for five Star Trek movies.

Star Trek Movies
AMT/ERTL

Star Trek: The Motion Picture models were the last made by AMT before being purchased by ERTL.

Enterprise, Star Trek: The Motion Picture, AMT, 1979, lights in saucer section, 12″ × 17″ box, shows movie Enterprise with lights..$50–$75

Enterprise, Star Trek II, ERTL, 1983, same basic box art still showing lights, though model was not equipped with them ....$25–$35

Enterprise, Star Trek III, ERTL, 1984, same model as Star Trek II. Box art now has lights removed..$15–$25

Enterprise, Star Trek IV, ERTL, 1986, new box art showing NCC 1701-A, same model.........
....$12–$18

Enterprise, Star Trek V, ERTL, 1989, new box art, same model of Enterprise. Small shuttlecraft model included..$12–$18

Enterprise, special edition, ERTL, 1991, lights and sound.............................$25–$30

Klingon Cruiser, Star Trek: The Motion Picture, 1979, AMT. Box 10″ × 12½″........$10–$15

Klingon Cruiser, ERTL, 1984, slightly different box art. Still in production..............$8–$10

Mr. Spock, AMT, 1979, 8½″ × 10″ box. Reworked mold of original TV model. Different base, no serpent..$40–$80

Vulcan Shuttle, AMT and ERTL, 1979, box 10″ × 12½″. Model had detachable sled. Box art changed from Star Trek: The Motion Picture to Star Trek III in 1984. Ceased production in 1989..$20–$30

Matchbox

Matchbox and AMT were both owned by the same parent company (Lesny) at the time of Star Trek: The Motion Picture and produced some models for the European market. Different box art from American models.

Klingon Cruiser, 1980, 10″ × 12½″ box, instructions in several different languages..............
....$45–$65

Vulcan Shuttle, 1980, 10″ × 12½″ box..$45–$65

MUSIC (SHEET)

Prices given are for individual pieces of music. Many variations of each piece may occur, not only for different instruments but also for degree of difficulty. Also, entire portfolios of sheet music for concert bands, marching bands, etc., can be found. This section is organized by publisher.

Almo Publications

Star Trek Theme (original TV), 1978, color photo cover of Enterprise, sheet ....$2–$5

Caterpillar Music

Sing a Song of Trekkin', 1979, book form, blue and white cartoon cover ....$8–$15
Visit to a Small Planet, 1979, sheet ....$2–$5

Columbia

Star Trek (original TV), 1970, Bruin Music, sheet ....$2–$5
Star Trek: The Motion Picture Main Theme, 1979, sheet..$2–$5
Star Trek II: The Wrath of Khan Main Theme, 1982, Famous Music, sheet, assorted covers depending on arrangement..$2–$5
Star Trek II: The Search for Spock Music Book, 1984, Famous Music, color cover and photo section followed by several music selections ....$10–$15
Star Trek IV: The Voyage Home, 1986, Famous Music, sheet ....$2–$5

Hal Leonard Publishing

Selections from Star Trek: The Motion Picture, 1980, Ensign Music, portfolio for entire orchestra ....$30–$40

Hansen House

Theme From Star Trek (original TV), 1970, Bruin Music, sheet....................................$2–$5
Theme From Star Trek/Space Race (original TV), 1970, Bruin Music, Super Fun Way Band portfolio...$20–$30
A Star Beyond Time (Ilia's Theme) From Star Trek: The Motion Picture, 1979, Famous Music, sheet ....$2–$5
A Star Beyond Time (Ilia's Theme) From Star Trek: The Motion Picture, 1979, Famous Music, photo cover booklet ....$3–$6
Complete Musical Themes: Star Trek: The Motion Picture, 1979, Ensign Music, sheet.....
....$2–$5
Star Trek: The Motion Picture, Hungry Five, Musical Themes, 1979, Ensign Music, portfolio, black and white photo cover ....$5–$10
Star Trek: The Motion Picture, Stage Band, Musical Theme, 1979, Ensign Music, portfolio, black and white photo cover ....$15–$20
Star Trek: The Motion Picture, Super Fun Way Concert Band, 1979, Ensign Music, color Enterprise photo cover, portfolio ....$25–$35
Star Trek: The Motion Picture, Selections, 1979, Bruin, book format, color photo cover.....
....$5–$10
Star Trek: The Motion Picture, Selections, 1979, Ensign, Roy Clark Big Note Guitar, book format, color photo cover...$4–$8
Star Trek: The Motion Picture, Elaine Sevin's Space Note Play and Color, 8½″ × 11″, horizontal book format, color photo cover...$4–$8
Star Trek: The Motion Picture, Music From Outer Space and Inner Space, 8½″ × 11″, horizontal book format, color photo cover ....$4–$8
Star Trek: The Motion Picture, Musical Themes, 1979, Ensign Music, spiral-bound book format, color photos throughout ....$5–$15

Petunia Music Co.

You Are Not Alone, 1967, sheet...$4–$8

Studio P/R Inc.

Main Theme From Star Trek: The Motion Picture, 1980, Ensign Music, band portfolio, black and white cover ....$25–$30

Warner Bros. Publications

Main Theme From Star Trek: The Motion Picture, 1980, Ensign Music, portofolio, Road Runner on cover ....$10–$15

PATCHES

All patches in this section are embroidered unless otherwise indicated. The values listed for these patches reflect current manufacturing prices. Most are still in production by the original manufacturer or others and will remain so as long as demand for them continues. Future appreciation of values is not likely since patches are easily reproduced.

Alpha Centauri Symbol, gold and purple from Tech Manual ....$3–$5
Borg Ship, Lincoln Enterprises, red symbol on gold background ....$9–$10
Borg Symbol, Lincoln Enterprises, symbol on front of ship ....$9–$10
Commendation Ribbons, set of 19 from TV show, small triangular patches ....$10–$15
Dreadnought, blue and yellow, NCC-1707 ....$3–$5
Enterprise
  Black background, Lincoln Enterprises ....$2–$4
  Black background with white silhouette captioned "Star Trek" ....$3–$5
  Dark blue background, cutout ....$3–$5
  Orbiting planet, six-color, fan-shaped, 4½″, Star Trek Welcommittee ....$2–$5
  With name and number, oval, 4″, white or black background, Star Trek Welcommittee ....
  ....$2–$5
Enterprise Cutout, movie version, Lincoln Enterprises ....$9–$12
Enterprise Cutout, Next Generation version, Lincoln Enterprises ....$9–$12
Enterprise Cutout, Next Generation version, Lincoln Enterprises, tiny stick-on patch ....
  ....$1–$3
Federation, word with Enterprise, 3″, Star Trek Welcommittee ....$2–$5
Ferengi Ship Cutout, orange, Lincoln Enterprises ....$6–$8
Figure Patch Cutouts, original TV characters
  Kirk ....$2–$5
  Spock ....$2–$5
  McCoy ....$2–$5
  Uhura ....$2–$5
Galileo, word, number, and picture, 2″, Star Trek Welcommittee ....$2–$5
IDIC Symbol, says "Peace in Our Galaxy," Lincoln Enterprises ....$2–$4
Insignia Patches, from original TV
  Command, black star with gold background ....$2–$4
  Science, black circle with round symbol inside ....$2–$4
  Engineering, black curved symbol ....$2–$4
  Nursing, red cross on gold background ....$2–$4

Examples of patches.

Pi symbol, on gold background ....$2–$4
Gamma symbol, on gold background ....$2–$4
Insignia Patches, from Star Trek: The Motion Picture
Command, black star with white background ....$2–$4
Science, orange background ....$2–$4
Engineering, red background..$2–$4
Medical, green background...$2–$4
Operations, yellow background ....$2–$4
Security, silver or blue background ....$2–$4
Keep on Trekkin', rectangular, red background, 3½", Star Trek Welcommittee ....$2–$5
Klingon, word with picture of Klingon Cruiser, 3", Star Trek Welcommittee ....$2–$5
Live Long and Prosper, words and Vulcan salute, 3" circle, Thinking Cap Co. ....$3–$6
Live Long and Prosper, words with Vulcan salute, hand 4", Star Trek Welcommittee..$2–$5
Mascot Patch, shows tribbles ....$2–$5
Medical Caduceus, green, Lincoln Enterprises..$2–$3
Star Trek: Next Generation Insignia Patch, gold and silver cutout, Lincoln Enterprises ......
....$2–$4
Phaser Patch, cutout...$2–$4
Photo Patches, from Star Trek: The Motion Picture, Aviva, 1979
Spock, Kirk, and McCoy ....$3–$5
Kirk in full dress uniform ....$3–$5
Worried Admiral Kirk...$3–$5
Spock and Kirk ....$3–$5
Spock in white ....$3–$5
Romulan, word with picture of Romulan Bird of Prey, 3", Star Trek Welcommittee......$2–$5
Space Station K-7, words and picture, 3", Star Trek Welcommittee ....$2–$5
Spock, with "Live Long and Prosper," square ....$2–$4
Spock Lives, 3" circle, Thinking Cap Co. ....$3–$6
61 Cygni Symbol, planetary system, copper bird from Tech Manual............................$3–$5
Star Trek III Commemorative Patch, embroidered, Lincoln Enterprises ....$6–$8
Star Trek IV, Enterprise and whales, multicolored, Lincoln Enterprises......................$9–$12
Star Trek IV, Bird of Prey and whale, multicolored, Lincoln Enterprises....................$8–$10
Star Trek IV, whales in insigna design, multicolored, Lincoln Enterprises.................$8–$10
Star Trek 20th Anniversary Patch, embroidered, Lincoln Enterprises ....$6–$8
Star Trek: The Next Generation, two styles: multicolored, and blue and silver, Lincoln En-
terprises ....$9–$12
United Federation of Planets
Silver and red banner (from original TV show) ....$2–$4
Silver and black banner...$2–$4
Silver and blue circle, 4", from Tech Manual..$4–$6
Silver and blue, 3" circle, Thinking Cap Co., from the movies ....$2–$5
Next Generation style, blue and red, Lincoln Enterprises................................$9–$12
U.S.S. Enterprise
Light blue background, dark blue border, lettering in orange, silver ship ....$3–$5
Yellow background, light blue border, lettering in orange, silver and gray ship ....$3–$5
Words and insignia in red, 3" circle, Thinking Cap Co. ....$2–$5
Words on yellow felt background, rectangle ....$3–$5
Zap, word with Enterprise firing phasers, rectangle, four-color, 3½", Star Trek Welcommittee
....$3–$5

PEWTER FIGURINES

Franklin Mint, 1989

An attempt was made on the part of this company, well known for other collectible
products, to produce high-quality, high-priced replicas. Ships come with hardwood
stands and are embellished with gold-plated trim and crystal insets.
Enterprise, original TV version, 10"..$190–$210
Klingon Cruiser, original TV version, 9" ....$190–$210

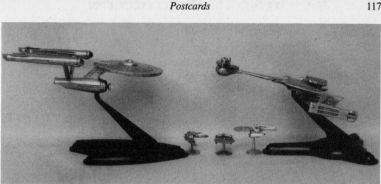

Large Franklin Enterprise and Klingon. Small ships in center are Rawcliffe.

Romulan Ship, original TV version, 9″ ....$190–$210
Three Ship Set, small original Enterprise, Klingon, and Romulan ships on one stand ....
....$190–$210
Note: *As of this writing, a pewter chess set is also planned to be released one piece at a time. Final cost would be in the $1,000 range.*

Rawcliffe, 1988

Rawcliffe, a manufacturer of all kinds of fine pewter figurines, made a series of Star Trek ships under FASA's (see Star Trek "Games and Accessories") license to produce gaming pieces. Paramount disagreed with this arrangement and forced Rawcliffe to cease production of the product. This short time on the market may affect future value. Though basically the same as the FASA gaming pieces, these ships are pewter instead of base metal and come in one piece. Ships came packaged in clear plastic boxes with blue velveteen inserts and silver embossed writing.
Chandley, 3″...$20–$25
Enterprise, 3″, original TV ....$20–$25
Enterprise, 3″, movie...$20–$25
Excelsior, 4¾″...$25–$30
Grissom, 2″ ....$20–$25
Klingon Bird of Prey (L-42), 1¾″...$20–$25
Klingon Cruiser, 2½″, original TV ....$20–$25
Regula 1, 2″..$20–$25
Reliant, 2½″...$20–$25

POSTCARDS

Anabas (British), 1987, color photos from the original TV show. Two different: Enterprise and Kirk, McCoy and Uhura. Price each...$1–$3
California Dreamers, 1985, color photos with captions
 Enterprise, "To seek strange new worlds—like you!" ....$1–$2
 Kirk, "Screens up full, magnification 10"..$1–$2
 Kirk with communicator, "Lock me in and beam me up, baby, I'm yours" ....$1–$2
 Kirk at party with aliens, " . . . Call me. We'll have lunch.".........................$1–$2
 Spock, "Bizarre . . . but I like it" ....$1–$2
 Spock touching wall...$1–$2
 Spock with headpiece, "Batteries may fail, but rock and roll will never die!".............$1–$2
 Sulu, "Control systems out, navigation out. Directional systems out . . . I'm so confused"
 ....$1–$2

Original and Star Trek III postcard books.

Engale (British), 1989, full-color photos from the original TV show and the first two seasons of the Next Generation. Backs identify them as sets of 16 but there is more than one set and not all are Star Trek. There are at least 30 different Star Trek cards. Price per card ....$1–$3
Foto Parjetas (Spanish), brown and white picture of cast on bridge ....$1–$3
Lincoln Enterprises, color, all still available, sold in sets, three different
   Original TV, Chekov, Kirk, McCoy, Scotty, Spock, Sulu, Uhura ....$3–$5
   Star Trek: The Motion Picture, Chapel, Chekov, Decker, Enterprise, Ilia, Kirk, McCoy, Rand, Scotty, Spock, Sulu, Uhura..$3–$5
   Star Trek III: The Search for Spock, Chekov, Kirk, McCoy, Saavik, Sarek, Scotty, Spock, Sulu, Tilar, Uhura..$3–$5
Impact, 1979, Movieland Wax Museum Star Trek exhibit ....$1–$2
National Air and Space Museum, color photo of original TV model now housed in museum.
....$2–$3
Prime Press, Star Trek Postcard Book, 1977, 48 color photo cards of the original TV series in oversize soft-cover book format, color cover...$15–$20
Simon and Schuster, Star Trek III: The Search for Spock Postcard Book, 1984, 22 color post-cards in book format ....$6–$10
TK Graphics, sets of eight silkscreened postcards, assorted colors.
   UFP banner, "Star Fleet Headquarters Tactical Center" ....$3–$6
   UFP emblem, "Star Fleet Headquarters Official Mail"..$3–$6
Miscellaneous
   Star Trek II: The Wrath of Khan poster art...$1–$2
   Star Trek III: The Search for Spock poster art...$1–$2
   Star Trek IV: The Voyage Home, reproductions of American one-sheet art, French, two different: advance poster art and Bird of Prey over San Francisco poster art. Price each...........
....$1–$2

POSTERS

Theatrical Release Posters

Theatrical release one-sheet posters are $27'' \times 41''$ and come both rolled (for promotions) and folded (for mailing to theaters). Often the rolled promotional ones are offered for sale by theaters or fan clubs.

Star Trek: The Motion Picture

One-sheet (advance), "The new adventure is about to begin," rainbow art
   Rolled...$25–$50
   Folded ....$15–$30
One-sheet (regular), "There is no comparison," rainbow art
   Rolled...$20–$40
   Folded ....$15–$25
   Smaller version, promotional...$5–$10

STAR TREK

Star Trek dolls and action figures

All of the Star Trek ceramic items produced by Ernst for Hamilton

Star Trek toys and games

Mego Star Trek toys and action figures

Franklin Mint fine pewter Star Trek ships

Assortment of products featuring all three versions of the **U.S.S. Enterprise**

Assortment of current and out-of-print Star Trek publications

Professional and homemade Star Trek uniforms and props

STAR WARS

Complete set of Kenner Star Wars large action figures

Star Wars housewares

Star Wars toys and games

Star Wars small action figures

Assortment of R2-D2 products

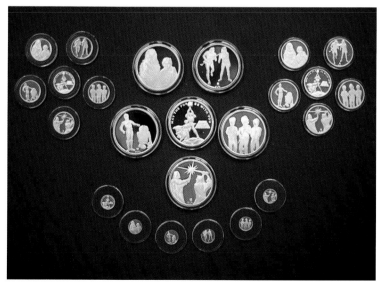

Complete set of Star Wars 1-ounce gold, 1/4-ounce gold, and 5-ounce silver collectors' coins

Assortment of Star Wars ceramic items

Star Wars saga advance and original release theatrical (1-sheet) posters

Star Trek IV theatrical one-sheet.

Foreign Editions of Rainbow Poster
German...$20–$40
Italian..$20–$40
Japanese ....$15–$30
French ....$20–$40
Mexican...$20–$40
Billboard Poster, Star Trek: The Motion Picture logo, says, "The new adventure is about to begin!," 8′ × 9′...$50–$100

Star Trek II: Wrath of Khan

One-sheet Style A (advance), Enterprise with Starburst in orbit around planet with rings
....$25–$50
Logo in silver...$25–$50
One-Sheet Collage
Rolled...$20–$40
Folded ....$15–$30
Smaller promotional version...$5–$10

Star Trek III: Search for Spock

One-sheet Outline of Spock in Space
Rolled...$20–$40
Folded ....$15–$25
Smaller promotional version...$5–$10
Montage, foreign artwork ....$20–$30

Star Trek IV: The Voyage Home

One-sheet (advance), dark blue
Rolled...$20–$30
Folded ....$15–$25
Smaller promotional version...$5–$10
One-sheet, orange, Bird of Prey and Golden Gate Bridge
Rolled...$15–$25
Folded ....$10–$15

Star Trek V

One-sheet, Drew Art, rolled...$6–$10

Mass Market and Commercial Promotional Posters

These are the posters that are generally sold in stores or displayed or given away as promotions.

Original TV

Dargis Associates, 1976, 17″ × 30″, black and white
Kirk ....$5–$10
Spock..$5–$10
Sulu ....$5–$10
McCoy...$5–$10
Door poster with Spock, Kirk, Enterprise, and Klingon, 6′ ....$10–$15
Dynamic Publishing, 1976, black light-flocked posters
Kirk ....$5–$10
Spock..$5–$10
Enterprise ....$5–$10
Huckleberry Designs, 1972, "Spock in Pain," 29″ × 23″, artwork by M. Beard ....$5–$10
Jeri of Hollywood, 1967, 22″ × 33″, black and white posters of early promotional pictures
Kirk ....$3–$5
Spock..$3–$5
McCoy...$3–$5
Langley Associates, 1976, did an extensive line of licensed color posters, 20″ × 24″ unless otherwise noted
Collage ....$4–$6
Crew in transporter ....$4–$6
Crew on bridge...$4–$6
Enterprise with enemy ships ....$4–$6
Enterprise firing on enemy ships ....$4–$6
Enterprise firing phasers ....$4–$6
Enterprise and crew ....$4–$6
Rigel Castle..$4–$6
Spock and Kirk ....$4–$6
Spock and Kirk (artwork) ....$4–$6
Kirk, 6′ door poster ....$10–$15
Spock, 6′ door poster ....$10–$15
Enterprise and Klingon (two-sided), 11″ × 15″, black and white....................$5–$8
Lincoln Enterprises, posters still available
Character collage, 16″ × 20″, color artwork ....$4–$6
Kirk as Romulan, 17″ × 22″, artwork by Little ....$4–$5
Spock, two faces, three-color artwork ....$3–$4
Color posters, 2′ × 3′, Kirk collage and Spock collage. Price each...................$5–$6
Star Trek Galore, 1976, manufactured a line of unlicensed color posters, 19″ × 23″
Kirk with Lirpa ....$3–$4
Party scene from "Journey to Babel" ....$3–$4
Landing party and Klingons ....$3–$4
City scene from "A Taste of Armageddon" ....$3–$4
Kirk ....$4–$6
Spock with harp ....$4–$6
Crew on bridge...$4–$6
Enterprise firing phasers ....$4–$6
Character collage, black and white artwork ....$3–$5
Character collage, black and white artwork with ship.....................................$3–$5
Klingon recruiting poster ....$5–$10
Federation recruiting poster...$5–$10
Steranko, Jim, 1974, color artwork collage of crew members and ships, 23″ × 32″.....$6–$12
Video Posters (American), color posters exist for all the movies and there are several different ones for the TV episodes. Price per poster (any)..$10–$20

Star Trek: The Motion Picture

Coca-Cola, 18″ × 24″ color promotional, Enterprise overhead with insets of crew below........
....$5–$10
Lincoln Enterprises, all posters still available
2″ × 3″
Spock, crying ....$5–$6
Enterprise ....$5–$6

17″ × 22″
    Group shot on bridge ....$2–$3
    Kirk ....$2–$3
    McCoy..$2–$3
    Kirk, Spock, and Enterprise..$2–$3
    Main characters and ship, "Human Adventure is Just Beginning" ....$2–$3
    Kirk, artwork by Little..$3–$4
    Spock, two faces, artwork by Little ....$3–$4
    Kirk and Spock, artwork by Little ....$3–$4
    Spock and Nixon, artwork by Little ....$3–$4
    Nixon and Klingon, artwork by Little ....$3–$4
    Enterprise and face..$3–$4
  Character portfolio, 12 11″ × 14″ color artwork posters, sold only in sets ....$9–$10
Proctor and Gamble, 17″ × 22″ color promotional posters
  No. 1 Enterprise ....$5–$7
  No. 2 Spock and Kirk ....$5–$7
  No. 3 Enterprise, crew overhead..$5–$7
  Set ....$15–$30
Sales Corp. of America
  Character collage, alien landscape and ships in background
    Regular..$4–$6
    Reversible 3-D with glasses...$5–$10
  Cutaway poster, color cross-section of Enterprise
    22″ × 48″ ....$15–$25
    22″ × 48″ Mylar ....$20–$35
    11″ × 23″ Coca-Cola promotion ....$5–$10
  Enterprise, Mylar, 22″ × 29″...$10–$15

Star Trek II: The Wrath of Khan

Lincoln Enterprises, all posters still available
  2″ × 3″
    Kirk ....$5–$6
    Group, with color insets from movie ....$5–$6
  17″ × 22″ color artwork posters by Doug Little
    Khan, with muppet...$3–$4
    Spock...$3–$4
    Spock and Enterprise ....$3–$4
Sales Corp. of America, 1982, 22″ × 30″, color.
  Enterprise, with insets of characters ....$5–$8
  Logo ....$4–$6
Sat Nam Kaur, 1982, 22″ × 30″, color artwork originally for fanzine cover ....$6–$10
Sega, 1983, 22″ × 34″, Enterprise and Klingon ships battling with "Star Trek" above and Sega
logo below, promotional ....$5–$10

Star Trek III: The Search for Spock

Bennett, 1984, 22″ × 28″ color artwork, montage similar to foreign one-sheet artwork ....
....$5–$10
Lever Bros., 1984, 16″ × 22″ color, promotional
  Bird of Prey and logo...$6–$10
  Enterprise and logo ....$6–$10
  Group ....$6–$10
  Kirk and Kruge ....$6–$10

Star Trek IV: The Voyage Home

Lincoln Enterprises, posters still available
  Montage, 18″ × 28″ color artwork, crew with ship and whales ....$6–$8
  One-sheet artwork, 24″ × 36″ ....$5–$7
Mind's Eye Press, 24″ × 36″, reprint of Enterprise cutaway poster updated with Star Trek IV
logo ....$10–$20
One Stop Publishing, 23″ × 35″, color, Enterprise at angle with inset picture................$4–$6

Personalities Twentieth Anniversary and British Next Generation video poster.

Twentieth Anniversary Posters

Anabas (British), 1987, 24″ × 35″, color, Kirk, Spock, and McCoy from original TV show ....$5–$8

Personalities, 1986, 22″ × 28″, color artwork by Gibson, Enterprise over planet with crew and logo, heavy paper stock ....$10–$20

Verkerkey Publishing, 1986, 36″ × 24″, color, Kirk, Spock, McCoy, and Uhura from original TV ....$6–$12

Video Poster, 1987, 26″ × 39″, color artwork, original Enterprise and characters with 20-year logo, promotional..$10–$15

Star Trek V: The Final Frontier

Lincoln Enterprises, 1989, 27″ × 40″, one-sheet artwork ....$6–$10

Star Trek: The Next Generation

Galoob, 1987, promotional. Next Generation Enterprise on one side, Galoob ad on other ....$8–$10

Lincoln Enterprises, 1987, 23″ × 34″, color
Next Generation Enterprise ....$8–$10
Crew in transporter ....$8–$10
One Stop Publishing, 1988, 22″ × 35″, artwork collage of characters.............$4–$6
Video Poster (British), 1989, 20″ × 32″, color, promotional for release of Encounter at Farpoint on British video ....$7–$10

Star Trek Poster Books

Original Television Poster Books, Paradise Press

This was a series of publications printed in full color on both sides of a 22″ × 33″ sheet that had a poster covering one side and pictures and articles on the other. It was sold folded down to a standard 8½″ × 11″ format. It lasted 17 issues and, like many finite series, fewer of the later issues were printed, making them more valuable.

Voyage 1, 1976. Cover, Enterprise. Poster, Enterprise in Tholian Web........................$10–$20
Voyage 2, 1976. Cover, Kirk, Spock, and McCoy. Poster same as cover.......................$8–$12
Voyage 3, 1976. Cover, Spock. Poster same as cover...$8–$12
Voyage 4, 1976. Cover, Kirk with Andorian. Poster, Kirk and Klingon.........................$6–$10
Voyage 5, 1977. Cover, Spock from "Amok Time." Poster, Spock with harp. ....$6–$10
Voyage 6, 1977. Cover, Enterprise. Poster, group on bridge ....$6–$10
Voyage 7, 1977. Cover, Kirk from "Miri." Poster, Kirk in dress uniform.......................$6–$10
Voyage 8, 1977. Cover, McCoy. Poster, Kirk, McCoy, and Rand ....$6–$10

Voyage One original TV, Star Trek: The Motion Picture, and British Star Trek II poster books.

Voyage 9, 1977. Cover, Kirk and Spock. Poster, Uhura ....$6–$10
Voyage 10, 1977. Cover, Enterprise. Poster, Klingons ....$6–$10
Voyage 11, 1977. Cover, Kirk as Romulan. Poster, Spock ....$6–$10
Voyage 12, 1977. Cover, Uhura and Sulu. Poster, Rand..`        `$8–$12
Voyage 13, 1977. Cover, Scotty. Poster same as cover..$10–$15
Voyage 14, 1977. Cover, Kirk and Spock playing chess. Poster, Kirk and Spock ....$15–$20
Voyage 15, 1978. Cover, Spock and Horta. Poster, Kirk and Sulu ....$15–$20
Voyage 16, 1978. Cover, Kirk and Spock from "Mirror, Mirror." Poster, bridge scene from
"Mirror, Mirror"..$15–$20
Voyage 17, 1978. Last issue. Cover, Kirk and McCoy. Poster, Enterprise model ....$20–$25

Movie Poster Books

Star Trek: The Motion Picture, Paradise Press, 1979. Same format as original TV poster
books. Cover and poster, Enterprise and crew..$8–$12
Star Trek II: The Wrath of Khan, Walkerprint Publications (British), 1982, 23″ × 32″.
Same format as American Posterbooks. Cover, logo, Enterprise, and Kirk. Poster, logo and col-
lage ....$8–$12

PROPS AND PROP REPRODUCTIONS

The aim of almost every collector is to own an original prop from the set of one of
the TV shows or movies. For ordinary collectors, this is not a realistic goal. Paramount is increasingly vigilant in regards to release of these items and anyone who
offers a prop as original should be suspect. If suitable authentication is provided, a
price in the thousands is not unreasonable. For this reason, prop reproductions have
become increasingly popular. Though not inexpensive themselves, they are at least
obtainable. In addition, they are almost always of superior quality to the originals.
This may seem surprising until you consider that most actual props are not intended
for lengthy use or close scrutiny. Unless a scene calls for a close-up of a particular
object, a rough unfinished version with no electronics or moving parts will usually
suffice. Though there have never been any licensed prop reproductions, there have
been several individuals who have produced professional quality pieces. Prices
listed below are for "state-of-the-art" items, as older pieces of lesser quality lose
value quickly. Kits are available but most customers find them unsatisfactory when

Prop reproductions.

compared to the finished pieces. Since prop reproductions are more or less custom products, any item from the TV shows or movies *could* be made. The following represents the more popular.

Communicators

Original TV, movable grid, no electronic functions ....$50–$75
Original TV, movable grid, light and sound effects ....$100–$125
Current Movie, movable grid, no electronic functions..$50–$100
Current TV, Next Generation, chirping sound ....$40–$50

Phasers

Original TV Hand Phaser, Phaser I, no electronics..$35–$50
Original TV Hand Phaser, lights and adjustable sound...$100–$125
Original TV Pistol Phaser, Phaser II, removable hand phaser, no electronics ......$125–$200
Original TV Pistol Phaser, lights and adjustable sound with removable hand phaser with independent lights and adjustable sound ....$300–$400
Early Movie Phaser, Phaser III, no electronics ....$75–$125
Early Movie Phaser, multiple light effects ....$125–$175
Current Movie Phaser, Phaser IV, removable hand phaser, no electronics ....$100–$150
Current Movie Phaser, Phaser IV, light effects, nonremovable hand phaser..........$125–$175
Current TV Hand Phaser, Next Generation, no electronics......................................$50–$75
Current TV Large Phaser, Next Generation, no electronics ....$125–$150

Tricorders

Original TV, flip-up screen, hinged control, and storage compartments, no electronics ....
....$100–$150
Original TV, flip-up screen, hinged control, and storage compartments, light and sound effects ....$200–$300
Current TV, Next Generation, flip-down control panel, removable scanner, no electronics ....
....$150–$200

PROMOTIONAL ITEMS

Studio

These are the items released by the studio to present an upcoming or current production to the public. Most of these items, such as press kits and lobby cards, are not designed for sale to the public but usually end up in circulation anyway, since the newspapers and theaters have little use for them once the movie is through running.

Star Trek: The Next Generation
promotional kit.

Television
ORIGINAL TV SERIES
Advance Brochure, 1966, 12-page booklet presenting the new television series to NBC affiliates. Rare...$200–$300
Second Season Publicity Folder, 1967, sent to NBC affiliates to promote Star Trek's second season. Rare ....$150–$250
Star Trek Mail Call, 1967, 20-page booklet of letters from viewers produced by NBC for network affiliates ....$150–$250
Star Trek Syndication Package, color folder with artwork of characters containing demographics designed to induce stations to carry Star Trek in syndication........................$40–$60
Promotional Flyer, early, NBC promotional art where the network had the points on Spock's ears airbrushed out ....$150–$175

STAR TREK: THE NEXT GENERATION
Advance Brochure, 1986, metal folder with etched title and "Captain's Log" on cover. Contains spiral-bound book of demographics on the original show and a 20th anniversary tee shirt. Came boxed ....$200–$400

UNIVERSAL STUDIOS TOUR, STAR TREK ADVENTURE
Plastic Briefcase, 1989, 13½″ × 16″ with color display on inside cover made to look like bridge station...$300–$500

Movies
LOBBY CARDS AND STILLS
These are the pictures designed for display in the lobbies of theaters. Lobby cards are generally 11″ × 14″. Lobby stills are 8″ × 10″. Sets usually are the same except for size. There are generally eight cards in each. Like the theatrical movie posters (*see* "Posters" section), they usually have foreign counterparts that are often different in content and form. German lobbies, for example, are larger sets printed on paper rather than card stock and come in perforated sheets of eight. As a general rule, foreign lobbies have the same approximate value. Values are for sets. Prices for individual cards from any film would be between $5 and $15, depending primarily on subject matter.
Star Trek: The Motion Picture
    Cards ....$50–$75
    Stills ....$40–$60
Star Trek II: The Wrath of Khan
    Cards ....$50–$75
    Stills ....$40–$60
Star Trek III: The Search for Spock
    Cards ....$45–$60
    Stills ....$35–$50

Star Trek IV: The Voyage Home
Cards ....$40–$50
Stills ....$30–$40
Star Trek V: The Final Frontier
Cards ....$25–$35
Stills ....$15–$25

PRESS BOOKS AND PRESS KITS

Press kits are the information packages given out by studios to promote an upcoming film. The general format is a folder containing stills and/or slides and biographies of the principal actors, a story outline, and additional information on producers, directors, proposed ad campaigns, etc. They can be more complex, if a studio deems a particular film of sufficient importance. Press books are primarily pages of pre-made ads of different sizes. These are for use in the newspaper movie schedule section.

Star Trek: The Motion Picture
Kit ....$75–$100
Giant kit, velcro closures, includes novel..............................$150–$250
Book..$20–$30
Star Trek II: The Wrath of Khan
Kit ....$75–$100
Book..$20–$30
Star Trek III: The Search for Spock
Kit ....$50–$75
Book..$15–$20
Star Trek IV: The Voyage Home
Kit ....$40–$60
Book..$10–$15
Star Trek V: The Final Frontier
Kit ....$25–$40
Book..$8–$12

STANDEES

These are color cardboard die-cuts of figures or scenes designed for display in theater lobbies. More complex ones may have lights. These should not be confused with store standees used for various products, which are much more common. Store standees will usually display a product name.

Star Trek: The Motion Picture, lights ....$200–$350
Star Trek II: The Wrath of Khan...$200–$300
Star Trek III: The Search For Spock......................................$150–$250
Star Trek IV: The Voyage Home ....$100–$200
Star Trek V: The Final Frontier ....$75–$125

PROGRAM BOOKS

Unlike most other studio promotional items, program books are designed for sale to the public. Theaters sell the books right along with the popcorn and candy. In recent years, however, program books have become less popular in the United States. Foreign program books are usually identical to the U.S. versions, except for language, and have about the same general value. Books are approximately $8'' \times 11''$ with color covers, usually the movie poster art, and color or black and white interior photos.

Star Trek: The Motion Picture ....$25–$45
Star Trek II: The Wrath of Khan..$25–$45
Star Trek III: The Search For Spock...$20–$30
Star Trek IV: The Voyage Home ....$15–$25
Star Trek V: The Final Frontier ....$10–$20

U.S. and foreign movie programs.

BROCHURES, CAST LISTS, AND NEWSLETTERS

These are all simple studio promotional items handed out in theaters. Brochures can be as simple as a color "Coming Soon" flyer. Newsletters are usually a little more complex with a page or two about the film. Cast lists are often given out at the premiere of the film and are usually just a list of credits on a card stock flyer. Any of these types of items sell from between $2 and $10 regardless of the film.

Commercial Promotional Items

Though the more common and collectible promotional items made available to the public are listed in their respective categories in this book (i.e. posters, glasses, trading cards, etc.), there are many unusual items used by stores and restaurants primarily for display. These include dumps for books and video tapes, standees, mobiles, banners, plastic window displays, counter cards, and dumps for jewelry, buttons, and other small items. While these types of things are undoubtedly collectible, they are very hard to assign a value to. On one hand, there are fewer of them, but on the other hand, they don't fit well into most people's collections. How do you display a large cardboard book rack? Probably the best rule of thumb to use is to use those criteria that apply to all collectibles. More valuable items are those that are older, in better condition, more elaborate, and the most appealing visually. This might mean a dollar or two for a counter dump that held buttons, $50 for a large store window banner, and $100 for an elaborate die-cut cardboard floor display.

PUZZLES

This section is organized alphabetically by manufacturer. Jigsaw puzzles with missing pieces, or missing or damaged boxes, have very little value.

Aviva, 1979

Star Trek: The Motion Picture, 18″ × 24″ color photo jigsaw puzzles, 551 pieces.
Mr. Spock ....$15–$20
Starship U.S.S. Enterprise ....$15–$20

Examples of Star Trek jigsaw puzzles.

H. G. Toys, First Series, 1974

Color cartoon-style artwork (not from the animated series), two different sizes.
Battle on the Planet Klingon, 150 pieces, 10″ × 14″ ....$5–$10
Battle on the Planet Romulon, 150 pieces, 10″ × 14″ ....$5–$10
Capt. Kirk and Officers Beaming Down, 150 pieces, 10″ × 14″................................$5–$10
Attempted Hijacking of the U.S.S. Enterprise and Its Officers, 300 pieces, 14″ × 18″........
....$8–$12
The Starship U.S.S. Enterprise and Its Officers, 300 pieces, 14″ × 18″ ....$8–$12

H. G. Toys, Second Series, 1976

Color artwork. More realistic style than first series. Boxes say "Series II." All are
150 pieces, 14″ × 10″.
The Alien...$8–$12
Capt. Kirk, Mr. Spock, Dr. McCoy ....$8–$12
Force Field Capture ....$8–$12

Larami, 1979

Star Trek: The Motion Picture, 15-piece sliding puzzles.
Kirk ....$5–$10
Spock...$5–$10
Enterprise ....$5–$10

Merrigold Press (See Whitman)

Milton Bradley, 1979

Star Trek: The Motion Picture, 19⅞″ × 13⅞″, 250-piece color photo puzzles. (Ar-
row in Britain did these puzzles in 100-piece versions.)
The Enterprise...$8–$12
Faces of the Future, collage...$8–$12
Sickbay ....$8–$12

Mind's Eye Press, 1986

U.S.S. Enterprise NCC 1701-A, Star Trek IV: The Voyage Home, 18″ × 24″, 551 pieces, color
cutaway artwork...$25–$30

Running Press, 1976*

Incredible Intergalactic Star Trek Crosswork Puzzle, color, 22″ × 34″ poster with puzzle in shape of Enterprise. Came packaged in color envelope with solution ....$5–$10
*See chapter on "Books" for other word and pencil puzzles.

Whitman Frame Tray Puzzles, 1978

Color cartoon-style artwork. Tray measures 8½″ × 11″. Four different. Puzzles with the Whitman brand name use the original TV Star Trek logo. Exact same artwork was used with Star Trek movie logo under Merrigold brand name.
Bridge Scene ....$4–$6
Kirk in Space Suit...$4–$6
Kirk, Spock, and Enterprise..$4–$6
Transporter Scene...$4–$6

Whitman Jigsaw Puzzles, 1978

Color cartoon artwork depicts major characters, ships, and alien planetscapes, 200 pieces each. All are 14″ × 18″.
Collage with Red Box ....$8–$15
Collage with Green Box..$8–$15
Collage with Purple Box...$8–$15
Collage with Yellow Box..$8–$15

RECORDS, TAPES, AND COMPACT DISCS

Audio Novels

This is a current series of dramatic readings, published by Simon and Schuster, by Star Trek personalities done on tape cassette only. All are based on Pocket Star Trek novels.
Enterprise: The First Adventure, 1988, Nimoy and Takei, one cassette.....................$9–$11
Entropy Effect, 1988, Nimoy and Takei, one cassette ....$9–$11
Final Frontier, 1989, Nimoy and Doohan, one cassette ....$9–$11
Gulliver's Fugitives, 1990, Jonathan Frakes, one cassette......................................$9–$11
Kobayashi Maru, 1990, Doohan, one cassette..$9–$11
Lost Years, 1989, Nimoy and Doohan, two cassettes...$14–$16
Spock's World, 1989, Nimoy and Takei, two cassettes ....$14–$16
Strangers from the Sky, 1987, Nimoy and Takei, one cassette...................................$9–$11
Time for Yesterday, 1989, Nimoy and Doohan, one cassette ....$9–$11
Web of the Romulans, 1988, Nimoy and Takei, one cassette ....$9–$11
Yesterday's Son, 1988, Nimoy and Doohan, one cassette...$9–$11
Star Trek IV: The Voyage Home, 1986, Nimoy and Takei..$9–$11
Star Trek V: The Final Frontier, 1989, Nimoy and Takei ....$7–$9

Audio novels.

Some more collectible Star Trek LPs.

Miscellaneous Audio

Captain of the Starship, Canadian pressing of William Shatner—Live!, two 12″ LP albums, Imperial Music, No. 9400 ....$20–$30

Captain of the Starship, another Canadian pressing of William Shatner—Live!, two 12″ LP albums, K-TEL Record, No. 9400 ....$20–$30

The Green Hills of Earth and Gentlemen, Be Seated, by Robert A. Heinlein, read by Leonard Nimoy, 12″ LP album or cassette, Caedmon Records, No. TC 1526 ....$15–$20

Halley's Comet: Once in a Lifetime, narrated by Leonard Nimoy with artificial space music and sound effects by Geodesium, notes by Dr. William Gutsch, Chairman of American Museum, Hayden Planetarium, audio cassette, Caedmon Cassette, No. S 1788, 1986...................
....$10–$15

The Ilustrated Man, by Ray Bradbury, read by Leonard Nimoy, 12″ LP album, Caedmon Records, No. TC 1479 ....$15–$20

Inside Star Trek, recorded by Gene Roddenberry, features William Shatner, Isaac Asimov, Mark Lenard, and DeForest Kelley. Discussion of the origin of the series, the personalities involved, and other insider's information. Selected musical themes, Columbia Records, No. 34279...$15–$20

The Martian Chronicles, by Ray Bradbury, read by Leonard Nimoy, 12″ LP album, Caedmon Records, No. TC 1466 ....$15–$20

Mimsy Were the Borogoves, by Henry Kuttner, read by William Shatner, 12″ LP album, Caedmon Records, No. TC 1509 ....$15–$20

The Mysterious Golem, Leonard Nimoy narrates the story of the Mysterious Golem which, in Jewish folklore, is an artificially created human being endowed with life by supernatural means, 12″ LP album, JRT Records ....$20–$30

The Psychohistorians, from Foundation, by Isaac Asimov, read by William Shatner, 12″ LP album or cassette, Caedmon Records, No. TC 1508 ....$15–$20

Star Fleet Beat, Phasers on Stun, special Star Trek 20th anniversary record, 12″ LP album, Penguin Records ....$15–$20

Star Trek Comedy: The Unofficial Album, collection of comedy skits and songs about Star Trek. Vince Emery Productions, 12″ album or cassette. Each ....$9–$12

Star Trekkin' by "The Firm," 12″, 45 rpm record featuring Star Trekkin' and Dub Trek. Precision Records and Tapes...$10–$12

Star Trekkin' by "The Firm," 7″, 45 rpm ....$6–$8

The Star Trek Philosophy and Star Trek Theme, performed by Gene Roddenberry and the Inside Star Trek Orchestra. From the Inside Star Trek album, 7″, 45 rpm, Columbia Records, No. 3-10448 ....$5–$10

Star Trek Tapes, a compilation of offical press recordings featuring the cast of Star Trek TV show, Jack M. Sell, producer ....$15–$20

Tape Cassettes, Inter Audio Associates, parody of Star Trek, Sterling Bronsan: Space Engineer. A series of four tapes started in 1973 as a lampoon for a college radio station, featuring James T. Clerk and Science Officer Spook, Vols. I–IV ....$25–$35

The Transformed Man, performed by William Shatner. Captain Kirk reads six selections with chorus and instrumental background, 12″ LP album, Decca Records, No. DL 75043 ....
....$40–$70

The Transformed Man and How Insensitive, from the album, The Transformed Man, read by William Shatner, 7″, 45 rpm, Decca Records, No. 32399 ....$10–$15

Trek Bloopers, compiled from unedited sound tapes of six "Third Season" episodes of Star Trek. Unusual record. Features audio bloopers made by original casts, 12″ LP album and cassette, Blue Pear Records, album or cassette ....$10–$15

Voice Tracks, U.S. Marine Corps Toys For Tots, readings by Leonard Nimoy, Clarence Williams III, Charlton Heston, Phyllis Diller, John Wayne, Jimmy Stewart, Jack Webb, Jimmy Durante. Introduction by Efrem Zimbalist, Jr. Music played by U.S. Marine Band. Edward Mulhare, Natalie Wood, Col. Frank Borman, 7″, 33⅓ rpm, Warner Bros.–Sevent Arts Records, No. PRO 381 ....$15–$20

The Voyage of Star Trek, coming attractions, 60-minute radio special, from The Source, NBC Radio's Young Adult Network. Promotional copy, not for sale. Discusses Star Trek from TV years to Star Trek: The Wrath of Khan, 12″ LP album, 1982 ....$20–$30

The War of the Worlds, by H. G. Wells, read by Leonard Nimoy, 12″ LP album, Caedmon Records, No. TC 1520 ....$15–$20

William Shatner—Live!, two-record LP album, dramatic narratives recited with musical background, William Shatner's college tour, Lemli Records, 9400 ....$30–$45

Whales Alive, by Paul Winter and Paul Halley, with narration by Leonard Nimoy and voices of the humpback whales, 12″ album, Living Music, No. 80013–1 ....$15–$20

Songs Performed by Star Trek Personalities

Beyond Antares and Uhura's Theme, sung by Nichelle Nichols, 7″, 45 rpm, R-Way Records, No. RW-1001 ....$5–$10

Consilium and Here We Go 'Round Again, sung by Leonard Nimoy from the album The Way I Feel, 7″, 45 rpm, Dot Records, No. 45–17175 ....$10–$15

Dark Side of the Moon, sung by Nichelle Nichols, two 7″ records, 45 rpm, four songs. EP album jacket opens out to a poster, Americana Records, EP-1 ....$5–$10

Disco Trekin' and Star Child, sung by Grace Lee Whitney (Yeoman Rand from Star Trek) and Star, 7″, 45 rpm, GLW Star Enterprises ....$5–$10

Down to Earth, sung by Nichelle Nichols, eight popular songs sung by Lt. Uhura, 12″ LP album, Epic Records, No. BNZ 6351 ....$15–$25

Leonard Nimoy, 12″ album from Sears, reissues previously recorded Dot records, No. SPS-491 ....$12–$15

Leonard Nimoy Presents Mr. Spock's Music From Outer Space, Leonard Nimoy sings and recites 11 songs, 12″ LP album, Dot Records, No. DLP 25794 ....$25–$50

   Same as above, British version, diffusion, 1973, No. 25156 ....$25–$50

Leonard Nimoy, You Are Not Alone, cassette, MCA. Features some of Nimoy's previously released material, MCA-20409 ....$9–$12

The New World of Leonard Nimoy, Leonard Nimoy sings eight popular songs, 12″ LP album, Dot Records, No. DLP 25966 ....$25–$40

Outer Space/Inner Mind, two-record album contains all of Leonard Nimoy Presents Mr. Spock's Music From Outer Space, and cuts from The Two Sides of Leonard Nimoy, The Touch of Leonard Nimoy, The Way I Feel, and The New World of Leonard Nimoy, two 12″ LP albums, Paramount Records Famous Twinsets PAS, No. 2-1030 ....$20–$30

Please Don't Try to Change My Mind, and I'd Love Making Love to You, sung by Leonard Nimoy, from the album The Way I Feel, 7″, 45 rpm, Dot Records, No. 45–17125 ....$5–$10

Space Odyssey, nine cuts from Leonard Nimoy's five Dot Records albums, Pickwick/33 Records, No. SPC 3199 ....$15–$30

The Sun Will Rise, and Time to Get it Together, sung by Leonard Nimoy from the album The New World of Leonard Nimoy, 7″, 45 rpm, Dot Records, No. 45–17330 ....$5–$10

Take a Star Trip, 45 rpm by Grace Lee Whitney ....$5–$10

The Touch of Leonard Nimoy, Leonard Nimoy sings 11 songs, Dot Records, No. DLP 25910.
....$25–$40

Two Sides of Leonard Nimoy, Leonard Nimoy sings and recites 13 songs, 12″ LP album, Dot Records, No. DLP 25835 ....$35–$60

Uhura Sings, nine songs by Nichelle Nichols, AR-WAY Productions, cassette, 1986..............
....$12–$15

Visit to a Sad Planet, and Star Trek Theme, sung by Leonard Nimoy from the album Leonard Nimoy Presents Mr. Spock's Music from Outer Space, 7", 45 rpm, Dot Records, No. 17038, 1967 ....$5–$10

The Way I Feel, 12 songs sung and narrated by Leonard Nimoy, 12" LP album and reel-to-reel, Dot Records, No. DLP 25883..$20–$35

Soundtracks and Themes

The Cage, and Where No Man Has Gone Before, original TV soundtrack, music composed and conducted by Alexander Courage, 12" LP album, CD, cassette, GNP Crescendo Records, No. GNPS 8006

    Album ....$10–$15
    Cassette ....$8–$11
    CD...$20–$25

Charlie X, The Corbomite Maneuver, Mudd's Women, and The Doomsday Machine, newly recorded from selected episodes of the Paramount Pictures Corp. TV series by the Royal Philharmonic Orchestra, conducted by Fred Steiner, 12" LP album, CD or cassette, Varese Sarabande Records, digital, No. 704.270

    Album ....$10–$15
    Cassette ....$10–$12
    CD...$20–$25

Children's TV Themes, by Cy Payne and His Orchestra, contains theme from Star Trek TV, 12" LP album, Contour Records, No. 2870–185 (English).......................................$15–$20

Classic Space Themes, by the Birchwood Pops Orchestra, includes the main theme from Star Trek: The Motion Picture, 12" LP album, Pickwick Records, No. SPC-3772, stereo ..$10–$15

Close Encounters, performed by Gene Page and His Orchestra, contains theme from Star Trek, 12" LP album, Arista Records, No. AB-4174...$10–$15

The Colors of Love, and Only Star Can Last, fan-produced album with original words and music, 12" LP album, Omicron Ceti Three ....$15–$20

Conquistador, performed by Maynard Ferguson and His Orchestra, contains theme from Star Trek TV, 12" LP album, trumpet solo by Maynard Ferguson, flute solo by Bobby Militello, 1977, Columbia Records, No. PC-34457 ....$10–$15

Dementia Royale, compiled by Dr. Demento, contains Star Trek, a parody of Star Trek by Bobby Pickett and Peter Ferrara, 12" LP album, Rhino Records, No. RNLP 010 ....$10–$15

Dyn-O-Mite Guitar, performed by Billy Strange, contains theme from Star Trek, 12" LP album, GNP Crescendo Record, No. LP 2094 ....$10–$15

Fifty Popular TV Themes, performed by The Bruce Baxter Orchestra, contains main theme from Star Trek TV, two 12" LP albums, Pickwick Records, No. 50 DA 315 ....$15–$20

Genesis Project, two-record album containing new expanded versions not in the original soundtracks of Star Trek II: The Wrath of Khan and Star Trek III: The Search For Spock. Composed and performed by Craig Huxley, two 12" LP albums, Sonic Atmo Spheres, No. 101

    Album ....$20–$30
    Cassette ....$15–$20

The Hustle, performed by Van McCoy and His Orchestra, contains theme from Star Trek TV, 12" LP album, 1976, H & L Records, No. HL69016 698, stereo ....$10–$15

I, Mudd, The Enemy Within, Spectre of the Gun, and Conscience of the King, newly recorded Star Trek, Vol. II. Symphonic suites arranged from the original TV scores, recorded by the Royal Philharmonic Orchestra, conducted by Tony Bremner, 12" LP album, CD or cassette, Label X Record, No. LXDR 704 (stereo-digital)

    Album ....$10–$15
    Cassette ....$10–$12
    CD...$20–$25

Is There in Truth No Beauty?, and Paradise Syndrome, newly recorded Star Trek, Vol. I. Symphonic suites arranged from original TV scores, recorded by the Royal Philharmonic Orchestra, conducted by Tony Bremner, 12" LP Album, CD or cassette, Label X Record, No. LXDR703 (stereo-digital)

    Album ....$10–$15
    Cassette ....$10–$12
    CD...$20–$25

Love Theme From Star Trek: The Motion Picture (A Star Beyond Time), sung by Shaun Cassidy, 7″, 45 rpm, Warner Bros. Records, No. WBS 49154 (not for sale, promotional record) ....$5–$10

Main Theme from Star Trek: The Motion Picture, arranged and conducted by Bob James, 7″, 45 rpm, Tappan Zee (Columbia) Records, No. 1–11171 ....$5–$10

Main Theme From Star Trek: The Motion Picture, from Music From the Original Soundtrack—Star Trek: The Motion Picture, composed and conducted by Jerry Goldsmith, 7″, 45 rpm, Columbia Records, No. 1–11212 ....$5–$10

Masterpiece, performed by Charles Randolph Grean Sounde, contains theme from Star Trek TV, 12″ LP album, Ranwood Records, No. 5–8105..$10–$15

Mirror, Mirror, By Any Other Name, The Trouble with Tribbles, The Empath—Vol. II, symphonic suites from the original TV scores, 1986, Varise Sarabande, 12″ LP, CD or cassette, No. 704-3001
    Album ....$10–$15
    Cassette ....$10–$12
    CD..$20–$25

Music From Return of the Jedi and Other Space Hits, performed by the Odyssey Orchestra, includes main theme from Star Trek TV, by Alexander Courage, 12″ LP album, Sine Qua Non Records, No. SQN 79065–1, stereo...$10–$15

Music From Star Trek and the Black Hole, disco music performed by Meco Monardo, Casablanca Record, No. NBLP 7196 ....$10–$15

Music From the Original Soundtrack—Star Trek: The Motion Picture, music by Jerry Goldsmith, 12″ LP album, CBS/SONY Record, No. 25AP, 1752, Japanese Pressing................
....$15–$20

Nadia's Theme, performed by Lawrence Welk and His Orchestra, contains theme from Star Trek TV, Ranwood Records, No. (S) 8165 ....$10–$15

1984—A Space Odyssey, performed by John Williams and The Boston Pops Orchestra, includes main theme from Star Trek TV and main theme from Star Trek: The Motion Picture, 12″ LP album, J & B Records, stereo, No. JB-177 ....$10–$15

Out of This World, performed by John Williams and The Boston Pops Orchestra, includes the main theme from Star Trek TV and main title from Star Trek: The Motion Picture, Phillips Digital Recording, No. 411-185-1 ....$10–$15

Spaced Out Disco Fever, contains main theme from Star Trek TV, 12″ LP album, Wonderland Records, stereo, No. WLP 315 ....$10–$15

Spectacular Space Hits, performed by The Odyssey Orchestra, contains theme from Star Trek TV, 12″ LP album, Sine Qua Non Records, stereo, NO. SQN 7808............................$10–$15

Starship, Frank Argus, 45 rpm, fan-produced, 1984..$5–$10

Star Tracks, performed by The Cincinnati Pops Orchestra, conducted by Erich Kunzel, contains main theme from Star Trek TV, Telarc Digital Records, stereo, No. DG-10094...............
....$15–$20

Star Trek: The Motion Picture, 7″, 45 rpm, Capital Expositions Record, 1981..........$5–$10

Star Trek: The Motion Picture, music from the original soundtrack, composed and conducted by Jerry Goldsmith, digital recording, Columbia Records, No. AL 36334, 12″ LP, CD or cassette
    Album ....$20–$30
    Cassette ....$15–$25
    CD..$25–$35

Star Trek—Main Theme From The Motion Picture, contains A Star Beyond Time (Love Theme from Star Trek: The Motion Picture) and Star Trek TV theme, performed by The Now Sound Orchestra, 12″ LP album, Synthetic Plastics Record, No. 6001 ....$10–$15

Star Trek—21 Space Hits, contains theme from Star Trek TV, 12″ LP album, Music World, No. EMS-1003 (Music World, Ltd., New Zealand) ....$15–$20

Star Trek II: The Wrath of Khan, original motion picture soundtrack, composed and conducted by James Horner, 12″ LP album, Atlantic Records, No. P-11301 ....$30–$50

Star Trek III: The Search for Spock, The Audio Movie Kit, kit contains transcripts of "The Movie for Radio" and "Behind the Scenes" narrative regarding the story of the movie. Two audio cassette tapes cover the same material, two audio cassette tapes and a script in folder, Riches/Rubinstein and Radio, Inc...$35–$60

Star Trek III: The Search For Spock, original motion picture soundtrack, music composed and conducted by James Horner, two 12″ LP albums, Capital-EMI Record, CD or cassette, No. SKBK 12360, 1984

Album ....$25–$45
Cassette ....$15–$25
CD ....$20–$25

Star Trek IV: The Voyage Home, soundtrack from the movie, MCA, 12″ LP, CD or cassette, MCAC-6195

Album ....$15–$20
Cassette ....$10–$15
CD ....$20–$25

Star Trek V: The Final Frontier, movie soundtrack, Epic, 12″ LP, CD or cassette

Album..$11–$15
Cassette ....$11–$15
CD ....$20–$25

Star Trek Sound Effects, from the original TV soundtrack, GNP Crescendo, 12″ LP, CD or cassette, No. GNPS-8010

Album ....$10–$15
Cassette ....$10–$12
CD ....$20–$25

Star Trek: The Next Generation, music from the original TV soundtrack, GNP Crescendo, 12″ LP, cassette or CD, GNPS-8012

Album ....$10–$15
Cassette ....$10–$12
CD ....$20–$25

Star Wars, performed by Ferrante and Teicher, contains theme from Star Trek TV, 12″ LP album, United Artists Record, No. UA-LA855-G, 1978...$15–$20

Themes From E. T. and More, arranged and conducted by Walter Murphy, contains main theme from Star Trek TV, 12″ LP album, MCA, No. MCA-6114 ....$10–$15

Theme From Star Trek TV, from the album Masterpiece, by The Charles Randolph Grean Sounde, 7″, 45 rpm, Ranwood Records, No. R-10444...$5–$10

Theme From Star Trek (TV), Greatest Science Fiction Hits, performed by Neil Norman and His Cosmic Orchestra, 12″ LP album, No. GNP-2128, 1979, also available on cassette ....
....$10–$15

Theme From Star Trek, performed by Tristar Orchestra and Chorus, produced by John Townsley, 7″, 45 rpm, Tristar Records, No. T-101 ....$5–$10

Theme From Star Trek, performed by The Jeff Wayne Space Shuttle, Wonderland Records, No. WLP 301 ....$10–$15

Theme From Star Trek, by Warp Nine, fan-produced electronically synthesized space music. Record was sold to make money to get Star Trek back on TV, 7″, 45rpm, Privilege Records
....$5–$10

Theme From Star Trek, performed by Ferrante and Teicher, 7″, 45 rpm, United Artists Record, No. UA-S1173-Y from the album Star Wars, United Artists, No. UA-LA-855-6, 1978
....$5–$10

Theme From Star Trek, performed by Meco Monardo from the album Music From Star Trek and the Black Hole, 7″, 45 rpm, Casablanca Record, No. NB2239DJ............................$5–$10

Theme From Star Trek, performed by Gene Page and His Orchestra, from the album Close Encounters, No. ARI (S) 4174, 7″, 45 rpm, Arista Record, No. ARI-0322....................$5–$10

Theme From Star Trek, performed by Billy Strange, from the album Dyn-O-Mite Guitar, 7″, 45 rpm, GNP Crescendo Record, No. GNP 800 ....$5–$10

Theme From Star Trek: The Motion Picture, on Greatest Science Fiction Hits II, performed by Neil Norman and His Cosmic Orchestra, 12″ LP album, GNP Crescendo Records, No. GNPS 2133, also available on cassette..$10–$15

Theme From Star Trek II: The Wrath of Khan, performed by James Horner and Orchestra, from the original soundtrack Star Trek II: The Wrath of Khan, 7″, 45 rpm, Atlantic Records, No. 4057, 1982...$10–$15

Theme From Star Trek III, by James Horner, from the original soundtrack Star Trek III: The Search for Spock, 7″, 45 rpm, Capital Records, No. P-B-5365 ....$8–$12

The Theme Scene, performed by Henry Mancini and His Orchestra, contains theme from Star Trek TV, 12″ LP album, Victor Records, No. AQLI-3052..$10–$15

TV Themes, performed by the Ventures, contains theme from Star Trek TV, 12″ LP album, United Artists Records, No. US-LA 717-G...$10–$15
Very Together, performed by Deodata, contains main theme from Star Trek TV, 12″ album, MCA Records, No. S-2219, 1976...$10–$15

Star Trek Stories

Star Trek: The Motion Picture, a read-along adventure record with 24-page color illustrated book, 7″, 33⅓ rpm, Buena Vista Record, No. 461, also available on cassette, Buena Vista Records, No. 161-DC...$10–$15
Star Trek II: The Wrath of Khan, a read-along adventure record with 24-page, full-color illustrated book, 7″, 33⅓ rpm, Buena Vista Records, No. 162-DC.................................$10–$15
Star Trek III: The Search for Spock, a read-along adventure record with 24-page, full-color illustrated book, 7″, 33⅓ rpm, Buena Vista Record, No. 463, also available on cassette, Buena Vista Records, No. 163-DC...$10–$15
Star Trek IV: The Voyage Home, a read-along adventure record with 24-page, full-color illustrated book, 7″, 33⅓ rpm, Buena Vista Records, No. 171DC, also available on cassette......
....$10–$15
Star Trek, book and record set, contains adventure story Passage to Moauv, 7″, 45 rpm record and 20-page illustrated book. Two different covers: one, a color photo of Spock, Kirk, and the Enterprise (Peter Pan, 1979); the other (an earlier edition), drawing of Kirk and Spock and a strange animal. Power Records, 1975, No. PR-25 ....$5–$10
Star Trek, book and record set, contains adventure story The Crier in Emptiness, 7″, 45 rpm record and 20-page full-color illustrated book. Two different covers: one, a color photo of Kirk, Spock, and McCoy (Peter Pan, 1979, No. 26); the other (an earlier edition), a drawing of Kirk, Spock, and Uhura. Power Records, 1975 ....$5–$10
Star Trek, book and record set, contains adventure story Dinosaur Planet, 7″, 45 rpm record and 20-page full-color illustrated book, Peter Pan Records, No. PR-45 ....$5–$10
Star Trek, book and record set, contains adventure story The Robot Masters, 7″, 45 rpm record and 20-page full-color illustrated book, Peter Pan Records, No. PR-46.........................$5–$10
Star Trek, book and record set, contains the two adventure stories A Mirror for Futility and The Time Stealer, 12″ LP album and 16-page, full-color comic book, Power Records, No. BR513. (These two adventure stories are also recorded on Peter Pan Records, No. 8168.).......
....$5–$10
Star Trek, book and record set, contains the two adventure stories The Crier in Emptiness and Passage to Moauv, 12″ LP album and 16-page, full-color comic book, Peter Pan Records, No. BR 522. (These two adventure stories are also recorded on Power Records, No. 8158.)...........
....$5–$10
Star Trek, five incredible all-new action adventures: The Time Stealer, In Vino Veritas, To Starve a Fleaver, Dinosaur Planet, and Passage to Moauv. 12″ LP album, Peter Pan Records, No. 1110...$5–$10
Star Trek, original stories for children, inspired by Star Trek—In Vino Veritas, 7″, 45 rpm, Power Records, No. F-1298..$3–$5
Star Trek, original stories for children, inspired by Star Trek—The Human Factor, 7″, 45 rpm, Peter Pan Records, No. 1516 ....$3–$5
Star Trek, original stories for children, inspired by Star Trek—The Time Stealer, 7″, 45 rpm, Power Records, No. 2305 ....$3–$5
Star Trek, original stories for children, inspired by Star Trek—To Starve a Fleaver, 7″, 45 rpm, Power Records, No. 2307 ....$3–$5
Star Trek, three exciting new complete stories: Passage to Moauv, In Vino Veritas, and The Crier in Emptiness. 12″ LP album, Power Records, No. 8158. (These stories are also recorded on Peter Pan Records, No. BR 522.) ....$5–$10
Star Trek, four exciting all-new action adventure stories: The Time Stealer, To Starve a Fleaver, The Logistics of Stampede, and a Mirror of Futility. 12″ LP album, Power Records, No. 8168. (This album appears in two different jackets.) ....$5–$10
Star Trek, four exciting all-new action adventure stories: The Man Who Trained Meteors, The Robot Masters, Dinosaur Planet, and The Human Factor. 12″ LP album, Peter Pan Records, No. 8236...$5–$10
Star Trek and Other Movie Songs, Kid Stuff Records. Contains Star Trek TV theme along with other TV (not movie, as the title implies) themes. Cover shows generic spaceship with planet in background, 1978...$5–$10

SCHOOL AND OFFICE SUPPLIES

Because they are extremely easy to produce (and virtually worthless as collectibles), the large volume of unlicensed and fan-made stationery items will be omitted from this section. Types of items in this category include writing paper, note cards, business cards, stickers, bookmarks, etc.; almost any one-color, printed paper product that can be made quickly and inexpensively.

Bookcovers, TK Graphics, lined vinyl in assorted colors with silkscreened design on front. Two sizes, 5″ × 7½″ and 6 × 9½″

Imperial Klingon Fleet	$3–$6
Star Fleet Command	$3–$6
Star Fleet Command, Intelligence Division	$3–$6
Star Fleet Headquarters Tactical Operations Center	$3–$6
United Federation of Planets Diplomatic Sevice	$3–$6
U.S.S. Enterprise (outline of ship)	$3–$6
U.S.S. Enterprise, NCC-1701	$3–$6
Vulcan Science Academy	$3–$6

Bookmark, One Stop Posters, 1987. Color photo of Next Generation Enterprise and logo at top. "Explore new worlds with books!" at bottom. 7″ long ....$1–$3
Checkbook Cover, Lincoln Enterprises, plush maroon vinyl checkbook/calculator. Small gold-plated original TV command symbol on outside lower left corner ....$20–$25
Checkbook Cover, TK Graphics, lined vinyl in assorted colors with silkscreened design on front, 6½″ × 3½″

Imperial Klingon Fleet	$2–$5
Star Fleet Command	$2–$5
Star Fleet Command, Intelligence Division	$2–$5
Star Fleet Headquarters Tactical Operations Center	$2–$5
United Federation of Planets Diplomatic Service	$2–$5
U.S.S. Enterprise (outline of ship)	$2–$5
U.S.S. Enterprise, NCC-1701	$2–$5
Vulcan Science Academy	$2–$5

Desk Set, Tel Rad, 1975. Gray plastic pen decorated with original TV Enterprise. Stand has nameplate ....$15–$20
Desk Set, Rarities Mint, 1990. Marble base with gold-plated silver Enterprise (original TV) clock coin. Includes gold-plated pen. Numbered limited edition............................$100–$125
Erasers, Diener Industries, 1983. Six different character heads and ships from Star Trek III. Assorted colors. Came blister packed on color header card with Star Trek III logo

Kirk	$2–$4
Spock	$2–$4
McCoy	$2–$4
Kruge	$2–$4
Enterprise	$2–$4
Excelsior	$2–$4

Memo Holder, Tal Rad, 1975. Pictures original TV Enterprise......................................$6–$12
Nameplates, One Stop Posters, 1988. Color photo of Next Generation Enterprise with words "Star Trek" below. Packaged in plastic bag of 24 with blue and yellow header ....$3–$5
Pencil, Lincoln Enterprises. Blue with star design and "Star Trek Lives" in gold..........$1–$2

Rarities Mint desk set.

Pen, Smithsonian, 1979. Floater pen containing Enterprise. From Air and Space Museum gift shop ....$5–$10
Portfolios, TK Graphics. Lined, vinyl zippered pouches. Assorted colors with silkscreened design, 10½″ × 16″
  Imperial Klingon Fleet...$8–$12
  Star Fleet Academy...$8–$12
  Star Fleet Command ....$8–$12
  Star Fleet Command, Intelligence Division...$8–$12
  Star Fleet Headquarters Tactical Operations Center.......................................$8–$12
  United Federation of Planets Diplomatic Service ....$8–$12
  U.S.S. Enterprise (outline of ship)..$8–$12
  U.S.S. Enterprise, NCC-1701..$8–$12
  Vulcan Science Academy ....$8–$12
Rubber Stamps, Aviva, 1979. White or blue plastic two-piece cylinders. Top is stamp, bottom is ink pad. Paper decal shows design. Came blister packed on header card with Star Trek: The Motion Picture logo and small inset picture of Spock, four different
  Kirk ....$3–$5
  Spock..$3–$5
  Vulcan salute ....$3–$5
  Enterprise ....$3–$5
Rubber Stamps, fan made. Blocks of wood with design affixed to bottom. Numerous designs or made to order...$5–$10
Stationery, Lincoln Enterprises
  Original Star Trek TV stationery, top has black Enterprise and and Star Trek logo on lined blue background
    Letter size (15)..$5–$10
    Envelopes (15) ....$5–$10
    Memo pad ....$2–$4
  Star Trek: The Motion Picture, blue movie Enterprise on light blue star background
    Letter size (15)..$5–$10
    Envelopes (15) ....$5–$10
    Memo pad ....$2–$4
  Star Trek III: The Search for Spock, standard logo with small silhouette of Enterprise above words
    Letter size (15)..$5–$10
    Envelopes (15) ....$5–$10
    Memo pad ....$2–$4
  Star Trek: The Next Generation, publicity memo. Logo on light blue background
    Letter size (15)..$5–$10
    Envelopes (15) ....$5–$10
    Memo pad ....$2–$4
  Star Trek: The Next Generation, logo over spiral galaxy design on dark blue
    Letter size (15)..$5–$10
    Envelopes (15) ....$5–$10
    Memo Pad ....$2–$4

SCRIPTS

Scripts are one of the most popular items among collectors and one of the hardest to authenticate. Unless you have positive proof to the contrary, you should assume the script is a copy, not an original. All scripts these days, including the ones the actors use, are photocopies. Different color pages, sometimes used for revisions, can be a clue, though by no means a conclusive one to authenticity. People using scripts on the set often write notes in the margin and an autograph, of course, adds to the value even if the script is a copy. Assuming it is a copy, a reasonable price for a TV script would be $10–$20, with any of the movies at $20–$30. If you are sure the script is original, $200–$500 would be reasonable depending on the episode or movie.

STILLS, SLIDES, AND PHOTOGRAPHS

There is a great deal of confusion about these items among collectors. To start with, many collectors do not realize the difference between lithographs and photographs. A photograph is a film process. A lithograph is a printing process. Lithographs are much cheaper to produce than photographs and are practical only in large quantities. Where it concerns films, all one needs to do to make slides is have a print of the film and a pair of scissors. Another slide or a photograph can be made easily from any frame of the film. For this reason, there are as many possible photographs and slides from a film as there are frames in that film. All of the "stills" in this section and others (including posters and lobby cards) are therefore lithographs. Fair prices for slides range from about $.50–$2 for mounted slides, less for unmounted film clips. Photographs should sell for $2–$4 for black and white photographs, $5–$10 for color.

Disney/MGM Studios, black and white cards with picture of characters for autographing when actor is present at the attraction..$1–$3
Fantasy House, set of six 4″ × 6″ mini-posters, Kirk, Sulu, Kirk and Chekov, McCoy, Spock, and Spock close-up. Each..$2–$5
Kelly Freas Portfolio, 1976. Set of seven color artwork stills of characters, 8½″ × 11″. (This set was also incorporated into a one-shot magazine, *Officers of the Bridge*.)...............$10–$15
Langley and Associates, 1976. All are 8″ × 10″ color on light card stock, licensed

Enterprise, surrounded by alien ships...$1–$2
Chekov, portrait ....$1–$2
Kirk, Spock, McCoy, and Scotty at conference table ....$1–$2
The crew on a barren planet..$1–$2
The crew in mid-beam ....$1–$2
The crew, portrait on bridge..$1–$2
Dr. McCoy, close-up portrait ....$1–$2
The Enterprise, captioned "Star Trek"...$1–$2
Enterprise firing phasers ....$1–$2
Enterprise following another Federation ship..$1–$2
Enterprise in starburst ....$1–$2
Kirk
   Cocked head, looking flirtatious...$1–$2
   Head shot of the captain ....$1–$2
   Looking seductive..$1–$2
   Surrounded by Tribbles..$1–$2
   Three-quarter shot in dress uniform...$1–$2
   Using communicators ....$1–$2
Lt. Uhura, color portrait..$1–$2
Mr. Scott in dress uniform, looking tense ....$1–$2
Spock
   Close-up with beard...$1–$2
   Color portrait..$1–$2
   Giving Vulcan hand signal...$1–$2
   Rare smile ....$1–$2
Spock and Kirk, seen through hole in cavern ....$1–$2
Sulu on the bridge..$1–$2

Lincoln Enterprises Art Prints, by Doug Little, color. Star Trek: The Motion Picture, 11″ × 14″

Chapel, Chekov, Decker, Ilia, Klingon, McCoy, Saavik, Scotty, Spock, Sulu, Uhura..$1–$3
Lincoln Enterprises Art Prints, by Probert, color. Star Trek TV show, 8½″ × 11″
Chapel, Chekov, Enterprise, Kirk, McCoy, Scotty, Spock, Sulu, Uhura......................$1–$2
Lincoln Enterprises, Evolution of the Enterprise, starship in different phases of conception, 12 different pictures per set ....$4–$6
Lincoln Enterprises, Star Trek: The Next Generation, 8½″ × 11″, color
Data, Dr. Crusher, Enterprise, Geordi, Picard, Riker, Tasha Yar, Troi, Wesley, Worf...$1–$3

Lincoln Enterprises, Wallet Pictures, color, 2″ × 3″, 15 per set

Costumes No. 1, per set ....$1–$3
Costumes No. 2, per set ....$1–$3
Kirk, per set...$1–$3
Make-up and aliens, per set ....$1–$3
Scenes from Star Trek: The Motion Picture, per set ....$1–$3
Scenes from Star Trek: The Motion Picture, action, per set...........................$1–$3
Spock, per set..$1–$3
Stars and groups (Star Trek: The Motion Picture), per set.............................$1–$3
Star Trek: The Wrath of Khan
   No. 1, per set...$1–$3
   No. 2, per set...$1–$3
   No. 3, per set...$1–$3
   No. 4, per set...$1–$3
Star Trek TV series No. 1, per set...$1–$3
Star Trek TV series No. 2, per set...$1–$3
Star Trek TV series No. 3, per set...$1–$3
Star Trek III
   No. 1, per set...$1–$3
   No. 2, per set...$1–$3
   No. 3, per set...$1–$3
   No. 4, per set...$1–$3
Lincoln Enterprises, Weapons and Field Equipment, color, 12 different pictures per set ....
....$3–$5

Note: *Lincoln also did several series of postcards. (See "Postcards" section.)*
Lobbie Cards and Stills (*See* "Promotional Items" section)
Print of U.S. Space Shuttle Enterprise, with the Starship Enterprise in background, "To Go Places and Do Things That Have Never Been Done Before . . ."......................................$3–$5
Star Trek Episode Cards, fan produced, large picture with three smaller insets on each card, color, 1978

All Our Yesterdays..$2–$4
Amok Time ....$2–$4
Bloopers ....$2–$4
The Cage..$2–$4
City on the Edge of Forever...$2–$4
Doomsday Machine ....$2–$4
Journey to Babel ....$2–$4
Mirror, Mirror ....$2–$4
Paradise Syndrome ....$2–$4
Patterns of Force ....$2–$4
Star Trek..$2–$4
Tholian Web...$2–$4
Trouble With Tribbles..$2–$4
What Are Little Girls Made Of?...$2–$4
Where No Man Has Gone Before...$2–$4
Star Trek Galore, 1976, unlicensed, color, 8″ × 10″ or 8½″ × 11″

Alien ship firing lasers..$1–$2
The bridge, Chekov and Sulu in forefront..$1–$2
The bridge, Kirk, Spock, Uhura, and Mr. Chekov..................................$1–$2
Captain Pike, early episode with Jeffery Hunter ....$1–$2
Chekov, portrait ....$1–$2
The crew, minus Captain Kirk ....$1–$2
The crew, on the bridge of the Enterprise...$1–$2
The crew, portrait on bridge...$1–$2
The crew, suspense on the bridge ....$1–$2
Dr. McCoy, Captain Kirk, and Mr. Spock ....$1–$2
The Enterprise firing phasers...$1–$2
The Enterprise looming overhead...$1–$2
The Enterprise surrounded by alien ships...$1–$2
The Galileo zooming through space ....$1–$2
Kirk drowning in Tribbles ....$1–$2

Kirk looking debonair..$1–$2
Kirk with Federation flag...$1–$2
Kirk and Spock shooting phasers at the Horta ....$1–$2
Mr. Scott looking worried...$1–$2
Scott on the bridge of the Enterprise ....$1–$2
Spock
   Aiming phaser...$1–$2
   Giving Vulcan hand gesture...$1–$2
   Making a point...$1–$2
   A rare display of emotion ....$1–$2
   With beard..$1–$2
   With child Vulcan ....$1–$2
   With harp..$1–$2
   With three-dimensional chess board ....$1–$2
Sulu, portrait..$1–$2
The Transporter Room, Kirk, McCoy, Uhura, Scotty, beaming.................$1–$2
The Tribbles, Captain Kirk looking dismayed...$1–$2
Uhura and Chekov smiling on the bridge...$1–$2

TOYS AND CRAFTS

Toys are one of the most intense areas of interest to Star Trek collectors. They are probably one of the best areas of investment, not only because of the demand within this field, but also because of the large market in general toy collecting. A toy is much more desirable in the original packaging, and the better the condition of the packaging, the more valuable the toy. A toy out of the box is worth about 25% of the value with box. Incomplete toys are to be avoided as they are of little interest to collectors. This section is organized alphabetically by product.

Note: *Galoob Toy Co. advertised several* Star Trek: The Next Generation *toys which were never produced. These included three cardboard action playsets (the bridge, the transporter room, and the alien planet), a plastic U.S.S. Enterprise Starship Action Playset, a flying Enterprise toy, and a Ferengi die-cast metal ship. Though pictured on many of the Star Trek products Galoob did produce, these items were never manufactured.*

Left: These and the ten different action figures are all of The Next Generation items made by Galoob. Right: Larami Star Trek binoculars.

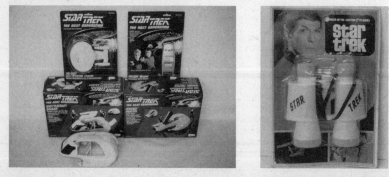

Mego bridges for original TV, 8″, and Star Trek: The Motion Picture 3¾″ action figures.

General Items

Action Fleet, Star Trek: The Motion Picture, 1979. Color cardboard mobile of various ships, candy promotion ....$20–$30

Astrotank, original TV show, Remco, 1967. Box pictures toy and color photos from show. Includes three figures and four shells for gun, very rare ....$900–$1,500

Belt, Buckle, and Insignia, Star Trek: The Motion Picture, South Bend, 1979. Thermal strip and storage compartment in buckle. Box has color photos on front top and header.....$15–$25

Binoculars, Larami, 1968. White and orange with "Star Trek" logo. Blister packed on color cardboard header depicting Spock...$35–$50

Bop Bag, Azrak-Hamway, 1975. Inflatable plastic Spock. Came packaged in 6″ × 5″ box. Color box art shows bag and Enterprise..$75–$100

Bridge, "Star Trek U.S.S. Enterprise Action Playset," Mego, 1975. Designed to be used with 8″ dolls. Blue plastic fold-out with picture of Enterprise on front. Accessories included two stools, console, captain's chair, and three screens. Box art showed toy with figures ....$150–$250

Bridge, Star Trek: The Motion Picture, "U.S.S. Enterprise Bridge," Mego, 1980. Designed to be used with 3¾″ action figures. White molded plastic. Box art shows toy and figures............ ....$125–$200

Cartoon Capers, Wiggins Teape, 1978. Made in France for British market. Battery-powered light box overlays and colored pins...$50–$75

Colorforms Star Trek Adventure Set, Colorforms, 1975. Plastic stick-ons and color cardboard bridge scene. Color box art shows Kirk, Spock, McCoy, and Enterprise ....$20–$30

Color N' Recolor Game Cloth, Star Trek, Avalon, 1979. 40″ × 36″ reusable plastic game cloth, eight crayons and sponge. Color box art shows children coloring cloth............$15–$25

Command Communications Console, Mego, 1976. Approximately 13″ long, blue plastic with light-up screen. Working toy base station to be used with walkie-talkies. Box art shows Spock and toy...$100–$150

Communicators, "Star Trek Astro-Walkie Talkies," Remco, 1967. Blue plastic cups with handgrip connected by string. Blister packed on cardboard header with line art of Kirk, Spock, and Enterprise ....$40–$50

Communicators, "Star Trek Inter-Space Communicator," Lone Star (British), 1974. Black and yellow plastic cups with handgrip connected by string. Came in blue 6″ × 9½″ box with line art of Kirk, Spock, and Enterprise ....$25–$35

Communicators, Mego, 1976. Blue plastic with flip-up grid and retractable antennae. Working toy walkie-talkies. Sold in pairs. Early models were boxed. Later packaging was 9″ × 14″ cardboard header. Both package styles utilized color art of characters and toy........$125–$200

Communicators, "Star Trek: The Motion Picture Wrist Communicators," Mego, 1980. Plastic wrist band walkie-talkies attached by wire to battery belt pack. Sold in pairs, 6½″ × 4½″ box. Color art shows toys. Low header shows logo and Enterprise....................................$175–$225

Communicators. Top: Mego, 1976. Bottom left to right: Lonestar, Star Trek V, and Mego wrist communicators.

Communicators, P.J. McNerney & Assoc., Inc., 1989. Black plastic with flip-up grid and retractable antennae. Working toy walkie-talkies. Proctor and Gamble Star Trek V promotion. Plain white box (mail order only item). Sold in pairs ....$40–$65
Controlled Space Flight, Remco (Burbank in Britain), 1976. Plastic Enterprise counterbalanced on hub connected by wire to control lever. Battery powered, includes color printed background board with "Star Trek" logo and pictures of ships and three objects to be retrieved, 23½" × 6" box shows photo of toy ....$150–$175
Figurine Painting, Crafts by Whiting (division of Milton Bradley), Star Trek: The Motion Picture, 1979. Blister packed, includes plastic figurine, brush, and five paints. Color header art, Kirk and Spock were produced..$15–$25
Frisbee, Remco, 1967. Flying U.S.S. Enterprise. "Star Trek" and Spock decal ....$25–$50
Happy Meals, McDonald's premium, 1979. Star Trek: The Motion Picture. Colorful cardboard boxes with games. Included small prize. Six different. Price each ....$6–$10
Helmet, Enco (Remco), 1976. Plastic with flashing red light on top. Included decals for characters. Electronic sound, color box art of child wearing toy ....$100–$150
I.D. Set, Star Trek: The Motion Picture, Larami, 1979. Red plastic folder. Blister packed on header with color photo art ....$5–$15
Kite, Hi-Flyer, 1975. Pictures original TV Enterprise or Spock................................$15–$25
Kite, Aviva, 1979. Star Trek: The Motion Picture. Pictures Spock, assorted colors ....$10–$20
Kite, Lever Bros. promotional, 1984. Star Trek III. Pictures movie Enterprise ....$10–$20
Magic Putty, Larami, 1979. Star Trek: The Motion Picture. Putty comes in blue plastic egg, blister packed with tube of transfer solution on cardboard header with photo of Kirk and Spock..$5–$10
Magic Slates, Whitman, 1979. Four different designs: Enterprise (original TV), Kirk, Spock, Kirk and Spock. Each ....$5–$10
Metal Detector, Jetco, 1976. Working toy metal detector. White with "Property U.S.S. Enterprise" decal. Red and white 24" × 10" box..$200–$350
Mission to Gamma VI, Mego, 1976. 18" high. Plastic "Cave Creature." Movable jaws, trap door, and cardboard base. Glove manipulator. Comes with four small, colored plastic "Gamma People." Comes in large dark blue box with photo of toy....................................$700–$1,000
Mix 'n Mold, plaster casting set, Catalog Shoppe, 1975. Mold, molding compound, paint, and brush to make character. Three separate kits available: Kirk, Spock or McCoy. Box shows color artwork of character...$25–$50

Assorted Mego toys from 1976.

Movie Viewer, Chemtoy, 1967. 3″ red and black plastic viewer toy. Includes toy film strips. Blister packed. Color header shows color photo of characters..$10–$15

Paint By Numbers, Hasbro, 1972. Canvas paint and instructions. Two sizes:

Large, 12″ × 19″ box, photo of Kirk, Spock, and Enterprise ....$50–$75

Small, 11″ × 11″ box, photo of Kirk, Spock, and Enterprise.......................................$35–$50

Pen and Poster Kit, Open Door, 1976. Four different: Enemies of the Federation, Journeys of the Enterprise, Star Trek Lives, Tour of the Enterprise. Line posters and felt-tipped pens, 14″ × 22″. Came boxed or bagged with header. Box art shows Enterprise, logo, and crew members. Each..$25–$40

Pen and Poster Kit, Open Door, "How Do You Doodle." Two original TV posters and pens ....$15–$25

Pen and Poster Kit, Aviva, 1979. Star Trek: The Motion Picture. One 14″ × 20″ poster and five pens ....$15–$20

Pen and Poster Kit, Placo, 1984. Star Trek III: The Search for Spock 3-D poster set. Comes with poster, 3-D plastic overlay, 3-D glasses, and four felt-tip pens. Cover photo of Enterprise with small insets of characters ....$15–$20

Phaser, Remco, 1967, "Star Trek Astro Buzz-Ray Gun." Early ray gun-type toy had three-color flash beam. Came packaged in box with color Star Trek TV artwork.............$125–$150

Phaser (Ray Gun), Larami, 1968. White plastic flashlight toy with "Star Trek" logo. Blister packed. Color header art ....$20–$35

Phaser, "Star Trek Phaser Gun," Remco, 1975. Flashlight toy projects target. Electronic sound. Black plastic shaped like pistol phaser, 8″ × 11″ box. Color art shows toy, Kirk, and Spock...$40–$75

Phaser, Azrak-Hamway, 1976. Plastic with "Star Trek" logo. Blister packed. Header art shows Enterprise ....$15–$25

Phaser, "Star Trek Super Phaser II Target Game," Mego, 1976. Target reflector game. Black plastic phaser-shaped toy and reflector with picture of Klingon ship, 8″ × 10″ box. Color art shows Kirk and Spock. Reverse pictures toy ....$30–$45

Phaser, South Bend, 1979. Star Trek: The Motion Picture. Set included two gray plastic phasers. Electronic dueling game. Box art depicts toys...$75–$125

Phaser, Daisy, 1984. Star Trek III. White and blue plastic gun has light and sound effects. "Star Trek" logo on handgrip, 6½″ × 10½″ window box. Color art shows Kirk, Spock, and Klingon from movies and toy ....$40–$75

Phaser, Galoob, 1988. Star Trek: The Next Generation. Gray plastic light and sound hand phaser toy. Blister packed. Color photo on header shows Yar, Riker, and Enterprise ..$15–$25

Phaser Battle Game, Mego, 1976. Battery-powered electronic target game. Black plastic. Approximately 13″ high. LED scoring lights, sound effects, and adjustable speed controls. Large red box with color artwork of Spock and toy ....$300–$500

Planetarium, Mego, 1976, "Star Trek Intergalactic Planetarium." Large plastic toy planetarium. Extremely rare. Possibly only prototypes made...$1,200–$1,500

Pocket Flix, Ideal, 1978. Hand-held movie viewer with film cartridge with scenes from original TV episode "By Any Other Name." Battery operated. Came packaged in window box...... ....$30–$50

Left: Assorted phaser toys. Right: Mego phaser battle game.

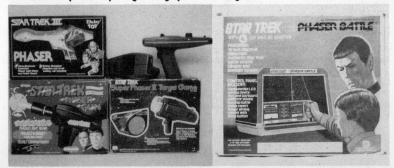

Left: Avalon Space Design Center. Right: Azrak Hamway Spock parachutist.

Saucer Gun, Azrak-Hamway, 1976. Plastic, phaser-shaped. Shoots 2″ plastic spinners. Three spinners included. Blister packed on color header picturing Kirk and Spock...............$25–$50

Space Design Center, Avalon, 1979. Star Trek: The Motion Picture. Craft kit consists of blue plastic tray, crew member cutouts, paints, pens, crayons, etc. and project book, 14½″ × 18½″ box shows photo of child and kit....................$125–$175

Space Viewer, Larami, 1979. Star Trek: The Motion Picture. Dome-shaped viewer toy with two film strips. Blister packed on color header with photos of Kirk, Spock, and aliens ....$15–$25

Sky Diving Parachutist, Azrak-Hamway, 1974. 4½″ painted weighted figure attached to plastic parachute with "Star Trek" logo. Blister packed on color header with artwork of Enterprise. Kirk or Spock....................$20–$35

Star Trekulator, Mego, 1976. Blue, plastic, battery-powered desk-top calculator. LED. and sound effects. Console shows bridge scene from original TV show. 6″ × 10″ box shows color artwork of Spock and toy....................$100–$150

String Art Kit, Open Door, 1976. Craft kit with pins and colored string to create picture on 18″ × 24″ background. Color box art shows completed work....................$40–$75

Telescreen, Console, Mego, 1976. Battery-operated target game. Light and sound effects. Plastic. Approximately 14″ × 10″. Black 10″ square box has artwork of Kirk, Spock, and toy. ....$125–$200

Tracer Gun, Rayline (Ray Plastic, Grand Toys in Canada), 1966. Plastic pistol, colored plastic discs. Discs included. Blister packed. Color header shows Kirk, Spock, and Enterprise ....$30–$50

Tracer Gun Discs (Jet Discs), Rayline, 1966. 100 replacement discs for "Tracer Gun." Blister packed on color header showing toy ....$5–$10

Tracer Scope, Rayline, 1968. Rifle version of "Tracer Gun." Included discs. Blister packed on color header showing Kirk, Spock, and Enterprise ....$100–$175

Transporter, Palitoy (British), 1976. Spinning cylinder allows figure to "dis-appear." This is actually the transporter part of the Mego 1976 bridge for the 8″ action figures. Comes in box with color artwork....................$60–$95

Tribbles, popular souvenir item. Balls of fur in various sizes and colors. Some with squeakers. All are fan produced. Mego advertised a boxed tribble along with its other toy line, but it is doubtful any were ever produced other than possible prototypes ....$2–$8

Tricorder, Mego, 1976. Blue, plastic, battery-operated working toy tape recorder. Flip-open top and plastic shoulder strap. Includes tape with excerpts from "The Menagerie" TV episode. 8″ × 11″ box displays color artwork of Kirk, Spock, and toy ....$125–$200

Utility Belt, Remco, 1975. Miniature black plastic phaser, tricorder, communicator, and belt with "Star Trek" buckle. Packaged in 8″ × 14½″ window box. At least two styles of box art are known. Both depict Kirk, Spock, and the Enterprise ....$75–$125

View-Master, GAF, 1968. Three viewer reels with scenes from "Omega Glory" TV episode. Includes 16-page story booklet. Color envelope shows photo of Enterprise and other starship ....$5–$10

Left: Tracer gun and extra package of discs. Right: Assorted water pistols.

View-Master, GAF, 1974. "Mr. Spock's Time Trek." Three viewer reels with scenes from "Yesteryear" animated episode. Includes 16-page story booklet. Color envelope art shows scenes from episode ....$5–$10
View-Master (Talking), GAF, 1974. "Mr. Spock's Time Trek." Three reels for talking viewer. Packed in 8″ × 8″ box with color scenes from "Yesteryear" episode ....$10–$20
View-Master, GAF, 1979. Star Trek: The Motion Picture. Three reels with scenes from movie. Includes story booklet. Color envelop shows movie logo...$5–$10
View-Master Double-Vue, GAF, 1981. Star Trek: The Motion Picture. Double plastic cassette with two film strips. Blister packed on color header with movie logo..........................$10–$20
View-Master Gift Pak, GAF, 1979. Star Trek: The Motion Picture. Set includes viewer, three reels, 3-D poster, and glasses. Packaged in cylindrical cardboard can with plastic lid. Container depicts child with toy and photos of characters in background.....................................$50–$75
View-Master, View-Master International, 1982. Star Trek II. Three viewer reels blister packed on color header with photo of Enterprise and logo ....$5–$10
Water Pistol, Azrak-Hamway, 1975. Plastic, phaser-shaped. Blister packed on color header with characters ....$20–$30
Water Pistol, "U.S.S. Enterprise Water Gun," Azrak-Hamway, 1976. White plastic shaped like Enterprise. Blister packed on color header with artwork of Enterprise and photos of Kirk and Spock..$35–$50
Water Pistol, Aviva, 1979. Star Trek: The Motion Picture. Gray plastic replica of early movie phaser. Blister packed on monotone header with artwork of Enterprise and Kirk........$20–$35
Yo-Yo, Aviva, 1979. Star Trek: The Motion Picture. Blue sparkle plastic with Enterprise and logo on side. Blister packed on monotone header with artwork of Spock ....$10–$20

Spaceships (by manufacturer)
Corgi (Mettoy), British

Enterprise, 1981. Star Trek II. Die-cast metal. Approximately 3″ long. Came blister packed on color header with photo of Kirk and Spock..$15–$20
Klingon Cruiser, 1981. Star Trek II. Blue die-cast metal with black and yellow decals. Approximately 3″ long. Came blister packed on color header with photo of Kirk and Spock........
....$15–$20
Double Pack, 1981. Star Trek II. Both 3″ die-cast ships blister packed together on color header with photo of Kirk and Spock...$30–$40

Dinky (Meccano), British

Enterprise, 1975. Original TV. Die-cast metal. Approximately 9″. Fires plastic discs from saucer section. Includes discs and plastic shuttlecraft. Packaged in window box with low header with color photo of Kirk and Spock (earlier packaging is solid box with artwork of toy) ....
....$75–$100

Assorted die-cast ships.

Klingon Cruiser, 1977. Blue die-cast metal. Approximately 9″ long. Fires plastic discs from front section. Comes with discs. Window boxed with low header. Color photo of Kirk and Spock on front of box ....$75–$100

Enterprise and Klingon Gift Set, 1978. Box 9″ die-cast ships come packaged together in window box with color header showing Kirk, Spock, and ships ....$250–$300

Enterprise, 1979. Star Trek: The Motion Picture. Die-cast metal. Movie Enterprise. Approximately 4″. Blister packed on color header with photo of Kirk, Spock, and Klingon ship ....
....$15–$20

Klingon Cruiser, 1979. Star Trek: The Motion Picture. Blue die-cast metal. Approximately 4″ long. Blister packed on color header with photo of Kirk, Spock, and Enterprise.........$15–$20

ERTL

Enterprise, 1984. Star Trek III. Movie Enterprise. Die-cast metal. Approximateldy 4″ long. Blister packed on color header with artwork of Kirk, Spock, and Klingon. Included black plastic stand ....$10–$20

Excelsior, 1984. Star Trek III. Die-cast metal. Approximately 4″ long. Blister packed on color header with artwork of Kirk, Spock, and Klingon. Included black plastic stand..........$10–$20

Klingon Bird of Prey, 1984. Star Trek III. Die-cast metal. Approximately 3½″ across. Blue with "Star Trek" logo on each wing. Blister packed on color header with artwork of Kirk, Spock, and Klingon. Included black plastic stand..$10–$20

Enterprise, 1989. Star Trek V. Reissue of Star Trek III 4″ die-cast with "A" added to NCC-1701 decal. Blister packed on color header wtih Star Trek V logo. Includes black plastic stand ....$5–$10

Klingon Bird of Prey, 1989. Star Trek V. Reissue of Star Trek III 4″ die-cast. Mottled green. Blister packed on color header with Star Trek V logo. Includes black plastic stand ......$5–$10

Galoob

Enterprise, 1988. Star Trek: The Next Generation. Die-cast metal Next Generation Enterprise. Approximately 6″ long. Detachable saucer section. Blister packed on color header with photo of ship ....$15–$25

Ferengi Fighter, 1989. Star Trek: The Next Generation. Orange plastic. Designed for use with 3¾″ action figures. Movable canopy and guns. Decals included, 8½″ × 12″ box. Color photo of toy and figures ....$30–$60

Shuttlecraft Galileo, 1989. Star Trek: The Next Generation. White plastic. Designed for use with 3¾″ action figures. Movable doors and sensor unit. Decals included, 8½″ × 12″ box. Color photo of toy and figures..$25–$50

Mego

Enterprise, 1980. Star Trek: The Motion Picture. White plastic movie Enterprise. Detachable saucer section. Includes decals. Approximately 12″ long. Box shows photo of toy. Made primarily for Pacific market ....$125–$200

Klingon Cruiser, 1980. Star Trek: The Motion Picture. Green plastic with decals. Approximately 8″ long. Box shows photo of toy. Made primarily for Pacific market...........$125–$200
Vulcan Shuttle, 1980. Star Trek: The Motion Picture. Yellow plastic. Approximately 8″ long with detachable sled and decals. Box shows photo of toy. Made primarily for Pacific market ....$125–$200

Other

General Mills, Enterprise, 1988. Star Trek: The Next Generation. Cereal prize. 4″ long, light blue plastic. Comes with decals and directions ....$15–$25
Paramount (Promotional), Enterprise, 1988. Color die-cut cardboard movie Enterprise. Came in five pieces. Approximately 4½′ long when assembled. "The Star Trek Video Collection" is printed on sides of primary hull ....$50–$75
South Bend, Enterprise, "Star Trek Electronic, U.S.S. Enterprise," 1979. Star Trek: The Motion Picture. White plastic. Battery-powered lights and sound. Approximately 20″ long. Included stand and decals. Modular design for conversion to other ships. Box shows picture of toy ....$150–$200
Sterling, Enterprise, 1986. Star Trek IV. Inflatable silver plastic. Approximately 24″ when inflated. Star Trek IV and Paramount 75th Anniversary logos on top and bottom of saucer section. Promotional item ....$20–$35
Sun, Enterprise, 1986. Star Trek IV. Inflatable blue plastic. Approximately 24″ when inflated. Star Trek IV logo on top, Star Trek and Paramount 75th Anniversary logos on bottom of saucer section. Promotional item ....$20–$35
Note: *For other ship representations, see sections on "Games and Accessories," "Model Kits," and "Pewter Figurines."*

TRADING CARDS AND STICKERS

This section is divided into three parts: gum cards (American), collectors' cards, and promotional and foreign cards. Each section is divided chronologically by TV and then movie. Values given are for excellent to mint cards. These cards have no creases or rounded edges. Defects like these can lower the value of the cards by 50–75%. The values for individual cards will often be higher than the average price per card of a complete set. This is because of the time involved in stocking single cards for collectors.

American Gum Cards
Original Star Trek TV Show
LEAF PHOTO CARDS
Star Trek 72-card set, withdrawn from the market because of contractual disputes, black and white photos from the TV series, captions in black panels below picture, story on back, 1967, 2⅜″ × 3⁷/₁₆″.

U.S. Star Trek trading cards. Clockwise from top left are first cards from Leaf, Topps original TV, Topps Star Trek: The Motion Picture, Fantasy trading cards Star Trek III, IV, and Star Trek II photocard sets.

Set ....$800–$1,200
Single Card ....$12–$15
    1 No Time for Escape, **2** Attempted Mutiny, **3** A Grup Appears, **4** Come In, Captain Kirk, **5** Muraski Mischief, **6** Beam Down to Dawn, **7** Beside Himself, **8** Back Through Time, **9** Horta Emerging, **10** Spock's Box, **11** Spock in Command, **12** Spock in Command, **13** Befuddled Bones, **14** Prepare to Fire Phasers, **15** Command Decision, **16** Kirk Battles a Gorn, **17** Phaser Daser, **18** Space Race, **19** Fight Fire with Fire, **20** Captain's Bluff, **21** Underground Pursuit, **22** The Bird, **23** Teeny Bopper, **24** Time Warp, **25** You're Kidding, **26** Beam Out, **27** Burn Out, **28** Interference Out, **29** Not So Funny, **30** Prisoner of the Mind, **31** Stalking a Killer, **32** The Earth Killer, **33** Fight for Lithium, **34** Destruction Decision, **35** "Return My Ship", **36** Frozen at the Controls, **37** Christmas Present, **38** Amnesia Victim, **39** Decoy, **40** Beyond Tomorrow, **41** Trapped, **42** Kirk Outside, Spock Inside, **43** Spock Takes a Job, **44** Kirk Held Hostage, **45** Big Joker, **46** A Scream of Pain, **47** Captain's Statue, **48** Call Me Senator, **49** Into a New World, **50** Tranquilized, **51** Time for Shore Leave, **52** Ice Age, **53** Ambushed, **54** Pain of Victory, **55** Cornered, **56** Jungle Hunt, **57** Collision Course, **58** Corbomite Maneuver, **59** You Give Me a Headache, **60** Shore Leave Surprise, **61** Killer Aboard, **62** Mindless Man, **63** Pirates at Bay, **64** Off Course, **65** Attack by Nothing, **66** Funny Little Enemies, **67** Poison Attack!, **68** Warp Out for Rescue, **69** Out of Control, **70** Return to the Living, **71** Space Prisoner, **72** Raspberries
Wrapper ....$150–$200
Display Box ....$250–$500

TOPPS PHOTO CARDS

88-card set, color photos from original TV show, "captain's log" on back with narrative and character profiles, 2½″ × 3½″, 1976.
Set ....$75–$100
Single Card ....$1–$2
    1 The U.S.S. Enterprise, **2** Captain James T. Kirk, **3** Dr. "Bones" McCoy, **4** Science Officer Spock, **5** Engineer Scott, **6** Lieutenant Uhura, **7** Ensign Chekov, **8** The Phaser—Tomorrow's Weapon, **9** The Shuttle Craft, **10** Opponents, **11** Energize!, **12** The Alien Mr. Spock, **13** Men of the Enterprise, **14** Story of Voyage One, **15** "Live Long and Prosper", **16** View from the Bridge, **17** Toward the Unknown, **18** Enterprise Orbiting Earth, **19** The Purple Barrier, **20** Outwitting a God, **21** Planet Delta Vega, **22** Charlie's Law, **23** Mysterious Cube, **24** Dwarfed by the Enemy, **25** Balok's Alter-Ego, **26** Last of Its Kind, **27** Frozen World, **28** Spock Loses Control, **29** The Naked Time, **30** The Demon Within, **31** "My Enemy . . . My Self!", **32** Monster Android, **33** Korby's Folly, **34** The Duplicate Man, **35** Balance of Terror, **36** Attacked by Spores, **37** Spock Unwinds!, **38** Duel at Gothos, **39** Timeship of Lazarus, **40** Dagger of the Mind, **41** The Lawgivers, **42** Hunting the Tunnel Monster, **43** Battling the Horta, **44** Strange Communication, **45** A Startling Discovery, **46** McCoy Insane!, **47** The Guardian of Forever, **48** Visit to a Hostile City, **49** Mystery at Star Base 6, **50** Fate of Captain Pike, **51** The Talosians, **52** Ordeal on Rigel Seven, **53** Capturing the Keeper, **54** Blasted by the Enemy, **55** Trapped by the Lizard Creature, **56** The Gorn Strikes!, **57** Earthman's Triumph, **58** Specimen: Unknown, **59** Mirror, Mirror, **60** Spock's Wedding, **61** Strangled by Mr. Spock, **62** Grasp of the Gods, **63** The Monster Called Nomad, **64** The Companion, **65** Journey to Babel, **66** Death Ship, **67** The Tholian Web, **68** The Architects of Pain, **69** The Mugato, **70** The Deadly Years, **71** Ancient Rome Revisited, **72** The Melkotian, **73** The Vulcan Mind Meld, **74** Possessed by Zargon, **75** Creation of a Humanoid, **76** Captured by Romulans, **77** A War of Worlds, **78** Space of Brains, **79** I, Yarneg!, **80** Death in a Single Cell, **81** The Uninvited, **82** The Lights of Zetar, **83** Invaded by Alien Energy, **84** Kirk's Deadliest Foe, **85** The Trouble with Tribbles, **86** The Nazi Planet, **87** The Starship Eater, **88** Star Trek Lives!
Wrapper ....$3–$5
Display Box ....$5–$10
Unopened Pack ....$5–$10
Unopened Box ....$200–$400

TOPPS STICKERS

Correspond with card set, from TV show, 1976.
Set ....$25–$50
Single Card ....$1–$2
    1 James Kirk, **2** Mr. Spock—Unearthly!, **3** Spock of Vulcan, **4** Dr. "Bones" McCoy, **5** Engineer Scott, **6** Lieutenant Uhura, **7** Ensign Chekov, **8** The Starship Enterprise, **9** Kirk

Beaming Up!, **10** Star Trek Lives!, **11** "Highly Illogical!", **12** The Keeper, **13** Commander Balok, **14** The Mugato, **15** Lai, the Interrogator, **16** The Parallel Spock, **17** Ambassador Gav, **18** Alien Possession!, **19** Spock Lives!, **20** Evil Klingon Kang, **21** Spock Forever!, **22** The Romulan Vessel

Star Trek: The Motion Picture

TOPPS PHOTO CARDS

Series of 88, color photos with white borders, captioned, 1979.

Set ....$15–$25
Single Card ....$.50–$1
    1 Star Trek: The Motion Picture, **2** Toward the Unknown, **3** Space Intruder, **4** Fate of the Klingons, **5** Warning from Space, **6** "Our Starcrafts—Annihilated!", **7** Enterprise in Drydock, **8** Rebuilding the Enterprise, **9** Filming "Drydock" Sequence, **10** James T. Kirk, **11** Captain Kirk's Mission, **12** Dr. "Bones" McCoy, **13** Executive Officer Decker, **14** Navigator Ilia, **15** Uhura, **16** Helmsman Sulu, **17** Engineer Scott, **18** Security Chief Chekov, **19** Dr. Christine Chapel, **20** Janice Rand, **21** The Vulcan Mr. Spock, **22** Spock on Planet Vulcan, **23** The UFP Assembled, **24** Being from Beyond, **25** The Face of Terror, **26** Lizard-Like Diplomat, **27** Not of This Earth, **28** Alien Insectoid, **29** The Unearthly, **30** The Andorians, **31** Advanced Life Form, **32** Betel's Attendent, **33** Andorian—Close-Up, **34** The U.S.S. Enterprise, **35** Back in Operation!, **36** Refurbished Starship, **37** Enterprise—Rear View, **38** Return to the Bridge, **39** The Senior Officer, **40** View from the Bridge, **41** Scotty's Domain, **42** Fantastic New Devices, **43** The Engineering Deck, **44** Investigating a Malfunction, **45** Heart of the Starship, **46** Incredible Explosion!, **47** Starship Under Attack!, **48** Assault on Chekov!, **49** Half Human, **50** Spock's Fight for Life, **51** Into the Nameless Void, **52** Terror in the Transporter Room, **53** The Surak Craft, **54** Transporter Malfunction, **55** Zero Gravity Adventure, **56** Symbol of Her People, **57** Exotically Beautiful Ilia, **58** Spock's Discovery, **59** The Phaser Battle, **60** Ilia in Sick Bay, **61** Stamina of the Alien, **62** Filming the Shuttlecraft, **63** Star Explorer, **64** Alien Menace, **65** Star Challengers, **66** "Beam Me Down, Scotty", **67** The Landing Party, **68** Portrait of a Vulcan, **69** Beyond Infinity, **70** The Encounter, **71** Its Secret Revealed, **72** On Spock's Native World, **73** Spectacular Starship, **74** Welcoming Dr. McCoy Aboard, **75** Kirk's Last Stand, **76** Landscape of Vulcan, **77** Klingon Warship—Rear View, **78** The Final Frontiersmen, **79** Klingon Warship, **80** Vulcan Starship—Overhead View, **81** Pride of the Star Fleet, **82** Duo for Danger, **83** The Unearthly Mr. Spock, **84** Woman from Planet Delta, **85** New Star Fleet Uniforms, **86** Men with a Mission, **87** The Deltan Beauty, **88** Klingon Commander

Wrapper ....$.50–$1
Display Box ....$2–$3
Unopened Pack ....$5–$8
Unopened Box ....$100–$150

TOPPS STICKERS

Correspond with Star Trek: The Motion Picture Set, 1979.

Set ....$10–$20
Single Card ....$.50–$1
    1 Engineer Scott, **2** Janice Rand, **3** On Spock's Native World, **4** Security Chief Chekov, **5** Navigator Ilia, **6** Helmsman Sulu, **7** Star Explorer, **8** Dr. Christine Chapel, **9** Portrait of a Vulcan, **10** Dr. "Bones" McCoy, **11** Uhura, **12** The Deltan Beauty, **13** The Face of Terror, **14** Being from Beyond, **15** Advanced Life Form, **16** Executive Officer Decker, **17** Betel's Attendant, **18** Lizard-Like Diplomat, **19** Pride of the Star Fleet, **20** Klingon Warship, **21** The Surak Craft, **22** Spectacular Starship

Collectors' Cards and Stickers

Cards in this section were designed to be sold to collectors directly, not through gum sales. This makes these cards much rarer due to limited distribution, but most of the cards issued got into the hands of collectors. These cards were designed for the collector, so they usually are of better quality and have more mature subject matter than gum cards.

Star Trek II: The Wrath of Khan

FANTASY TRADING CARD CO.

Thirty-card set, color photos, no stickers, no captions, print run limited to 7,500 possible sets, 1982, 5″ × 7″.

Set ....$20–$30
Single Card ....$1–$2

    1 Kirk with book under arm, **2** Sulu, **3** Scott, **4** Uhura, **5** Kirk, **6** David Marcus, **7** Khan inside cargo bay, **8** Saavik on bridge, **9** Saavik, **10** Chekov aiming phaser, **11** Khan, **12** Terrell aiming phaser, **13** Kirk and Spock, **14** Carol Marcus, Kirk, David Marcus, and Saavik, **15** McCoy, **16** Khan on wrecked bridge of U.S.S. Reliant, **17** Chekov in cargo bay holding S.S. Botany Bay belt, **18** Carol Marcus, Genesis control, and David Marcus, **19** Saavik with communicator, **20** David Marcus and Kirk, **21** Space Lab Regula I, **22** Khan and Chekov on Reliant Bridge, **23** U.S.S. Reliant, **24** Group photo, shows original eight characters, **25** Kirk, Spock, and Saavik on bridge, **26** Saavik and Spock, **27** Sulu, Kirk, Uhura, and McCoy in travel pod, **28** McCoy, Scott, and crewman holding Kirk back, **29** Spock at bridge station, **30** Saavik at bridge station

Wrapper, four different, each ....$1–$2
Display Box..$4–$6

Star Trek III: The Search for Spock

FANTASY TRADING CARD CORP.

Sixty scene cards and 20 spaceship cards, no stickers, subject titles on the back of each card, 20 spaceship cards have a glossy finish, 2½″ × 3½″, 1984.

Set ....$12–$20
Single Card ....$.50–$1

    1 William Shatner stars as Adm. James T. Kirk, **2** Leonard Nimoy as Captain Spock, **3** DeForest Kelley stars as Dr. Leonard "Bones" McCoy, **4** Chief Engineer M. Scott played by James Doohan, **5** Capt. Hikaro Sulu played by George Takei, **6** Acting Science Officer Commander Pavel Chekov, **7** Nichelle Nichols as the beautiful Uhura, **8** Introducing Robin Curtis as Lt. Saavik, **9** Ambassador Sarek, Spock's father, portrayed by Mark L., **10** Vulcan High Priestess T'Lar played by Dame Judith Anderson, **11** Star Fleet Comm. Morrow played by Robert Hooks, **12** Klingon Battle Comm. Kruge played by Christopher Lloyd, **13** Kruge's Pet, Warrigul, **14** The Enterprise returning home for repairs, **15** The Enterprise berthed next to the Excelsior, **16** Sarek mind-melds with Kirk, **17** Kirk replaying the Enterprise's engine room flight record, **18** Kirk viewing the tape of Spock transferring his Katra, **19** Morrow tells Kirk the bad news—Genesis is off limits, **20** Conspirators in conference, **21** Visiting Bones in prison, **22** Liberating Bones from prison, **23** Sabotaging the prison's communications console, **24** Kirk and crew find Saavik and Spock held prisoner, **25** Commander Chekov at the helm, **26** Lt. Saavik and Dr. David Marcus view the Genesis, **27** Dr. David Marcus arrives on his creation, **28** Locating Spock's torpedo tube coffin, **29** Spock's burial robe, but no body, **30** What could have happened to Spock's body?, **31** Tracking . . . Spock?, **32** The Spock child lost in the snow, **33** Rescuing the Spock child from the hostile elements, **34** Uncloaking itself, Kruge's Klingon ship fires, **35** The Spock child resting, **36** Klingon landing party, **37** Kruge subduing a Genesis mutation, **38** Kruge planning his next strategy against the Enterprise, **39** Deadly enemies crippled in space, **40** Scotty and Chekov worrying over instrument readings, **41** Young Spock in the agony of Pon Farr, **42** Saavik soothing young Spock from the effects, **43** Spock, now a young adult, and still aging, **44** Which one shall I execute?, **45** David attracts the Klingon's fatal hand, **46** Turning certain death into a fighting chance of life, **47** Watching the Starship Enterprise blaze into history, **48** Kruge in rage after Kirk outwits him, **49** Kirk and Kruge duel as Genesis convulses, **50** Fighting on the brink of destruction, **51** The death throes of Genesis, **52** Kirk bargaining for the lives of his crew, **53** Escaping the exploding Genesis planet, **54** The Enterprise crew and their stolen Bird of Prey land, **55** The Enterprise crew returning Spock to his Vulcan home, **56** Sarek, at the foot of Mount Seleya, asking T'Lar, **57** McCoy's friendship for Spock is put to the ultimate test, **58** T'Lar performs the ritual of Fal Tor Pan—The Refusion, **59** Spock and Kirk face to face after Fal Tor Pan, **60** Spock's memories finally restored; the search is over

1 U.S.S. Enterprise, NCC-1701, left view, **2** U.S.S. Enterprise, rear view, **3** U.S.S. Enterprise leaving spacedock pursued, **4** U.S.S. Enterprise, front view, **5** Spacedock orbiting space station, top view, **6** Spacedock, side view, **7** NX-2000 U.S.S. Excelsior, **8** U.S.S. Excelsior, right rear view, **9** U.S.S. Excelsior, top view, **10** U.S.S. Excelsior, bottom view, **11** The Merchantman merchant ship destroyed, **12** The Merchantman, bottom view, **13** The Merchantman, top view, **14** The Merchantman, rear view, **15** Kruge's ship Klingon Bird of Prey, **16** Klingon Bird of Prey captured by Kirk, **17** U.S.S. Grissom NCC-638 destroyed by Kruge, **18** U.S.S. Grissom, rear view, **19** U.S.S. Grissom, top view, **20** U.S.S. Grissom, bottom view

Wrapper..$1–$2
Display Box..$2–$4
Unopened Pack..$5–$10
Unopened Box ....$50–$100

Star Trek IV: The Voyage Home

Set..$10–$15
Single Card ....$.50–$1

1 Title Card/Checklist, **2** Admiral James T. Kirk played by William Shatner, **3** Captain Spock in Vulcan robes played by Leonard Nimoy, **4** Dr. Leonard "Bones" McCoy played by DeForest Kelley, **5** Chief Engineer Montgomery Scott played by James Doohan, **6** Commander Chekov played by Walter Koenig, **7** Klingon Ambassador played by John Schuck, **8** Amanda, wife of Sarek and mother of Spock, played by Jane Wyatt, **9** Federation Headquarters, **10** Alien visitor to Star Fleet, **11** The Klingon Ambassador in Federation Council Chambers, **12** Extraterrestrials witness Genesis, **13** Klingon Ambassador demands extradition of Kirk, **14** Sarek and Commander Chapel, **15** Aliens listen to Sarek, **16** Spock tests his memory, **17** Admirak Kirk before his departure from Vulcan, **18** Bridge equipment on the Bird of Prey, **19** Scotty gets the ship ready, **20** Leaving Vulcan, heading for Earth, **21** Captain Spock prepares to leave for Earth, **22** A mysterious alien probe orbits Earth, **23** The president of Earth broadcasts a warning, **24** Matching whale songs with the probe, **25** Kirk wants to take whales to the future, **26** Bones tries to talk Kirk out of his scheme to bring whales from the past, **27** Warping towards a time jump, **28** During time travel, Kirk experiences hypnotic dreams, **29** Disembarking in Golden Gate Park, **30** Scotty explains that the dilithium crystals are decrystalizing, **31** Experiencing 20th-century San Francisco, **32** Kirk tells crew that he'll have to find money, **33** Kirk hocks his 18th-century spectacles, **34** Gillian and Kirk drop Spock off at the park, **35** Now what can I do?, **36** Gillian discovers Kirk's spaceship, **37** A call for help, **38** Uhura and Chekov waiting for their photon collector, **39** Bones and Kirk as Gillian tries to help them, **40** Chekov's rescue, **41** Watching spellbound as the crew does their job, **42** Free in the sun, oblivious to the danger, **43** Scaring the whales, would-be executioners, **44** The whales in their spacebound aquarium, **45** Scotty, amazed at the sight of the whales, **46** Kirk tells Gillian that mankind was destroying its own future by killing whales, **47** After re-entry, the ship is rocked by turbulence, **48** Abandoning ship, **49** The whales are set free, **50** Making sure everyone is safe, **51** The whales sing their song, **52** The Enterprise crew on trial, **53** Kirk is demoted to captain, **54** Gillian and Kirk say their farewells, **55** The Enterprise crew shuttling to its new commission, **56** Coming home to the new U.S.S. Enterprise, NCC 1701-A, **57** Bridge control panel on the new Enterprise, **58** Sulu contemplating going boldly where no man has gone before, **59** Uhura ready at her communications console, **60** Kirk and crew ready for the unknown

Wrapper..$1–$2
Display Box..$2–$4
Unopened Pack..$5–$10
Unopened Box ....$30–$50

Promotional and Foreign Cards

Promotional cards were issued in conjunction with the sale of a product in hopes of boosting sales. All foreign cards are listed here because not enough information is available about foreign sets to distinguish between gum (or other product), collectors', and promotional cards. This section is organized chronologically by TV show and movie.

Star Trek TV Series

Morris, Canadian, 4½″ × 3¼″, brown-backed stickers on thin stock and mostly black puzzle cards, each sticker is comprised of three or four smaller numbered stickers depicting TV scenes or new art, the title and Enterprise on a starry black front and a colored puzzle piece behind, copyright 1975 Paramount, issued without gum

Set ....$40–$80
Album for 35 stickers, issued with Canadian Morris set, different albums distinguished by the colored centerfold: Kirk portrait, Spock with phaser, Kirk and Gorn, Robot .....$10–$20
Panini, made in Italy for European market, 400 stickers plus album, color, 1979 .....$75–$150
Phoenix Candy Co. Boxes, United States, folded box with all flaps about 8″ × 3½″ when flattened, front photo about 3″ × 2¼″, color photo with number below on front, labeled photo of Enterprise on back of all boxes, copyright 1976 Paramount, issued as individual boxes with candy and two plastic prizes, eight boxes in set, each..$4–$8
Primrose Confectionery, English, 1970, 2½″ × 1⅜″, thin white stock with color print on front, number and story on back, all say "Issued A.S. 2307," copyright PPC (Paramount), assumed issued with candy cigarettes, all cards on the market are mint remainders, 12 cards in the set ....$20–$30

1 The Enterprise Incident, **2** Plato's Stepchildren, **3** Operation Annihilate, **4** Man Trap, **5** Spock, **6** Taste of Armageddon, **7** Dr. McCoy, **8** Kirk, **9** Enterprise and planet, **10** Enterprise in meteor storm, **11** Enterprise, **12** Doomsday Machine
Topps A and BC, English, 3¼″ × 2¼″, color photos, blue border with caption in white, rocket at bottom, story and number on pale bluish-green back, copyright 1969 Paramount, issued in packs with bubble gum, 55 cards in the set, very uncommon

Per card ....$5–$8
Wrapper...$100–$150

Star Trek: The Motion Picture

General Mills Collectors' Series, United States and England, 5⅛″ × 3½″, plain-backed heavy stock, color photos in silver and white borders, numbered, no issuer information once cut from package, copyright 1979 Paramount, issued on back of General Mills cereal boxes: Cocoa Puffs, Trix, Count Chocula, Frankenberry, Boo-Berry, and Lucky Charms. Two vertical cards were on large boxes (close-ups) and on horizontal card on small boxes (action shots), 18 cards in set, scarce, per card ....$4–$6
General Mills Starship Door Signs, United States and England, 6½″ × 3½″, plain-backed heavy card with angled corners, orange and silver borders around various art and photos with titles, no numbers, no issuer information once cut from package, copyright 1979 Paramount, issued on the back of Cheerios boxes, seven cards in the set, scarce

Authorized Personnel Only, Captain's Quarters, Danger! Keep Out, Do Not Enter, Engine Room, Intermix Chamber, Medical Officer Dr. Leonard "Bones" McCoy, U.S.S. Enterprise, per card ....$4–$6
Lyons Maid, English, 3″ × 1⅜″, color photos, number and story on back, copyright 1979 Paramount, issued on packs of Lyons Maid ice lollies, wrapper dark blue, flattens out to about 5″ × 3″, 25 with spaces for the cards. Were issued as a premium, uncommon, per set .$25–$50
Rainbow Bread, series of cards numbered 1–33, white borders, either red, blue or yellow trim, photographs from the first movie, distributed wtih Rainbow Bread, one card with one loaf of bread, 3½″ × 2½″, 1979

Set ....$5–$10
1 Title Card, **2** Toward the Unknown, **3** Space Intruder, **4** Fate of the Klingons, **5** Warning from Space, **6** Our Starcraft's Annihilated, **7** Enterprise in Drydock, **8** Rebuilding the Enterprise, **9** Filming Drydock Sequence, **10** James T. Kirk, **11** Captain Kirk's Mission, **12** Dr. "Bones" McCoy, **13** Executive Officer Decker, **14** Navigator Ilia, **15** Uhura, **16** Helmsman Sulu, **17** Engineer Scott, **18** Security Chief Chekov, **19** Dr. Christine Chapel, **20** Janice Rand, **21** The Vulcan Mr. Spock, **22** Spock on Planet Vulcan, **23** The UFP Assembled, **24** Being from Beyond, **25** The Face of Terror, **26** Lizard-Like Diplomat, **27** Not of This Earth, **28** Alien Insectoid, **29** The Unearthly, **30** The Andorians, **31** Advanced Life Form, **32** Betel's Attendant, **33** Andorian Close-Up ....$.25–$.50
As Above, **Kilpatrick's Bread,** United States, like Rainbow Bread issue but with Kilpatrick's Bread logo on back of each card, 33 cards in set, per set...$5–$10
As Above, **Colonial Bread,** United States ....$5–$10

As Above, **Monitor Bread**, United States ....$5–$10

Swizzels Refreshers Stickers, English, 1½″ × 1¼″, stickers with rounded corners, color photos with caption below and number on side, copyright 1979 Paramount, issued in packs of Swizzels Star Trek Refreshers—Flavored Fizzy Sweets, wrapper black with starburst and rainbow, about 4¼″ × 3⅟₁₆″ when flattened, each sticker..$2–$4

Topps United Kingdom T.M.P., English, same format as U.S. cards but on a thinner and whiter stock that gives the red and blue backs a much brighter appearance (backs dull on grayish stock on U.S. cards), some differences in content, no stickers, copyright 1979 Paramount, wrapper very similar to United States but says "Movie Photo Cards Bubble Gum," 88 cards per set, uncommon, per set ....$20–$30

Note: *This set is not identical to the U.S. issue, differing in several cards as follows:*
  1 The Final Frontiersmen, **2** Klingon Ship in Red Border, **11** Mr. Spock, **52** Vulcan Spaceship, **55** A Pensive McCoy, **76** Speeding at Warp Seven, **78** Klingon Warship.........$.50–$1

Vending Stickers, United States, 3⅛″ × 2⅟₁₆″, color photos with gold borders, not numbered, no issuer information, backs say only "peel off backing, stick on window or outside of glass," title on front, copyright 1979 Paramount, issued in transparent bubbles (folded) from vending machines at 25 cents each, remainders show no traces of folds, four stickers in set
  Set ....$10–$20
  Enterprise, Kirk, Kirk, Spock, and Enterprise, Spock ....$3–$6

Weetabix, United Kingdom, 3½″ × 1⅝″, color art with caption on front, color photo in oval on purple back, cards scored at bottom to stand up, issued perforated on one or two long sides, issued in large packs of Weetabix cereal, usually in strips of three cards, 18 cards in the set, uncommon
  Set ....$20–$30
  Andorian man, Andorian woman, Arcturian (these six share a common background of blue V'ger floor panels), Betelgeusian Chief Ambassador, Captain Kirk, Commander Decker, Commander Scott, Commander Uhura, Dr. McCoy, Klingon Captain, Lieutenant Chekov, Lieutenant Ilia, Lieutenant Sulu, Megarite (these six share a common background of Federation Headquarters), Mr. Spock, Rigellian, Shamin Priest (these six share a common background of red panels), Vulcan Master..$1–$2

Star Trek II: The Wrath of Khan

Monty Gum, English, 100 cards, smaller than American cards
  Set ....$40–$60

Star Trek: The Next Generation

Panini, Italian, sticker books with set of 240 color stickers printed in several languages for the world market, only test marketed in the United States..$35–$45

Star Trek: The Next Generation Panini stickers.

STAR WAR LISTINGS

ACTION FIGURES

Small Action Figures, Kenner, 1978–1985

This line of figures was an extremely successful product for Kenner at the time of their production and has become an extremely successful collectible today. The figures came blister packed on color photo headers and ranged in size from approximately 2¼″ to 4¼″ in height. They were released in series, new figures being added with each new film. Older figures were not dropped from production but were repackaged to display the logo of the most current film. Consequently, figures that had been in production longer accumulated more package variations. Some of the oldest had five different packagings before Kenner discontinued the line. These were Star Wars, Empire Strikes Back, Return of the Jedi, Power of the Force (a reissue series), and Triple Language (for foreign markets).

Prices listed here are for figures in Return of the Jedi packages. Empire Strikes Back packaging is worth about twice that of Jedi packaging and Star Wars more still. Power of The Force packaging, while later chronologically, is not as common as Jedi and the last series of figures, which are the rarest, are primarily Power of The Force. In addition, many Power of The Force figures came with a special collectors' coin which makes them more collectible. Triple Language packages are almost as common as Jedi, especially in some areas. Unpackaged figures do have collectors' value, generally about ⅓ that of packaged figures, but should be complete. Almost all the figures had clothing, helmets, weapons, or other implements which were easily lost once the package was opened. Prices reflect popularity and scarcity of figure.

Figures are organized alphabetically by name for ease of reference. Kenner released them chronologically in series (I–VIII) and that number is listed also.

Characters

Admiral Ackbar, fish eyes, white outfit, short staff (VI) ....$20–$30
Amanaman, green and buff reptile, ornamented staff (VIII) ....$75–$100
Anakin Skywalker, long gray outfit. This figure was available in the United States only through Sears mail order. Packaged ones are all foreign (VIII) ....$75–$100
AT-AT Commander, gray uniform and hat, gun (V) ....$15–$25

Kenner small action figure packaging, left to right: Star Wars, Empire Strikes Back, Return of the Jedi, Triple Language, and Power of the Force.

Stormtrooper figures, left to right: Large Kenner action figure, Takara (Japanese) action figure, small Kenner action figure, and Kenner die-cast metal figure from Micro toy series.

AT-AT Driver, gray outfit, white helmet, and gloves, rifle with shoulder strap (IV) ..$15–$25
AT-ST Driver, light gray uniform, dark gray hat, goggles, gun (VII)...........................$15–$25
A-Wing Pilot, green flight suit, gun (VIII)...$75–$100
Barada, green-skinned, brown trousers, white shirt, bandolier, long-handled weapon (VIII)...
....$75–$100
Ben (Obi-Wan) Kenobi, removable brown plastic robe, retractable lightsaber (I) .....$25–$35
Bespin Security Guard (Black), black uniform, gun (V)..$25–$35
Bespin Security Guard (White), black uniform, gun (III)......................................$25–$35
Bib Fortuna, long tentacles on head, removable brown cloth robe, long ornate staff (VI).......
....$35–$50
Biker Scout, white armor, black gloves and leggings, squarish hand weapon (VI).....$30–$40
Boba Fett, green and gray armor, short rifle (II) ....$25–$35
Bossk, brown skin, tan and white jumpsuit, short rifle (III) ....$15–$25
B-Wing Pilot, red flightsuit, gun (VII)...$20–$30
Chief Chirpa, solid gray Ewok, cowl, staff (VI)..$15–$25
C-3PO, tall gold droid (I)..$30–$40
C-3PO, removable limbs, black plastic carrier (V)..$20–$30
Chewbacca, crossbow rifle (I)..$20–$30
Cloud Car Pilot, white flightsuit, wide white and orange helmet, gun (V)................$30–$40
Darth Vader, black plastic removable cape, retractable lightsaber (I)........................$35–$50
Death Star Droid, tall silver droid (II) ....$35–$45
Dengar, tan outfit and headgear, darker breastplate and leggings, long rifle (IV) ....$25–$35
Droopy McCool (*See* "Action Figure Toys" section)
8D8, tall white droid (VII)..$15–$25
Emperor, stooped, black outfit, cane (VII)...$20–$30
Emperor's Royal Guard, red cloth robe, long staff (VI) ....$35–$45
EV-9D9, tall, bronze metallic droid (VIII)..$75–$100
4-LOM, bug-eyed, tan cloth outfit, short weapon (V)..$40–$50
FX-7, gray, metallic cylindrical droid with nine white sensor arrays (III)....................$15–$25
Gammorrean Guard, green with horns, brown tunic, short ax (VI)............................$25–$35
General Madine, tan and blue outfit, short staff (VI) ....$25–$35
Greedo, green skin and outfit, horns, gun (II) ....$35–$50
Hammerhead, long brown snout, blue outfit, gun (II)..$45–$60
Han Solo
    Vest, gun (I)..$50–$75
    Hoth gear, tan legs, dark parka, gun (III)..$45–$60
    Bespin outfit, long-sleeve jacket, gun (IV)..$35–$45
    Carbonite, light color shirt, translucent plastic box (VIII) ....$75–$100
    Trenchcoat, long camouflage coat, gun (VII)...$40–$50
IG-88, tall silver droid, bandolier, long rifle (III) ....$25–$35
Imperial Commander, dark uniform and hat, gun (IV) ....$20–$30
Imperial Dignitary, long purple outfit and hat (VIII)..$75–$100
Imperial Gunner, black jumpsuit and helmet, gun (VIII) ....$75–$100
Imperial Stormtrooper white armor, gun (I)..$50–$75

Imperial Stormtrooper (Hoth Gear), long removable white plastic apron, rifle (III)............
....$35–$50
Imperial TIE Fighter Pilot, black flight suit, gray gloves and boots, gun (V)...........$35–$50
Jawa, short, brown, with gun. Early U.S. and foreign figures had removable plastic cloak.
Most are cloth (I) ....$50–$75
Klaatu, green skin, vest, bandolier, helmet, cloth apron, short forked weapon (VI)....$30–$40
Klaatu (Skiff Guard), light colored jumpsuit, long weapon (VII) ....$25–$35
Lando Calrissian, blue shirt, short gray cloak, gun (III) ....$25–$35
Lando Calrissian (General Pilot), long tan cloth cloak, gun (VIII) ....$75–$100
Lando Calrissian (Skiff Guard), removable helmet, long forked weapon (VI)........$20–$30
Lobot, bald with earphonelike headpiece, gun (IV)..$15–$25
Logray, tan striped Ewok, cowl, shoulder bag, elaborate staff (VI)...........................$20–$30
Luke Skywalker
   Tattooine outfit, retractable lightsaber (I)...$50–$75
   Stormtrooper outfit, white armor, removable helmet (VIII)...................................$75–$100
   X-wing outfit, orange flightsuit, gun (II)..$25–$35
   Hoth gear, light colored jumpsuit, hat, binoculars, rifle with shoulder strap (V)......$35–$50
   Bespin outfit, tan outfit, brown boots, gun (III) ....$45–$65
   Jedi outfit, black outfit, long brown cloak, green lightsaber, gun (VI) ....$45–$65
   Battle poncho, short cloth camouflage poncho, helmet (VIII)...............................$75–$100
Lumat, gray Ewok, dark gray cowl, shoulder bag, bow (VII) ....$45–$65
Max Rebo (*See* "Action Figure Toys" section)
Nien Numb, gray skin, red jumpsuit, dark vest, gun (VI) ....$15–$25
Nikto, brown wrinkled skin, green tunic, gray pants and breastplate, long elaborate weapon
(VII) ....$15–$25
Paploo, brown Ewok, tan cowl, forked staff (VII) ....$45–$65
Power Droid, dark, box-shaped droid (II) ....$40–$50
Princess Leia
   Star Wars outfit, white plastic removable robe, gun (I)..$50–$75
   Hoth outfit, tan and white jumpsuit, gun (IV) ....$40–$60
   Bespin outfit, brown outfit, pink plastic removable robe, gun (III) ....$45–$65
   Boushh disguise, removable helmet, long elaborate weapon (VI)...........................$20–$30
   Poncho, short cloth camouflage cloak, helmet, gun (VII)...$15–$25
Prune Face, eye-patch, long tan cloth cloak, rifle (VII)..$15–$25
Rancor Keeper, bare-chested, headpiece, weapon (VII)..$15–$25
Rebel Commander, light colored jumpsuit, hat, mustache, scarf, rifle with shoulder strap
(IV)...$15–$25
Rebel Commando, green fatigues, hat, rifle with shoulder strap (VI).......................$40–$60
Rebel Soldier, brown and tan outfit, hat, gun (III)...$15–$25
Ree-Yees, brown outfit, three eyes, rifle (VI) ....$45–$65
R5-D4, short white barrel-shaped droid, white top (II)..$45–$65
Romba, brown Ewok, dark cowl, spear (VIII) ....$45–$65
R2-D2, short white barrel-shaped droid, silver top (I)...$40–$60
R2-D2 (Sensorscope), pull-out sensor on top (V) ....$20–$30

**Some harder to find small
action figures. Left to right:
Anakin Skywalker, Yak Face,
and Sears Snaggletooth.
Regular Snaggletooth is last.**

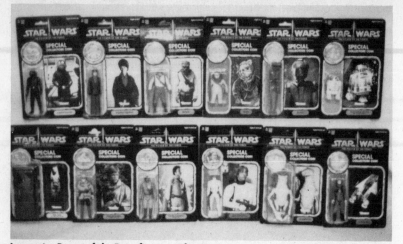

Last series Power of the Force figures with coins.

R2-D2 (Pop-Up Lightsaber), removable from top (VIII) ....$50–$75
Snaggletooth, regular version had red outfit, gun (II).............................$15–$25
Snaggletooth, blue outfit with silver boots originally available only through a Sears promotion. Never available in blister pack ....$75–$100
Squid Head, tan cloth apron, brown cloak, gun (VI) ....$35–$45
Star Destroyer Commander, gray outfit, wide black helmet, gun (I).........................$30–$40
Sy Snootles (*See* "Action Figure Toys" section)
Teebo, gray striped Ewok, pink animal head helmet, shoulder strap and stone ax (VII) ....
....$15–$25
Tusken Raider, tan outfit, removable plastic cloak, sticklike weapon (I)..................$45–$60
2-1B blue and gray droid with cable running from face to torso, short staff (IV) ....$15–$25
Ugnaught, short, pig-snouted, blue cloth apron, black rope, white carrying case (IV) ....
....$40–$50
Walrus Man, green skin, orange and blue outfit, gun (II)............................$45–$65
Warok, gray Ewok, brown cowl, shoulder bag, bow (VIII)............................$45–$65
Weequay, brown skin, bald with ponytail, gray tunic with blue sleeves, long ax (VI) ....
....$30–$40
Wicket, small brown Ewok, cowl, spear (VII) ....$15–$25
Yak Face, tall long-faced alien, dark pants, tan top. This figure was never released in the United States. All are foreign (VIII)...$150–$200
Yoda, small, green, cloth robe, snake, cane (III)....................................$35–$50
Zuckuss, dark gray bug-eyed droid, rifle (V) ....$15–$25

COINS

Sixty-two silver-colored aluminum coins were made to go along with many figures and some action figure-related toys. The coins were blister packed on the cards along with some Power of the Force figures and increase the value of a figure about 50%. The coins by themselves are worth between $5 and $15. Fronts of coins showed the character; backs had short descriptions of the character under either original "Star Wars" or "Power of The Force" logos. Though designed to go with the figures, it should be noted that many were never packaged with their figure and were available only through the mail from Kenner. Coins manufactured are as follows:

Amanaman, Anakin Skywalker, AT-ST Driver, A-Wing Pilot, AT-AT, Barada, Bib Fortuna, Biker Scout, Boba Fett, B-Wing Pilot, Chewbacca, Chief Chirpa, Creatures, C-3PO, Darth

Vader, Droids, Emperor, Emperor's Royal Guard, EV-9D9, FX-7, Gammorrean Guard, Greedo, Han Solo, Han Solo (Carbon Freeze), Han Solo (Rebel), Han Solo (Rebel fighter), Han Solo (Rebel hero), Hoth Stormtrooper, Imperial Commander, Imperial Dignitary, Imperial Gunner, Jawas, Lando Calrissian (Bespin), Lando Calrissian (Millennium Falcon), Luke Skywalker, Luke Skywalker (Tatooine outfit), Luke Skywalker (X-wing outfit close-up), Luke Skywalker (X-wing in background), Luke Skywalker (Jedi knight, close-up), Luke Skywalker (Jedi knight, Dagobah), Luke Skywalker (On Taun-Taun), Luke Skywalker (On speeder bike), Logray, Lumat, Millennium Falcon, Obi-Wan Kenobi, Paploo, Princess Leia (Boushh), Princess Leia (Wearing Helmet), Princess Leia (Original Hair Style), Romba, R2-D2, Sail Skiff, Star Destroyer Commander, Stormtrooper, Teebo, TIE Fighter Pilot, Too-Onebee, Tusken Raider, Warok, Wicket, Yak Face, Yoda, Zuckuss

Droids, 1985

This series of figures is based on the animated TV series. Figures came blister packed on color headers showing scenes of the character from the show. All packages included a gold-color aluminum coin of the character. Kenner, at one time, announced that it was going to add figures to the series but apparently dropped those plans. "Boba Fett" and an "A-Wing Pilot" are included as part of this series, but these are the figures from the movie series. Though a few were put in "Droids" packaging, the figures themselves are no different from the movie ones.

C-3PO, flat yellow finish (as opposed to the gold metallic used on the movie figure)..............
....$10–$20
Jann Tosh, gray pants, brown vest, rifle...$10–$20
Jord Dusat, purple tunic, red sleeves, belt and boots, rifle ....$8–$15
Kea Moll, green and white outfit, rifle ....$10–$20
Kez Iban, purple skin, bandolier, gun...$5–$10
R2-D2, differs from movie version in nonmetallic finish on dome, pop-up lightsaber..$5–$10
Sise Fromm, green skin, purple cloth robe...$8–$15
Thall Joben, dark jumpsuit, yellow boots, gun ....$8–$15
Tig Fromm, green skin, gray and purple outfit, short staff ....$10–$20
Uncle Gundy, tan outfit, mustache, hat, rifle..$5–$10

Ewoks, 1985

Based on the animated series, this figure series was also supposed to be expanded but never was. Packaging is like the "Droids" packaging except that character coins were copper colored.

Dulok Scout, green with white eye paint, short club...$5–$10
Dulok Shaman, brown and yellow eye paint, necklace, long brown staff....................$5–$10
Logray, Ewok in blue outfit, long ornate staff...$4–$8
King Gorneesh, brown legs, necklace, headpiece, long gray staff ....$4–$8
Urgah Lady Gorneesh, yellow-green, brown shawl ....$4–$8
Wicket W. Warrick, differs from movie version by having painted-on nonremovable cowl, spear ....$4–$8

Large Action Figures, Kenner, 1977–1980

When originally marketed, this series of figures did not compete well against Kenner's own line of small action figures, which were selling concurrently with these. Consequently, Kenner soon lost interest in the large action figure line and discontinued its production. Because of this relative scarcity, these dolls have become extremely collectible.

Dolls come packaged in window boxes with side panels depicting a photograph of the character. Boxes originally came with colored cardboard liners which were slotted to hold accessories (if any). All boxes, except one, carry the "Star Wars" logo. Though others were originally planned, only IG-88 was packaged in an *Em-*

pire Strikes Back box. (Though the character of Boba Fett was introduced in *Empire*, the figure packaging is still *Star Wars*.)

Boxes can double the value of a figure, and particularly nice condition boxes add an extra premium. Because of the high collector demand for these items, however, unpackaged figures are still extremely collectible (as long as they are complete). For this reason, values will be listed for both packaged and unpackaged dolls.

Ben (Obi-Wan) Kenobi, 12″ tall, white hair and beard. White robe with black collar, brown robe with hood, brown boots, yellow lightsaber. Boxed ....$250–$350
  Unboxed...$150–$200

Boba Fett, 13½″ tall, gray and green outfit, helmet with swing-up "range-finder." Cape, rifle, backpack, two "Wookie-scalps," belt. Boxed..$250–$350
  Unboxed...$100–$200

Chewbacca, 15″ tall, brown. Crossbow rifle, bandolier with 16 removable gray plastic inserts. Boxed ....$125–$175
  Unboxed...$50–$75

C-3PO, 12½″ tall, metallic gold finish, no clothing or accessories. Boxed ....$100–$150
  Unboxed...$40–$65

Darth Vader, 15″ tall, black finish with helmet. Black cape, red lightsaber. Boxed ....
  ....$150–$200
  Unboxed...$75–$100

Han Solo, 12½″ tall, brown hair. Black pants, white shirt, black vinyl vest, boots, pistol, holster, gold plastic medallion on red ribbon. Boxed ....$450–$600
  Unboxed...$250–$350

IG-88, 15″-tall silver droid. Brown bandolier with four red "grenades," pistol (approximately 3½″ in length) and rifle (approximately 7½″ in length). Boxed ....$400–$500
  Unboxed...$200–$300

Jawa, 8″ tall, tan with yellow eyes and brown boots. Brown hooded robe, X-shaped bandolier, rifle (approximately 4″ long). Boxed...$200–$300
  Unboxed...$100–$150

Luke Skywalker, 12″ tall, blond hair. Tan pants, white shirt, white boots, belt, grappling hook, blue lightsaber. Boxed...$300–$400
  Unboxed...$150–$250

Princess Leia, 12″ tall, fiber hair held in original bun style by two plastic rings. White dress with hood, silver plastic belt, white stockings. White plastic shoes, blue plastic comb and brush (a hairstyle booklet also originally came with this figure). Boxed...........................$300–$400
  Unboxed...$150–$250

R2-D2, 7½″ tall, white barrel-shaped droid with silver domed top. Back panel opens to hold two removable "circuit boards." Boxed ....$150–$250
  Unboxed...$50–$75

Stormtrooper, 12″ tall, white armor with black details. Rifle (approximately 5″ long) can be secured to waist of figure with black thread loop. Boxed ....$200–$300
  Unboxed...$100–$150

Complete large Han Solo action figure.

Foreign small action figures, left to right: Mexican, Brazilian, Japanese, and British package with sticker in Dutch.

Foreign Star Wars Figures

Both the small and large action figures were sold throughout Europe variously under Palitoy, Meccano, and Denys Fisher brand names. Despite the different names and slight variations in packaging, these are essentially the same figures as were sold in the United States and elsewhere.

There was a series of figures manufactured in Japan by Takara primarily for the Pacific market, which are different from the Kenner versions. These are vary rare in the United States. It apparently included only four figures, all approximately 8″ in height. Figures originally came blister packed on cardboard headers. They are as follows:

Chewbacca	$150–$300
C-3PO	$150–$300
Darth Vader	$150–$300
Stormtrooper	$150–$300

ACTION FIGURE TOYS

All toys in this section were designed by Kenner to be used with the 3¾″ action figures. Values listed are for complete toys in the original box. Toys without boxes are worth considerably less, regardless of condition. Equally, boxes in extremely good condition are worth more. Boxes show color photos of toy depicted in action scenes with figures. Like the small action figures, toy packaging was updated as each film in the series was released. A toy in earlier packaging is worth more than the same toy displaying a later movie logo. Power of the force packaging was done after the completion of the movie trilogy and was apparently designed as a general title. In actuality, very few toys were done in Power of the Force boxes and these also are more valuable. There was also a late series where original toys were reissued in packaging identical to the original, except for a "Collector's Series" seal printed on the box. These are worth approximately the same as their original counterpart. Droids packaging was limited to a few very late toys and, while Ewok packaging is shown in Kenner advertising of the time, it is unlikely it was used except for items in Kenner's preschool line.

X-Wing toys, action figure toy, Micro toy, and die-cast toy.

Many of the action figure toys were done in Britain by Palitoy. In most cases, toys have only minor changes and prices are comparable to the U.S. versions. Palitoy also often combined toys and action figures into sets unique to the British market, especially in the case of smaller toys. Packaging is similar but not identical to U.S. counterparts.

Action Figure Accessories, 1983

These came boxed in 4½″ × 6″ boxes with color photo of toy similar to the Mini-Rigs, but without the side headers. Manual functions.

Ewok Assault Catapult, simulated wood, two boulders ....$20–$30
Ewok Combat Glider, tan "wings," two boulders..$20–$30
Tri-Pod Laser Cannon, dark gray plastic ....$15–$25
Vehicle Maintenance Energizer, white plastic...$15–$25

Action Figure Holders

Collector's Case, 1979–1983, black vinyl, illustrated cover. Holds 24 figures. Updated to Star Wars, Empire Strikes Back, and Return of the Jedi versions ....$15–$20
Chewbacca Bandolier Strap, 1983, holds ten figures plus two containers for accessories. Came boxed ....$15–$25
C-3PO Collector's Case, 1983, gold plastic bust of C-3PO. Holds 40 figures, wrapper with color photos around base ....$15–$25
Darth Vader Collector's Case, 1980, black plastic bust of Darth Vader. Holds 31 figures, wrapper with color photos around base ....$15–$25
Laser Rifle Case 1984, shaped like rifle. Holds 19 figures, came packaged in color cardboard base ....$30–$50
Note: *Action figure cases came with paper inserts showing color photos of small action figures.*
Action Display Stand, 1977, gray plastic stand for action figures with cardboard backdrops. ....$20–$30

Action Figure Toys

AT-AT (All-Terrain Armored Transport), 1981, posable legs, movable control center, 17½″ high, battery functions ....$100–$150
ATL (Air-To-Land) Interceptor Vehicle, 1985, Droids packaging............................$40–$60
A-Wing Fighter, 1985, battery-operated sound. Droids packaging, approximately 12″ long ...
....$85–$125
B-Wing Fighter, 1983, battery-operated sound. Many manual functions, approximately 22″ long ....$75–$95

Different kinds of TIE Fighter toys. TIE Fighter, battle-damaged TIE, Darth Vader's TIE, and TIE Interceptor.

Cantina Adventure Set, 1978, Sears promotional set. Base and backdrop plus four figures: Greedo, Hammerhead, blue Snaggletooth, and Walrusman ....$175–$250
Cloud City Playset, 1981, included base, backdrop, and four figures: Han Solo, (Bespin), Ugnaught, Lobot and Dengar, and Boba Fett. Relatively rare ....$175–$250
Creature Cantina, 1977, consisted of base and scenic backdrop with lever-activated functions (no batteries). No figures included with set..$50–$75
Dagobah Action Playset, 1981, plastic set with lever-operated functions. Includes two "cargo boxes" ....$50–$85
Darth Vader's Star Destroyer, 1980, approximately 20″ long. Cross-section of ship. Manual functions and battery light. No figures included ....$100–$150
Darth Vader's TIE Fighter, 1977, approximately 11″ across. Battery light and sound. Pop-off solar panels ....$60–$85
Death Star Space Station, 1978, approximately 23″ high when assembled. Three-story playset with many manual features. Contains many small plastic parts and "trash monster," which make set hard to obtain in complete condition. (*Note*: Palitoy (British) version of this toy is made primarily of cardboard instead of plastic. Price is comparable.)..................$125–$175
Display Arena, 1981, four-L-shaped plastic stands for action figures and eight two-sided backdrop cards with scenes from Star Wars and Empire. Mail-order item (plain shipping box) ....$25–$40
Droid Factory, 1977, plastic base with movable crane. Includes 38 plastic robot parts. No battery functions. (*Note:* Palitoy (British) version has manually operated conveyer belt instead of crane. Price is comparable.)..$75–$100
Early Bird Package, 1977, envelope with certificate to purchase soon-to-be-manufactured action figures and scenes to be used with them ....$75–$100

Early bird package.

Kenner preschool Ewok action figure toys.

Ewok Assault Catapult, 1983, approximately 5" long. Came with two plastic "boulders" .....
....$25–$40
Ewok Battle Wagon, 1984, approximately 12" long. Free rolling. Many manual functions ....
....$65–$85
Ewok Family Hut, 1984, Ewoks animated series (Kenner Preschool). Hut plus 15 separate accessories including four nonposable figures. Approximately 12" high.........................$60–$95
Ewok Fire Cart, 1984, Ewoks animated series (Kenner Preschool). Cart plus accessories and two nonposable figures ....$40–$75
Ewok Village Action Playset, 1983, approximately 12" high. Two-story plastic playset with many manual functions. No figures included ....$75–$100
Ewok Woodland Wagon, 1985, Ewoks animated series (Kenner Preschool). Covered two-wheel cart, horse, and accessories ....$40–$75
Hoth Ice Planet Adventure Set, 1980, cardboard AT-AT backdrop, plastic base with several manual functions. No figures or battery functions ....$75–$100
Hoth Wampa, 1981, 6" tall, movable arms and legs..$15–$25
Imperial Attack Base (Hoth Scene), 1980, white plastic base with several smaller plastic accessories. Several lever-activated functions. No figures or battery functions...............$60–$85
Imperial Cruiser (*See* Imperial Troop Transporter)
Imperial Shuttle, 1984, approximately 18" tall with wings folded, several movable features, battery sound...$100–$125
Imperial Side Gunner, 1985, from Droids animated series. Several manual functions............
....$40–$60
Imperial Sniper Vehicle, 1984, small one-figure vehicle with overhead wings. Came blister packed on color artwork header...$45–$75
Imperial TIE Fighter, 1977, approximately 12" wide. Pop-off solar panels. Battery light and sound, white plastic...$60–$85
Imperial TIE Fighter (Battle Damaged), 1983, battery functions. Same mold as original TIE but in blue plastic with "battle damage" decals ....$50–$75
Imperial Troop Transporter, 1979, compartments for figures (not included) plus manual functions. Six different battery-operated sounds in some. Also called "Imperial Cruiser" on some packaging...$75–$100
Jabba the Hutt Playset, 1983, includes Jabba action figure, Salacious Crumb molded figure, and platform with several manual functions...$25–$40
Jabba the Hutt Dungeon Action Playset, two different variations, both utilize reworked base

Two different Jabba the Hutt dungeon variations.

Motorized action figure toys, left to right: Radio-controlled JAWA Sandcrawler and Sonic Landspeeder with smaller, regular Landspeeder for comparison.

and crane from earlier "Droid Factory" toy. Difference in value is due primarily to scarcity of different action figures included with sets.

1983, includes Klaatu (Skiff Guard), Nikto, and 8D8 action figures. Box has red background ....$75–$100

1984, includes EV-9D9, Amanaman, and Barada figures. Box has green background ....$150–$200

Land of the Jawas Action Playset, 1977, plastic base, plastic escape pod, cardboard sandcrawler backdrop, manual functions, no figures included ....$75–$100

Landspeeder, 1977, rolls on spring wheels, hood opens, holds four action figures, no figures included...$50–$75

Mini-Riggs, 1981–1983, these are small one-figure vehicles which came uniformly packaged in 6″ × 4½″ boxes with side headers showing color photos of the toy. All had many manual functions. None had battery functions

Armored Sentinel Transport (AST-5), orange, two side cannons.............................$20–$30

Captivator (CAP-2), dark gray, many arms...$20–$30

Desert Sail Skiff, green with orange "sail" ....$25–$35

Endor Forest Ranger, green, drum-shaped ....$25–$35

Interceptor (INT-4), dark gray, podlike..$20–$30

Imperial Shuttle Pod (ISP-6), white, dorsal fin ....$20–$30

Mobile Laser Cannon (MLC-3), white mini-tank ....$20–$30

Multi-Terrain Vehicle (MTV-7), white on high wheels...$20–$30

Personnel Deployment Transport (PDT-8), white with front and back openings .....$20–$30

Millennium Falcon Spaceship, 1977, 23″ long movable canopy, radar dish, and retractable landing gear. Battery sound, no figures ....$125–$175

One-Man Sand Skimmer, 1984, small one-figure vehicle. Figure stood on platform with single orange sail behind. Came blister packed on color artwork header..........................$45–$75

Patrol Dewback, 1977, approximately 10″ long. Movable head, legs, and tail. Includes saddle and reins, no figures...$35–$50

Radio-Controlled Sandcrawler, 1978, 17″ long. Hinged top and side panels, side elevator ... .$300–$500

Rancor Monster, 1983, approximately 10″ high. Movable joints, spring-loaded arm section.. ....$30–$50

Rebel Command Center Adventure Set, 1981, includes cardboard playset and three action figures, R2-D2 (Sensorscope), Luke (Hoth), and AT-AT Commander ....$175–$250

Rebel Transport, 1982, approximately 20″ long. Removable front and back hatches and cannons. Top is removable. Includes five backpacks and four gas masks.......................$75–$100

Sonic-Controlled Land Speeder, 1977, slightly larger than regular Land Speeder. Battery operated with rotating front wheel. Direction is controlled with a mechanical clicker shaped like R2-D2...$200–$250

Scout Walker, 1982, approximately 10″ tall. Hand-operated walking mechanism. Many movable parts ....$45–$75

Security Scout, 1984, small one-man vehicle. Camouflage colored. Figure was placed in front with guns on either side. Came blister packed on color artwork header.......................$45–$75

Slave I, 1982, approximately 12″ long. Movable wings and ramp. Adjustable seat. No battery functions. Includes one-piece Han Solo in carbonite figure exclusive to this set (not the same as two-piece action figure)...$85–$125

Snowspeeder package variations. One on right was probably later, to promote Tauntaun toy.

Snow-speeder, 1982, approximately 12″ long. Movable canopy and harpoon. Battery light and sound ....$75–$100

Speeder Bike, 1983, approximately 8″ long. Movable flaps, brakes, and handle bars ....$15–$25

Survival Kit, 1980, mail order only. Packet of accessories for action figures. Grappling hook, belt, Jedi training harness, two backpacks, three gas masks, and five different weapons. Came in clear plastic bag ....$3–$6

Sy Snootles and the Rebo Band, 1983, set includes three action figures that could only be purchased in this set: Droopy McCool, Max Rebo, and Sy Snootles. Set also includes Max's pianolike instrument, Droopy's flute, and two microphones......................................$15–$25

Tattoine Skiff, 1985, approximately 12″ long. No battery functions. Not to be confused with the Desert Sail Skiff Mini-Rig...$175–$250

Tauntaun, 1980, approximately 8″ tall. Movable front and rear legs. Removable saddle and reins. Trap door in back for placement of action figure ....$25–$35

Tauntaun (Open Belly), 1980, same as the regular model except for slot in belly for placement of action figure...$20–$30

TIE Interceptor, 1983, approximately 12″ wide. Pop-off solar panel. Battery light and sound ....$50–$70

Turret/Probot, 1980, white plastic base, swiveling turret with cannon and trap doors and probot on stand. Many lever-activated functions. No battery functions or figures included in set ....$75–$100

Left: Desert sail skiff mini-rig. Right: Tatooine skiff toy.

X-Wing Fighter in original Star Wars box.

Twin Pod Cloud Car, 1980, approximately 10″ wide, molded in orange plastic. Movable canopies and landing gear. No battery functions ....$70–$95
X-Wing Fighter, 1977, approximately 14″ long. Movable wings, landing gear, and canopy. Battery-operated light and sound..$65–$90
X-Wing (Battle Damaged), 1980, battery functions. Same as original X-Wing with "battle damage" decals ....$50–$75
Y-Wing Fighter, 1983, approximately 20″ long. Removable engine pods, cannons, and bomb. Battery sound ....$60–$85

ART

Star Wars art is much less available to the collector than similar Star Trek items (*see* "Star Trek Artwork"). While some fan-made traditional art (i.e., paintings, sketches, etc.) does turn up at conventions, Lucasfilm retains most of the professional work themselves. Artwork for such items as book covers, games, promotional posters, etc., that tend to turn up in the Star Trek field never make it into public circulation in the case of Star Wars. In addition, Lucasfilm has traditionally been very protective of the rights of its numerous product licensees. As a result, this discourages a large body of craft art that in the Star Trek field has usually been regarded by the studio as "fan art." These same kinds of Star Wars items are likely to be viewed as possible "license infringements."

BADGES, BUTTONS, BUMPER STICKERS, AND DECALS

Badges

Badges were hard plastic, came with pinback, and were unlicensed. All of the following were manufactured by Star Trek Galore.
Ambassador to Alderon, Brotherhood of the Jedi, Droid Technician, Imperial Senator, Jedi Knight, Jedi Training Academy, Millennium Falcon Crew, Sisterhood of the Jedi, Terror Squad, Wookie Translator, X-Wing Fighter Pilot, Y-Wing Fighter Pilot ......$1–$3

Buttons

For reasons explained in the "Star Trek" section of this book, we are listing only those buttons done in large quantities for promotional purposes or sale to the public. A button should cost between $1 and $2. Size and subject matter have no effect on button prices.

Word Buttons

Darth Vader Lives, 3″, Factors, Etc. ....$1–$2
May the Force Be With You, 2¼″, Factors, Etc...$1–$2
May the Force Be With You, 3″ Factors, Etc...$1–$2
May the Force Be With You, promotional word button given away at Star Wars premiere, manufactured for 20th Century Fox by L.A. Button, no value as a collectible due to ease of reproduction, 2¾...$1–$2

Logo Buttons

Tenth Anniversary Logo, color logo button on silver rectangular pinback ....$1–$2
Revenge of the Jedi, promotional logo button. Red on black, 2¼″. No collector value due to ease of reproduction..$1–$2

Picture Buttons

Star Wars, Factors, Etc., 3″, all with words identifying characters
     Chewbacca, C-3PO, C-3PO/R2-D2 (with Star Wars Logo), Darth Vader, Luke Skywalker,
     Obi-Wan, Princess Leia, R2-D2, Han and Chewie...$1–$2
Star Wars, Star Trek Galore, 2½″ artwork character "Sparkle buttons." Unlicensed. Several
different designs and variations. Price each ....$1–$2
Empire Strikes Back, Factors, Etc., 3″, no words
     Boba Fett, Chewbacca, Darth Vader, Luke Skywalker, R2-D2/C-3PO, Yoda ....$1–$2
Return of the Jedi, Adam Joseph, 2¼″, came on cardboard headers.
     Baby Ewok, Chewbacca, Darth Vader (artwork from pre-release, one-sheet), Darth Vader,
     Droopy (from Rebo Band), Gammorrean Guard, Group shot (heroes in woods), Imperial
     Guard, Jabba the Hutt, Logo from Return of the Jedi, R2-D2 and C-3PO, Yoda.........$1–$2

Star Wars Fan Club Buttons

Picture with logo and character name, 1″, 1978.
First Series
     Chewbacca, George Lucas, Han Solo, Luke, Princess Leia, Tusken Raider.................$1–$2
Second Series
     Ben Kenobi, Moff Tarkin, Darth Vader, R2-D2, C-3PO, Jawa ....$1–$2

Star Tours Buttons

Star Tours Logo, 3″ glow-in-the-dark..$1–$2
Star Tours and Disney-MGM Logos, on blue ....$1–$2
Star Tours Logo and C-3PO/R2-D2 ....$1–$2
Star Tours, Disney-MGM Logos, and C-3PO/R2-D2 ....$1–$2

Bumper Stickers

Let the Wookie Win ....$1–$2
May the Force Be With You ....$1–$2
Support the Rebels...$1–$2
Wookies Need Love Too...$1–$2
Star Tours
     Star Tours, Disney-MGM logos, and Droids, on silver...$1–$2
     Commander Rebel Alliance, Luke, red on white ....$1–$2
     Moon of Endor, Ewok village, white on red ....$1–$2
     Millennium Falcon, battle station, white on red..$1–$2
     Headquarters, X-Wing Fighter Squadron, white on green ....$1–$2
     Imperial Lord Darth Vader, white on black ....$1–$2

Decals (Stickers)

This refers to the peel-and-stick variety as opposed to rub-off transfers found elsewhere in this book.

APS, 1983

Set, includes two sheets, 4″ × 7½″ each with 11 1″ character stickers from Return of the Jedi.
Per set..$2–$5
Set. includes two sheets, 6″ × 9″ each with eight 1″- and 3″-round character stickers from Jedi.
Per set...$3–$6

Fun Products, 1982

Sold in sets of six (two Chewbaccas).
Darth Vader ....$5–$8
Chewbacca ....$5–$8

R2-D2/C-3PO...$5–$8
C-3PO...$5–$8
R2-D2..$5–$8

Star Wars Fan Club (Original)

All full color.
New Hope triangular design ....$1–$2
Vader-in-Flames ....$1–$2
Yoda..$1–$2
Bounty Hunters, McQuarrie Art ....$1–$2

Star Tours

Star Tours Triangular Logo, glow-in-the-dark.............................$1–$2

BLUEPRINTS

Star Wars Blueprints, shows detailed designs for interior of Death Star, the Millennium Falcon, the Sandcrawler, and others, 15 prints in set. Ballantine Books, 1977, 13″ × 19″ ....
....$10–$15
Corellian Freighter Blueprints, Selayana class S starship, interior and exterior details, fan produced, four sheets...$6–$8
Imperial Shuttle Blueprints, L. Miller, exterior and interior views, fan produced, three sheets...$5–$7
Star Destroyer, exteriors, fan produced, four sheets......................$3–$5
X-Wing Blueprints, fan produced...$5–$8

BOOKS

Adult Books

Books are divided first chronologically by movie and then alphabetically within each movie section. Other Star Wars-related books are at the end. Many books have also been translated into foreign language editions including German, Dutch, French, Spanish, and Japanese. Prices are comparable to U.S. editions.
Note: *Ballantine, Del Rey, and Random House are all divisions of the same publishing company.*

Star Wars

Art of Star Wars, The, Ballantine, 1979. Illustrations, stills, and artists' concepts from the movie. Includes script. Oversize hardback ....$35–$45
   Trade paperback...$20–$35
Star Wars, from The Adventures of Luke Skywalker, Ballantine (Sphere in Britain), George Lucas
   Original novel, 1976, paperback...$15–$25
   Later paperback version, 1977, 16-page color photo section .....$4–$8
   Original hardback edition, 1977 ....$15–$20
   Hardback book club edition, 1977 ....$10–$15
Star Wars Album, Ballantine (Sphere in Britain), 1977. Trade paperback.............$15–$25
Star Wars Iron-On Transfer Book, Ballantine, 1977. Sixteen color tee-shirt transfers in book form..$10–$15
Star Wars Portfolio, Ballantine, 1977. Twenty color production prints in folder by Ralph McQuarrie ....$20–$30
Star Wars Sketchbook, Ballantine, 1977, Joe Johnston. Trade paperback.............$25–$30

Assorted Star Wars books for adults.

The Empire Strikes Back

Art of The Empire Strikes Back, The, Ballantine, 1981. Artistic and technical accomplishments of the movie. Does not include script. Oversize hardback..................................$30–$40
   Trade paperback..$20–$30
Empire Strikes Back, The, Del Rey (Sphere in Britain), 1980. Donald F. Glut. Paperback novel..$4–$6
   Hardback book club edition ....$10–$15
Empire Strikes Back, The (Illustrated Edition), Del Rey, 1980, Donald F. Glut. Illustrations by Ralph McQuarrie. Trade paperback..$8–$12
Empire Strikes Back Notebook, Ballantine, 1980. Illustrated script, trade paperback ....
....$15–$25
Empire Strikes Back Portfolio, The, Ballantine, 1980, Ralph McQuarrie. Twenty-four color prints in folder...$20–$30

Art of hardbacks.

Empíre Strikes Back Sketchbook, The, Ballantine, 1980, Joe Johnston and Nilo Rodis-Jamero. Trade paperback ....$20–$25
Once Upon a Galaxy: A Journal of the Making of The Empire Strikes Back, Del Rey, 1980, Alan Arnold ....$10–$12

Return of the Jedi

Art of Return of the Jedi, Ballantine, 1983. Art and photos plus complete script. Oversize hardback ....$30–$40
   Trade paperback ....$20–$30
Jedi Master Quizbook, The, Del Rey, 1982, Rusty Melter...........................$5–$10
Making of Return of the Jedi, The, Ballantine (Sphere in Britain), 1983. Softcover............
....$10–$12
My Jedi Journal, Ballantine, 1983. Blank book ....$5–$7
Return of the Jedi, Del Rey (Futura in Britain), 1983, Novel, James Kahn. Paperback...........
....$4–$6
   Hardback book club edition..$10–$15
Return of the Jedi (Illustrated Edition), Del Rey, 1983. Trade paperback ....$8–$12
Return of the Jedi Portfolio, Ballantine, 1983. Twenty color prints in folder by Ralph McQuarrie ....$20–$30
Return of the Jedi Sketchbook, Ballantine, 1983, Joe Johnston and Nilo Rodis-Jamero. Trade paperback ....$15–$20

Miscellaneous Adult Books

All About the Star Wars, Japanese, Shueisha, 1983. Oversize softcover..................$20–$30
A Guide to the Star Wars Universe, Del Rey (Sphere in Britain), 1984, Raymond L. Velasco
....$3–$5
Force of Star Wars, The, Bible Voice, 1977, Frank Allnutt....................................$5–$10
425 Questions and Answers About Star Wars and The Empire Strikes Back, Del Rey, 1977..$5–$10
Han Solo and The Lost Legacy, Del Rey (Sphere in Britain), 1980, Brian Daley. Original novel. Hardback..$10–$15
   Paperback..$5–$8
Han Solo At Stars' End, Del Rey (Sphere in Britain), 1979, Brian Daley. Original novel. Hardback..$10–$15
   Paperback..$5–$8
Han Solo's Revenge, Del Rey (Sphere in Britain), 1979, Brian Daley. Original novel. Hardback..$10–$15
   Paperback..$5–$8
How to Draw Star Wars Heroes, Creatures, Spaceships, and Other Fantastic Things, Random House, 1984, Lee J. Ames. Softcover ....$8–$12
Industrial Light and Magic: The Art of Special Effects, Del Rey, 1986, Thomas G. Smith. Oversize hardback with dust jacket ....$55–$65
Lando Calrissian and The Flamewind of Osceon, Del Rey, 1983, L. Neil Smith. Hardback
....$10–$15
   Paperback..$5–$8
Lando Calrissian and The Mindharp of Sharu, Del Rey, 1983, L. Neil Smith. Hardback
....$10–$15
   Paperback..$5–$8
Lando Calrissian and The Starcave of Thonboka, Del Rey, 1983, L. Neil Smith. Hardback.
....$10–$15
   Paperback..$5–$8
Return of The Jedi (Japanese Picture Book), Keibunsha, 1983. Small softcover with dust jacket..$10–$15
Skywalking, Harmony (Elm Tree in Britain), 1983, Dale Pollock. George Lucas biography. Hardback..$10–$20
   Paperback..$4–$7
Splinter of the Mind's Eye, Del Rey, 1978, Alan Dean Foster. Original novel. Hardback ......
....$10–$15
   Paperback..$4–$7

Star Wars Intergalactic Passport, Ballantine, 1983. Passport-style booklet with stamps from Star Wars saga locations ....$2–$4
Star Wars Movie Storybook Trilogy, Random House, 1987. Tenth anniversary reprint of storybooks from all three movies ....$12–$15
Star Wars, Star Trek, and the 21st-Century Christians, Bible Voice, 1978, Winkie Pratney ....$10–$15
Star Wars Trilogy, Random House, 1987. Special 10th anniversary edition. All three stories in one book..$10–$20

Children's Books

Activity Books

All softcover.
Star Wars, Random House, 1979
    R2-D2, Chewbacca, Darth Vader, Luke Skywalker, each ....$5–$10
Empire Strikes Back, Random House, 1981. Yoda's Activity Book, James Razzi ......$5–$10
Return of The Jedi, Random House, 1983
    Dot-to-Dot Fun, Mazes, Monster Activity Book, Picture Puzzle Book, Word Puzzle Book, each ....$5–$10

Annuals

These are British oversize hardbacks containing articles and comic reprints.
Star Wars Annual No. 1, 1978, Brown Watson ....$15–$20
Star Wars Annual, 1979, Grandreams...$12–$18
The Empire Strikes Back Annual, 1980, Grandreams.............................$10–$15
The Empire Strikes Back Annual No. 2, 1981, Grandreams ....$10–$12
Star Wars Annual, Featuring Droid World, Marvel/Grandreams, 1982 ....$10–$12
Return of The Jedi, Movie Adaptation, Marvel/Grandreams, 1983.........................$10–$12
Return of The Jedi Annual, Marvel/Grandreams, 1984 ....$10–$12
Star Wars, Featuring Ewoks Annual, Marvel/Grandreams, 1985............................$10–$12

Coloring Books

Star Wars, Kenner, 1977. Several different
    Chewbacca and Han, R2-D2, Chewbacca, each..$5–$10
Empire Strikes Back, Kenner, 1980. Eight different with the following covers
    Cast, Chewbacca and C-3PO, Chewbacca and Leia, Darth Vader and Stormtroopers, Han, Chewbacca, Lando, and Leia, Luke Skywalker, R2-D2, Yoda, each ....$4–$6
Return of the Jedi, Kenner, 1983
    Lando, Lando amd Skiff Guard, Luke, Max Reebo Band, Wicket, Wicket and Kneesa, Wicket, Kneesa and Logray, each..$3–$5

Educational Books

Star Wars Attack on Reading, Random House, 1977
    Comprehension No. 1, Comprehension No. 2, Word Study, Study Skills, each.........$8–$15
Star Wars Book About Flight, Random House, 1983. Softcover...............................$6–$12
Star Wars: C-3PO's Book About Robots, Random House, 1983. Softcover.............$6–$12
Star Wars Question and Answer Book About Computers, Random House, 1983. Softcover..$6–$12
Star Wars Question and Answer Book About Space, Random House, 1983. Softcover...... ....$6–$12
Return of The Jedi Educational Wookbooks, Happy House (Random House), 1983. Six different
    ABC Readiness, Addition and Subtraction, Early Numbers, Spelling, Multiplication, Reading and Writing, each..$3–$5
Ewok Books, Random House, 1985
    ABC Fun, Learn-to-Read, each ....$3–$6

Pop-Up Books

Star Wars Pop-Up Book, Random House (Collins in Britain), 1978. Hardback, 12 scenes ....
....$20–$25
Empire Strikes Back, The, Random House, 1980. Hardback, 14 scenes ....$20–$25
Empire Strikes Back Panorama Book, The, Random House, 1981. Two pop-up scenes plus
punch-out figures ....$20–$25
Return of The Jedi Pop-Up Book, Random House, 1983. Hardback, ten scenes .....$20–$25
Ewoks Save the Day, The, Random House, 1983. Little pops, 5¼″ × 6″ hardback, six scenes
....$8–$15
Han Solo's Rescue, Random House, 1983. Little pops, 5¼″ × 6″ hardback, six scenes ....
....$8–$15
Empire Strikes Back Mix or Match Storybook, Random House, 1980. Flip book with differ-
ent scenes, spiral bound ....$15–$20

Punch-Out Books

Star Wars Punch-Out and Make It Book, Random House, 1978 ....$10–$15
Empire Strikes Back Punch-Out and Make It Book, The, Random House, 1980 ..$10–$15
Return of The Jedi Punch-Out and Make It Book, Random House, 1983 ....$10–$15
Star Wars Book of Masks, The, Random House, 1983. Nine punch-out masks..........$8–$12

Step-Up Books

These are illustrated easy-to-read books for children who are slightly above the be-
ginning reader stage.
Star Wars Step-Up, Random House, 1985 ....$6–$10
Empire Strikes Back, The, Random House, 1985 ....$6–$10
Return of The Jedi, Random House, 1985 ....$6–$10
Star Wars, The Making of the Movie, Random House, 1980....................................$10–$15

Storybooks

Star Wars Storybook, Ballantine, 1978. Oversize hardback.......................................$10–$15
Star Wars Storybook (British), Collins, 1978. Plain blue hardback with dust jacket picturing
R2-D2 and C-3PO..$25–$35
Empire Strikes Back Storybook, The, Random House (Armada in Britain), 1980. Oversize
hardback..$10–$15
Return of The Jedi Storybook, Random House (St. Michael in Britain), 1983. Oversize hard-
back ....$10–$15
Return of the Jedi "Special Junior Edition", Futura (British), 1983 ....$15–$20
Note: *Softcover versions of the U.S. movie adaptation storybooks were done by Scholastic.*
Ewoks and the Lost Children, The, Random House, 1985. Hardback, based on an Ewoks tel-
evision movie (there is also a softcover Japanese version of this book)........................$8–$12
Wookie Storybook, The, Random House, 1979. Hardback.......................................$10–$15

**Assorted Star Wars children's
books.**

Softcover Illustrated Stories, Random House (Armada in Britain). Color artwork

Droid Dilemma, The, 1979, Star Wars ....$4–$8

Maverick Moon, The, 1979, Star Wars...$4–$8

Mystery of the Rebellious Robot, The, 1979, Star Wars.......................................$4–$8

Ewoks Join the Fight, The, 1983, Return of the Jedi ....$4–$8

Softcover Mini-Storybooks, Random House, 1984. 5″ × 5½″ format. Return of the Jedi logo.

Baby Ewoks' Picnic Surprise ....$2–$4

Ewoks' Hang-Gliding Adventure ....$2–$4

Three Cheers for Kneesa..$2–$4

Wicket Finds a Way ....$2–$4

Droids Storybooks, Random House, 1985

Escape from the Monster Ship...$3–$6

Lost Prince, The..$3–$6

Pirates of Tarnoonga, The ....$3–$6

Red Ghost, The ....$3–$6

Shiny as a Droid..$3–$6

Ewoks Storybooks, Random House, 1985

Fuzzy as an Ewok ....$3–$6

How the Ewoks Saved the Trees ....$3–$6

School Days...$3–$6

Wicket and the Danelion Warrior ....$3–$6

Wicket Goes Fishing...$3–$6

Young Readers Editions

Sphere (British)

Star Wars, 1978 ....$15–$20

Empire Strikes Back, The, 1980 ....$10–$20

CALENDARS

Ballantine Books

1978, black cover with "Star Wars" in blue and photos of Han, Luke, Leia, and X-Wing chasing TIE Fighter. Interior has photos from movie, came boxed ....$25–$30

1979, black cover with "Star Wars" in red. Interior has photos from first movie, last boxed calendar...$25–$30

1980, blue cover with triangular "A New Hope" art. Interior has different movie posters from around the world ....$20–$25

1981, cover shows color "Kissing Scene" art from Empire. Interior has photos from second movie..$10–$15

1984, Return of the Jedi. Black cover with "Lightsaber" movie art. Interior has photos from Jedi ....$8–$12

Assorted Star Wars calendars.

1984, Ewok Calendar, Random House (affiliated with Ballantine). Yellow cover with cartoon artwork of Ewoks hang-gliding. Interior has Ewok animated artwork and 48 peel-off stickers ....$4–$7

Miscellaneous
Cedco Publishing

1990, cover shows color artwork of characters originally done as promotional art for Return of the Jedi. Interior has photos from all three of the original Star Wars saga films ....$10–$12
1991, Cedco Publishing. Cover art shows montage of characters originally used as promotional art for first movie ....$10–$12

Thomas Forman and Sons (British)

1982, 12 color scenes from Star Wars and Empire...$20–$25

CLOTHING AND ACCESSORIES

Belts and Belt Buckles

Basic Tool & Supply, 1977. Made a series of buckles in heavy brass. Unlicensed copies of these also exist
  C-3PO and R2-D2, Darth Vader, Star Wars (logo), X-Wing with Star Wars logo....$15–$20
Character Belt, characters engaged in scenes from Star Wars imprinted on belt........$15–$20
Character Belt, characters alternate with Star Wars and Jedi logos imprinted on belt..............
....$15–$20
Lee Co., 1979/83. Made elastic and leather belts and belt buckles.
  Buckle, 1979. C-3PO and R2-D2-. 3″ rectangular with blue enamel background. Adult size
  ....$10–$15
  Elastic belts, packaged on metal hangers
    May the Force Be With You, elastic with word printed onto belt ....$15–$25
    Star Wars, elastic with logo printed on belt. Tan or blue with small magnetic enamel Star Wars logo buckle...$15–$25
    Star Wars/Empire Strikes Back, alternating logos on elastic belt. Tan or blue .....$15–$25
    Star Wars/Return of the Jedi, alternating logos on elastic belt. Tan or blue with small, round, color artwork character buckle ....$15–$25

Assorted clothing accessories: hats, Jedi belt, and Darth Vader sandals.

Star Wars belts.

Leather belts, came in box with clear plastic lid. Star Wars logo, R2-D2, and C-3PO on box lid. Children's sizes. Included small brass character buckles. Three styles:
    Darth Vader, oval ....$20–$30
    Jabba the Hutt, rectangular ....$20–$30
    Yoda, round..$20–$30
Leather belt, brown, child's size with red enamel Empire logo buckle....................$15–$20

Billfolds, Coin Holders, and Wallets

Billfolds, Adam Joseph, 1983. Color vinyl. Horizontal folding style. Came blister packed on cardboard header with Jedi logo.
    Darth Vader and Imperial Guards on black billfold, R2-D2 and C-3PO on blue background, Yoda on red background ....$10–$15
Coin Holders, Adam Joseph, 1983. Small pouches with color artwork of characters. Vertical fold-over with velcro closure. Packaged in clear plastic bag attached to header with Jedi logo
    Darth Vader and Imperial Guards on black, R2-D2 and C-3PO on blue, Yoda on red...........
....$5–$10
Coin Holder, Touchline (British), 1983. Plastic 3″ oval in assorted colors. Eight different characters. Price each...$5–$10
Pocket Pals, Adam Joseph, 1983. Similar to coin holders but with extra compartment for photos and ring for keys. More square in shape
    Darth Vader and Imperial Guards on black, R2-D2 and C-3PO on blue, Yoda on red...........
....$5–$10
Wallet, Adam Joseph, 1983. Color vinyl. Similar to billfolds but with side snap closure
    Darth Vader and Imperial Guards on black, R2-D2 and C-3PO on blue, Yoda on red...........
....$10–$15
Wallet, Adam Joseph, 1983. Vinyl with cartoon Ewok artwork. Came blister packed on header card
    Kneesa, Wicket ....$10–$15
Wallet, Adam Joseph, 1983. Velcro closure-type. Vertical foldover. Packaged similar to coin holders
    Darth Vader and Imperial Guards on black, R2-D2 and C-3PO on blue, Yoda on red...........
....$10–$15
Wallet, Star Tours. Black nylon with velcro closure and "Star Tours" words screen-printed in corner ....$5–$8

Caps and Hats

Thinking Cap Co., 1980–81
    Empire Strikes Back logo cap, embroidered white, red, and black emblem on front of adjustable baseball-style cap. Assorted colors ....$10–$15

Imperial Guard hat, solid black hat with short bill styled after those worn by Imperial offi-
cers in the movies. Metal silver medallion on front of hat said "Star Wars" and "Imperial
Guard." Adult sizes...$15–$25
Rebel Forces cap, tan billed cap with flap in back. Round red, blue, and yellow embroidered
patch on front says "Star Wars" and "Rebel Forces." Adult sizes............................$15–$20
Yoda ear cap, red, adjustable baseball-style cap. Green stuffed cloth "ears" and artificial hair
on sides. Yellow and black embroidered "Yoda" patch on front...............................$15–$20
Sales Corp. of America, 1983. Adjustable children's size baseball-style caps with solid fronts
and mesh backs in assorted colors. Color artwork design was silkscreened on hat
    Admiral Ackbar, name and picture of character...$8–$12
    Darth Vader and Emperor's Guards...$8–$12
    Gammorrean Guard, name and four guards ....$8–$12
    Jabba the Hutt, name and picture of Jabba..$8–$12
    Luke and Darth, logo and characters dueling ....$8–$12
    Return of the Jedi, logo..$8–$12
Sales Corp. of America, 1983. Ski cap with "Jedi" knit into hat. White with red and black
trim..$15–$20
Sales Corp. of America, 1983. Knit child's hat with Ewok pictured in color on front .$10–$15
Star Tours
    "Star Tours," words embroidered on black baseball cap...$6–$8
    Logo, in orange artwork burst design on black baseball cap..$6–$8
    Logo, orange and blue on white baseball cap..$7–$9
    "Star Tours and Disney–MGM," logos on front, Droids on side. Color artwork on white
    painter's cap..$7–$9
Star Wars Fan Club Hat, special promotional item ....$10–$15

Carrying Bags

Back Packs, Adam Joseph, 1983
    Darth Vader and Imperial Guards on red pack, R2-D2 and C-3PO on blue pack, Yoda on red
    nylon pack..$20–$30

**Left: Tote bags, Velcro billfold and coin holder, and backpack.
Right: Luke Skywalker jacket.**

Back Pack, Bags of Character. Blue canvas with small outside pocket. Darth Vader and two Stormtroopers on flap, Luke, Leia, C-3PO, and R2-D2 on front along with Jedi logo ....
....$20–$30
Back Pack, Star Tours. Black with blue and silver "Star Tours" logo ....$25–$30
Duffle Bags, Adam Joseph, Barrel, 1983
  R2-D2 and C-3PO on blue bag...$20–$30
  Yoda on red bag ....$20–$30
Fanny Pack, Star Tours. Black with blue and silver "Star Tours" logo.....................$10–$15
Gym Bag, Star Tours. Horizontal design with blue and silver "Star Tours" logo........$25–$30
Toilette Case, Star Tours. Black with blue and silver "Star Tours" logo ....$12–$15
Tote Bags, Adam Joseph, 1983. Canvas with handles and snap closure.
  Darth Vader and Imperial Guards on red bag ....$15–$25
  R2-D2 and C-3PO on blue bag...$15–$25
Tote Bag, Star Tours. Black open design with blue and silver "Star Tours" logo........$15–$20

General Items

Jacket, fatigue type. Features Luke Skywalker and Bespin Guard ....$50–$75
Jacket, short, tan fitted style. Copy of jacket worn by Luke in Empire Strikes Back. Fan Club promotion ....$75–$100
Jacket, Star Tours. Embroidered pocket logo on black and blue nylon jacket with half zipper front..$40–$50
Jacket, Star Tours. Pocket front logo and full back logo. Silver satin jacket with blue piping and lining ....$80–$90
Leg Warmers, Sales Corp. of America, 1983. 22″ long, black with red and white stitching. "Jedi" knit into item..$15–$20
Pajamas, three different styles
  Star Wars, C-3PO, and X-Wing, gold..$10–$20
  Star Wars, Darth Vader, C-3PO, and R2-D2, blue...$10–$20
  May the Force Be With You, Darth and R2-D2, blue ....$10–$20
Pajamas, Sleepers, and Nightshirts, several different one- and two-piece outfits in children's sizes with Ewok artwork. Price each ....$10–$15
Polo Shirt, Star Tours. Color embroidered pocket logo on white or black shirt ....$20–$25
Poncho, 1983. Plastic, children's, with Jedi logo..$10–$20
Raincoat, 1983. Plastic, children's, with Jedi logo..$15–$20
Sandals, flip-flop variety
  Darth Vader, 1977, Vader head, Star Wars logo ....$15–$20
  Yoda, "May the Force Be With You" on sides ....$10–$20
Shoes, Stride Rite. Sneakers, decorated with cutouts of characters. Assorted colors ...$15–$25
Shoelaces, Stride Rite, 1983. Came blister packed on header card with spaceships and Jedi logo
  Ewoks...$3–$5
  Return of the Jedi, logo...$3–$5

Examples of boys' tube socks.

Underoos.

Star Wars logo, with Darth Vader ....$3–$5
Star Wars logo, with R2-D2 and C-3PO..$3–$5
Slipper Socks, Stride Rite, 1983. Character on front
C-3PO, Darth Vader..$10–$15
Socks, 1980. Boys, tube style with small, square, color photo transfers on cuff
C-3PO, Chewbacca, "Darth Vader Lives," R2-D2, Space Battle, Snowspeeder ....$5–$10
Socks, Charleston Hosiery, 1983. Color transfer on cuff
R2-D2 and Wicket, R2-D2 and Darth Vader..$5–$10
Socks, 1977. Girls knee-highs with Star Wars logo......................................$5–$10
Suspenders, Lee Co. 1980. Children's suspenders with circular plastic badge with raised Empire logo and color picture of character
Darth Vader, Yoda..$15–$20
Sweatshirt, Star Tours. Word logo in glitter on black shirt ....$30–$35
Sweatshirt, Star Tours. Embroidered pocket logo on gray shirt....................$30–$35
Sun-Visor, Star Tours. White plastic with logo on bill ....$3–$5
Underwear, Union Underwear, 1983, Underoos. Children's shirt and pants sets. Color decals on shirts. Packaged in flat square cardboard envelope with color photo of product and Underoos and Jedi logos. Includes "Jedi Knight Certificate"
Boba Fett, C-3PO, Darth Vader, Han Solo, Luke Skywalker, Princess Leia, R2-D2, Wicket, Yoda ....$10–$20
Umbrellas, Adam Joseph, 1983
Darth Vader, R2-D2 ....$15–$25
Vest, black with pockets. Replica of one worn by Han Solo in movies. Fan Club promotion ...
....$75–$100

Tee Shirts and Tee-Shirt Transfers

At the time the Star Wars movies were first being shown, the popular method of applying a design to a tee shirt was by means of iron-on decals made primarily from plastisal, a thin rubberlike material. Unfortunately for collectors, these transfers do not age well, either on or off of shirts. They are sensitive to both temperature and humidity and often crack, peel, or bubble. Another type of transfer, done by a method called sublimation, was used for the *Star Wars Transfer Book* (*See* "Books"), but these could only be used on polyester shirts and never gained much popularity. By the end of the Star Wars saga, the much more durable silkscreen shirt process was coming into general usage, but very few Star Wars shirts utilize this process.

Transfers, Factors, Etc., 1977. Color photo or artwork designs. Usually sold to the retail customer on shirts. Price here is for transfer alone
Chewy, Darth Vader helmet (with ships), "Darth Vader Lives" (with Vader helmet), Darth Vader (full figure), Droids (blue background), Han Solo and Chewbacca, "May the Force Be

With You," Jawas, Luke and C-3PO, Poster art (Hildebrandt), Princess Leia, R2-D2 and C-3PO in ship corridor, Star Wars logo (glitter)..$1–$3

Transfers, Factors, Etc., 1980. Color photo or artwork designs. Empire designs were glossier transfer material than earlier ones and made greater use of glitter detail

Boba Fett, Empire Strikes Back (logo), Han Solo, Lando Calrissian, Luke on Tauntaun, Luke with X-Wing, Millennium Falcon, Poster art (kissing scene), Star Destroyer, The Way of the Force (Luke and Yoda), TIE Fighter, X-Wing, Yoda ....$1–$3

Tee Shirts, Junior Stars, 1983. A tee shirt with photo transfers applied. Transfers were not sold separately even to wholesalers. Shirts came in assorted colors

Chewbacca, R2-D2, and C-3PO ....$5–$10
Han Solo, insets of Sarlacc and Ewok..$5–$10
Luke Skywalker and Darth Vader..$5–$10
Luke, Darth, and Emperor ....$5–$10
Princess Leia, inset of Leia and Han ....$5–$10
R2-D2 and Wicket ....$5–$10
Wicket ....$5–$10

Tee Shirt and Cap, Hi-C, 1983. Promotional set. Shirt had montage of Jedi characters. White and navy hat showed Luke and Darth Vader...$15–$20

Tee Shirts, Color-Me-Tee, Patti M. Productions, 1987. Four different line drawings of Ewoks. Comes packaged in clear plastic box with four markers. Price each ....$12–$15

Tee Shirt, Star Wars Fan Club. Promotional. Shows Club's Bantha logo....................$10–$15

Tee Shirt, Studio promotional. Star Wars logo on front and "May the Force Be With You" on back...$10–$15

Tee Shirts, Star Tours. Star Tours at both Disneyland and Disneyworld carry extensive lines of Star Wars- and Star Tours-related shirts. All are silkscreened. Prices reflect current shirt prices only since Disney will undoubtedly continue making any design for as long as it sells. Most designs come in adult and children's sizes

10th anniversary logo, blue, lavender, and yellow on white shirt ....$10–$12
Star Tours logo, triangular logo puffy design on black shirt with stylized white star pattern
....$18–$22
Robot, with "Star Tours" background wording on navy shirt....................................$12–$14
TIE Interceptor, with Star Tours triangular logo below and word logo on side........$12–$14
C-3PO, stylized color artwork and name. White shirt...$24–$26
R2-D2, stylized color artwork and name. White shirt...$24–$26
Ewoks, color artwork and name on white shirt ....$14–$16
Darth Vader, color artwork with smaller inset of silhouette of Darth and Luke in lightsaber duel..$12–$14
C-3PO, artwork with parts labeled and name at side on white shirt ....$12–$14
R2-D2, artwork with parts labeled and name at side on white shirt ....$12–$14
"Jedi and Master Yoda," words and color artwork on red shirt ....$12–$14
Darth Vader, outlined head in glitter on name background ....$12–$14
Ewok, color cartoon artwork on white shirt ....$12–$14
Imperial Walker, name and color artwork on white shirt ....$12–$14
"Star Tours," name with color artwork of R2-D2, C-3PO, and vehicle below stylized logo. Child's size only...$10–$12
"Star Tours," name and Star Tours droid in color circular design. Child's size only....$7–$9
"Star Tours," words in glitter on black shirt..$17–$19
"Star Tours," words around artwork view down trench...$10–$12
R2-D2 and C-3PO, stylized line artwork with vehicles and "Star Tours" below .....$10–$12
X-Wing, color artwork with triangular logo below and "Star Tours" on side. Tank top ....
....$10–$12

Note: *All of the above shirts and transfers are licensed. Though a few unlicensed Star Wars shirts and transfers have been made, they never reached the epidemic proportions that unlicensed Star Trek shirts have.*

COINS, RARITIES MINT (1987–1988)

This series of limited edition, numbered collectors' coins in fine metals was released over a period of time by the manufacturer. Coins are .999 pure gold or silver with proof finishes. All coins are encased in plastic containers. The five-oz. silver coins come in hinged velveteen jewelry boxes. For all others, the plastic coin cases are embedded in a cardboard card which is slipped into a pocket of a paper folder. Both the card and the folder show color artwork of the characters depicted on the coin. The front of the folders of all coins show the Star Wars Tenth Anniversary logo. In the case of all but the one-oz. silver coins, mintages are probably very low.

One-Oz. Silver Coins

I The Epic Begins..$75–$100
II R2-D2 and C-3PO...$75–$100
III Han Solo and Chewbacca..$75–$100
IV Imperial Stormtroopers...$75–$100
V Mos Eisley Cantina Band..$75–$100
VI Darth Vader and Ben (Obi-Wan) Kenobi............................$75–$100

Five-Oz. Silver Coins

I The Epic Begins...$200–$300
II R2-D2 and C-3PO...$200–$300
III Han Solo and Chewbacca..$200–$300
IV Imperial Stormtroopers...$200–$300
V Mos Eisley Cantina Band..$200–$300
VI Darth Vader and Ben (Obi-Wan) Kenobi............................$200–$300

One-Quarter-Oz. Gold Coins

I The Epic Begins...$400–$500
II R2-D2 and C-3PO...$400–$500
III Han Solo and Chewbacca..$400–$500
IV Imperial Stormtroopers...$400–$500
V Mos Eisley Cantina Band..$400–$500
VI Darth Vader and Ben (Obi-Wan) Kenobi............................$400–$500

One-Oz. Gold Coins

I The Epic Begins...$2,000–$5,000
II R2-D2 and C-3PO...$2,000–$5,000
III Han Solo and Chewbacca..$2,000–$5,000
IV Imperial Stormtroopers...$2,000–$5,000
V Mos Eisley Cantina Band..$2,000–$5,000
VI Darth Vader and Ben (Obi-Wan) Kenobi............................$2,000–$5,000

Note: *A series of aluminum coins was made by Kenner in conjunction with the Star Wars, Droids, and Ewoks series of small action figures. See "Action Figures" section for these coins.*

COLLECTORS' PLATES

This series of plates was released in intervals between 1986 and 1988. Their manufacture was totally discontinued in 1989. Plates are 8¼″ in diameter, numbered limited editions, designed by the Hamilton Collection with artwork by Thomas Blackshear. Never as available as the Star Trek plates, they went out of production very suddenly and values rose accordingly. As with most numbered series, lower numbers can be worth considerably more.

Star Wars commemorative plate (bottom center) and eight plates of series.

Crew in Cockpit of Millennium Falcon, Darth and Luke, Han Solo, Imperial Walkers, Luke and Yoda, Princess Leia, R2-D2 and Wicket, Space Battle..........................$75–$125
Note: *A series of mugs was done to go along with the collectors' plates with identical artwork. Originally, mugs were only sold in sets, but were later made available individually in some outlets. Price each* ....$10–$15
Star Wars 10th Anniversary Plate, 1988, designed by Hamilton, artwork by Thomas Blackshear, 10¼″ numbered, limited edition. Last of the Star Wars plates to go out of production ....$75–$100
Note: *For other ceramics and glassware, see appropriate section under "Housewares."*

COMICS

Marvel Comics Group, 1977–1986

Star Wars
  No. 1, 30 cents cover price ....$5–$10
  No. 2, 35 cents cover price ....$50–$300
  No. 2–4...$4–$8

Star Wars Treasury #3, Star Wars #1, and Star Wars Annual #1.

No. 5–10...$3–$5
No. 11–19...$2–$4
No. 20–37...$1–$2
No. 38–44..$1.50–$3
No. 45–107...$1–$2
Star Wars Annual No. 1, 1979 ....$1–$2
Star Wars Annual No. 2, 1980 ....$1–$2
Star Wars Annual No. 3, 1981 ....$1–$2
Star Wars: Return of the Jedi, No. 1–4..$1–$2

Marvel Comics (British)

This long-running series published first on a weekly, then on a monthly basis. Any issue cost between ....$1–$2

Marvel Illustrated Books

Star Wars, 1981. Four original adventures: Way of the Wookie, The Day After the Death Star, Weapons Master, and War on Ice...$3–$6
Star Wars 2, 1982. World of Fire ....$2–$4
Star Wars Treasury 1, 1977. 11″ × 14″, story of Episode IV (A New Hope), part one of two
....$2–$4
Star Wars Treasury 2, 1977. 11″ × 14″, completes story in part one............................$2–$4
Star Wars Treasury 3, 1978. 11″ × 14″, complete story from one and two in one volume......
....$3–$5
Empire Strikes Back, Marvel Super Special No. 2, 1980. 8½″ × 11″ magazine format. Complete story...$3–$5
Star Wars: Return of the Jedi, 1983. 8½″ × 11″ magazine format. Marvel Super Special. Complete story. ....$3–$5

Star Comics (Juvenile Division of Marvel)

Droids, based on the animated TV series, No. 1–8............................$.50–$1.50
Ewoks, based on the animated TV series, No. 1–15..........................$.50–$1.50

Blackthorne 3-D Series

No. 30, Star Wars in 3-D, No. 1 ....$2.50–$6
No. 47, Star Wars in 3-D, No. 2 ....$2.50–$5
No. 48, Star Wars in 3-D, No. 3 ....$2.50–$5

COSMETICS

Beauty Bag, Omni, 1981. Princess Leia Beauty Bag. Contains two-oz. shampoo, cream rinse, and cologne in regular-shaped plastic bottles decorated with Star Wars logo and line drawing of Leia. Also contains Leia character soap and comb. Comes in clear plastic carry bag with handles decorated with Star Wars logo and "Princess Leia Beauty Bag" on front.......$25–$40
Belt Kit, Omni, 1981. Luke Skywalker Belt Kit. Contains two-oz. bottles of shampoo, cream rinse, and cologne in regular-shaped plastic bottles decorated with Star Wars logo and line drawing of Luke. Also includes Luke character soap, comb, and toothbrush. Comes in clear plastic snap-shut pouch with Star Wars logo and "Luke Skywalker Belt Kit" on front ....
....$25–$40
Bubble Bath, Addis (British), 1983. Character bubble bath. Eight different
    Luke, Leia, R2-D2, Darth Vader, Chewbacca, C-3PO, Ben Kenobi, Wicket............$10–$15
Bubble Bath Gift Sets, Addis (British), 1985. Two different
    R2-D2, C-3PO, and two soaps..$20–$30
    Ewoks bath and soap ....$15–$25

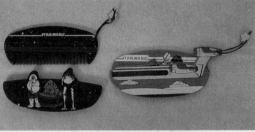

Left: Star Wars soap (top) and examples of bubble bath/shampoo containers with bubble bath refill. Right: Comb-and-keepers.

Bubble Bath, Omni, 1981–83. Containers were colored plastic shaped like characters from Star Wars, 4½″ × 9½″ tall. Most were introduced in 1981 but Wicket and Jabba were added after Return of the Jedi in 1983.

Chewbacca, Darth Vader, Jabba the Hutt, Luke Skywalker (X-Wing Pilot outfit), Princess Leia, R2-D2, Wicket, Yoda..$10–$15

Note: *Omni used these same containers to hold their line of shampoo which was being marketed the same time as the bubble bath.*

Bubble Bath Refueling Station, Omni, 1981. Regular-shaped plastic bottle, 6½″ tall decorated with ships in space and Star Wars logo ....$3–$5

Combs

Comb-N-Keepers, Adam Joseph, 1983. Colorful plastic combs fit into base (keeper), small plastic star is attached by string to one end. Two different

Speeder, R2-D2 and C-3PO on comb, keeper is shaped like landspeeder ....$10–$15

Rebo Band, band is shown on keeper..$10–$15

Pop-Up Combs, Adam Joseph, 1983. Combs come with flip-up mirror which locks closed when comb is inserted. Three different

C-3PO and R2-D2 Star Wars logo..$10–$15

Darth Vader, Jedi logo..$10–$15

Leia, Jedi logo...$10–$15

Personal Care Kit, Adam Joseph, 1983. Ewok Personal Care Bag. Zippered bag with silk-screened picture of Princess Kneesa. Includes comb and mirror ....$15–$25

Shampoo, Omni, 1981. Character shampoo (*see* Bubble Bath in this section). The same containers were used for both. Prices are comparable ....$10–$15

Shampoo Refueling Station, Omni, 1981. Regular-shaped plastic bottle, 6½″ tall, decorated with space-ships and Star Wars logo ....$3–$5

Soap, Cliro (British), 1977. Character soap. 4″ high. Packaged in illustrated box

C-3PO, R2-D2 ....$5–$10

Soap, Omni, 1981–83. Character soaps. Individual soap was bath size in assorted colors with character in relief on one side and Star Wars logo on other. Came packaged in window boxes with headers displaying Star Wars logo and character's name. Short description of character on back of box

C-3PO, Chewbacca, Darth Vader, Gammorrean Guard, Lando Calrissian, Leia, Luke, R2-D2, Wicket, Yoda...$5–$10

Soap Collections, Omni, 1981. Four different character soaps packaged together in window box with header saying "Star Wars Soap Collection" and picturing spaceships. Two different

No. 1, Leia, Luke, Yoda, and Chewbacca...$20–$30

No. 2, R2-D2, C-3PO, Darth, and Lando ....$20–$30

Sponge, British. Shaped like Darth Vader...$5–$10

Toothbrushes (See "Housewares")

Costumes. Top: Don Post masks.
Bottom: Ben Cooper costumes
and mask, McCall's pattern.

COSTUMES

Acamas (British), 1983

Sets included mask and plastic outfit in illustrated box.
C-3PO, Stormtrooper, Darth Vader, Yoda, Wicket, Luke, Gammorrean Guard,
Chewbacca ....$25–$35

Ben Cooper

Costumes

Between 1977 and 1983, Ben Cooper manufactured traditional Halloween-type costumes in children's sizes. Costume generally consisted of a one- or two-piece vinyl
suit and a thin plastic mask. Packaging was in 8½″ × 11″ thin cardboard window
boxes with color artwork and logo from most current movie. Characters were added
and box logos updated with each new film. Values assume costume and box are in-
tact.
Admiral Ackbar ....$20–$30
Boba Fett..$25–$35
Darth Vader ....$25–$35
C-3PO...$25–$35
Chewbacca...$25–$35
Gammorrean Guard..$20–$30
Klaatu, displays Revenge of the Jedi logo on costume ....$50–$75
Luke Skywalker ....$25–$35
Obi-Wan Kenobi ....$25–$35
Princess Leia...$25–$35
R2-D2...$25–$35
Stormtrooper ....$25–$35
Wicket ....$20–$30
Yoda...$25–$30

Poncho

Darth Vader Fun Poncho, 1977. Waterproof yellow vinyl poncho and matching mask..........
....$30–$40

Masks

Adult Masks (no costume), 1977. Vacuformed plastic
   C-3PO, Chewbacca, Darth Vader, Stormtrooper, Tusken Raider..............................$25–$35

Don Post, 1980–1983 and 1990 (Reissue)

Manufacturer of quality adult masks. Don Post's original series of Star Wars character masks came packaged in square blue boxes with movie logo. Seven of the masks were reissued in 1990. Reissue masks come unboxed and some have minor changes from the originals. Values reflect difficulty of production (real fiber was used for hair) and devaluation of originals by reissues.

1980

C-3PO	$75–$100
Cantina Band Member	$60–$75
Chewbacca	$80–$100
Darth Vader, rounded points either side of breathing grid	$50–$75
Stormtrooper, hard plastic, solid eye-pieces	$75–$100
Tusken Raider	$50–$75
Ugnaught	$50–$75
Yoda	$50–$60

1983 Additions

Admiral Ackbar	$60–$75
Gammorrean Guard	$75–$100
Klaatu	$75–$100
Weequay	$75–$100
Wicket	$75–$90

1990 Reissues

Admiral Ackbar	$50–$60
Cantina musician	$50–$60
Chewbacca	$75–$85
Darth Vader, indentations either side of breathing grid	$50–$60
Stormtrooper, soft plastic, grid eye-pieces	$55–$65
Wicket	$65–$75
Yoda	$40–$50

McCall's

Patterns to make children's costumes. Small-, medium-, and large-size patterns were available. Came packaged in standard pattern envelope with color photo of completed outfit.

1981, included patterns for Chewbacca, Leia, Yoda, Jawa, and Darth Vader ....$8–$12
1983, pattern for Ewok costume ....$8–$12

Palitoy

(British), 1978, five different masks.
C-3PO, Chewbacca, Darth Vader, Stormtrooper, Tusken Raider ....$15–$25

FAN CLUBS

There has never been the plethora of small fan clubs in Star Wars that there has been in Star Trek. This is partially due to Lucasfilm's policy of being very selective as regards use of the "Star Wars" name. They much prefer an official fan club whose standards and policies they could supervise and direct. There have been two such clubs. The first, now defunct, put out 31 issues of a club subscription newsletter, *Bantha Tracks*, and distributed club membership kits and merchandise (found under appropriate chapters in this book). The current club, The Lucasfilm Fan Club, puts out a glossy news magazine very similar to the *Official Star Trek Fan Club* magazine. This is not surprising since they are both run by the same people. Like its Star

Fan club kit from original Star Wars fan club (left) and first issue of current Lucasfilm fan club newsletter.

Trek counterpart, this is a good source of interesting news articles that, because of Lucasfilm's support, is "straight from the horse's mouth." Their address is as follows:

> **The Lucasfilm Fan Club**
> **P. O. Box 111000**
> **Aurora, CO 80011**

FANZINES

As with Star Trek fanzines, several different types of Star Wars fanzines exist: Action/Adventure (AA), Mixed Media (MM), and Adult. Lucasfilm was not very happy with the subject matter of some fanzines and has taken an active part in directing fanzine editors not to produce Adult Graphic Star Wars stories. As a result, the vast majority of Star Wars fanzines are Action/Adventure. The Adult Star Wars fanzines that do exist command much higher prices than their Action/Adventure counterparts. Fanzine editors (zineds) are a feisty lot and somehow find ways of distributing their erotic stories at local conventions and amongst each other. It is due to their relative unavailability that racy fanzines consistently out-price generic Star Wars fanzines.

Below are listed some of the more collectible and well-written fanzines. Most Star Wars fanzines are out of print and can only be purchased at science fiction conventions from people selling their personal collections. New Star Wars fanzines are relatively rare; however, with the announcement of additional Star Wars movies, a resurgence in the publications of Star Wars fanzines is expected. It is generally expected that the prices of the fanzines listed below will rise accordingly. All prices listed are for single issues of *original* issue copies only.

Against the Sith, N. Duncan, AA...$15–$18
Alderaan, Kzinti Press, AA..$10–$12
Besbin Times, P. Nolan, AA...$10–$12
Beta Antares, Interplanetary Fizbin Society, MM ....$10–$12
Combining Forces, K. Gianna, AA...$15–$18
Crossed Sabres, K. Harkins, AA..$18–$22
Empire Review, S. Barrett, AA...$12–$15
Esper!, T'Kuthian Press, AA..$10–$12
Facets, J. Firmstone, AA..$18–$22
Far Realms, J. Henning, MM..$18–$20
Flip of a Coin, J. McAdams, AA..$18–$25
Imperial Entanglements, K. Osman, AA ....$12–$15
Incident on Ardnor, N. White, AA..$18–$20
Jedi Journal, E. Dougherty, AA...$12–$15
Kessel Run, M. Malkin, AA..$18–$20

Legends of Light, S. Voll, AA ....$18–$22
Lighter Side of the Force, S. Crites, AA ....$10–$12
Mos Eisley Tribune, AA ....$18–$20
Multiverse, N. White, AA ....$18–$20
Outland Chronicles, C. Jeffords, AA...$12–$15
Pegasus series, J. Hendricks, AA...$35–$40
Princes Tapes, J. Lowe, AA..$25–$30
Showcase Special, S. Emily ....$15–$18
Skywalker, B. Deer, AA ....$50–$60
Slaysu Series, C. Siebrant, Adult ....$20–$25
Thunderbolt, J. Hicks, AA ....$12–$15
Twin Suns, J. Hicks, AA ....$15–$18

The list below represents a cross-section of the short stories, novels, newsletters, commentaries, and correspondence circulating around the world of Star Wars. If you would like to contact any of the people on this list, please enclose a self-addressed, stamped envelope with your correspondence.

Abode of Strife
Bill Hipe
6273 Balfour
Lansing, MI 48911

Just Deserts
Ann Wortham
1402 Allison Ave.
Altamonte Springs, FL 32701

Comlink
Allyson M. Dyar
40-A Cecil Lane
Montgomery, AL 36109

Knights of Shadows
Poison Pen Press
627 E. 8th St.
Brooklyn, NY 11218

Datazine Fanzine Listing
P. O. Box 24590
Denver, CO 80224

Partisans
Wendy Rathbone
13101 Sudan Rd.
Poway, CA 92064

Dragon's Teeth
Poison Pen Press
627 E. 8th St.
Brooklyn, NY 11218

Revenge of the Jedi
Melody Rondeau
1853 Fallbrook Ave.
San Jose, CA 95130

Flip of a Coin
Jenny McAdams
502 McKeithan #4a
Tallahassee, FL 32304

FIGURINES

Ceramic

Produced by Sigma, 1983. Figures are hand-painted porcelain bisque and range in height from 3½″ to 5″. Figurines came in silver-colored boxes with photo of item and Jedi logo on front.

Bib Fortuna ....$25–$40
Boba Fett...$25–$40
C-3PO and R2-D2 ....$30–$50
Darth Vader ....$30–$50
Galactic Emperor, seated ....$25–$40
Gammorrean Guard ....$25–$40
Han Solo..$30–$50
Klaatu..$25–$40

Ceramic figures by Sigma.

Lando Calrissian ....$25–$40
Luke Skywalker, Jedi knight ....$30–$50
Princess Leia, Boush disguise ....$25–$40
Wicket W. Warrick ....$25–$40

Metal Miniatures

Produced from 1977–78, figures are pewter, 1″ to 2″ in height. All but one of the figurines (Han Solo) was originally produced by Heritage. Star Trek Galore redid all of the original Heritage figures and added the Han Solo figure. In addition to selling them strictly as figures, Star Trek Galore adapted a number of the pieces to different types of jewelry—keychains, charms, etc. Neither company was licensed and when Twentieth Century Fox forced manufacturing to cease, most were destroyed. Figures were sold either painted or unpainted. No packaging.

Bantha Set, Bantha ridden by two Sand people. Sand people were removable but wouldn't stand alone ....$35–$45
C-3PO ....$10–$15
Chewbacca ....$15–$20
Darth Vader ....$15–$20
Han Solo ....$10–$15
Jawa ....$10–$15

Heavier figures on right are Star Trek Galore's. Figures on left are for Kenner Micro toys.

Luke Skywalker ....$15–$20
Obi-Wan Kenobi ....$15–$20
Princess Leia..$15–$20
R2-D2 ....$15–$20
Sand Person, not the same as in Bantha set ....$10–$15
Snitch..$10–$15
Storm Trooper ....$15–$20

Plastic

Produced by Comics Spain, 1986, figurines are 2″ to 3″ nonposable. Based on animated shows.
C-3PO ....$2–$4
R2-D2 ....$2–$4
Ewok..$2–$4
Note: *For other metal miniature figurines see Micro Collection Toys under "Toys and Crafts" and West End Games in the Role-Playing Games section under "Games."*

FILM AND VIDEO

All the Star Wars saga movies were released in Europe on videotape as they were in the United States. Some of the Droids and Ewoks cartoons were released there as well. It should be noted, however, that U.S. and European video systems are incompatible, and tapes from one system cannot be viewed on the other.

Film, 8mm

Usually came boxed with color photo and logo of film. Ken Films
Star Wars, 1977, 8-min. excerpts..$10–$15
Star Wars, 1977, 17-min. excerpts ....$15–$20
Empire Strikes Back, 1980, 8-min. excerpts ....$10–$15
Empire Strikes Back, 1980, 17-min. excerpts ....$15–$20
JEF Films, commercial releases of theatrical film trailers (teasers for upcoming movies) for the public
Star Wars ....$10–$15
Empire Strikes Back ....$10–$15
Revenge of the Jedi..$10–$15

Video Tape and Discs, CBS Fox Video

Star Wars..$20–$30
Empire Strikes Back ....$20–$30

Back: Super 8 and video packaging. Front: 35mm theatrical Star Wars trailer compared with 8mm film reel.

Return of the Jedi ....$20–$30
Making of Star Wars ....$20–$30
Making of Empire Strikes Back ....$20–$30
Star Wars: The Making of a Saga...$12–$15
Ewoks: The Battle for Endor..$75–$85
Ewok Adventure..$75–$85

Note: *Value on Ewoks video is as of this writing. Price will undoubtedly go down when sales to video rental stores decline.*

GAMES

Board Games

Adventures of R2-D2, Kenner (Palitoy in Britain), 1977. Color-coded game for small children. Includes color game board, spinner, and four R2-D2 game pieces......................$15–$25

Destroy Death Star, Kenner, 1979. Game includes game board, spinner, 12 X-Wing tokens, and four bases ....$20–$30

Escape from the Death Star, Kenner (Palitoy in Britain), 1979. Game includes game board, eight playing tokens, spinner, and move cards ....$15–$25

Hoth Ice Planet Adventure, Kenner, 1980. Game includes playing board, four Millennium Falcon tokens, spinner, and move cards ....$15–$25

Star Wars, Parker Bros., 1982. Game includes game board, four X-Wing puzzle/markers, one TIE marker, one Force card, and two spinners...$20–$30

Wicket the Ewok, Parker Bros., 1983. Includes game board, four Ewok tokens with stands, five transportation cards, and 25 food chips...$15–$20

Yoda the Jedi Master, Kenner, 1981. Includes game board, four Luke Skywalker tokens with stands, spinner, and move cards..$15–$25

Electronic Games

Destroy Death Star, Palitoy (British), 1978. Battery-powered game board has controls for range finding and firing on enemy TIE Fighters. Large 17″ × 25″ box has color artwork of X-Wing and TIE fighting. Not to be confused with the Kenner Destroy Death Star board game ....$100–$150

Left: Assorted Star Wars saga board games. Right: Kenner X-Wing Aces game and box.

Electronic Battle Command and Electronic Laser Battle games.

Electronic Battle Command Game, Kenner (Palitoy in Britain), 1977. Battery-powered tactical combat game. White plastic console with control console and vertical LED display, 9½″ × 7″ box shows color photo of game ....$60–$75
Electronic Laser Battle Game, Kenner, 1977. Electronic reaction game. Black plastic with control panels for two players. Includes AC adaptor. Decorated with paper decals of X-Wings, 20″ × 6½″ box shows color photo of game ....$50–$75
X-Wing Aces Target Game, Kenner, 1978. Large white plastic electronic target game. Gun is mounted on top of controls at one end. Screen displays TIE fighter targets with Death Star as backdrop. Star Wars logo on side. Box shows color photo of game. Rare..........$1,500–$2,500

Miscellaneous

Battle at Sarlacc's Pit, Parker Bros., 1983. Includes 3-D cardboard diorama of Sail Barge and Sarlacc's pit plus 16 plastic playing figures and deck of move cards. 12″ square box has artwork of characters battling over pit..$20–$30
Card Trick, Nick Trost, 1978. Star Wars Card Trick ....$5–$10
Ewok Card Games, Parker Bros., 1984. Several different, came boxed.....................$10–$15
Return of the Jedi Card Game, Parker Bros., 1983. Play-For-Power. Two decks, five different games. Came boxed in 3½″ × 4½″ silver box decorated with color art of Jedi characters...
....$5–$10
Top Trumps New Spacecraft, Waddington (British). Card game employing five picture cards of Star Wars ships ....$10–$15

Role-Playing Games (West End Games, 1987 to present)

West End has produced an extensive line of boxed games, game supplements, game books, playing pieces, and other accessories. While all West End Star Wars products are, strictly speaking, associated with their role-playing games (which is what West End's license specifies), many would just as easily fit into other categories such as reference books, metal figurines, etc.

Boxed Games

West End Star Wars board games all come in 9″ × 11½″ boxes with color art or photos.
Star Warriors, 1987. Starfighter Combat. Includes color map, 80 ship counters, 100 game markers, asteroid and Star Destroyer sheets, record sheet, stand-up charts and table screen, rules booklet, counter storage tray, and six dice...$20–$25
Assault on Hoth, 1988. Adventure board game. Two-person battle game. Includes terrain map, over 55 stand-up playing pieces, two decks of move cards, eight picture dice, and rules book..$25–$30

West End Star Wars game products.

Battle for Endor, 1989. Solitaire adventure board game. Includes terrain map, 62 playing pieces, two decks of move cards, six picture dice, and rules book ....$25–$30
Escape Death Star, 1990. Solitaire or multiplayer adventure board game. Includes Death Star schematic, four stand-up character cards, deck of sector cards, four score pads, three dice, and rules book...$25–$30

Hardback Books

All are 8½″ × 11″, approximately 140 pages with color artwork or photo covers.
Star Wars, The Role-Playing Game, 1987. Primary rules book ....$18–$22
Star Wars Sourcebook, 1987. Background supplement to basic role-playing game ..$18–$22
Imperial Sourcebook, 1989. Supplemental background information on the Empire..$18–$22

Softcover Books

8½″ × 11″ with color artwork or photo covers. Between 70 and 80 pages in length.
Rules Companion, 1989. Supplemental rules for basic role-playing game.................$15–$20
Galaxy Guides, these are supplemental background books on assorted subjects, five different
No. 1 A New Hope, 1989 ....$13–$15
No. 2 Yavin and Bespin, 1989 ....$13–$15
No. 3 The Empire Strikes Back, 1989 ....$13–$15
No. 4 Alien Races, 1989..$13–$15
No. 5 Return of the Jedi, 1990...$13–$15
No. 6 Tramp Freighters, 1991..$13–$15
Jedi's Honor, 1990. Solitaire plot-your-own-adventure game book. Player takes the part of
Luke ....$13–$15
Scoundrel's Luck, 1990. Solitaire plot-your-own-adventure game book. Player takes the part
of Han Solo ....$13–$15

Adventure Modules

Scenarios for different adventures using the rules of the basic role-playing game. Modules typically contain booklet with adventure script and other supplemental information, pertinent maps and/or charts, and gamemaster notes; 8½″ × 11″ modules come shrink-wrapped and have color artwork or photo covers.
Tatooine Manhunt, 1988..$10–$12
Strike Force: Shantipole, 1988..$10–$12
Battle for the Golden Sun, 1988...$10–$12
Starfall, 1989...$10–$12
Otherspace, 1989...$10–$12
Scavenger Hunt, 1989...$10–$12

Riders of the Maelstrom, 1989..$10–$12
Crisis on Cloud City, 1989..$10–$12
Black Ice, 1990..$10–$20
The Game Chambers of Questal, 1990 ....$10–$20

Other West End Games and Accessories

Campaign Pack, 1988. Includes supplemental guidelines and adventures, floor plans, and gamemaster screen. Packaged like adventure modules ....$12–$15
Lightsaber Dueling Pack, 1988. Two-player game utilizing two "flip" books and two score cards to play. Comes shrink-wrapped in color folder...$12–$15
Starfighter Battle Book, 1989. Flip-book game similar to Lightsaber Dueling Pack. Two books come in slipcase with color artwork of X-Wing and TIE Fighter.......................$12–$15
Metal Figure Sets, 25mm sculpted metal miniature gaming pieces. Come unpainted in $4'' \times 8''$ boxes with color artwork or photos on lid.

Heroes of the Rebellion, 1988, ten figures ....$12–$15
Imperial Forces, 1988, ten figures ....$12–$15
Bounty Hunters, 1988, ten figures ....$12–$15
A New Hope, 1988, ten figures ....$12–$15
The Empire Strikes Back, 1989, ten figures .... $12–$15
Return of the Jedi, 1989, ten figures..$12–$15
Stormtroopers, 1989, ten figures...$12–$15
Rebel Characters, 1989, ten figures ....$12–$15
Mos Eisley Cantina, 1989, ten figures..$12–$15
Jabba's Palace, 1989, eight figures..$12–$15
Rancor Pit, 1990, two figures ....$12–$15
Rebel Troopers, 1990, ten figures..$12–$15

Video Games

Arcade Games, Parker Bros. The large electronic games found in commercial video arcades.
Star Wars, stand-up version ....$400–$600
Star Wars, sitting (cockpit) version...$800–$1,200
The Empire Strikes Back ....$400–$600
Return of the Jedi..$400–$600
Computer Games, Domark (British), 1988. Software for home computer. Tape or disc. Several brands available
Star Wars..$15–$20
Empire Strikes Back ....$15–$20
Return of the Jedi ....$15–$20
Mastertronic (British), 1988. Droids cartoon game for home computers...................$15–$20
Home Video Games, Parker Bros. Cartridges for Atari (or Sears) home video systems. Came packaged in $7\frac{1}{2}'' \times 5\frac{1}{2}''$ boxes with color artwork from movies
Star Wars, 1983..$10–$20
The Empire Strikes Back, 1982 ....$10–$20
Jedi Arena, 1983 ....$10–$20
Return of the Jedi, 1984..$10–$20

GREETING CARDS

General

Color-Me-Cards, Patti M. Productions, 1987. Eight cards and envelopes plus four markers. Line drawings of Ewoke. Come packaged in clear plastic box. Three different assortments. Per assortment ....$7–$10

Assorted Star Wars cards.

Star Wars

Birthday and Everyday Cards

Drawing Board, 1977. Full-color photos from Star Wars with text on front and inside.

C-3PO, "Sorry I haven't written . . . But I'm only human!" .... $2–$3
C-3PO, "Feeling kinda rusty? How about a warm lubrication bath? Get Well Soon!" .... $2–$3
C-3PO and Luke, "They don't make them like you anymore!" .... $2–$3
C-3PO In Desert, ". . . Lost without you!" .... $2–$3
Chewbacca, "You're weird . . . But wonderful!" .... $2–$3
Chewbacca, "Not feeling well? May you soon have the strength of a Wookie!" .... $2–$3
Darth Vader, "When I say have a nice day, I *mean* have a nice day!" .... $2–$3
Darth Vader, "Happy Birthday, earthling!" .... $2–$3
Darth Vader, "Don't play games with me . . . WRITE!!!" .... $2–$3
Luke, "Hold it right there! . . . And have a Happy Birthday" .... $2–$3
Luke in Trash Compactor, "There's no escaping . . . Another birthday!" .... $2–$3
Millennium Falcon, "Greetings from Tatooine!" .... $2–$3
Obi-Wan, "May the Force be with you" .... $2–$3
R2-D2, "From your faithful Droid; . . . Within me is a message expressly beamed to you from one of your fellow humanoids, Happy Birthday" .... $2–$3
R2-D2 and C-3PO, "29 Again? . . . It boggles the memory bank! Oh well, Happy Birthday!" .... $2–$3
Space Battle, "Would have written sooner . . . But I just haven't had a minute!" .... $2–$3

Die-Cut Birthday and Everyday Cards

Drawing Board, 1977. Full-color artwork.

C-3PO, "Happy Birthday from your friendly Droid!" .... $3–$4
Chewbacca, "That's Wookie talk for Happy Birthday" .... $3–$4
Darth Vader, "The Empire commands you to have a Happy Birthday" .... $3–$4
Luke, Leia, and Han, "Happy Birthday from the Alliance!" .... $3–$4
Obi-Wan, "Happy Birthday and may the force be with you!" .... $3–$4
R2-D2, "That's Droid talk for Happy Birthday!" .... $3–$4
R2-D2 and C-3PO, "Sorry to hear about your malfunction! Hope all systems are functioning soon!" .... $3–$4
Stormtrooper, "Have a Happy Birthday! Darth Vader wants it that way!" .... $3–$4

Christmas Cards

Drawing Board, 1977. 5½″ × 8″. Color photo or artwork covers.

C-3PO, "For an out-of-this-world grandson . . . From our galaxy to your galaxy, Happy Holidays!" .... $2–$3
Chewbacca, "Merry Christmas, earthling" .... $2–$3

Chewbacca, "Happy Holidays . . . To a favorite bipedal earthling" ....$2–$3
Luke, Han, and Chewbacca, "From the Alliance . . . Happy Holidays" ....$2–$3
Obi-Wan, "MERRY CHRISTMAS . . . And may the Force be with you" ....$2–$3
R2-D2, "VREEP ADOOT BLEEP . . . That's Droid talk for Happy Holidays!" ....$2–$3
R2-D2 (Projecting Image of Leia), "For an out-of-this-world granddaughter . . . The code is broken and the message is clear—Have a Merry Christmas and a Happy New Year".....$2–$3
R2-D2-and C-3PO, "PEACE and GOODWILL towards all mankind . . . and to their faithful androids!" ....$2–$3
R2-D2 and C-3PO, "For an earthling girl . . . In keeping with the ancient humanoid custom. Christmas kisses to you!" ....$2–$3
X-Wings, "Intergalactic greetings . . . For a fantastic holiday season" ....$2–$3
X-Wings, "To an out-of-this-world boy . . . Intergalactic greetings and may the Force be with you" ....$2–$3

Juvenile Birthday Cards

Drawing Board, 1977. Color artwork.
C-3PO, "You're 12 . . . Hope it's the best day on Earth since you were born!" ....$2–$3
Chewbacca, "Now that you're 7 . . . Wishing you 7 gronks and one to grow on" ....$2–$3
Darth Vader, "I've uncovered information that says you are 11 . . . And I will see to it that it's celebrated thoughout the far reaches of the galaxy!" ....$2–$3
Obi-Wan, "Honored one, now that you are 10 . . . May the Force be with you on your birthday and for many years to come" ....$2–$3
R2-D2, "Earthling, my calculations confirm that you are 9 . . . Hope it's your finest day on the planet yet" ....$2–$3
Stormtrooper, "You're 8 . . . So join the troops and have the best birthday in the universe!" ....$2–$3

Halloween Cards

Drawing Board, 1977. Color photos or artwork on cover.
C-3PO, "Trick or Treat, Earthling" ....$2–$3
Chewbacca, "Do not fear . . . Your Wookie friend is here" ....$2–$3
Darth Vader, "This is MY kind of holiday! Happy Halloween" ....$2–$3
Han, Luke, and Chewbacca, "From the Alliance . . . Happy Halloween" ....$2–$3
Leia, "For an out-of-this-world daughter . . . Intergalactic wishes for a Happy Halloween!" ... .$2–$3
Luke, "For an out-of-this-world son . . . May your deflector shields protect you this Hallow-een!" ....$2–$3
Millennium Falcon, "For an earthling girl . . . All Hallows Eve greetings from Tatooine!" ....$2–$3
Obi-Wan, "Happy Halloween . . . And may the Force be with you" ....$2–$3
X-Wing and TIE Fighter, "For an earthling boy . . . Intergalactic greetings for a Happy Hal-loween!" ....$2–$3

The Empire Strikes Back
Die-Cut Birthday Cards

Drawing Board, 1980. Color artwork covers.
Boba Fett, "May you get your share of bounty on your birthday" ....$3–$4
Luke (on Tauntaun), "Wishing you the happiest birthday in the galaxy!" ....$3–$4
Yoda, "Happy Birthday . . . And may you live to be 800" ....$3–$4

Birthday Game Cards

Drawing Board, 1980. Three different fold-out cards.
Birthday Greetings Maze Card, Darth Vader in asteroid belt..$3–$4
Happy Birthday Maze Card, Leia, Chewy, and Han on cloud city ....$3–$4
Yoda Birthday Puzzle Card, Hidden objects in Dagobah swamp ....$3–$4

Return of the Jedi

Greeting and Birthday Cards

Drawing Board, 1983. Die-cut with color artwork on cover.

C-3PO and Ewoks, "Hope you have a Royal time! Happy Birthday!"..........................$3–$4
Darth Vader, "I want *you* to have a Happy Birthday".......................................$3–$4
Darth Vader and Imperial Guards, "May the Force be with you" ....$3–$4
Ewoks, "Have a birthday filled with happy surprises!"......................................$3–$4
Ewoks and R2-D2, "Happy Birthday to a wonderful friend!"..................................$3–$4
Ewok and Leia, "It's so special having a friend like you!" ....$3–$4
Rebo Band, "Droopy, Sy, Max, and I hope your birthday strikes a happy note!" ....$3–$4

Greeting Cards

Westbrook (British), 1983.

No. 1, Lightsaber (Poster Design), "May the Force be with you" ....$3–$4
No. 2, Luke in Bespin Fatigues, "Happy Birthday, rebel" ....$3–$4
No. 3, Stormtroopers, "If the universe is immeasurably vast, why are you so close to me?"
....$3–$4
No. 4, Luke (Jedi Knight), "Happy Birthday to the universe's blue-eyed boy" ....$3–$4
No. 5, Han Solo, "Happy Birthday, rebel!"..$3–$4
No. 6, Wicket and R2-D2, "You're the right height, why aren't you furry?" ....$3–$4
No. 7, Revenge of the Jedi, "May the Force be with you"....................................$3–$4
No. 8, Vader in the Stars, "You're the embodiment of all that is mean, nasty, malevolent, and evil in the universe. I guess that's what makes you so lovable" ....$3–$4
No. 9, Princess Leia, "Happy Birthday, princess"...$3–$4
No. 10, Darth Vader, "So it's your birthday. What do you expect me to do, blow up a planet?"
....$3–$4
No. 11, Yoda, "I like you, you've got cute ears" ....$3–$4
No. 12, Vader and Boba Fett on Cloud City, "Right, I'll have the sauna now and the manicure afterwards!" ....$3–$4
No. 13, Han Solo, "Happy Birthday, hero"..$3–$4
No. 14, Luke and Vader, "Don't jump, it's only another birthday" ....$3–$4
No. 15, R2-D2 and C-3PO (With Broken Leg), "You think you've got problems".....$3–$4
No. 16, R2-D2 and C-3PO Approaching Jabba's Palace, "Are you sure this is the right way to the party?"...$3–$4
No. 17, C-3PO, Jabba, Leia, and Bibb Fortuna, "It's your birthday. Bring on the dancing girls"...$3–$4
No. 18, Luke, Han, and Leia, "I could travel the universe and not find friends like you".$3–$4
No. 19, Baby Ewok, "Hear's to the cutest thing in four galaxies" ....$3–$4
No. 20, B-Wing Fighter, "Hope your birthday is a blast!" ....$3–$4
No. 21, Han and Chewie Shoot It Out, "We have this trouble every time you come to the barbers" ....$3–$4
No. 22, Millennium Falcon in the Asteroid Field, "Even at light speed, your birthday's got to catch up with you sometime" ....$3–$4
No. 23, Gammorrean Guard, "If you had my dentist bills, you wouldn't smile either"
....$3–$4
No. 24, Luke and Vader, "Is this your first lesson in how to use chopsticks?".............$3–$4

HOUSEWARES

Banks

Ceramic

Roman, 1977. Approximately 8″ tall. Plug-in bottom for removal of coins. All use shiny glazes

C-3PO, waist-up, metallic gold...$100–$150

Assorted housewares: Chein metal tray and wastebasket, wallpaper trim, R2–D2 radio, record tote, and Darth Vader phone in box.

Darth Vader, head only...$100–$150
R2-D2, entire figure...$100–$150
Sigma, 1982–1983. Store packaging was silver box with color photo of bank on front. Many were sold in plain white mail boxes, however. All use shiny glazes
   Chewbacca, 10½″ tall, kneeling with gun ....$50–$75
   Jabba the Hutt, 6″ tall...$35–$50
   Yoda, 8″ tall ....$50–$75

Metal

Leonard Silver Mfg., bust of Darth Vader, 6″ high ....$75–$100
Metal Box Co., 1980. Tin combination banks had color photo fronts with two combinations on face and slot at top for coins. Two different
   Darth Vader ....$50–$75
   Yoda ....$50–$75
Metal Box Co., 1980. Tin octagonal bank has photos of characters on side panels and removable lid with slot for coins. Lid has Empire logo and word "Bank" ....$35–$50

Plastic

Adam Joseph, 1983. Return of the Jedi banks. In the shapes of characters. Came in red and black window boxes with Jedi logo
   Darth Vader, 9″ tall ....$15–$25
   Emperor's Royal Guard, 9″ tall ....$15–$25

Roman Darth Vader bank.

Gammorrean Guard, 9″ tall (rare)..$50–$75
R2-D2, 6″ tall...$20–$30
Adam Joseph, 1983. Wicket the Ewok. Character banks came in blue window boxes with cartoon illustrations of Ewoks, 6″ tall
    Princess Kneesa, playing tamborine ....$10–$15
    Wicket, playing drum...$10–$15

Clocks

Bradley Time

This company made several table clocks with 3-D figures designed primarily for children. Clocks came packaged in window boxes.
Clock/Radio, 1984. R2-D2 and C-3PO on face of quartz clock with built-in AM/FM radio....
....$75–$100
Talking Alarm Clock, 1980. R2-D2 and C-3PO stand on base with speaker on bottom. Clock is wind-up. Voice is battery operated, 9″ tall...$60–$90
3-D Sceni-Clock, free-standing R2-D2 and C-3PO in front of backdrop with space scene. Clock is in middle of TIE Fighter, 8″ tall, battery operated ....$50–$75

Kenner Preschool

Ewok Teaching Clock, colorful plastic shaped like Ewok village with picture of Wicket on face and pop-up counters at base. Came packaged in green window box ....$50–$75

Welby Elgin, 1981

Wall clocks. Two different. Both models have blue plastic cases and come either as cord or battery operated.
Star Wars, round, pictures R2-D2 and C-3PO ....$45–$65
Empire Strikes Back, square, shows Darth Vader, Stormtroopers, and Empire logo ....
....$45–$65

Furniture

Bookcase, American Toy and Furniture Co., 1983. Wood and fiberboard with scenes from Return of the Jedi on back panel, 20″ × 18″ × 41″ ....$100–$150
Bookcase/Toy Chest, American Toy and Furniture Co., 1983. Shelves above, toy chest below with slanted chalkboard sliding cover. Decorated with Ewoks and droids, 32″ × 18″ × 41″......
....$125–$175
Coat Rack, American Toy and Furniture Co., 1983. Base decorated with picture of Darth Vader and Jedi logo. Pegs above. Approximately 47″ tall ....$75–$100
Desk and Chair, American Toy and Furniture Co., 1983. Child's desk with shelf above. Movie scenes on back and sides. Approximately 32″ high ....$125–$175
Nightstand, American Toy and Furniture Co., 1983. Scalloped edges with scenes from Return of the Jedi, 20″ × 16½″ × 25″ ....$100–$150
Picnic Table, American Toy and Furniture Co., 1983. Pedestal table with benches on either side attached to base. Movie scenes on top. Approximately 36″ long ....$125–$175
Table and Chair Set, American Toy and Furniture Co., 1983. 25½″ round table with scenes from movie on top. Two chairs with Jedi logo on back ....$125–$175
Toy Chest, American Toy and Furniture Co., 1983. Shaped like R2-D2. Wooden base on wheels with plastic lid, 28″ tall..$100–$150

Glasses (Drinking)

Star Wars Promotional, Burger King/Coca-Cola, 1977. Four different with color silk-screened artwork. Designs were: Luke Skywalker, Han Solo, Darth Vader, and R2-D2/C-3PO. (Burger King also issued a set of matching promotional posters.)
    Per glass ....$10–$15
    Set of all four ....$50–$60

Left: R2–D2 toy chest.
Right: California Originals: Darth Vader mug (top center). Two types of ceramic mugs by Sigma and Star Wars series promotional drinking glasses. Unusual Jedi set is made of plastic.

The Empire Strikes Back Promotional, Burger King/Coca-Cola, 1980. Four different silk-screened artwork scenes from Empire. Scenes include Luke, Lando, R2-D2 and C-3PO and Darth Vader. Descriptions are on back of glass

    Per glass ....$8–$12

    Set of all four ....$40–$50

Return of the Jedi Promotional, Burger King/Coca-Cola, 1983. Four different silkscreened artwork scenes: Sand barge fight scene, Jabba's palace scene, Ewok village, and Luke and Darth Vader fighting

    Per glass ....$5–$10

    Set of all four ....$30–$40

Return of the Jedi Promotional, set of three with color artwork of characters made for the European market. Per set ....$35–$50

Linens

Star Wars

Bedspread, 1977. Predominantly light blue with Star Wars characters in action poses. Twin, bunk or full sizes..$45–$65

Blanket, matches bedspread..$45–$65

Drapes, assorted sizes ....$20–$40

Pillow Cases, two different

    Blue background ....$5–$10

    White background ....$10–$15

Sheet Sets, matches bedspread

    Sheets ....$15–$25

    Pillow Case ....$5–$10

Towels, Bibb, 1977

    Bath towel, Luke, Leia, and Droids...$15–$20

    Bath towel, Darth Vader..$15–$20

    Face cloth, R2-D2 and C-3PO ....$5–$10

Empire Strikes Back

Bed Set, Black Falcon (British), 1979. Shows characters. Includes pillow case and duvet (European sheet) ....$25–$35

Bedspread, Bibb, 1980, 63″ × 108″

    Darth Vader's chamber from the movie...$35–$45

    Characters from movie..$35–$45

Empire bedspread.

Bedspread, Black Falcon, 1979. Blue background with characters from the movie. Several sizes..$35–$45
Pillow Case, Room Concepts, 1980. Reversible character designs
    Darth Vader and Boba Fett ....$10–$15
    R2-D2 and C-3PO...$10–$15
Towels, Canon, 1979–80
    Beach towel, Yoda or Darth Vader ....$15–$20
    Bath towel ....$10–$15
    Hand towel, Darth Vader and Boba Fett..$8–$12
    Face cloth, Yoda...$5–$10

Return of the Jedi

Bed Set, Bibb, 1983. Three-piece for twin size ....$35–$45
Bed Set, Hay Jax (British). Duvet (European sheet) and pillow case. Brown or white background ....$35–$40
Bedspread, 1983. Characters from the movie. Assorted sizes ....$30–$40
Blanket, 1983. Scenes from movie ....$30–$40
Drapes, main characters on red background...$15–$25
Sheet Set, Marimekko, 1983. Characters from the movie, twin size............$25–$35
Towels, Bibb, 1983. Beach, two different designs ....$10–$15

Star Wars Saga

Bedset, Bibb, 1983. Three-piece twin set...$30–$40

Sleeping Bags

Bibb, 1983. Jedi, shows Darth Vader ....$60–$95
Marrimekko, 1983. Two different styles
    Luke and Leia ....$60–$95
    Characters from Empire ....$60–$95

Lunch Boxes

All lunch boxes in this section were done by King Seeley-Thermos. Prices listed are for boxes complete with thermos bottle.
Star Wars, Metal, 1977. Color silk-screened artwork shows space battle on cover and Tatooine scene on reverse. Plastic thermos has silkscreened design of Droids ....$20–$35
Star Wars, Plastic, 1977. Red box with paper decal. Color artwork shows Darth Vader, R2-D2, and C-3PO. Picture on one side only. Plastic thermos has silkscreened artwork of Droids..$20–$35

Metal Star Wars saga lunch boxes with thermoses.

Empire Strikes Back, Metal, 1980. Color silkscreened artwork shows scene in Millennium Falcon on lid, Luke, Yoda, and R2-D2 on back. Plastic thermos has silkscreened artwork of Yoda ....$20–$35

Empire Strikes Back, Metal, 1980. Color photo shows Dagobah scene on lid, Hoth battle on back. Plastic thermos has silkscreened artwork of Yoda..$30–$40

Empire Strikes Back, Plastic, 1980. Red with color photo silkscreened on lid only. Shows Chewbacca, Han, Leia, and Luke. Thermos has silkscreened artwork of Yoda............$20–$35

Empire Strikes Back, Plastic, 1980. Silkscreened photo cover has logo and small hexagonal inset pictures. Plastic thermos has silkscreened picture of Droids and logo.................$25–$40

Return of the Jedi, Metal, 1983. Color silkscreened artwork shows Luke in Jabba's Palace on lid, space scene on reverse. Plastic thermos has silkscreened artwork of Ewok...........$15–$30

Return of the Jedi, Plastic, 1983. Red with cartoon-style artwork of Wicket and R2-D2 on lid only. Plastic thermos has silkscreened artwork of Ewok...$20–$35

Miscellaneous Housewares

Candleholder, Sigma, 1981. Ceramic. Yoda standing by tree stump (which holds candle), 4½" tall ....$20–$30

Flashlight, General Mills, 1977. Promotional. Black plastic with foil decal with color artwork of Luke and Leia, logo, and words "Lightsaber" ....$5–$10

Sigma ceramic housewares. Top: Picture frame, toothbrush holder, soapdish, teapot, Yoda salt and pepper shakers. Bottom: Yoda vase, bookends, cookie jar, Chewbacca bank.

Lamps, Windmill Ceramics, 1979. Unlicensed ceramic accent lamps contained color blinking lights. These different

Chewbacca, 9½" tall...$35–$60
Darth Vader, 12" tall ....$50–$75
R2-D2, 8½" tall...$40–$60

Lampshade, Hay Jax (British), 1983. Main characters from Return of the Jedi on brown background. For ceiling light ....$25–$35

Light Switch Covers (Switcheroos), Kenner, 1979. Snap-on covers in shapes of characters with eyes which glow in the dark. Came blister packed on header card with movie logo. Three different

C-3PO, head only..$8–$15
Darth Vader, head only..$8–$15
R2-D2, full figure ....$8–$15

Luggage, Adam Joseph, 1983. Three different size suitcases. Came as set packaged one inside another. Per set..$50–$75

Magnets, Adam Joseph, 1983. Four 1" color plastic magnets of Darth Vader, Chewbacca, R2-D2, and Yoda. Came blister packed on cardboard header with Jedi logo. Per set ....$7–$12

Magnets, Adam Joseph, 1983. Two 1" color plastic magnets of Ewoks. Came blister packed on cardboard header with Wicket, the Ewok logo.....................................$4–$8

Magnets, Howard Eldon, 1987. Flexible plastic 1½" × 2" rectangular. Color movie logo art on white background. No packaging

Star Wars, triangular "A New Hope" logo ....$5–$8
The Empire Strikes Back, Vader head in flames ....$5–$8
Return of the Jedi, Yoda head in circle...$5–$8

Magnets, Star Tours, Disney

Star Tours logo...$2–$4
R2-D2, picture and name, cutout design ....$2–$4
C-3PO, picture and name, cutout design ....$2–$4

Mat, Becticel Sutcliffe, Ltd. (British), 1983. Cartoons of main characters and vehicles ....
....$30–$45

Mirror, Sigma, 1981. Approximately 10" tall mirror in black ceramic frame with Darth Vader head at top..$30–$50

Mirror, Lightline Industries, 1977. 20" × 30" in silver plastic frame

C-3PO and R2-D2..$45–$60
Han and Chewbacca..$45–$60
Darth Vader ....$45–$60

Music Box, Sigma, 1981. Hoth turret with C-3PO on top, 8" tall. Ceramic, turns and plays Star Wars theme..$40–$60

Music Box, Sigma, 1983. Ewoks, ceramic, 6" high. Turns and plays Star Wars theme.............
....$35–$50

Music Box, Sigma, 1983. Max Rebo Band, ceramic. Turns and plays Star Wars theme ....
....$40–$60

Nightlights (Dimensional), Adam Joseph, 1983. Three different flat nightlights in colored plastic. Came carded. Cards display Return of the Jedi logo

C-3PO, head in circle..$4–$9
R2-D2, full figure ....$4–$9
Yoda, full figure...$4–$9

Nightlights (Domed), Adam Joseph, 1983. Three different domed plastic lights in the shape of figures' heads. Came carded. Cards display Return of the Jedi logo

C-3PO ....$5–$12
Darth Vader...$5–$12
Yoda ....$5–$12

Pennant, 1987. Color artwork of Darth Vader head and Jedi Deathstar with 10th anniversary logo on cloth pennant. Approximately 2" long...$4–$8

Pennant, Star Tours, Disney. Color artwork of Star Tours and Disney-MGM logos with R2-D2, C-3PO, and Star Tours Droid and vehicle ....$2–$4

Picture, Icarus (British), 1982. Silver plastic framed artwork prints. Six different

Luke ....$5–$10
R2-D2 and C-3PO..$5–$10
Boba Fett...$5–$10
Yoda ....$5–$10

Windmill ceramics accent light and Adam Joseph domed and dimensional nightlights.

Darth Vader ....$5–$10
Chewbacca ....$5–$10
Picture Frames, Sigma, 1981. Ceramic, three different
C-3PO, 5″ × 7″, head in bottom right corner, arms and legs around sides, word "help" at top
....$25–$40
Darth Vader, 10″ tall ....$35–$50
R2-D2, 7″ × 10″, full figure of R2-D2 in bottom right corner ....$30–$45
Pillow (Throw), 15″ square, quilted cover. R2-D2 and C-3PO on one side, Darth Vader on other. Star Wars logo both sides. Matches Star Wars linens...$10–$15
Pillow (Throw), Adam Joseph, 1983. Small die-cut accent pillows. Two different
Darth Vader, black figure on red background...$15–$25
R2-D2, white figure on blue background decorated with Return of the Jedi logos ..$15–$25
Pillow (Throw), 1983. Jabba the Hutt. Small die-cut, fuzzy tan with black silkscreened features...$10–$15
Place Setting, Sigma, 1981. "The World of Star Wars Fantasy Childset." Ceramic plate, bowl, and mug set. Plate has color artwork of Chewbacca, R2-D2, and C-3PO. Bowl has color artwork of R2-D2. Mug has same color artwork as Droid mug from 1981 Sigma mug set (*See* Mugs, this section) but with rounded rather than square handle. Came boxed. Box art shows color picture of plate ....$50–$85
Radio, 1978, Kenner. Luke Skywalker head-set radio. Uses 9V battery. Ear piece has Star Wars logo, mouth piece extends from right side. Rare.............................$250–$600
Radio, 1978, Kenner. R2-D2, shaped like R2-D2. Hand strap on back, 6½″ tall. Uses 9V battery ....$75–$125
Record Tote, Disneyland-Vista, 1982. Lacquered cardboard box with plastic handle for 45s. Scenes from Empire Strikes Back on side panels...$30–$45
Soap Dish, Sigma, 1981. Ceramic. Shaped like landspeeder. Shiny glaze, 7″ long (See "Cosmetics" section for soap, shampoo, etc.) ....$40–$60
Tape (Audio) Carrier, Disneyland-Vista, 1983. Take-a-Tape-Along. Holds six tapes. Decorated with photos from Return of the Jedi ....$15–$25
Tissues (Facial), Puffs (Proctor and Gamble), 1980. Color photo on front of box, cutout on bottom. Six different. Price each ....$3–$7
Telephone, American Telecommunications, 1983. Darth Vader Speakerphone. Darth Vader statuette on touchtone base, 14″ high. Came in box with photo of phone and Darth Vader artwork on front panel. Plastic handle at top. Limited edition collectible.................$150–$200
Toothbrush, Kenner, 1978. Electric with Star Wars logo and characters on handle. Came blister packed on header with color photos from Star Wars and child using toothbrush. Included two brushes ....$50–$75
Toothbrush, Kenner, 1980. Electric, similar to Kenner's Star Wars toothbrush but Empire instead ....$40–$65
Toothbrushes, Oral-B, 1983. Regular toothbrushes with decal of character and Jedi logo on handle. Box displayed character and had windows to show brush. Box was either shrink-wrapped or blister packed on header card showing X-Wing. Six different
Chewbacca and Han Solo ....$5–$10

C-3PO and R2-D2..$5–$10
Darth Vader..$5–$10
Leia...$5–$10
Luke..$5–$10
Ewoks...$5–$10

Toothbrush, Kenner Preschool, 1984. Electric, handle molded in shape of Ewok on tree trunk with words "Wicket the Ewok." Green box with side flap with photo of toothbrush...$25–$35

Toothbrush Holder, Sigma, 1981. Ceramic, shaped like snowspeeder. Toothbrushes slide in sides. Shiny white glaze, 7" long...$40–$60

Tote Bag, Adam Joseph, 1983. Ditty Bag. Clear vinyl with drawstring. Decorated with artwork of R2-D2 and C-3PO. Jedi logo around top ....$15–$25

Tray, Chein, 1983. Metal, 12" × 14½". Color artwork montage of characters and logo from Return of the Jedi ....$15–$30

Vase, Sigma, 1981. Ceramic, shaped like Yoda standing by tree. Shiny glaze, 9" high.............
....$40–$60

Wallpaper, characters and scenes distinctive to their respective movies. Prices per roll
Star Wars...$45–$60
Empire Strikes Back ....$35–$50
Return of the Jedi..$30–$45

Wallpaper (Trim), for room borders. Color photos of characters set in ovals of various sizes. Per roll..$20–$30

Waste Basket, Chein, 1983. Metal, montage of characters and Return of the Jedi logo in color on black background...$35–$50

Miscellaneous Kitchenware

Cake Candles, Wilton, 1980. 3½"-high character candles with paper inset at base with character's name. Came blister packed on color cardboard header. Chewbacca, Darth Vader or R2-D2. Price each..$3–$8

Cake Decorating Kits, Wilton, 1983. Included molded aluminum pan in shape of character plus tools for decorating. Came boxed. Box shows photo of decorated cake
Darth Vader..$15–$20
R2-D2...$15–$20

Cake Pans, Wilton, 1980. Molded reusable aluminum in shape of character. Paper sticker affixed to bottom of pan showed photo of finished decorated cake
Boba Fett..$10–$15
C-3PO ....$5–$10
Darth Vader..$5–$10
R2-D2...$5–$10

Cake Put-Ons, Wilton, 1980. Plastic figures of characters for decorating cakes. Came boxed with header describing item and photo of product on front
C-3PO and R2-D2..$10–$15
Darth Vader and Stormtrooper..$10–$15

Wilton R2–D2 cake pan and
Darth Vader cake decorating kit.

Candy Heads, Topps, 1980. Empire Strikes Back
First series, red box contained candy dispensers in shapes of Stormtrooper, Boba Fett, Chewbacca, C-3PO or Darth Vader
    Individual head ....$.50–$1
    Box...$15–$25
Second series, yellow box contained candy dispensers in shape of 2-1B, Bossk, Tauntaun or Yoda
    Individual head ....$.50–$1
    Box...$15–$20
Candy Heads, Topps, 1983. Return of the Jedi. Contained candy dispensers in shapes of Admiral Akbar, Jabba, Ewok, Darth Vader or Sy Snoodles
    Individual head ....$.50–$1
    Box...$15–$20
Candy Mold, Wilton, 1980. 8″ × 7½″ plastic sheets. Two sets
    Star Wars I, Darth Vader, Boba Fett, and Stormtrooper ....$10–$15
    Star Wars II, C-3PO/R2-D2, Yoda, Chewbacca ....$10–$15
Candy Mold, Wilton, 1983. 8″ × 7½″ sheet for making C-3PO, Chewbacca, Darth Vader, R2-D2, Stormtrooper, Ewok, and Yoda suckers...$10–$15
Cereal Boxes, C-3PO Cereal, Kellogg, 1984. Picture of C-3PO on front, back had six different cutout masks or promotion for stickers included in box. Masks were C-3PO, Chewbacca, Darth Vader, Luke, Stormtrooper or Yoda. Per box...$5–$10
Cereal Boxes, Nabisco, 1978. Star Wars Shreddies (British). Back has scenes from movie. Included sheets of transfers as prize ....$10–$15
Containers (Cheese Spread), Dairylea (British), 1988. Plastic, illustrated with Droids and Ewok characters...$2–$5
Containers (Yogurt), Dairylea (British), 1983–88. Plastic, illustrated with different characters for different flavors
    Chewbacca, fudge...$2–$5
    Jabba the Hutt, peach melba ....$2–$5
    Ewoks, banana ....$2–$5
    Darth Vader, black cherry ....$2–$5
    Admiral Ackbar, pineapple ....$3–$5
    Luke Skywalker, raspberry ....$2–$5
    Yoda, gooseberry ....$2–$5
    Princess Leia, strawberry ....$2–$5
Cookie Boxes, Pepperidge Farm, 1983. Eight-oz. boxes of molded cookies in three different shapes and flavors
    The Imperial Forces (chocolate), Darth Vader, Gammorrean Guard, Jabba, Emperor's Royal Guard...$5–$10
    The Rebel Alliance I (vanilla), Luke, Leia, Han, and Yoda ....$5–$10
    The Rebel Alliance II (peanut butter), Admiral Ackbar, Chewbacca, R2-D2, Max Rebo......
    ....$5–$10
Note: *Values on food products are for empty containers. For obvious aesthetic reasons, elderly edibles have limited appeal to most collectors.*
Cookie Jars, Roman Ceramics, 1977
    C-3PO, gold glazed ceramic. Head and shoulders lift off ....$150–$200
    R2-D2, blue and white glazed ceramic. Head lifts off ....$125–$175
Cookie Jars, Sigma, 1981. Ceramic hexagonal design shows Darth Vader on one side and R2-D2 and C-3PO on the other ....$75–$100
Placemats, Dixie, 1980. Plastic, set of four: AT-AT, Luke, Darth Vader, space scene, and Yoda. Price each..$5–$10
Placemats, Icarus (British), 1982. Set of three 9″ × 10″ laminated placemats. Two different sets
    Set 1, R2-D2/C-3PO, Lando, Han, and Chewie, Bounty Hunters............$15–$20
    Set 2, Yoda, Darth and Stormtroopers, Luke on Tauntaun ....$15–$20
Placemats, Icarus (British), 1983. Illustrations by Andrew Skilleter. Two different with story summaries
    Luke, Vader Helmet, Guards, and Speeder Bikes.....................................$5–$10
    Leia, Lando, Jabba, and Wicket...$5–$10

Placemats, Sigma, 1981. Vinyl, 11″ × 17. Four different color artwork scenes from The Empire Strikes Back. Luke and Yoda, R2-D2 and C-3PO, Darth and Leia, and Chewbacca and Boba Fett. Price each ....$10–$20

Plates (*See* "Collectors' Plates" section)

Salt and Pepper Shakers, Sigma, 1981. Ceramic
    R2-D2 and R5-D4...$50–$75
    Yoda (both) ....$35–$50

Squeeze Bottle, Star Tours, Disney. Translucent white with black and silver Star Tours logo on front...$3–$5

Teapot, Sigma, 1981. Ceramic. Luke riding Tauntaun. Luke's body comes off to add water. Tauntaun's tail is handle and its head and neck are the spout. Approximately 10½″ tall ....
....$100–$125

Wrapper, Burtons (British), 1984. Star Wars Biscuits (Cookies). Plastic, illustrated with artwork of Vader on one side and Luke on the other..$2–$4

Wrappers, Dairylea (British), 1988. Cheese wedges. Paper, 12 different. Droids and Ewoks characters
    Baga ....$1–$2
    Teebo...$1–$2
    Malani ....$1–$2
    C-3PO ....$1–$2
    Winda..$1–$2
    Wicket ....$1–$2
    Kneesa...$1–$2
    Chirpa..$1–$2
    R2-D2..$1–$2
    Logray...$1–$2
    Latara ....$1–$2
    Shodu ....$1–$2

Mugs (Ceramic)

California Originals, 1977. Three different large mugs in the shape of character heads from Star Wars. All are approximately 7½″ tall
    Ben Kenobi, matte brown glaze outside. Shiny blue glaze lining............................$75–$100
    Chewbacca, matte brown glaze outside. Shiny blue glaze lining............................$75–$100
    Darth Vader, shiny black glaze inside and out..$75–$100

Earnst/Hamilton (*See* "Collectors' Plates" section)

Sigma, 1981. Set of four standard size and shape mugs with color silkscreened artwork scenes
    Chewbacca and Boba Fett..$15–$20
    C-3PO and R2-D2...$15–$20
    Darth Vader, Leia, and Stormtroopers ....$15–$20
    Yoda and Luke ....$15–$20

Sigma, 1982–83. Character mugs molded in the shape of figures' heads. Came boxed for stores in silver box with color photo of mug, though many not intended for store sales are in simple white mailing boxes. Shiny full color glaze
    Biker Scout ....$30–$40
    C-3PO ....$20–$30
    Chewbacca..$20–$30
    Darth Vader ....$25–$35
    Gammorrean Guard ....$20–$30
    Han Solo, Hoth gear..$25–$35
    Klaatu...$20–$30
    Lando, Skiff Guard outfit..$20–$30
    Leia ....$25–$35
    Luke, X-Wing pilot gear ....$25–$35
    Wicket ....$20–$30
    Yoda ....$20–$30

Star Tours, Disney, 1986. Glass mug with silver metallic finish and glitter Star Tours logo, 6″ tall ....$5–$10
Star Tours, Disney. Star Tours logo and character. Two different
    C-3PO and Star Tours logo..$5–$10
    R2-D2 and Star Tours logo..$5–$10
Star Wars Fan Club, 1987. Ceramic 10th anniversary logo. Gold on black ....$5–$10

Plastic Tableware

Deka

This company produced an extensive line of plastic tableware for all three movies in the Star Wars saga. Pieces are heavy-duty plastic with full-color photo scenes in the case of Star Wars and Empire, and color artwork for Return of the Jedi. Pieces included 6-oz., 11-oz., and 17-oz. tumblers, soup bowls, cereal bowls, mugs, plates, and pitchers.
Star Wars, 1977. Items depicted major characters with labels identifying each. One design throughout
    Bowls, soup or cereal..$5–$10
    Compartment plate..$4–$8
    Mug...$4–$8
    Pitcher..$15–$20
    Tumbler, any size..$2–$5
The Empire Strikes Back, 1980. Items depict major characters set in circles
    Bowls, soup or cereal..$4–$8
    Compartment plate..$3–$6
    Mugs, four different styles..$3–$6
    Pitcher..$10–$15
    Tumbler, any size..$2–$4
Return of the Jedi, 1983. Items show artwork of scenes from the movie
    Bowls, soup or cereal..$4–$6
    Compartment plate..$3–$5
    Mugs, two different styles..$3–$5
    Pitcher..$8–$10
    Tumbler, any size..$2–$3
Wicket the Ewok Three-Piece Set, Deka, 1983. Boxed set has mug, plate, and bowl with color artwork of Ewok scenes and Return of the Jedi logo...$15–$25

Coca-Cola, Promotional

1977, large (18 oz.) plastic tumblers with color artwork scenes from the movie. Eight different. Price each..$1–$3
1977, small (12 oz.) tumblers with color artwork scenes from the movie. Twenty different. Price each..$1–$3
1979, large (18 oz.) tumblers with color artwork of characters and scenes primarily from Star Wars, though Boba Fett is shown on one ....$1–$3
1982, pitcher. Logo and characters from Empire Strikes Back.........................$1–$3
1983, 18-oz. tumbler with scenes from Return of the Jedi................................$1–$3
1983, pitcher with scenes from Return of the Jedi (matches tumbler above)..................$3–$5

Miscellaneous, Promotional

Pepperidge Farm, 1983. Small tumblers with scenes from Return of the Jedi. Four different. Price each..$1–$2
Star Tours, Disney, 1986. Thermal mug with Star Tours logo.....................................$5–$10
Star Tours, Disney. Thermal mug with Star Tours logo and R2-D2, C-3PO, and Star Tours Droid. Color artwork..$5–$10

Assorted Metal Box (top) and Chein (bottom) products.

Storage Containers
Ceramic

Sigma, 1982. Came packaged for stores in silver boxes with color photo of product. Many were sold in plain white mail boxes, however. Shiny glazes

Stormtrooper box, head only ....$40–$60
Yoda backpack box, Yoda is lid...$35–$50

Metal
CHEIN (CHEINCO), 1983
This company made an assortment of tin containers featuring characters and scenes from Return of the Jedi. All feature a black background with color artwork and Jedi logo.

Trinket Tins, 3½" round, 1" deep. Artwork on lid. Six different

Darth Vader ....$8–$15
Droids..$8–$15
Ewoks...$8–$15
Jabba ....$8–$15
Luke, Leia, and Han...$8–$15
Max Rebo Band ....$8–$15

Mini-Tins, 3½" round, 3½" deep. Artwork on lid and sides. Six different (same subjects as trinket tins). Price each ....$10–$20

Cookie Tin, 6" round, 4" deep. Artwork on lid and sides shows montage of characters and scenes ....$20–$30

Carry-All Tin, 6" × 5" rectangular, 4½" deep. Two hinged metal handles. Artwork on lid and sides shows montage of characters and scenes...$25–$40

METAL BOX CO., 1980
This company made an assortment of storage tins in various sizes. All are decorated with color photos of characters and things from The Empire Strikes Back. Made in England.

Micro Tins, small (2¼" × 1¾"), shallow rectangular boxes with photos on lids. Reverse had Empire logo. Six different

AT-ATs...$5–$10
Boba Fett..$5–$10
Lando Calrission ....$5–$10
Luke fighting Darth Vader ....$5–$10
Luke on Tauntaun ....$5–$10
Yoda ....$5–$10

Micro Tins, shallow, 3½" square tins with photos on hinged lids. Eight different

Chewbacca..$8–$15

Darth Vader ....$8–$15
Han Solo ....$8–$15
Imperial Cruiser ....$8–$15
Leia ....$8–$15
Luke ....$8–$15
Probe Droid...$8–$15
Yoda ....$8–$15

Tall Square Storage Tin, 4″ high, logo on hinged lid, photos of R2-D2, Darth Vader, Yoda, and Probot on side panels ....$15–$25

Oval Storage Tin, 4½″ tall, front and back panels show Cloud City (Bespin). Hinged lid with logo ....$25–$35

Space Trunks, large, tall square container tins. Lid has Empire logo and words "Space Trunk." Side panels have character photos. Two different

Luke on front panel..$45–$75
Droids on front panel ....$45–$75

JEWELRY

When Star Wars first came out in 1977, the costume jewelry industry was, by nature, somewhat informal. As a result, many of the earlier pieces of jewelry are either unlicensed or are indistinguishable copies of licensed products.

Assorted Items

Belt Buckles (*See* "Clothing and Accessories")
Bracelet, gold link bracelet with character charms. Several different combinations ...$10–$15

Earrings

Factors, Etc., 1977. ½″ figure earrings in metal. Earrings were either pierced or clip-on and were sold on padded earring mounts with Star Wars logo, usually from open displays

C-3PO, gold-plated heads ....$15–$20
Darth Vader, black painted heads...$15–$20
R2-D2, full figure in unfinished metal ....$15–$20

Factors, Etc., 1977. ¾″ metal full-figure earrings with moving arms and/or legs

C-3PO, gold plated ....$20–$25
Chewbacca, brown painted...$20–$25
R2-D2, unfinished metal..$20–$25

Assorted Star Wars jewelry items.

Keyrings

Adam Joseph, 1983. Heavy brass, 2″ high. Figure is in relief
Millennium Falcon..$10–$15
R2-D2..$10–$15
Yoda ....$10–$15
Adam Joseph, 1983. Ewok keyrings, 3-D, 2″ high. Hard plastic, molded in color and painted
Boy Ewok ....$3–$5
Girl Ewok ....$3–$5
Howard Eldon, 1987. Flexible, plastic, magnetic 1½″ × 2″ rectangles. Color movie logo art on white backgrounds
Star Wars, triangular "A New Hope" design ....$5–$8
Empire Strikes Back, Vader head in flames..$5–$8
Return of the Jedi, Yoda in circle ....$5–$8
Star Trek Galore (*See* "Figurines" section)
Weingeroff, 1977
Darth Vader head, 1¼″ black painted metal ....$5–$10
Stormtrooper head, 1″ white painted metal ....$5–$10
X-Wing, 2″ unpainted metal ....$5–$10
Tenth Anniversary Logo, 1987. 1½″ square plastic, promotional ....$3–$5

Medals

Wallace Berrie, 1980. Color enamel two-piece jewelry items. Top portion pinned to wearer, bottom is attached to top by a jump ring and dangles freely. Between 1″ and 1½″ total length. Pins came affixed to blue backing with Empire logo in blue box with clear lid. Six different
Boba Fett, figure above, name below ....$20–$25
Chewbacca, figure above, name below ....$20–$25
Darth Vader, Empire logo above, Darth head below ....$20–$25
Millennium Falcon pilot, words above, ship below ....$20–$25
X-Wing Fighter pilot, words above, ship below..$20–$25
Yoda, "May the Force Be With You" above, figure below ....$20–$25

Pendants

Adam Joseph, 1983. Photo-etched black and gold colored. Die-cut, came mounted on black plastic jewelry card with Jedi logo for display on rack. Included chain
May the Force Be With You, words, 1½″ ....$5–$10
Return of the Jedi, logo, 1½″...$5–$10
X-Wing Pilot, round rebel logo from movies...$5–$10

Wallace Beerie Empire medal and ring.

Adam Joseph, 1983. Figure pendants. Gold color characters in relief. Came carded like photo-etched pendants. Included chain

C-3PO, bust, 1″ ....$5–$10
Emperor's Royal Guard, 1¼″ ....$5–$10
Ewok, 1″ ....$5–$10
R2-D2, 1″ ....$5–$10
Salacious Crumb, 1¼″ ....$5–$10
Yoda, 1″ ....$5–$10

Adam Joseph, 1983. Painted, metal full-figure pendants, 1½″ high. Came blister packed on red header card with Jedi logo. Includes chain

Darth Vader ....$5–$10
R2-D2 ....$5–$10
Yoda ....$5–$10

Howard Eldon, 1987. Magnetic plastic rectangles with color logo art, leather neck cord

Star Wars ....$5–$10
Empire Strikes Back ....$5–$10
Return of the Jedi ....$5–$10

Miscellaneous, manufacturers and dates unknown

C-3PO, 1¼″ enamel ....$5–$10
R2-D2, ¾″ enamel ....$5–$10
Millenniem Falcon, small ....$5–$10
TIE Fighter, small ....$5–$10
Star Wars, logo, flat trapezoidal design ....$5–$10
Star Wars, logo and stars, cutout ....$5–$10

Wallace Berrie, 1980. Color enamel pendants came affixed to blue backing with Empire logo packaged in 3″ × 2¼″ blue box with clear plastic lid. Chain included

Chewbacca, 1″ octagonal design ....$15–$20
Darth Vader, 1″ outline of head ....$15–$20
R2-D2, 1″ full-figure cutout ....$15–$20
R2-D2 and C-3PO, 1″ on circular background ....$15–$20

Weingeroff, 1977. Articulated figure pendants. Arms and/or legs move, two sizes

Large
C-3PO, 2″, gold plated ....$10–$15
Chewbacca, 2″, painted ....$10–$15
R2-D2, 1½″, unplated metal ....$10–$15

Small
C-3PO, 1½″, gold plated ....$5–$10
Chewbacca, 1½″, painted ....$5–$10
R2-D2, 1″, unplated metal ....$5–$10

Weingeroff, 1977

Darth Vader head, 1¼″, black painted metal ....$5–$10
Darth Vader head, ¾″, black painted metal ....$5–$10
Stormtrooper head, 1″, painted metal ....$5–$10
X-Wing, 2″, unplated metal ....$5–$10

Pins

Adam Joseph, 1983. Photo-etched gold and black. Came affixed to black plastic header card with red Jedi logo ....$5–$10

May the Force Be With You, 1½″ ....$5–$10
Return of the Jedi, logo, 1½″ ....$5–$10
Star Wars, 1½″ ....$5–$10
The Force, 1½″ ....$5–$10
X-Wing Fighter Pilot, 1″ round, rebel symbol ....$5–$10

Adam Joseph, 1983. Character pins. Gold plate, in relief, came packaged similarly to photo-etched pins. Between 1″ and 1½″

C-3PO, bust ....$5–$10
Emperor's Royal Guard ....$5–$10

Ewok ....$5–$10
R2-D2 ....$5–$10
Salacious Crumb ....$5–$10
Yoda ....$5–$10
Adam Joseph, 1983. Ewok pins. Painted plastic, 1¼″, came blister packed on blue header card
with color artwork of Ewok
    Boy Ewok ....$3–$5
    Girl Ewok..$3–$5
Atari, promotional pins, metal, black and silver
    C-3PO ....$5–$10
    Darth Vader ....$5–$10
    R2-D2..$5–$10
Factors, Etc., 1977. Scatter pins, ½″ metal. R2-D2, C-3PO head, and Darth Vader head. Sold
as set of three on padded backing with Star Wars logo. Designed to be sold in open display.
Price per set..$15–$20
Howard Eldon, 1987. Color polycoat figure pins
    C-3PO, 1½″ high ....$5–$8
    Darth Vader, 1½″ high ....$5–$8
    R2-D2, 1¼″ high...$5–$8
Howard Eldon, 1987. Color polycoat logo pins
    Star Wars, black and silver ....$5–$8
    The Empire Strikes Back, blue and silver ....$5–$8
    Return of the Jedi, red and silver..$5–$8
Howard Eldon, 1987. Pewter 10th anniversary pins
    Original design, round with dates set inside circle.....................................$10–$15
    Later design, dates set outside circle ....$6–$10
Star Tours (Disney), triangular Star Tours logo..$5–$10

Rings

Adam Joseph, 1983. X-Wing Fighter Pilot. Photo etched. Gold plated, adjustable. Circular design featuring rebel symbol with words around it ....$10–$15
Factors, Etc, 1977. Set of three different (Darth, C-3PO, and R2-D2) in box with Star Wars
logo. Set ....$35–$45
Wallace Berrie, 1980. Color enamel designs on adjustable ring. Came affixed to blue card
with Empire logo inside blue box with clear lid
    Darth Vader, head on blue circular background ....$20–$25
    May the Force Be With You, words on blue square background............................$20–$25
    R2-D2, on blue circular background ....$20–$25
    R2-D2 and C-3PO, blue circular background..$20–$25
    X-Wing, blue circular background ....$20–$25
    Yoda, orange circular background, name below head ....$20–$25

Watches

Bradley, 1977. Full-figure Darth Vader analog watch on gray background. Came in cylindrical
blue plastic case with decals of Vader and Star Wars logo.........................$75–$90
Bradley, 1982. R2-D2 and C-3PO. Digital with rectangular face, Star Wars logo below..........
....$40–$60
Bradley, 1982. R2-D2 and C-3PO. Analog, round stainless steel case, black strap.....$40–$60
Bradley, R2-D2 and C-3PO. Blue face with two ships and Star Wars logo. Black case and
band, musical alarm...$50–$70
Bradley, 1982. Darth Vader double-image watch. Star Wars logo alternates with picture of
Darth when watch is moved, digital..$50–$70
Bradley, radio watch. Digital watch/radio set came complete with headphones. Packaged in
window box showing headphones with artwork of R2-D2 above................................$50–$75

Early Bradley Analog Darth Vader watch (left) and Texas Instrument digital watch with decal strip to change decorations on face.

Bradley, 1982–83. Series of watches with round faces and stainless steel cases. Watches displayed color artwork and movie logo on face. Black vinyl bands. Watches were either blister packed on card with movie logo or, in some cases, just bagged in clear plastic envelopes. Watches were either battery digital style or wind-up analog with minor variations in artwork to accommodate watch face

    C-3PO and R2-D2, black background with Star Wars logo ....$25–$50
    Darth Vader, head and name on gray ....$25–$50
    Darth Vader, figure with lightsaber..$25–$50
    Ewoks, with Jedi logo ....$25–$50
    Jabba the Hutt ....$25–$50
    Star Wars, logo...$25–$50
    Yoda, head and name on gray ....$25–$50
Bradley, 1983. Stopwatch/timer with cord. Stormtroopers on speeder bikes. Came boxed ......
....$30–$40
Star Tours (Disney), Darth Vader head. Outline in gold on black-faced analog watch, no numerals..$50–$75
Texas Instrument, 1977. Digital watch with gray band and decals of Star Wars scenes and characters around face, red faceplate. Came packaged in clear plastic vertical display box that fit into slipcase with color artwork. Included strip of ten extra artwork stickers that could be applied to watch..$125–$150
1983, series of analog watches with round faces show artwork of character and stars around rim

    Darth Vader ....$30–$50
    Ewok ....$30–$50
    Yoda ....$30–$50
Zeon, British. Alarm, date, time, calendar. C-3PO, R2-D2, X-Wing, and TIE Fighter on face, came boxed ....$50–$100
Zeon, British, 1982. Logo with R2-D2 and C-3PO. Promotion with British Star Wars/Empire weekly and monthly comic magazines ....$50–$100

MAGAZINES

Amazing Heroes, No. 13. "Star Wars in Comics," cover...$3–$5
American Cinematographer
    Star Wars issue, cover..$75–$100

Assorted Star Wars magazines.

Empire Strikes Back issue, June 1980, cover..$15–$25
American Cinematographer, R2-D2 and C-3PO on cover, profiles Return of the Jedi inside
....$6–$8
American Film
   April, 1977, "George Lucas Goes Far Out" ....$5–$10
   June, 1983, Lucas cover, Jedi special effects article ....$4–$6
Best of Starlog, The
   Vol. 1, Luke Skywalker with blaster in photographs from Empire Strikes Back on cover, as-
sorted articles...$6–$8
   Vol. 2, Yoda on cover, assorted articles ....$6–$8
   No. 4, Jabba on cover ....$6–$8
   No. 5, Luke and Vader fighting scene on cover.....................................$6–$8
Chicago Tribune, May 4, 1980, Empire Strikes Back ....$3–$5
Cinefantastique, F. S. Clark, Publishers, the magazine with a "sense of wonder"
   Vol. 6, No. 4, Vol. 7, No. 1, double issue, "Making Star Wars," 23 interviews with the actors,
technicians, and artists ....$15–$25
   Vol. 10, No. 2, review of Empire..$5–$10
   Vol. 12, No. 5 and 6, July/August 1982, "Star Trek II" and "The Revenge of the Jedi".......
....$5–$10
   Vol. 13, No. 4, Jedi plot revealed...$5–$10
Cinefex
   No. 2, Aug. 1980, special effects articles ....$10–$15
   No. 3, Empire cover...$10–$15
   No. 13, Jedi film production ....$10–$15
Comic Collector's Magazine, No. 139, Oct. 1977, this issue devoted to Star Wars, interviews,
behind the scenes and comic art ....$5–$8
Comics Journal
   No. 2, Empire issue..$3–$5
   No. 37, Articles on Star Wars comics and movie......................................$3–$5
Comics Scene, Vader cover and article on Jedi comic ....$3–$5
Commodore User Magazine (Dutch Computer Magazine), No. 3, 1988. Star Wars cover art
and game information ....$3–$5
Cracked
   No. 146. Nov. 1977, R2-D2/C-3PO cover, Star Wars spoof ....$5–$10
   No. 173, Nov. 1980, "The Empire Strikes It Out" ....$5–$7
   No. 174, Dec. 1980, "The Empire Strikes It Rich".....................................$5–$7
   No. 199, Nov. 1983, "Returns of the Jed Eye"...$5–$7
Crash (British Computer Magazine), No. 54, July 1988. Cover and article on Empire com-
puter game...$3–$5
Crazy, Vol. 1, No. 32, Dec. 1977, cover and Star Wars spoof......................$5–$10
Creative Computing, Vol. 8, No. 8, Aug. 1982, cover photograph of Darth Vader........$3–$5
Delap's F and SF Review, a review of fantasy and science fiction, Fredric Pattern Publisher,
Vol. 3, No. 7, July 1977, a cover story on Star Wars plus reviews of the movie ....$8–$12
Der Nederlandse Mad (Dutch Version of Mad), No. 87, March 1978, Star Wars spoof........
....$5–$10

Die Ruckkehr Der Jedi—Ritter: Das Offizielle Magazin Zum Film, German version of the Return of the Jedi collector's magazine ....$5–$10

Die Sprechblase, German comic fan magazine
    Oct. 1981, Star Wars cover and articles...$3–$5
    Dec. 1981, Star Wars cover and articles...$3–$5

Discover, Vol. 5, No. 8, Aug. 1984, Lucus, C-3PO and R2-D2 on cover, contains article entitled "Computerizing the Movies"...$4–$6

Dynamite
    No. 41, 1977, articles on Star Wars ....$3–$5
    No. 63, preview of Empire, cover ....$3–$5
    No. 76, 1980, Scholastic Magazine, Luke with saber on cover, article on The Empire Strikes Back ....$3–$5
    No. 114, Luke and Leia on cover, 1983..$3–$5

Electric Company, The, April/May 1983, Yoda on cover, Star Wars articles.................$3–$5

Empire Strikes Back Official Collector's Edition...$5–$8

Enterprise Spotlight, No. 4, Star Wars special...$3–$5

Eppo, Dutch comic fan magazine
    No. 11, 1983, Star Wars cover art and comics...$3–$5
    No. 22, 1983, Jedi cover and comics..$3–$5
    No. 32, 1983, Jedi cover art and comics...$3–$5

Famous Monsters
    No. 137, Star Wars special issue, Sept. 1977..$5–$8
    No. 138, Star Wars cover ....$5–$8
    No. 140, Star Wars article ....$5–$8
    No. 142, Darth Vader cover ....$5–$8
    No. 145, Empire article ....$4–$6
    No. 147, Star Wars cover ....$4–$6
    No. 148, Darth Vader cover ....$4–$6
    No. 153, David Prouse interview ....$3–$5
    No. 156, Empire cover ....$3–$5
    No. 165, Empire Strikes Back special issue ....$3–$5
    No. 166, Empire cover ....$3–$5
    No. 167, Empire cover ....$3–$5
    No. 174, Star Wars cover ....$3–$5
    No. 177, Yoda cover ....$3–$5
    No. 190, Empire cover ....$3–$5
    Movie aliens, Special reprints of *Famous Monsters* articles, Darth Vader cover ....$4–$6

Fantascene, Fantascene Productions, No. 3, 1977, "The Star Wars," an article on the technical aspects of the film..$10–$15

Fantastic Films, Blake Publishing
    Vol. 1, No. 1, April 1978, Star Wars, "Let the Wookie Win," "The Ships of Star Wars," "Interview with Rick Baker," and "Animating the Death Star Trench"............................$6–$10
    Vol. 1, No. 3, May 1978, the latest on behind the scenes during the making of Star Wars ....$6–$10
    Vol. 1, No. 8, April 1979, "Star Wars Strikes Back," news on sequel ....$4–$8
    Vol. 2, No. 2, June 1979, Star Wars: "One Last Time Down the Death Trench" with never-before-seen photos ....$4–$8
    Vol. 3, No. 2, July 1980, "An Interview With Larry Kasdan, the Screenwriter for Empire Strikes Back," "An Interview With Special Effects Photographer Dennis Muren"......$4–$8
    Vol. 3, No. 3, Sept. 1980, "Gary Kurtz Interviewed," the producer of Star Wars and Empire Strikes Back, a Wookie on the cover ....$4–$8
    Vol. 3, No. 4, Oct. 1980, "The Empire Talks Back," "Painting the Empire," Yoda on the cover...$4–$8
    Vol. 3, No. 5, Dec. 1980, "Speculation Concerning The Future History of the Star Wars Saga," clone wars explained ....$4–$8
    Vol. 3, No. 7, Feb. 1981, "From Star Wars to Empire," "The Weapons of Star Wars," "Rick Baker," "Animating the Death Star Trench," "The Best of Fantastic Films"...............$4–$8
    Vol. 3, No. 8, April 1981, part two of "From Star Wars to Empire," "The Mystery Behind Darth Vader's Prosthetic Armor"...$4–$8
    Vol. 3, No. 9, June 1981, "Star Wars Comes to Radio," illustrated cover of characters making radio program...$4–$8

Vol. 4, No. 1, Aug. 1981, "The Voice of Vader," "Nevana Limited," "From Star Wars to Empire" ....$4–$8

Vol. 4, No. 4, April 1982, "From Star Wars to Empire to Revenge of the Jedi" ....$4–$8

Vol. 5, No. 2, "Revenge of the Jedi," partial cover ....$4–$8

Vol. 5, No. 3, Return of the Jedi, cover ....$4–$8

Vol. 6, No. 4, Return of the Jedi article and cover ....$4–$8

Vol. 6, No. 5, Return of the Jedi, cover ....$4–$8

Fantasy Film Preview, 1977, special effects ....$4–$6

Fantasy Modeling, No. 6, Star Wars miniature models ....$4–$6

Film Review, British

June 1980, "Star Wars Rage Again Against the Empire," cover ....$4–$8

July 1980, "More Photos From the Empire Strikes Back," ¼ cover ....$4–$8

Aug. 1980, "Carrie Fisher and Mark Hamill Talk About Their Roles in Empire" ....$4–$8

July 1983, "Star Wars—The Final Force-Filled Phase" ....$4–$8

Films and Filming, Hansom Books, London, Vol. 23, No. 11, Aug. 1977, preview of Star Wars ....$6–$10

Finescale Modeler, No. 43, Summer 1983, Jedi diorama cover ....$3–$5

Fortune, Oct. 6, 1980, "The Empire Pays Off" ....$3–$5

Future, the magazine of science adventure, Future Magazine, Inc., NY

No. 1, April 1978, advertising posters of Star Wars ....$4–$8

No. 19, Empire preview ....$4–$8

No. 20, Empire cover and article ....$4–$8

Gateways, No. 6, Star Wars role-playing game ....$3–$5

Hollywood Studio Magazine, D. Denny, Publisher, Vol. 12, No. 5, June 1978, "New 15 Million Star Trek Movie," "Star Wars, a Sequel" ....$6–$10

Hot Dog, No. 17, 1983, article on Star Wars action figures ....$2–$4

House of Hammer, British

No. 13, article ....$4–$8

No. 16, articles plus poster ....$4–$8

Kuifje (Belgian), Vol. 38, No. 5, Return of the Jedi issue ....$4–$8

LA Times, June 14, 1977, "George Lucas on Opening Night" ....$3–$5

Ladies Home Journal, Sept. 1983, contains article entitled "Jedimania: Why We Love Those Star Warriors" ....$4–$6

L'ecran Fantastique (French)

No. 13, Empire Strikes Back issue ....$4–$8

No. 31, Jedi cover ....$4–$8

No. 33, Empire Strikes Back cover, special effects ....$4–$8

No. 37, Return of the Jedi cover ....$4–$8

No. 38, Return of the Jedi cover ....$4–$8

No. 86, 10th anniversary article ....$4–$8

L'Express (French), No. 1519, 23 Aug. 1980, cover story, "La Guerre Pour Rire," Star Wars II ....$4–$8

Life

Vol. 4, No. 1, Jan. 1981, features Yoda on cover, titled "The Year in Pictures" ....$4–$8

Vol. 6, No. 6, June 1983, "George Lucas: A Man and His Empire" ....$5–$10

Look-In (British), The Junior TV Times, June 4, 1983, Return of the Jedi, cover, articles and poster ....$4–$8

Mad

No. 196, Jan. 1978, "Star Bores," *Mad* plot synopsis ....$5–$10

No. 197, March 1979, "A *Mad* Look at Star Wars" ....$5–$10

No. 203, Dec. 1978, "The *Mad* Star Wars Musical" ....$5–$10

No. 220, Jan. 1981, "The Empire Strikes Out" ....$5–$10

No. 230, April 1982, "The Star Wars Log," *Mad*'s version of Lucas' personal log ...$5–$10

Mad Superspecial, Summer 1983, Star Wars spoofs ....$5–$10

No. 242, Oct. 1983, "Star Bores—Rehash of the Jedi" ....$5–$10

Mad Movies (French), No. 20, Empire Strikes Back cover, 1980 ....$4–$6

Mediascene Preview, supergraphics

Vol. 1, No. 22, Nov. 1976, the first Star Wars feature news, color cover, and center spread art ....$12–$15

Vol. 2, No. 4, Aug. 1980, The Empire Strikes Back, an interview with Mark Hamill, a profile of Harrison Ellenshaw, creator of unknown worlds ....$8–$12

Vol. 2, No. 11, "Darth Vader Returns With a New Ally, Boba Fett," and new costume designs ....$6–$10

Vol. 3, No. 2, Star Wars interview with Brian Johnson, special effects ....$4–$8

Midnight Marquee, No. 29, Yoda cover, Empire review ....$3–$5

Military Modeler, Vol. 7, No. 11, Nov. 1980, cover photograph of Millennium Falcon, "Han Solo's Millennium Falcon"...$4–$6

Modesto Bee, June 5, 1977, Star Wars...$5–$10

Movie Monsters, Vol. 1, No. 3, Fall 1981, Darth and Bounty Hunters on cover, article: "Star Wars: The Legend of Darth Vader" ....$4–$6

Muppet Magazine, Vol. 1, No. 3, Summer 1983, cover features Kermit as Luke, Gonzo as Darth, Piggy as Leia, article: "Super Star War: Battle of the Space Heroes" ....$4–$6

National Enquirer, June 21, 1983, cover photograph of stolen shuttle scene from Return of the Jedi, article: "Top Psychiatrists Explain the Amazing Appeal of Return of the Jedi" ....
....$4–$6

Newsweek, Newsweek, Inc., Vol. 89, No. 22, May 30, 1977, "Fun in Space," a review of Star Wars ....$15–$20

New Voyager (British), No. 4, Summer 1983, Jedi articles..$3–$5

NY Times, Dec. 20, 1980, the saga beyond Star Wars ....$3–$5

Orbit (Dutch), No. 13, Winter 1981, Empire cover and articles ....$4–$8

Orbit and SF Tera Presenteren Return of the Jedi, Dutch collaboration between two magazines to publish a Return of the Jedi special issue..$5–$10

People

July 18, 1977, article: "The Talented Folks Who Gave Us C-3PO and the Summer's Box Office Sizzler," with photographs...$5–$10

Vol. 8, No. 26, "The 25 Most Intriguing People of 1977," R2-D2 on cover, "The Shyest Guy in Hollywood Creates Star Wars"...$5–$10

July 7, 1980, Empire cover and article ....$5–$10

June 6, 1983, cover shows Carrie Fisher from Return of the Jedi ....$5–$10

Vol. 19, No. 24, June 20, 1983, Darth Vader on cover, "Match Wits With the Jedi Quiz Kid"
....$5–$10

Vol. 16, No. 9, Aug. 31, 1981, Mark Hamill and Yoda on cover, story on Mark Hamill ....
....$5–$10

Aug. 14, 1978, contains article about Carrie Fisher entitled "Star Wars Strikes Again," cover photo shows Carrie and Darth Vader...$5–$10

June 9, 1980, contains article entitled "Star Wars Strikes Back," cover shows Yoda.............
....$5–$10

Photoplay, British

Jan. 1978, Star Wars cover...$5–$10

Feb. 1978, Star Wars cover...$5–$10

June 1980, Empire Strikes Back cover ....$5–$10

Pizzaz, No. 1, R2-D2 and C-3PO cover..$3–$5

Questar, William Wilson, Publisher

No. 1, 1978, "The Triumph of Star Wars," "Close Encounters With Star Wars" ....$8–$12

No. 8, Aug. 1980, cover story "The Making of an Empire: Star Wars Returns"..........$4–$8

Reel Fantasy, No. 1, Star Wars issue ....$3–$5

Review

Vol. 2, No. 14, interview with Billy Dee Williams, "Rogue's Eye View of Star Wars Adventure"..$4–$8

Vol. 2, No. 12, double-length interview with Richard Marquand, Luke and Leia on cover ...
....$5–$10

Return of the Jedi Official Collector's Edition, Lucasfilm, 1983 ....$5–$10

Return of the Jedi Giant Collector's Compendium, magazine with poster and stories on production and the actors...$5–$10

Rolling Stone

Aug. 25, 1977, "The Force Behind George Lucas" ....$8–$12

Aug. 12, 1980, The Empire Strikes Back ....$8–$12

No. 322, July 24, 1980, cover features Luke, Leia, Han, and Lando in street clothes, article entitled "Slaves to (of) the Empire" ....$6–$10

No. 400/401, Darth Vader, Jedi monsters, and Princess Leia on cover, "George Lucas: The Rolling Stone Interview," "Space Cadet: A Few Words With Carrie Fisher" ....$6–$10

Science and Fantasy, R. Finton, Publisher, no date, interviews with the stars of Star Wars and an article on the music ....$4–$6

Science Fiction, Horror and Fantasy, Douglas Wright Publishing, Los Angeles, CA, Star Wars collector edition, Vol. 1, No. 1, Fall 1977, the making of Star Wars: the secrets behind the special effects, official blueprints, discussions with all the main characters....................$5–$8

Scintillation, the magazine of science-fiction people, Carl Bennet, Publisher, No. 13, June 1977, "George Lucas Brings the Excitement Back" ....$6–$10

Screen Superstars, No. 8, 1977, Star Wars issue..$5–$10

Seventeen, March 19, 1973, interview on location...$4–$6

SFTV, No. 7, Star Wars costume article...$3–$5

Space Wars

Oct. 1977, Star Wars ....$3–$5

June 1978, Star Wars, Close Encounters comparison..$3–$5

Star Blaster, Vol. 1, No. 2, article on Droids, Darth cover.......................................$4–$6

Starblazer, Dec. 1986, special issue, Vader cover..$3–$5

Starburst, British

No. 1, Feb. 1978, Star Wars cover...$10–$15

No. 2, "3PO Unmasked" article ....$8–$12

No. 3, Star Wars article ....$5–$10

No. 8, Empire Strikes Back ....$5–$10

No. 22, Empire Strikes Back ....$5–$10

No. 23, Empire articles plus poster...$5–$10

No. 24, Star Wars interviews ....$5–$10

No. 25, Empire interviews ....$5–$10

No. 26, Empire special effects ....$5–$10

No. 43, Star Wars article ....$5–$10

No. 58, Jedi articles...$5–$10

No. 59, Jedi articles...$5–$10

No. 60, C-3PO ....$5–$10

No. 61, Carrie Fischer interview..$5–$10

No. 93, Return of the Jedi video..$4–$8

Winter Special 1987, Star Tours and 10th anniversary articles..........................$4–$8

Star Encounters, April 1978, Vol. 1, No. 1, making of Star Wars article ....$4–$6

Starfix (French), Return of the Jedi special issue, 1980...$4–$6

Star Force

Vol. 1, No. 2, Oct. 1980, features Star Wars, Empire Strikes Back and other creepy crawlies ....$4–$6

Vol. 2, No. 3, Aug. 1981, Darth Vader, Lando, and scenes from Empire Strikes Back on cover, contains article "Star Wars III: The Sci-Fi Success Story Continues"...............$4–$6

Oct. 1981, Revenge of the Jedi..$4–$6

Starlog

No. 7, features an X-Wing Fighter and a TIE fighter on the cover.............................$6–$10

No. 16, "Invisible Visions of Star Wars" article, 1978.....................................$5–$8

No. 17, miniature explosion and R. Mcquarrie articles....................................$5–$8

No. 19, Star Wars TV special, 1979 ....$5–$8

No. 19, Cantina Creatures on cover, Star Wars TV special............................$5–$8

No. 31, ESB on cover, report on movie inside ....$5–$8

No. 35, Darth Vader on cover..$5–$8

No. 36, Vader and Boba Fett on cover...$5–$8

No. 37, Millennium Falcon on cover..$5–$8

No. 40, features Luke Skywalker and Yoda on cover ....$5–$8

No. 41, cover photograph of Luke and Yoda on Dagobah, interview with Mark Hamill.......
....$5–$8

No. 48, features Luke Skywalker and Yoda on cover ....$5–$8

No. 50, features Boba Fett on cover ....$5–$8

No. 51, features Luke Skywalker on cover...$5–$8

No. 56, features Darth Vader on cover .... $5–$8
No. 65, cover photograph of Luke with lightsaber; interview with Mark Hamill, "I Was Mark Hamill's Stand-In," Dec. 1982 .... $5–$8
No. 69, features Return of the Jedi cast on cover .... $5–$8
No. 71, assorted articles on Return of the Jedi, interviews with Carrie Fisher and Richard Marquand, cover photograph of Han, Luke, and Leia, June 1983 .... $5–$8
No. 72, Mark Hamill interview .... $5–$8
No. 74, Jedi creature manufacture .... $5–$8
No. 76, Preview of Jedi .... $5–$8
No. 80, Jedi special effects, cover .... $5–$8
No. 82, Jedi effects, Emperor interview .... $5–$8
No. 84, Frank Oz on Yoda .... $5–$8
No. 86, Jedi special effects .... $5–$8
No. 90, Ewok Adventure .... $5–$8
No. 93, Jedi bike special effects .... $5–$8
No. 94, Jedi special effects .... $5–$8
No. 96, Peter Cushing interview .... $5–$8
No. 99, C-3PO cover .... $5–$8
No. 100, Lucas interview .... $5–$8
No. 104, Peter Mayhew article, Chewbacca cover .... $5–$8
No. 115, Star Tours .... $5–$8
No. 118, Lucas/Star Tours cover .... $5–$8
No. 120, Star Wars 10th anniversary special, cover .... $5–$8
No. 127, Lucas interview .... $5–$8
Starlog Poster Magazine, Vol. 2, 1984, contains ten 16″ × 21″ color posters, includes close-up of Darth Vader .... $3–$5
Star Warp, April 1978, includes posters .... $3–$5
Star Wars Compendium
World of Star Wars—A Compendium of Fact and Fantasy From Star Wars and The Empire Strikes Back, Paradise Press, 1981 .... $6–$10
Vol. II, June 1981, compilation of information on the Star Wars poster book (minus the posters) .... $6–$10
Vol. III, June 1982, reset of the poster book on The Empire Strikes Back .... $5–$8
Star Wars Newspaper, Star Fleet Productions, Inc., 1977 .... $3–$5
Star Wars, The Making of the World's Greatest Movie, Paradise Press, 1977, an entire magazine devoted to the making of Star Wars, with special effects, who's who in Star Wars ...
.... $6–$10
Star Wars Spectacular, a Warren magazine, special edition of *Famous Monsters*, 1977, issue devoted to the motion picture, articles on robots, special effects, a tribute to George Lucas .....
.... $6–$8
Stripschrift (Dutch), No. 142, Dec. 1980, Empire cover and article on McQuarrie artwork ....
.... $3–$5
Time Magazine, R. Davidson Publishing
Vol. 109, No. 22, May 30, 1977, "The Year's Best Movie—Star Wars," profile of the movie and stars .... $15–$20
Vol. 115, No. 20, May 19, 1983, "The Empire Strikes Back," profiles of the movie, behind the scenes production, George Lucas .... $6–$8
Vol. 121, No. 21, May 23, 1983, "Star Wars III: The Return of the Jedi," profiles of the movie and its stars, a second article profiles George Lucas .... $4–$6
True, UFOs and Outer Space Quarterly, No. 19, Fall 1980, AT-ATS on cover, story: "The Empire Strikes Back . . . But Not Out!" .... $3–$5
US
Vol. 4, No. 7, July 22, 1980, cover story: "The Good Guys of Star Wars" .... $4–$8
Vol. 8, No. 13, June 20, 1983, cover photograph and articles on Return of the Jedi .... $4–$8
Videofilmmagazine (Dutch), No. 3, 1986, Return of the Jedi cover art and article .... $3–$5
Video Games, Vol. 2, No. 2 .... $3–$5
Videogaming Illustrated, Feb. 1983, cover illustration of Darth Vader, articles: "Star Wars Spectacular: First Look at the Jedi Arena Videogame," "Revenge of the Jedi Film and Videogame," "Darth Vader Interviewed" .... $3–$5
Weird Worlds, No. 6, 1980, Scholastic Magazine, Vader cover, Empire article .... $3–$5

Assorted Star Wars saga models.

MODELS

Estes

Flying Models

These were actual flying rocket kits built in the shape of the ship or character. Models were packaged in plastic bags with color headers and a color cover sheet.

R2-D2 ....$15–$25
TIE Fighter ....$20–$30
X-Wing ....$20–$30

Left: Y-Wing Mirr-A-Kit (top), Snap Kit Model (middle) and action figure toy. Right: Current (top) and original X-Wing model packaging.

Rocket Kits

Included not only rocket but complete launching kit. Came boxed.
Proton Torpedo ....$50–$75
X-Wing ....$50–$75

MPC
Model Kits

MPC was the major model licensee for the Star Wars saga. Box art showed color picture of the subject and movie logo. Movie logos were often updated to depict the most recent film. Models in earlier boxes tend to be slightly more valuable, though in all cases except the Millennium Falcon, whose original production run had lights, the model remained the same. Recently the ERTL company purchased MPC, reissued several of the models, and is planning to reissue more. Box art is nearly identical to the original except for the MPC/ERTL logo and some very minor changes. A silver "Commemorative Edition" sticker is affixed to the outside of the shrink-wrapping but could be easily removed.

The reissues have drastically affected the collectibility of those models, reducing their value considerably. Prices shown here for models that have not yet been reissued would undoubtedly be similarly affected should ERTL elect to redo them. Assembled models or incomplete kits have very little collectors' value. In Europe, Airfix issued many of the models done by MPC in the United States. In addition to the individual kits we are familiar with, they also combined some of the smaller kits into large assortments for sale in some countries.

AT-AT, 8″ tall, posable front legs, 1982 ....$15–$20
AT-AT, reissue, MPC/ERTL, 1990 ....$9–$11
Battle on Ice Planet Hoth, glue or snap-together, diorama, 11¾″ × 17¾″, 1982 ....$40–$60
C-3PO, 10″ tall, 1977 ....$15–$25
Darth Vader Action Model, bust, 10¾″ tall, snap-together, illuminated eyes and rasping breathing sound, 1978 ....$30–$60
Darth Vader's TIE Fighter, 7½″ wide, 1977 ....$15–$25
Darth Vader's TIE Fighter, reissue, MPC/ERTL, 1990 ....$9–$11
Darth Vader, molded in black, full figure, glow-in-the-dark lightsaber, movable arm, height 11¾″, 1979 ....$15–$25
Darth Vader Van, 1979 ....$25–$35
Encounter With Yoda on Dagobah, glue or snap-together, 5¾″ × 10″, 1982............$30–$40
Jabba the Hutt Throne Room, diorama, 1983...$20–$25
Luke Skywalker Van, snap-together, molded-in color, 1977 ....$20–$30
Millennium Falcon, 18″ long, original version with lights, 1977.........................$100–$125
Millennium Falcon, no lights, 1982..$20–$30
Millennium Falcon, reissue, MPC/ERTL, 1990..$11–$13
R2-D2 Model Kit, 6″ tall, 1977 ....$10–$20
R2-D2 Van, snap-together, molded-in color, 1977 ....$20–$30
Shuttle Tyderium, 20″ wingspan, 1983 ....$20–$30
Slave I, movable parts, 1982 ....$35–$50
Snowspeeder, 8″ long, 1980 ....$20–$25
Snowspeeder, reissue, MPC/ERTL, 1990..$7–$9
Speeder Bike Vehicle, 12″ long, 1983 ....$10–$20
Speeder Bike Vehicle, reissue, MPC/ERTL, 1990 ....$7–$10
Star Destroyer, 15″ long, 1980...$20–$25
Star Destroyer, reissue, MPC/ERTL, 1990 ....$11–$13
X-Wing Fighter, glue or snap-together, 12½″, 1982.......................................$15–$25
X-Wing Fighter, reissue, MPC/ERTL, 1990 ....$9–$11

Mirr-A-Kits, 1984

Small, easy snap-kits where half a vehicle is affixed to a mirror surface to give the allusion of a whole ship. Came in 4½″ × 5½″ header boxes showing color artwork of subject.

AT-ST ....$10–$15
Shuttle Tyderium ....$10–$15
Speeder Bike ....$10–$15
TIE Interceptor ....$10–$15
Y-Wing ....$10–$15
X-Wing ....$10–$15

Snap Kits

Small, easily built kits requiring no glue. These come in 7″ × 9½″ boxes with box art similar to the larger models.

AT-ST, 6″ high (scout walker), 1983 ....$10–$20
A-Wing Fighter, 1983 ....$10–$15
A-Wing, reissue, MPC/ERTL, 1990 ....$7–$10
B-Wing Fighter, 1983 ....$10–$20
TIE Interceptor, 1983 ....$10–$15
TIE Interceptor, reissue, MPC/ERTL, 1990 ....$7–$10
X-Wing Fighter, 1983 ....$10–$15
X-Wing Fighter, reissue, MPC/ERTL, 1990 ....$7–$10
Y-Wing, 1983 ....$10–$15
Y-Wing, reissue, MPC/ERTL, 1990 ....$7–$10

Structors, 1984

Simple snap-kits included wind-up motor. Completed model "walked." Came in 5½″ × 8″ header boxes showing color artwork of subject in action pose.

AT-AT, 4½″ high ....$15–$25
AT-ST, 4½″ high ....$15–$25
C-3PO, 4¾″ tall ....$15–$25

Miscellaneous

Takara

(Japan), cutout models made of wood.

Landspeeder ....$75–$100
R2-D2 ....$75–$100
TIE Fighter ....$75–$100
X-Wing ....$75–$100

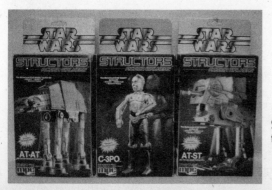

Structor Walkers. Wind-up toys.

Star Wars music book.

Tskuda

(Japan), standard injection molded plastic models made for the Japanese market.
AT-AT ....$75–$100
AT-ST ....$75–$100
Star Destroyer ....$75–$100

MUSIC (SHEET)

Music Books

All are from Fox Fanfare Music by John Williams.
Star Wars, 1977. Includes "Main Title" piano solo and sketch score, "Princess Leia's Theme," and "Cantina Band." Numerous pictures with extensive outlines ....$15–$20
Star Wars Music Picture Book, 26 pages, color cover ....$10–$15
The Empire Strikes Back, 1980. "Star Wars" (main theme), "The Imperial March" (Darth Vader's theme), "Yoda's Theme," "Han Solo and the Princess," "May the Force Be With You," and "Finale." Numerous photos...$10–$15
Star Wars Saga Book, 100 pages, black cover, black and white interior photos ....$15–$20

Sheet Music

All are from Fox Fanfare Music by John Williams.
Star Wars, 1977. Main theme from the movie...$3–$5
Princess Leia's Theme, 1977 ....$3–$5
Empire Strikes Back Medley, 1980, Darth Vader/Yoda's theme ....$3–$5
Han Solo and the Princess, 1980..$3–$5

PARTY GOODS

Prices on party goods assume a complete package, if applicable, since the price on individual paper goods is negligible. Packaging is generally very basic. Usually shrink-wrapping with either a sticker or simple header describing product.

Balloons
British, 1979–1983

Assorted characters and colors, sold separately.
C-3PO...$1–$3

Star Wars saga party supplies.

R2-D2 ....$1–$3
Stormtrooper ....$1–$3
Darth Vader ....$1–$3
Millennium Falcon ....$1–$3
AT-AT ....$1–$3
Chewbacca ....$1–$3

Drawing Board

1980, package of ten character balloons packaged in plastic bag with color Empire logo and artwork ....$3–$5
1983, package of ten character balloons packaged in plastic bag with color Jedi logo and artwork ....$3–$5
1983, Ewok balloons, package of six, assorted colors ....$3–$5

Gift Tags, Drawing Board

1978, R2-D2 and C-3PO, package of five self-sticking ....$1–$3
1978, four different Star Wars scenes
    Space battle ....$1–$2
    Luke, Leia, and Han, with Star Wars logo ....$1–$2
    R2-D2 and C-3PO, artwork, "A Gift For You" ....$1–$2
    R2-D2 and C-3PO, photo, "Happy Birthday" ....$1–$2
1981, Empire Strikes Back motif ....$1–$3

Hats, Drawing Board

1978, package of eight open-top paper party hats with pointed front and back flange to resemble Darth Vader's helmet ....$5–$8
1981, package of eight pointed paper party hats with color artwork of characters and Empire logo ....$5–$8
1983, package of eight pointed paper party hats with color artwork of Luke and Vader dueling ....$5–$8

Invitations, Drawing Board

1978, package of eight die-cut cards shaped like R2-D2 ....$5–$8
1978, package of eight greeting card-style invitations picturing R2-D2 and C-3PO ....$3–$5
1978, package of 16 postcard-style invitations with R2-D2, C-3PO, and Darth head ......$3–$5
1981, package of eight greeting card-style invitations with artwork of characters and Empire logo ....$3–$5
1981, package of eight fold-out-style invitations with artwork of characters and Empire logo ....$4–$8
1983, package of eight greeting card-style invitations with artwork of Luke and Darth dueling ....$3–$5

Napkins, Drawing Board

1978, 5″ beverage napkins, package of 16 has artwork of R2-D2 and C-3PO ....$2–$5
1978, 6½″ dinner napkins, package of 16 has artwork of R2-D2 and C-3PO ....$3–$6
1981, 5″ beverage napkins, package of 16 has artwork of Empire characters and logo ...$2–$5
1981, 6½″ dinner napkins, package of 16 has artwork of Empire characters and logo ....$3–$6
1983, 5″ beverage napkins, package of 16 has artwork of Luke and Vader dueling........$2–$5
1983, 6½″ dinner napkins, package of 16 has artwork of Luke and Vader dueling..........$3–$6
1983, package of 16 napkins with artwork of Ewok ....$2–$4

Paper Cups

Deeko (British) 1977

Package of eight, illustrated with Star Wars scenes.......................................$10–$15

Dixie

1980, box of 100 five-oz. cups, 40 different scenes on cups. Color box art of characters and Star Wars logo
   Darth Vader ....$5–$10
   Han and Chewbacca...$5–$10
   Leia ....$5–$10
   Luke ....$5–$10
   Obi-Wan..$5–$10
   R2-D2 and C-3PO...$5–$10
   Stormtrooper ....$5–$10
   X-Wing and TIE Fighter..$5–$10
1981, box of 100 five-oz. cups with Empire artwork. Box art of Empire subject and logo
   AT-AT..$5–$10
   Bespin and Cloud Car ....$5–$10
   Darth Vader ....$5–$10
   Luke on Tauntaun ....$5–$10
   Millennium Falcon...$5–$10
   Star Cruiser ....$5–$10
   X-Wing on Dagobah ....$5–$10
   Yoda ....$5–$10
1983, box of 100 five-oz. cups with Jedi artwork. Box art of Jedi characters and logo
   Ewoks...$5–$10
   Emperor and Darth Vader ....$5–$10
   Leia and Jabba ....$5–$10
   Luke and Yoda ....$5–$10
1984, box of 100 five-oz. cups with photos from movies and Star Wars Saga logo.......$5–$10

Star Wars, Empire, and Jedi dixie cups.

Drawing Board

1978, package of eight with Star Wars motif and logo..$3–$6
1981, package of eight with Empire characters and logo...$3–$6
1983, package of eight with Luke and Darth Vader dueling ....$3–$6
1983, package of eight with animated Ewok...$2–$4

Paper Plates, Drawing Board

1978, package of eight 7″ luncheon size. Artwork of Darth Vader and Star Wars logo ...$4–$8
1978, package of eight 9″ dinner size. Artwork of R2-D2 and C-3PO with Star Wars logo......
....$5–$10
1981, package of eight 7″ luncheon size. Artwork of Chewbacca and Empire logo........$4–$8
1981, package of eight 9″ dinner size. Artwork of Boba Fett and Darth Vader with Empire
logo ....$5–$10
1983, package of eight 7″ luncheon size. Artwork of Luke and Darth dueling................$4–$8
1983, package of eight 9″ dinner size. Artwork of Luke and Darth dueling...................$5–$10
1983, package of eight 7″ luncheon size. Artwork of animated Ewok ....$3–$6
1983, package of eight 9″ dinner size. Artwork of animated Ewok................................$4–$8

Table Covers

Deeko (British)

1978, Star Wars design, sold in packages of three ....$10–$15

Drawing Board

1978, 60″ × 96″ paper with color artwork of C-3PO and R2-D2 with Star Wars logo...$5–$10
1981, 60″ × 96″ paper with color artwork of characters in front of city ....$5–$10
1983, 54″ × 96″ paper with color artwork of Luke and Darth Vader dueling ....$5–$10

Wrapping Paper, Drawing Board

1978, color artwork of space battle scenes. Rolls or sheet..$3–$8
1978, color artwork of R2-D2 and C-3PO. Rolls or sheets...$3–$8
1978, color artwork of assorted characters. Rolls or sheets ....$3–$8
1978, color photos of assorted scenes and logo. Rolls or sheets....................................$3–$8
1981, color artwork of Yoda and Ben..$3–$8
1983, sheets showing color artwork of Luke and Darth Vader. Set included wrap, tag, ribbon,
and bow...$3–$8

Miscellaneous

Banner, Drawing Board, 1981. "Happy Birthday" with characters off to sides. Small Empire
logo below...$5–$8
Blowouts, Drawing Board, 1980. Darth Vader head at mouthpiece end, star design on
streamer. Packaged in fours ....$5–$8
Cake Decorating Accessories (*See* "Housewares" section)
Centerpiece, Drawing Board, 1980. Die-cut color cardboard, shows characters in city scene,
14″ tall. Packaged in paper envelope with color photo of product....................................$5–$8
Centerpiece, Drawing Board, 1983. Die-cut color cardboard scene of Luke and Darth dueling
....$5–$8
Name Badges, Drawing Board, 1978. Package of 16 with Darth Vader head on left-hand side
....$1–$3
Name Badges, Drawing Board, 1978. Package of 16 with Star Wars logo in lower left-hand
corner ....$1–$3
Package Decorations, Drawing Board, 1981
   R2-D2...$1–$2
   Yoda ....$1–$2

Party Bags, Drawing Board, 1983. Package of eight with artwork of Luke and Darth Vader dueling...$3–$5
Placecards, Drawing Board, 1978. Package of eight with artwork of R2-D2 and C-3PO on left-hand side..$1–$3
Placemats, Drawing Board, 1978. Package of eight. Designed as maze decorated with Star Wars characters ....$4–$8
Thank You Notes, Drawing Board, 1981. Package of eight pictures R2-D2 and says "Thanks" on cover, "From the bottom of my circuits" inside ....$5–$10

PATCHES

As with several other categories of merchandise, patches are too easy to reproduce for them to accumulate much collectors' value. Though Lucasfilm has been diligent in the protection of its licensees, a well-made counterfeit patch is virtually indistinguishable from the original.

Factors, Etc., 1977

Embroidered patches with iron-on backing.
Brotherhood of Jedi Knights, 2″ × 3″ rectangular, words and stylized lightsaber, blue on white...$3–$6
Darth Vader Lives, 3″ circle. Words and Darth's head, white on black background.....$3–$6
May the Force Be With You, 2″ × 3″ rectangular, words only, white on black.............$3–$6
Star Wars, 2″ × 3″ rectangular, outline logo, white on black...$3–$6
Star Wars, 2″ × 3″ rectangular, logo, red, yellow, black, and blue ....$3–$6

Lucasfilm Fan Club, 1987

Tenth Anniversary Star Wars, 4″ wide, "Star Wars" in yellow on shades of blue in center of circle. "The First Ten Years" on purple border around outside of circle. Side bars with "1977" and "1987" ....$5–$6

Star Tours, Disney

Star Tours, word embroidered in silver on black rectangular patch ....$3–$5
Star Tours, blue and black triangular logo ....$2–$4

New Hope, Empire, Return, and Revenge patches. Revenge patch is original crew patch.

Star Wars Fan Club

These embroidered patches were first made by the original Fan Club. Though this club disbanded, the current Lucasfilm Fan Club continues to produce the patches. All are embroidered and have iron-on backings.

Empire Strikes Back, logo, 2″ × 3″ rectangular, white and red on black........................$4–$5
Empire Strikes Back, "Crew patch," Darth Vader head surrounded by flames with logo on shield-shaped patch, seven colors, 4¼″ high
(Note: *This is a copy of the patch originally worn by the film crew of the movie. Though theoretically an original would be considerably more valuable, it would be difficult to authenticate)*..$8–$10
Return of the Jedi, logo, 2½″ × 4¼″ rectangular, red on black......................................$6–$7
Return of the Jedi, "Crew patch," Yoda in circle surrounded by logo on rectangular background. Ten colors, 5¼″ high.
(Note: *As with the Empire "crew patch," originals theoretically exist which could be worth more if authenticated. There also existed a "Revenge" crew patch similar to this which would be worth more still, but which has almost surely been duplicated.)*.................$8–$10
Star Wars, logo, 2″ × 3¾″ rectangular, white on black..$4–$5
Star Wars, "A New Hope," figure in front of orange planet on light blue triangular background, 4¾″ high ....$8–$10

Thinking Cap Co.

Empire Strikes Back, logo, 2½″ × 4″ rectangular, white and red on black, iron-on backing. Though designed to be applied to hats, this patch was sold separately.............................$5–$6

POSTERS

Theater Posters

In this section, posters are arranged chronologically by movie. You will find *Star Wars* first, followed by *Empire Strikes Back*, and then *Return of the Jedi*. The "Ewok Adventure" TV movie is also included.

All movie posters are printed at contracted printing plants called National Screen Services, which are generally located near areas of distribution. These distribution points have been sending out advertising material for films from most studios since 1942. Today, movie posters come in five basic sizes. The one-sheet (27″ × 41″) is usually printed on a thin clay-coated paper stock, in use since 1970. The insert size (14″ × 36″) is printed on a heavy card stock paper which lends itself to greater durability. The half-sheet or display poster is also printed on the more durable paper stock and is the only movie poster format with a horizontal composition. The thirty-forty (30″ × 40″) is printed on the heavy card stock paper. In most cases, the printing plates used to print the one-sheets are also used for the thirty-forty. The last of the standard movie poster sizes is the forty-by-sixty (40″ × 60″) and it, too, is printed on the heavy card stock paper. Larger sizes exist, usually for sign and billboard use. These are usually designated as a multiple of one-sheets (three-sheet or six-sheet), each being three or six times the standard size of a one-sheet.

A popular movie will often release more than one style of artwork or photograph for theater posters. When this is done they will letter the posters (A, B, C, etc.) on the lower border where the title is printed. Prices and descriptions are for U.S. posters. Foreign posters which generally have different, though similar, artwork are comparable in value.

Special thanks to Jeff Killian of *L'Affiche* for descriptions and pricing in this section (L'Affiche, 2352 S. Osage, Wichita, KS 67213). His magazine is highly recommended.

Star Wars Saga

This two-sided, full-color poster shows every theater poster from the Star Wars trilogy.

One-sheet rolled ....$5–$10
One-sheet folded ....$4–$8

First Advance (First Version), this was the first one-sheet-size poster to be released for *Star Wars*. It was printed on silver Mylar paper, which has a chrome finish and is very reflective. It features the phrase "Coming to Your Galaxy This Summer—Star Wars." The Star Wars logo featured on this poster is different than the standardized logo that was adopted a few months later.

One-sheet rolled ....$300–$600
One-sheet folded ....$150–$250

First Advance (Second Version), similar to first version but on white paper and with standard trademark logo

One-sheet rolled ....$150–$300
One-sheet folded ....$50–$200

Advance (Style "B"), blue ink on white paper, "A Long Time Ago in a Galaxy Far, Far Away . . . Star Wars"

One-sheet rolled ....$100–$200
One-sheet folded ....$50–$100

Style "A", illustration by Tom Jung. Luke with lightsaber and Leia in front of large Darth Vader helmet

One-sheet rolled ....$75–$150
One-sheet folded ....$50–$100
Insert rolled ....$40–$100
Insert folded ....$20–$50
30″ × 40″ rolled..$60–$100
30″ × 40″ folded..$40–$60
40″ × 60″ rolled..$100–$150
40″ × 60″ folded..$50–$100
Three-sheet folded ....$75–$150
Six-sheet folded ....$100–$200
Standee..$75–$150

Style "A," Half-Sheet, different artwork from regular style "A"

Half-sheet rolled ....$60–$100
Half-sheet folded..$40–$60

Style "C", illustrated by Tom Cantrell. Artwork used on many foreign posters

One-sheet rolled ....$150–$300
One-sheet folded ....$75–$150

Style "D", illustration by Drew Struzan and Charles White III. Done in 1930s' style of circus posters

One-sheet rolled ....$100–$200
One-sheet folded ....$75–$150
30″ × 40″ rolled..$100–$200
30″ × 40″ folded..$50–$75
40″ × 60″ rolled..$100–$200
40″ × 60″ folded..$50–$100
Standee..$75–$150

Happy Birthday, at the end of the first year of Star Wars distribution, a special birthday poster was released to theaters still playing the movie. Probably less than 500 printed

One-sheet rolled ....$300–$600
One-sheet folded ....$150–$300

1979 Reissue, cropped style "A" artwork with red band across the middle containing information on new Star Wars toys

One-sheet rolled ....$75–$100
One-sheet folded ....$40–$60

1981 Reissue, cropped version of style "A" artwork with bright red banner proclaiming that "The Force will be with you for two weeks only"

One-sheet rolled ....$40–$60

One-sheet folded ....$20–$40
Half-sheet rolled ....$20–$35
Half-sheet folded...$10–$20
Insert rolled ....$20–$35
Insert folded ....$10–$20
30″ × 40″ rolled ....$30–$50
30″ × 40″ folded ....$15–$25
40″ × 60″ rolled ....$40–$60
40″ × 60″ folded ....$15–$25
Standee ....$30–$50

1982 Reissue, "Star Wars is Back" with "Revenge of the Jedi" trailer advertisement
One-sheet rolled ....$35–$60
One-sheet folded ....$20–$30
Half-sheet rolled ....$25–$40
Half-sheet folded...$10–$20
Insert rolled ....$25–$40
Insert folded ....$10–$20
30″ × 40″ rolled ....$25–$40
30″ × 40″ folded ....$10–$20
40″ × 60″ rolled ....$30–$45
40″ × 60″ folded ....$15–$25
Standee ....$35–$55

Tenth Anniversary
One-sheet, Mylar ....$150–$250
One-sheet, Drew Art ....$100–$150
16″ × 36″, Mind's Eye Press, McQuarry Art...........................$20–$40

The Empire Strikes Back

Advance Style "A", Darth Vader's helmet superimposed on a field of stars
One-sheet rolled ....$60–$120
One-sheet folded ....$25–$75

Style "A", illustration by Rodger Kastel, dubbed the "Love Story" or "Kissing Scene" poster due to the "Gone With the Wind"-style artwork
One-sheet rolled ....$60–$100
One-sheet folded ....$30–$60
Half-sheet rolled ....$30–$60
Half-sheet folded...$10–$20
Insert rolled ....$30–$50
Insert folded ....$20–$30
30″ × 40″ rolled ....$40–$80
30″ × 40″ folded ....$20–$35
40″ × 60″ rolled ....$40–$80
40″ × 60″ folded ....$25–$40
Standee ....$50–$100

Style "B", illustration by Tom Jung, light blue background
One-sheet rolled ....$30–$50
One-sheet folded ....$20–$35
Half-sheet rolled ....$20–$40
Half-sheet folded...$10–$20
Insert rolled ....$20–$40
Insert folded ....$10–$20
30″ × 40″ rolled ....$25–$45
30″ × 40″ folded ....$10–$24
40″ × 60″ rolled ....$30–$50
40″ × 60″ folded ....$12–$25
Standee ....$20–$60

1981 Summer Rerelease
One-sheet rolled ....$20–$40
One-sheet folded ....$15–$25
Half-sheet rolled ....$20–$35

Half-sheet folded...$8–$18
Insert rolled ....$20–$35
Insert folded ....$8–$18
30″ × 40″ rolled...$20–$40
30″ × 40″ folded..$10–$20
40″ × 60″ rolled...$30–$45
40″ × 60″ folded..$12–$24
Standee..$30–$55
1982 Rerelease
One-sheet rolled ....$15–$30
One-sheet folded ....$10–$20
Half-sheet rolled ....$15–$25
Half-sheet folded...$8–$12
Insert rolled ....$15–$25
Insert folded ....$8–$12
30″ × 40″ rolled...$20–$30
30″ × 40″ folded..$10–$15
40″ × 60″ rolled...$25–$35
Standee..$20–$40
Tenth Anniversary
One-sheet, Mylar ....$100–$150
One-sheet, Mobile Art ....$15–$25

Revenge of the Jedi

Advance (First Version), no release date on bottom
One-sheet rolled ....$100–$200
One-sheet folded ....$50–$100
Advance (Second Version), release date May 25, 1983, on bottom. Most of the print run was distributed through the Star Wars Fan Club
One-sheet rolled ....$40–$100
One-sheet folded ....$30–$60
Note: *Counterfeit versions of the two posters above exist. Printing quality is poor so the poster looks muddy and out of focus.*

Return of the Jedi

Style "A", illustration by Tim Reamer, lightsaber artwork
One-sheet rolled..$25–$40
One-sheet folded ....$10–$25
Half-sheet rolled ....$15–$30

Revenge of the Jedi theatrical one-sheet poster.

Half-sheet folded...$10–$25
Insert rolled ....$15–$30
Insert folded ....$10–$20
30″ × 40″ rolled...$20–$35
30″ × 40″ folded..$10–$20
40″ × 60″ rolled...$25–$35
40″ × 60″ folded..$15–$25
Standee..$25–$50

Style "B", illustration by Kazuhiko Sano
One-sheet rolled..$20–$40
One-sheet folded...$15–$25
Half-sheet rolled..$10–$20
Half-sheet folded...$10–$20
Insert rolled ....$25–$35
Insert folded ....$10–$20
30″ × 40″ rolled...$30–$40
30″ × 40″ folded..$10–$25
40″ × 60″ rolled...$20–$40
40″ × 60″ folded..$10–$20
Standee..$30–$50

1985 Reissue, illustration by Tom Jung
One-sheet rolled..$15–$25
One-sheet folded...$10–$20
Half-sheet rolled..$10–$20
Half-sheet folded...$10–$20
Insert rolled ....$10–$20
Insert folded ....$8–$15
30″ × 40″ rolled...$15–$25
30″ × 40″ folded..$10–$15
40″ × 60″ rolled...$20–$30
40″ × 60″ folded..$15–$20
Standee..$25–$40

The Caravan of Courage

Style "A", illustration by Kazuhiko Sano, foreign release and distribution by Star Wars Fan Club
One-sheet rolled..$20–$40
One-sheet folded...$15–$25
Style "B", illustration by Drew Struzan, Fan Club distribution and foreign release
One-sheet rolled..$20–$40
One-sheet folded...$15–$25

Foreign Theatrical Posters

Often in different sizes, sometimes with different art. This listing is not complete but should give a feel for pricing.
Star Wars
British, Quad poster, 30″ × 40″...$100–$150
Italian, 54″ × 39″...$50–$100
German, Style "A"...$50–$100
German, Style "B"...$50–$100
Japanese, Teaser...$30–$50
Japanese, reissue..$15–$20
French ....$50–$100
Empire Strikes Back
German, Style "A"...$30–$60
Italian, 54″ × 39″...$30–$50
Japanese, Style "A" or "B"..$15–$20
Return of the Jedi, British, Quad, 30″ × 40″ ....$30–$40
Triple Feature, British, Quad, 30″ × 40″...$20–$30

Star Wars and Empire radio posters.

Promotional Posters

Many of these posters are much rarer than some of the theatrical posters. Limited or regional distribution adds to their desirability and value. Many were only available for a short period of time. Posters are listed chronologically by movie.

Star Wars

Luke Skywalker Poster, Howard Chaykin, artist. "Star Wars" in red letters on lower right. Images of Luke, Leia, and others superimposed over aqua and orange circle, black background. First promotional poster, distributed at the World Science Convention in Kansas City. Star Wars Corp., 1976, 20″ × 29″

    Rolled ....$150–$250
    Folded ....$40–$100

Star Wars Style "A" Record Promotion Poster, Tom Jung, artist. Design is basically the same as regular style "A" with the rearranging of the credits at the bottom and the enlargement of the phrase "Original Motion Picture Soundtrack on 20th Century Record and Tapes," 1977, 27″ × 41″

    Rolled ....$50–$100
    Folded ....$40–$60

Star Wars Style "D" Record Promotion Poster, Drew Struzan and Charles White III, artists. Similar to style "D" theater poster with record promo added, 1978, 27″ × 41″

    Rolled ....$60–$100
    Folded ....$40–$75

Star Wars Concert Poster, illustrated by John Alum. Sold only at Hollywood Bowl on November 30, 1978, 24″ × 37″

    Rolled ....$100–$200
    Folded ....$25–$75

Star Wars Radio Drama Poster, illustration by Celia Strain. Sent only to National Public Radio Stations for promotion. Lucasfilms Ltd., 1979, 17″ × 29″

    Rolled ....$40–$100
    Folded ....$20–$50

Burger Chef/Coca-Cola Promotional Posters, set of four full-color posters (Luke Skywalker; Darth Vader, C-3PO, and R2-D2; Chewbacca; and Han Solo). 20th Century Fox, 1977, 18″ × 24″

    Each..$5–$10
    Set of four ....$15–$30

Burger King/Coca-Cola Promotional Posters, set of four with same art as above but with white borders. 20th Century Fox, 1977 18″ × 24″

    Each..$4–$8
    Set of four ....$10–$20

General Mills, two-sided, set of four, Star Destroyer, R2-D2 and C-3PO, Space Battle, Hildebrandt art, 1978, 9″ × 14½″. Each ....$6–$10

Immunization Poster, from U.S. Department of Health, Education, and Welfare/Public Health Service, promotes immunization of children. Features R2-D2 and C-3PO, 1979 ....$10–$15
Kenner Promotional Poster, captioned "Star Wars is forever," montage on one side and Star Wars toys advertised on the back..$6–$10
Proctor and Gamble Promotional Posters, set of three (Ben Kenobi and Vader fighting; C-3PO and R2-D2; Leia, Han, Chewbacca, and Luke collage). 20th Century Fox, 1978, 17½″ × 23″
    Each..$5–$10
    Set of three ....$15–$30
Star Wars Record Mylar Poster, included in Star Wars Soundtrack Album. Darth Vader's helmet in Mylar, black background
    Rolled..$6–$10
    Folded ....$3–$4
Topps Bubble Gum Press Sheets, often the gum card art is printed first on paper to test it. Sometimes offered as a promotion on gum wrappers, often 22″ × 28″
    Star Wars ....$15–$30
    Empire Strikes Back ....$15–$30
    Return of the Jedi..$15–$30

Empire Strikes Back

American Library Association Promotional Poster, captioned "Read and the Force is with you." Features Yoda, 22″ × 34″ ....$6–$10
Coca-Cola Boris Poster, art by Boris Valejo. Sold in theaters, Lucasfilm, 1980, 24″ × 33″.....
....$8–$12
Coca-Cola Promotional Posters, set of three by famous artist Boris Valejo (Darth Vader, Luke on Dagobah, Luke and Han on Hoth). Lucasfilm, 1980, 17″ × 23″
    Each...$5–$8
    Set of three ....$10–$20
Palitoy (British), 1981, two-sided, toy AT-AT on front, information on reverse..........$10–$15
Palitoy (British), 1981, two-sided, shows product line (toys) on both sides ....$10–$15
Proctor and Gamble Promotional Posters, set of four (Luke, Darth Vader, C-3PO and R2-D2, Han and Leia in Bespin Freeze Chamber). Photographic, Lucasfilm, 1980, 17″ × 23″
    Each...$4–$8
    Set of four ....$12–$20
Empire Strikes Back Radio Drama Poster, illustration by Ralph McQuarrie. Sent only to National Public Radio Stations for publicity. Much rarer than Star Wars version. Lucasfilm, 1982, 17″ × 28″
    Rolled..$50–$100
    Folded...$25–$45
Star Wars Fan Club, Empire Issue, kissing scene, membership kit, 22″ × 28″ ....$5–$10
Video Promotion, main characters and AT-AT battle scene, given to video shops to promote cassette ....$6–$12
Weekly Reader Book Club, montage of characters, 1980, 14½″ × 20½″.....................$6–$10

Return of the Jedi

Return of the Jedi Hi-C Promotional Poster, front: painted Jedi montage; back: selection of photographs from the film. Free with purchase of four cans of Hi-C, 1983, 17″ × 22″ ...$3–$6
Marvel Comics, Jedi Promotional Poster, issued to promote Marvel Super Special No. 27, 1983
    Rolled..$6–$10
    Folded...$3–$5
Oral-B Toothbrush Jedi Poster, free with purchase of two Oral-B adult toothbrushes..........
....$4–$8
Palitoy (British), 1983, only given away with £10 or more toy purchase ....$15–$25
Palitoy (British), 1984, advertises up-coming toy line, only available from manufacturer ....
....$10–$15
Proctor and Gamble Jedi Posters, set of four (Leia and Jabba; Lando and Skiff guard; Luke with blaster at Jabba's; R2 and Teebo the Ewok), 1983, 18″ × 22″
    Each...$4–$6
    Set ....$10–$20

Scholastic, Inc., mother and baby Ewok, 1983, 22″ × 15″..............................$4–$8
Star Wars Fan Club, Jedi Issue, Death Star, B-Wing, and other vehicles, in membership kit, 22″ × 28″..$4–$8
Video Poster, 24″ × 14½″ horizontal poster, 3-D effect has tapes appearing to fly out of forest
....$20–$25
Weekly Reader Book Club, montage of characters, 1983, 14½″ × 20½″......................$4–$8
Weekly Reader Book Club, Wicket the Ewok, 14½″ × 20½″, 1983 ....$4–$8

General Public Posters
Anabas (British)

Return of the Jedi, 1983
   The Team of Endor ....$5–$10
   Lord Darth Vader ....$5–$10
   Darth Vader..$5–$10
   Luke and Leia ....$5–$10
   Wicket the Ewok..$5–$10

Factors, Etc.

The first Star Wars poster licensee, full color, 20″ × 28″.
Star Wars
   Hildebrandt artwork ....$10–$15
   Cantina Band poster, limited distribution ....$20–$30
   Ship battle scene, limited distribution ....$10–$20
   Darth Vader...$5–$8
   Princess Leia..$5–$8
   Luke Skywalker ....$5–$10
   C-3PO and R2-D2...$5–$10
Empire Strikes Back
   Darth Vader and Stormtroopers ....$5–$8
   Boba Fett...$5–$8
   Montage of characters...$5–$8
   R2-D2, C-3PO, with Empire logo ....$5–$8
   Yoda ....$5–$8
Stand-Up Posters, color silhouettes backed with cardboard
   Boba Fett, 69″ × 26″..$15–$25
   Chewbacca, 69″ × 30″...$15–$25
   C-3PO, 69″ × 26″...$15–$25
   Darth Vader, 69″ × 43″..$15–$25
   R2-D2, 41″ × 30″...$15–$25

Sales Corp. of America

Animated TV Posters, each is full color, 17″ × 22″
   Droids, the adventure of R2-D2 and C-3PO...$5–$10
   Ewoks, "Friends Come in All Shapes and Sizes" ....$5–$10
Full Color, 22″ × 34″
   Star Wars, Style "D" ....$5–$10
   Empire Strikes Back, advance ....$5–$10
   Return of the Jedi, teaser ....$5–$10
   Return of the Jedi, Style "A"..$5–$10
   Darth Vader, montage ....$5–$10
   Vehicle battle scene..$5–$10
   Ewok, montage ....$5–$10
   Endor, portrait ....$5–$10
   Return of the Jedi, Style "B" ....$5–$10
Full Color, 24″ × 72″, Darth Vader door poster...$8–$15
Return of The Jedi Poster Art Mini-Posters, full color, 11″ × 14″, 1983
   No. 0021 Jabba and Friends..$2–$4

No. 0023 Vehicle battle scene...$2–$4
No. 0025 Jedi teaser..$2–$4
No. 0027 Vehicle shuttle landing ....$2–$4
No. 0029 Laser, one-sheet ....$2–$4
No. 0031 Ewok montage ....$2–$4
No. 0033 Darth Vader montage ....$2–$4
No. 0035 Luke Skywalker ....$2–$4
No. 0037 Emperor montage..$2–$4
No. 0039 Creature montage ....$2–$4
No. 0041 Speeder bike..$2–$4
No. 0043 Montage, one-sheet ....$2–$4
Return of the Jedi Stand-Up Posters
Darth Vader with Imperial Guards..$10–$20
Ewoks...$10–$20
R2-D2 and C-3PO...$10–$20

Scanlite (British)

The Empire Strikes Back
Snowspeeder Model...$4–$8
Imperial Star Destroyer Model ....$4–$8
Luke Skywalker ....$4–$8
Yoda on Dagobah...$4–$8

Portal Publications

Full color, 24″ × 36″.
Star Wars, style "C" ....$8–$10
Empire Strikes Back, advance ....$8–$10
Return of the Jedi, advance ....$8–$10

Star Tours

Travel posters, all have a small "Star Tours" logo at the bottom center. Each depicts color artwork of the planet to be visited.
Yavin landscape below a red planet..$3–$6
Dogobah, view of swamp ....$3–$6
Endor, view of Ewok village ....$3–$6
Tatooine, Jabba's palace ....$3–$6
Hoth, Luke on Taun-Taun...$3–$6
Promotional Poster, Star Tours ship chased by TIE Fighters over Magic Kingdom ..$10–$15

Star Wars Poster Books

Star Wars Poster Monthly, a giant poster on back of interviews, stories, inside looks at production and special effects
No. 1, R2-D2 and C-3PO, plus the stories of the stars................................$5–$10
No. 2, Darth Vader, plus how the dogfights were made ....$5–$8
No. 3, R2-D2 and C-3PO in the Death Star, plus Han Solo, rogue space pilot ....$5–$8
No. 4, Chewbacca, plus soldiers of the Empire and the building of R2-D2 ....$5–$8
No. 5, Darth Vader, portrait of evil, plus inside stories of Chewbacca and Tarkin ....$5–$8
No. 6, C-3PO, plus the secrets of R2-D2 and the spaceships.......................$5–$8
No. 7, R2-D2, plus the Droids of Star Wars ....$5–$8
No. 8, Imperial stormtrooper, plus Ben Kenobi, man or legend, also space travel secrets.....
....$5–$8
No. 9, the dark lord, plus the brains of the Droids ....$5–$8
No. 10, Star Wars montage, plus what it takes to be a space pilot and the return of evil ....
....$5–$8
No. 11, R2-D2, plus the men behind the masks ....$6–$10
No. 12, space dogfight, plus the Cantina aliens and the Soundmaster......................$6–$10

No. 13, Luke and C-3PO, plus the shooting of Star Wars and the model squad.........$6–$10
No. 14, attacking the Death Star, plus the machines that made lines move................$6–$10
No. 15, C-3PO, plus "Empire's latest" and the Orbiter 102 Space Freighter.............$8–$15
No. 16, R2-D2 with C-3PO, plus the Star Wars quiz and fan club facts...................$10–$20
British Star Wars Poster Magazine, Galaxy Press, 1978. Ran at least five issues. Price each
....$15–$20
Empire Strikes Back Poster Album, Bantha tracks, an Official Star Wars Fan Club publication, featuring all the characters...$10–$20
Empire Strikes Back Poster Book, giant poster with editorials and information on back
No. 1, "Back in Action," Princess Leia, Han Solo, and Chewbacca on bridge ....$5–$8
No. 2, "The Dark Lord, The Forces of the Empire," Darth Vader...............................$5–$8
No. 3, "The Mysteries of Yoda, The Indignities of R2-D2" ....$5–$8
No. 4, "AT-AT Attack, The Magic Factory"..$5–$8
No. 5, "Han Solo—Hero and Scoundrel," laser weapons..$5–$8
Return of the Jedi Poster Book, Paradise Press
No. 1...$4–$8
No. 2...$4–$8
No. 3...$4–$8
No. 4...$4–$8

PROMOTIONAL ITEMS, STUDIO

Note: *See "Star Trek Promotional Items" section for descriptions of promotional material and other additional information. See appropriate section for commercial promotional items.*

Lobby Cards and Stills

Star Wars
Cards ....$50–$75
Stills ....$40–$60
Empire Strikes Back
Cards ....$40–$60
Stills ....$30–$50
Return of the Jedi
Cards ....$30–$50
Stills ....$25–$40

Star Wars theatrical program book (left), Caravan of Courage (Ewok movie) lobby card (center), and Empire Strikes Back lobby still (right).

Caravan of Courage (Ewok Movie), released theatrically in foreign markets
Cards ....$25–$35
Stills ....$15–$25

Press Kits and Press Books

Star Wars
Kit, rare ....$250–$350
Book...$25–$35
Empire Strikes Back
Kit ....$75–$100
Book...$15–$25
Return of the Jedi
Kit ....$50–$75
Book...$10–$20

Program Book

Star Wars, only the first movie had an actual theater program book. Subsequent movies licensed special magazines (*see* "Magazines" section), which the studio felt took the place of programs. Horizontal format with artwork of Vader and X-Wings.
First printing, slick cover...$25–$35
Subsequent printings, pebble-tone cover ....$15–$25

Other Items

Promotional Book, Star Wars, black cover with early Star Wars logo. Color interior photos. Came packaged in white box. Early promotional item ....$125–$175
Star Wars Cast Flyer, 1977 ....$5–$10
Empire Strikes Back Art Portfolio, not available to general public. Long black cardboard outer box embossed with Darth Vader design. Black inner envelope sealed with lead Darth Vader medallion. Contains two color McQuarrie art prints......................................$100–$150
Promotion Guide for Revenge of the Jedi, 1982, white cover with Revenge artwork by Ralph McQuarrie ....$100–$150

Early Star Wars promotional book (left) and The Empire Strikes Back promotional portfolio.

Assorted Star Wars jigsaw puzzles.

PUZZLES

A puzzle in collectible condition should be complete and in the box.

Star Wars

Capiepa (French), 1977

150 Piece Puzzle, 17″ × 11″, puzzles also appeared in France under Waddington name

Entre Dans LaVille	$15–$20
Dans Le Millennium Condor	$15–$20
Yan Solo et Chiquetaba	$15–$20
C-3PO et D2-R2	$15–$20

Kenner, 1977

Color photo puzzles in 140-, 500-, 1,000-, and 1,500-piece sizes. Earlier packaging was blue or purplish star border around photo of puzzle. Later packaging had black star border. Though 140- and 500-piece black border puzzles have series numbers, they were probably released at or near the same time. Series number (if any) is in parentheses.

Early and more common Kenner jigsaw packaging.

140-Piece Puzzles, 14″ × 18″

Bantha ridden by sand person (IV)..$5–$10
C-3PO and R2-D2 (I)...$5–$10
Han Solo and Chewbacca (I)..$5–$10
Jawas capture R2-D2 (IV)..$5–$10
Luke and Han in trash compactor (II) ....$5–$10
Sand person (III)..$5–$10
Stormtroopers (I)..$5–$10

500-Piece Puzzles, 15½″ × 18″

Ben Kenobi and Darth Vader dueling (II) ....$8–$12
Cantina Band (IV)..$8–$12
Luke and Leia (II)..$8–$12
Luke on Tatooine (I)..$8–$12
Jawas selling Droids (IV) ....$8–$12
Space battle (I)...$8–$12
Victory celebration (III)..$8–$12
X-Wing fighter in hanger (III) ....$8–$12

1,000-Piece Puzzles, 21½″ × 27½″

Crew aboard the Millennium Falcon ....$10–$15
Movie art poster...$10–$15

1,500-Piece Puzzles, 27″ × 33″

Millennium Falcon in space...$15–$20
Stormtrooper in corridor ....$15–$20

Waddington (British)

150-Piece Puzzle, 17″ × 11″, 1977

R2-D2 and C-3PO..$10–$15
Han and Chewie..$10–$15
Entering the city..$10–$15
Inside the Millennium Falcon ....$10–$15

350-Piece Star Wars Toy Puzzles, 14″ × 19″, 1979

Small action figures and landspeeder ....$15–$20
Small action figures, landspeeder, X-Wing and TIE Fighter...............................$15–$20

Return of the Jedi
Craft-Master, 1983

Fundimensions, 170 pieces, 16″ × 20″

Battle of Endor..$6–$12
Ewok leaders...$6–$12

Fundimensions, 70 pieces, 12″ × 18″

Jabba's friends..$5–$10
Jabba's throne room ....$5–$10
Death Star...$5–$10

Frame Tray Puzzles, 15 pieces, 8″ × 11″

Darth Vader...$3–$5
Ewoks on hang gliders...$3–$5
Ewok village ....$3–$5
Gammorrean Guard ....$3–$5
Jedi characters (nine match blocks)...$3–$5
Leia and Wicket..$3–$5
R2-D2 and Wicket ....$3–$5
Wicket...$3–$5

Match Block Puzzles, nine blocks and tray

Ewoks (cartoon)..$5–$10
Luke and Jabba ....$5–$10

Miscellaneous

Schmid (Germany), 1983, two-in-one Return of the Jedi jigsaw puzzle. Jabba the Hutt and
Luke in Jabba's court ....$15–$20

Tamara (Japan), six different jigsaw puzzles. Price each...$10–$15
Waddington (British), 1983, 150 pieces, 17″ × 11″
 Darth Vader ....$10–$15
 Crew of Millennium Falcon...$10–$15
 Jabba's throne room ....$10–$15
 Luke with blaster ....$10–$15

RECORDS AND TAPES

The records are divided into two sections: Soundtracks and Music, and Story Records. Values are for records in excellent condition with dust jackets.

Soundtracks and Music

Bienvenido, E.T., arranged and directed by Rafael Acosta, contains theme from Star Wars, 12″ LP album, Orfeon Records, No. LP–20–TV–019, Spanish album...............................$10–$15
Big Daddy, contains theme from Star Wars, 12″ LP album, Rhino Records, No. RHI (S) 852 ....$9–$11
 Also available on cassette, No. RNC 852 ....$9–$11
Classic Space Themes, including music from The Empire Strikes Back, performed by the Birchwood Pops Orchestra. Contains Star Wars, Main Theme from The Empire Strikes Back, The Imperial March (Darth Vader's Theme), and Yoda's Theme, 12″ LP album, Pickwick Records, No. SPC–3772, stereo, 1980..$9–$10
Classic Space Themes, includes Star Wars Theme (disco version), 12″ LP album, Pickwick Records, No. SPC–3172, stereo, 1980..$9–$11
Chewie, The Rookie Wookie, from the album Living in These Star Wars, performed by The Rebel Force Band, 7″ 45rpm, Bonwhit Records ....$5–$7
Cinema Gala, Star Wars/Close Encounters, John Williams and the Los Angeles Philharmonic Orchestra, 1987, Decca, cassette only ....$8–$12
Close Encounters of the Third Kind and Star Wars, composed by John Williams, performed by the National Philharmonic Orchestra, conducted by Charles Gerhardt. Contains Main Title, The Little People Work, Here They Come!, Princess Leia Theme, The Final Battle, The Throne Room, and End Title, 12″ LP album, RCA Red Seal Record, No. ARL 1–2698, stereo, 1978...$12–$15
Disco Excitement, performed by Enock Light and His Light Brigade, contains disco version of theme from Star Wars, 12″ LP album, Lakeshore Music, No. LSM 107, 1978 ....$15–$18
 Also available on eight-track tapes and cassettes......................................$15–$18
Dune, arranged by David Matthews, contains Princess Leia's Theme and the Main Theme from Star Wars, 12″ LP album, CTI Records, No. 7–5005, 1977 ....$9–$12
 Also available on stereo eight-track tape and cassette ....$9–$12

Assorted Star Wars records.

Empire Jazz, produced and arranged by Ron Carter from the original soundtrack from the motion picture Star Wars/The Empire Strikes Back, composed by John Williams. Contains The Imperial March (Darth Vader's Theme), The Asteroid Field, Han Solo and the Princess (Love Theme), Lando's Palace, Yoda's Theme, 12″ LP album, RSO Records, No. RS–1–3085, 1980 ....$8–$10

    Also available in eight-track tape, No. RS–8T–1–3085 ....$8–$10
    Also available in cassette, No. RS–CT–1–3085 ....$8–$10
The Empire Strikes Back, the original soundtrack from the motion picture, composed and conducted by John Williams with the London Symphony Orchestra, two 12″ LP albums, RSO Records, No. RS–2–4201, 1980..$12–$15
    Also available on eight-track tape, No. RS–8T–2–4201 ....$12–$15
    Also available on cassette, No. RS–CT–2–4201 ....$12–$15
The Empire Strikes Back (Medley), performed by Meco. Contains Darth Vader's Theme, Yoda's Theme, and The Force Theme, RSO Records, No. RS–1038, stereo, 7″ 45rpm, 1980 ....$3–$5
The Empire Strikes Back, performed by Boris Midney and His Orchestra. Contains Yoda's Theme, The Imperial March (Darth Vader's Theme), Han Solo and the Princess (Love Theme), and Star Wars (Main Theme), RSO Records, No. RS–1–3079 ....$8–$10
    Also available on eight-track tape, No. RS–8T–1–3079 ....$8–$10
    Also available on cassette, No. RS–CT–1–3079 ....$8–$10
The Empire Strikes Back (Meco Plays Music From), contains The Empire Strikes Back (Medley), Darth Vader/Yoda's Themes, The Battle in the Snow, The Force Theme, The Asteroid Field/Finale, 10″ LP album, RSO Records, No. RO–1–3086, 1980 ....$8–$10
The Empire Strikes Back, music from the original soundtrack of the motion picture. Music composed and conducted by John Williams, performed by The London Symphony Orchestra, 12″ LP album, RSO Records, No. RSO Super RSS–23, 1980, British pressing ....$10–$12
The Empire Strikes Back, Symphonic Suite, from the original motion picture soundtrack, performed by The National Philharmonic Orchestra, conducted by Charles Gerhardt, 12″ LP album, Chalfont Digital Records, No. SDG 313, 1980, pressed in Japan....................$15–$17
E.T. and Star Wars: The Best 12 Arts of John Williams, Victor Musical Industries, 1987, 12″ LP, No. VIP 7321 ....$15–$20
Ewoks: Original Soundtrack, 1986, Varese Sarabande Records, 12″ LP. Original soundtracks from Caravan of Courage and Battle for Endor, No. STV 81281 ....$15–$20
Flip Side of Red Seal, performed by Tomita, contains theme from Star Wars, 12″ LP album, Victor(S) Records, No. XRL1–5173...$9–$10
Greatest Science Fiction Hits II, conducted by Neil Norman and His Cosmic Orchestra, contains Star Wars: The Empire Strikes Back (Medley), 12″ LP album, GNP Crescendo Records, No. GNPS–2133, 1980 ....$9–$12
    Also available on cassette, GNP Crescendo Records, No. GNPS–2133....................$9–$12
Great Movies—There's Something Going On Out There, contains Main Title from Star Wars, performed by the National Philharmonic Orchestra, 12″ LP album, His Master's Voice Records, No. OPL 1–0003..$13–$16
Horspiel Nach Dem Gleichnamigen Film Mit Den Originalsprechern Krieg Der Sterne (The Story of Star Wars in German), with music and sound effects from the original soundtrack from the motion picture, 12″ LP album, Fontana Records, No. 9199535, full color, eight-page photo booklet ....$10–$12
The Imperial March (Darth Vader's Theme) and The Battle in The Snow, performed by the London Symphony Orchestra, conducted by John Williams. From the original soundtrack of the motion picture The Empire Strikes Back, 12″ LP album, RSO Records, No. RS–1033 ....$9–$12
John Williams Symphonic Suites, E.T.—The Extraterrestrial, Close Encounters of the Third Kind, and Star Wars, performed by The London Symphony Orchestra and The National Philharmonic Orchestra, conducted by Frank Barber, 12″ LP album or cassette. EMI–Angel Records, No. RL–32109, British recording ....$12–$15
La Guerre Des Etoiles (Star Wars in French), 7″ 33⅓rpm, Buena Vista Records, No. LLP–455F ....$10–$12
Living in These Star Wars, country-western version of Star Wars, performed by the Rebel Force Band, 12″ LP album, Bonwhit Records..$10–$12
Main Theme—Star Wars, performed by David Matthews, from the album Dune, 7″ 45rpm, CTI Records, No. 7–5005, CTI Records, No. OJ–39, 1977..$5–$7

Main Title Themes From The Empire Strikes Back, Star Wars, 2001: A Space Odyssey, and Close Encounters, 12″ LP album, Peter Pan Records, No. 1116...........................$8–$10

Meco—Ewok Celebration, contains themes from Star Wars: The Motion Picture, 12″ LP album, Arista Records, No. AL 8–8098 ....$8–$10

  Also available in abridged 45rpm, No. AS1–9045...$4–$8

Music From John Williams—Close Encounters of the Third Kind and Star Wars, performed by The National Philharmonic Orchestra, conducted by Charles Gerhardt, 12″ LP album, RCA Records, No. AGLI–3650, stereo...$10–$12

Music From Other Galaxies and Planets, featuring the Main Theme and Princess Leia's Theme from Star Wars, performed by Don Ellis and Survival, 12″ LP album, Atlantic Records, No. SD 18227, 1977 ....$10–$12

Music From Star Wars, performed by The Electric Moog Orchestra, arranged and conducted by Jimmy Wisner, 12″ LP album, Musicor Records, No. MUS–8801...........................$8–$10

Music From the Galaxies, CBS Masterworks, 1980, London Symphony Orchestra. Music from Star Wars and other science-fiction movies...$10–$15

1084—A Space Odyssey, performed by John Williams conducting The Boston Pops Orchestra. Includes Parade of The Ewoks from Return of The Jedi, Star Wars Main Theme, The Empire Strikes Back, The Asteroid Field, The Forrest Battle from Return of the Jedi, Star Trek: The Main Theme from TV, and the Main Theme from Star Trek: The Motion Picture, 12″ LP album, J & B Records, No. JB–177...$9–$11

Pops in Space, performed by The Boston Pops Orchestra, conducted by John Williams. Contains The Asteroid Field, Yoda's Theme, and The Imperial March from The Empire Strikes Back, 12″ album, Philips Digital Record, No. 9500 921, 1980.....................................$12–$15

Pops in Space, The Boston Pops Orchestra, conducted by John Williams, contains Star Wars Main Theme and The Princess Leia Theme, 12″ LP album, Philips Digital Record, No. 9500 921, 1980 ....$12–$15

Princess Leia's Theme, from Star Wars, performed by David Matthews. From the album Dune, 7″ 45rpm, CTI Records, No. 7–5005, CTI Records, No. OJ–40, 1977.................$5–$7

Return of the Jedi, soundtrack, RSO, 1983, No. 0704...$10–$15

Return of the Jedi, symphonic rendition, National Philharmonic, RCA Red Seal .....$15–$20

Sounds of Star Wars, Pickwick (British), 1977, LP, performed by the Sonic All-Stars, synthesizer, No. SHM 941 ....$10–$12

Space Organ, performed by Jonas Nordwall, contains medley from Star Wars—Main Title, Princess Leia's Theme, Cantina Band, 12″ LP album, Crystal Clear Records, No. CCS–6003, 1979...$10–$12

Spaced-Out Disco Fever, contains theme from Star Wars, Star Trek Theme, Bionic Woman Theme, Six-Million-Dollar-Man Theme, Theme from 2001: A Space Odyssey, Beyond the Outer Limits, Rocket Man, Space Race, and Star Light, 12″ LP album, Wonderland Records, No. 315, stereo...$6–$8

Spectacular Space Hits, performed by the Odyssey Orchestra, includes themes from 2001, Star Trek, Star Wars, Superman, Close Encounters, and The Empire Strikes Back, 12″ LP album, Sina Qua Non Records, No. SQN 7808, stereo...$10–$12

Star Tracks, performed by Erich Kunzel and The Cincinnati Pops Orchestra. Includes Main Title from Star Wars, The Imperial March from The Empire Strikes Back, Luke and Leia (Love Theme) from Return of the Jedi and Main Theme from Star Trek TV, 12″ LP album, Telarc Digital Record, No. DG–10094, stereo ....$12–$15

Star Trek, Main Theme from the motion picture, performed by The Now Sound Orchestra, contains Theme From Star Wars: Part I and Theme From Star Wars: Part II, 12″ LP album, Synthetic Plastic Records, No. 6001..$9–$10

Star Trek—21 Space Hits, contains theme from Star Wars, 12″ LP album, Music World Ltd. Record, No. EMS–1003, 1979 (this is a New Zealand record album)..........................$12–$15

Star Wars and Close Encounters of the Third Kind, suite conducted by Zubin Mehta and The Los Angeles Philharmonic Orchestra. Star Wars suite contains Main Title, Princess Leia's Theme, The Little People, Cantina Band, The Battle, Throne Room, and End Title, 12″ LP album, London Records, No. 7M1001, 1978 ....$10–$12

Star Wars/Close Encounters, performed by Richard "Groove" Holmes, contains theme from Star Wars, 12″ LP album, Versatile Records, No. P 798, 1977.....................................$10–$12

Star Wars, selections from the film, performed by Patrick Gleeson on the world's most advanced synthesizer. Contains Star Wars Theme, Luke's Theme, The Tatooine Desert, Death

Star, Star Wars Cantina Music, Princess Leia's Theme, Droids, and Ben Kenobi's Theme, Mercury Records, No. SRM–1–1178, 1977 ....$10–$12
   Also available on eight-track tape and cassette ....$10–$12
Star Wars, John Rose playing the Great Pipe Organ at the Cathedral of St. Joseph in Hartford, CT, 12″ LP album, Delos Records, No. DEL/F 25450...$9–$11
Star Wars, Main Title, from the 20th-Century Fox film Star Wars, performed by Maynard Ferguson, 7″ 45rpm, Columbia Records, No. 3–10595..$3–$5
Star Wars Main Theme, from the album Not Of This Earth by Neil Norman and His Cosmic Orchestra, 7″ 45 rpm, GNP Crescendo Records, No. GNP 813, 1977..............................$4–$6
Star Wars and Other Galactic Funk, performed by Meco, 12″ LP album, Casablanca Records, No. MNLP–8001 (Meco Millennium Record Co., Inc.), 1977 ....$8–$12
Star Wars and Other Space Themes, Music for Pleasure, 1978, performed by Geoff Love and Orchestra, 12″ LP, No. MFP 50355 ....$5–$10
The Star Wars Stars, 7″ 45rpm, Lifesong Records, No. LS 45031 ....$5–$7
Star Wars/The Empire Strikes Back, special in-store play disc featuring excerpts from Star Wars/The Empire Strikes Back, 12″ LP album (promotion copy, not for sale), RSO Records, No. RPO–1025...$10–$15
Star Wars Dub, English recording, Burning Sounds Record, No. BS–1019...............$10–$12
Star Wars, Music from the Sci-Fi Film, composed by John Williams, performed by the London Philharmonic Orchestra, conducted by Colin Frechter. Contains Main Title, Imperial Attack, Princess Leia's Theme, Fighter Attack, Land of the Sand People, The Return Home, 12″ LP album, Damil Records, No. SGA 1000, 1977...$15–$20
   Also available on cassette, Ahed Records, No. C–SGA 1000 ....$15–$20
   Also manufactured in the United Kingdom by Damont Records, Ltd., Hayes, Middlesex, 12″ LP album, Damont Records, No. DMT–2001 ....$9–$11
Star Wars, performed on two pianos by Ferrante and Teicher, contains Main Title from Star Wars, 12″ LP album, United Artists Record, No. UA LA 855–G................................$20–$25
   Also available on cassette, 20th-Century Records, No. RSO–541...........................$20–$25
Star Wars—Main Title and Cantina Band, from the original soundtrack performed by The London Symphony Orchestra, conducted by John Williams, 7″ 45rpm, 20th-Century Records, No. TC–2345, 1977, play time 2:20 ....$5–$7
   As above, longer version, play time 5:20 ....$7–$10
Star Wars—Main Title, from the original soundtrack of the motion picture, performed by The London Symphony Orchestra, conducted by John Williams, 7″ 45rpm, 20th-Century Records, No. TC–2358, 1977...$5–$7
The Star Wars Trilogy—Return of the Jedi, The Empire Strikes Back, and Star Wars, music by John Williams from the original motion picture scores. Varuan Kojian conducting the Utah Symphony Orchestra, 12″ LP album, Varese Sarabande Digital Record, No. 704.210, 1983 (contains Darth Vader's Death and Fight With the Tie Fighters, only available recording of these two themes) ....$17–$20
Themes From the Movies, contains Main Theme from Star Wars and The Princess Theme, 12″ LP album, Peter Pan Records, No. 8201...$7–$9
Themes From Star Wars, New York, New York, The Deep, Black Sunday, The Greatest, A Bridge Too Far, Annie Hall, Exorcist II, The Heretic, and Roller Coaster, performed by The Birchwood Pops Orchestra, contains Main Theme from Star Wars, 12″ LP album, Pickwick Record, No. SPC–3582, stereo ....$8–$10

Star Wars Story Records

The Adventures of Luke Skywalker, from The Empire Strikes Back, featuring the voices of Mark Hamill, Harrison Ford, Carrie Fisher, Billy Dee Williams, Anthony Daniels, James Earl Jones, and Frank Oz. Music performed by The London Symphony Orchestra, conducted by John Williams, 12″ LP album, RSO Records, No. RS–1–3081, 1980 ....$10–$15
   Also available on eight-track tape, RSO Records, No. RS–8T–1–3081 ....$10–$15
   Also available on cassette, RSO Records, No. RS–CT–1–3081 ....$10–$15
Christmas in the Stars, Star Wars Christmas album, featuring the original cast: R2–D2 and C-3PO (Anthony Daniels). Album concept by Meco Monardo, 12″ LP album, RSO Records, No. RS–1–3093...$10–$12
Droid World–The Further Adventures of Star Wars, adapted from Marvel Comics, story by Archie Goodwin, illustrated by Dick Foes, 7″ 33⅓rpm record and 24-page full-color illustrated booklet, Buena Vista Records, No. 453...$5–$7

The Empire Strikes Back, read-along book and record. Story, music, sound effects, and photos from the original motion picture, 7″ 33⅓rpm record and 24-page full-color illustrated book, Buena Vista Records, No. 451, 1979 ....$5–$6

    Also available on cassette, Buena Vista Records, No. 151–DC ....$5–$6

Ewoks Join the Fight Book and Record Set, 7″ 33⅓rpm, Buena Vista Records, No. 460, 1983 ....$5–$6

L'Empire Contre-Attaque (The Empire Strikes Back), in French, 7″ 33⅓rpm, Buena Vista Records, No. LLP–458–F ....$10–$12

La Guerre des Etoiles, L'Empire Contre-Attaque, raconte par Dominique Paturel, livre–disque, 24-pages du film (Star Wars, The Empire Strikes Back, narrated by Dominique Paturel, book and record, 24 pages of photos from the original motion picture), 12″ LP album, Buena Vista, No. ST–3984–F ....$10–$12

La Guerra De Las Galaxias (Star Wars), story, music, and sound effects from the original motion picture (in Spanish), 7″ 33⅓rpm record and 24-page full-color illustrated booklet, Buena Vista Records, No. 450–M, 1979 ....$5–$7

    Also available on cassette, Buena Vista Records, No. 150–SC ....$5–$7

La Guerra De Las Galaxias, read-along book and record (in Spanish), story, music, and sound effects from the original motion picture, 7″ 33⅓rpm record with 24-page full-color illustrated booklet, Buena Vista Records, No. 450–S...$7–$10

    Also available on cassette, Buena Vista Records, No. 150–SC ....$7–$10

L'Histoire De La Guerre Des Etoiles, raconte par Dominique Paturel, bande originale de la musique et des effets sonores du film (The Story of Star Wars, narrated by Dominique Paturel, music and sound effects from the original soundtrack of the motion picture, in French), 12″ LP album, Buena Vista Records, No. ST–3893–F ....$10–$12

    Also available on cassette ....$10–$12

Planet of the Hogibs—The Further Adventures of Star Wars, adapted from Marvel Comics, story by David Micheline, illustrated by Greg Winters, 7″ 33⅓rpm record and 24-page full-color illustrated booklet, Buena Vista Records, No. 454...$5–$7

    Also available on cassette, Buena Vista Records, No. 154–DC, 1983 ....$5–$7

Rebel Mission to Ord Mantel, A Story From The Star Wars Saga, script by Brian Daley, author of Star Wars and The Empire Strikes Back radio series, Buena Vista Records, No. 2104 ....$8–$12

    Also available on cassette, Buena Vista Records, No. 2104–B, 1983........................$8–$12

Return of the Jedi, Read-a-Long Book and Record, music and photos, 33⅓rpm, Buena Vista Records, No. 455, 1983 ....$5–$6

Return of the Jedi Dialogue and Music, Buena Vista Records, 1983, includes 16-page souvenir book, No. 62103 ....$10–$15

Return of the Jedi, picture disc, story record, RSO...$10–$15

Return of the Jedi, story record, RSO ....$8–$10

Star Wars Read-Along Adventure Series, story, music, and photos from the original motion picture, 7″ 33⅓rpm record and 24-page full-color illustrated booklet, Buena Vista Records, No. 450...$5–$7

    Also available on cassette, Buena Vista Records, No. 150–DC, 1979........................$5–$7

Star Wars Adventures in Colors and Shapes, 7″ 33⅓rpm record, Buena Vista Records, No. 480...$5–$7

Star Wars Adventures in ABC, 7″ 33⅓rpm record, Buena Vista Records. Also available on cassette, No. 481 ....$5–$7

Star Wars and The Story of Star Wars, two four-track reel-to-reel tapes with beautifully illustrated full-color 16-page booklet and program, 20th-Century Records, No. RN–541 (this is an extremely rare item; the record manufacturer that bought out 20th-Century Records has no record of its existence)..$100–$125

Star Wars Cassette Storybook, book and cassette, Black Falcon, Ltd......................$10–$12

Star Wars Saga Book/Cassette Set, Buena Vista Records, books and cassettes from all three movies packaged together...$15–$20

The Story of The Empire Strikes Back, dialogue, music, and sound effects from the original motion picture soundtrack. Includes 16-page full-color souvenir photo booklet. Features the voices of Mark Hamill, Harrison Ford, Carrie Fisher, Billy Dee Williams, Anthony Daniels, James Earl Jones, Alec Guinness, and Frank Oz. Narration by Malachi Throne, 12″ LP album, Buena Vista Records, No. 62102, 1983 ....$8–$10

The Story of Star Wars, dialogue, music, and sound effects from the original motion picture soundtrack. Includes 16-page full-color souvenir photo book, audio tape cassette, Buena Vista Records, No. 6101B, 1977...$10–$15
The Story of Star Wars, from the original soundtrack. Contains 12″ LP record and 16-page full-color photo booklet. Narration by Roscoe Lee Brown. Contains voices, music, and sound effects from original motion picture, 12″ LP album or eight-track tape with booklet, 20th-Century Fox Records, No. T–550...$15–$20

SCHOOL AND OFFICE SUPPLIES

Binders, Notebooks, and Portfolios

Doodle Pad, Stuart Hall, 1983. 12″ × 7″ horizontal format, cover shows Max Rebo Band and Jedi logo...$2–$5
File Binders, Mead, 1978
   C–3PO and R2–D2, Han and Chewbacca ....$5–$10
Learn to Letter and Write Tablets, Stuart Hall, 1980–83. 11¾″ × 7″ horizontal design, color photo covers with movie logos
   Boba Fett, Darth Vader, Ewoks, Luke, Stormtroopers, Yoda.......................................$2–$5
Notebooks, Letraset (British), 1977
   Chewbaccas Space Notes, Stormtrooper Manual, R2–D2's Memory Book.................$3–$5
Notebooks, Stuart Hall, 1980. 8½″ × 11″, color photo covers with Empire logo
   Boba Fett, Bounty Hunter and 2–1B, C–3PO and R2–D2, Darth Vader, Darth Vader and Stormtroopers, Han with Leia and Luke, Hoth and Bespin scenes, Luke, Yoda...........$2–$5
Notebooks (Mini), H.C.F. (British), 1983. Color cover art with Jedi logo, several different styles. Each ....$1–$2
Pencil Tablets, Stuart Hall, 1980–83. 8″ × 10″, 50 sheets each with color photo covers with movie logos
   C–3PO and R2–D2, Space scene, Empire montage, R2–D2 and Ewok ....$2–$5
Pocket Memos, Stuart Hall, 1980. Spiral-bound vertical 3″ × 5″ notebooks, color photo cover.
   Boba Fett, C–3PO and R2–D2, Character montage, Darth Vader and Stormtroopers, Luke..
....$1–$4
Pocket Memos, Stuart Hall, 1983. Return of the Jedi color artwork covers
   Space battle scenes, Biker scouts, C–3PO with R2–D2 and Wicket, Jabba the Hutt, Luke and Darth, Max Rebo Band...$1–$4
Pocket Memo, H.C.F. (British), 1983. Luke and Yoda, C–3PO or Han and Chewbacca. Price each ....$2–$4
Portfolios, Mead Corp., 1977. 9½″ × 12″, different color photos front and back, inside pocket
   Leia front, Luke back..$3–$5
   Obi-Wan front, Stormtroopers back...$3–$5
   Darth Vader ....$3–$5
   C–3PO and R2–D2 ....$3–$5

Assorted school notebooks.

Portfolios, Stuart Hall, 1980. 9¾″ × 11″ folders with color photo covers, same photo front and back, inside pockets
    Bounty Hunters, Character montage, Chewbacca, C–3PO and R2–D2, Darth Vader, Darth Vader and Stormtroopers, Luke, Yoda...$2–$4
Portfolios, Stuart Hall, 1983. Return of the Jedi color artwork scenes
    Battle scene, Biker scout, C–3PO with R2–D2 and Wicket, Jabba the Hutt, Luke and Darth, Max Rebo Band...$2–$4
Themebooks, Stuart Hall, 1980. Spiral-bound in two different sizes, either 8″ × 10½″ or 8½″ × 11″, color photo
    Boba Fett, C–3PO and R2–D2, Chewbacca, Character montage, Darth Vader and Boba Fett, Han with Luke and Leia, Luke, Space scene, Yoda ....$2–$5
Themebooks, Stuart Hall, 1983. Return of the Jedi color artwork scenes
    Space battle scene, Biker scout, C–3PO with R2–D2 and Wicket, Jabba the Hutt, Luke and Darth Vader, Max Rebo Band...$2–$5
Three-Ring Binders, Stuart Hall, 1980. Flexible plastic, color photo covers, five different
    C–3PO and R2–D2, Darth Vader and Stormtroopers, Luke, Montage, Yoda ....$3–$5

Bulletin Boards, Manton Cork, 1980–1983

All boards have color artwork.

First Series, 1980

All approximately 17″ × 23″.
Rectangular
    Star Wars, logo with spaceships, horizontal format...$15–$25
    Darth and Company, Darth and Stormtroopers ....$15–$25
    Good Guys, group picture...$15–$25
Die-Cut
    Darth Vader ....$15–$25
    Yoda, glow in the dark ....$15–$25
    R2–D2 and C–3PO, two separate boards to set...$20–$30

Second Series, 1981

Glo-Dome, glow in the dark, arched vertical design, 11″ × 17″.
AT–AT, C–3PO and R2–D2, Chewbacca, Darth Vader, Luke on Tauntaun, Yoda ....
....$15–$20

Third Series, 1982

All are rectangular with Return of the Jedi logo across top.
Horizontal, 17″ × 23″ format
    Ewok village, group with main characters ....$20–$30
    Jabba's Palace, group with main characters ....$20–$30
Vertical, 11″ × 17″ format
    Darth and Luke, Ewoks and Droids, Jabba's Palace, Rebo Band ....$15–$20

Miscellaneous

Book Bag, Adam Joseph, 1983. Black with Jedi logo and artwork of Darth Vader and Imperial Guard..$20–$35
Book Covers, Butterfly Originals, 1983. Laminated, packages of two...........................$4–$6
Book Cover, Factors, Etc., 1978. 13″ × 21″, Original Fan Club logo in color................$1–$2
Bookends, Sigma, 1982. Ceramic, Darth Vader and Chewbacca (kneeling) in pair. Per pair....
....$35–$50
Bookmarks, Random House, 1983. Color artwork, 16 different
    Luke, Darth Vader, Leia (Boush), R2–D2, C–3PO, Lando (Skiff Guard), Chewbacca, Yoda, Admiral Ackbar, Ben Kenobi, Han Solo, Boba Fett, Wicket the Ewok, Emperor's Royal Guard, Stormtrooper, Jabba the Hutt ....$1–$3
Bookplates, Random House, 1983. All are captioned "This book belongs to . . ." Four different
    Darth Vader, black border ....$1–$3

Jedi book bag.

C–3PO and R2–D2, blue border..$1–$3
Wicket, brown border ....$1–$3
Yoda, green border..$1–$3
Business Cards, Fan made, set of 12 mythical business cards for Star Wars characters. Per set
....$3–$5
Chalkboard, Manton, 1983. 11″ × 17″ horizontal format, R2–D2 and Wicket in lower left cor-
ner, Jedi logo at top..$20–$30
Clip-A-Longs, Craft Master (Fundimensions), 1983. Children's desk tools designed to clip to
pocket. Colored plastic with artwork paper decal of character. Came blister packed on header
with Jedi logo. Three different
Darth Vader, crayon holder and sharpener...$4–$10
Ewok, magnifying glass...$4–$10
R2–D2, crayon drawing compass ....$4–$10
Drawing Set, Helix (British), 1978. Tin containing drawing instruments, lid illustrated with
photo of C–3PO and R2–D2...$15–$20
Glue, Butterfly Originals, 1983. "Color Glue," tube of blue glue with illustration of X-Wing
and Jedi logo. Came blister packed on header with X-Wing and Jedi logo.....................$2–$4
Labels, Introduct (Dutch), 1983. School labels, sheet consisting of six labels each with a different character ....$2–$4

Assorted school supplies.

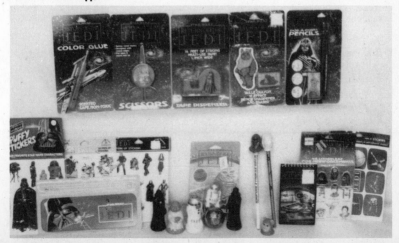

H. C. F. and Butterfly original kits.

Marker, Butterfly Originals, 1983. Felt tip, shaped like Darth Vader, 3½″ tall ....$2–$4
Memo Board, Icarus (British), 1982. 8½″ × 12″, wipe clean, with felt-tip marker
   Han, Chewbacca, and Lando in Skiff Guard outfit ....$20–$30
   Darth and Stormtroopers...$20–$30
   Luke, Leia, and Han..$20–$30
Memo Holder, Union, 1987. Blue or purple plastic with pocket for paper and pen, magnetic
backed, 10th anniversary logo ....$5–$10
Paper Clip, 1987. Spring-hinge-type with magnetic back, 10th anniversary logo ....$2–$4
Ruler, Butterfly Originals, 1983. 6″ with changing space battle scene ....$1–$4
Ruler, Butterfly Originals, 1983. 12″, decorated with characters and Jedi logo ....$2–$5
Ruler, Bradley Time, 1983. Built-in LCD calculator and clock, decorated with characters and
Jedi logo...$10–$15
Ruler, H.C.F. (British), 1983. 15cm long, illustrated...$1–$4
Ruler, Helix (British), 1978. 30cm long, blue, illustrated with Stormtroopers on reverse.........
....$2–$5
School Kit, Butterfly Originals, 1983. Pencil pouch, ruler, eraser, pencil, and pencil sharpener
in clear plastic bag with Jedi header ....$10–$15
School Sets, Helix (British), 1978. Padded front with illustration, contains assorted school
supplies. Two sizes
   Large, pictures Han and Chewie...$15–$20
   Small, pictures a Star Destroyer ....$10–$15
Scissors, Butterfly Originals, 1983. Red plastic adorned with round medallion that changed
between Darth Vader head and shuttle Tydirium. Blister packed on header card with Jedi logo
....$5–$10
Scrapbook, H.C.F. (British), 1984. Large size ....$10–$15

C–3PO tape dispenser and pencil tray, and R2–D2 string dispenser from Sigma ceramics.

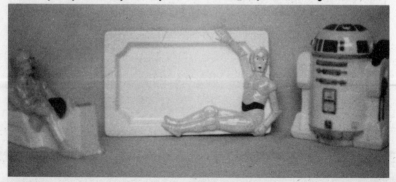

Stationery Sets, H.C.F. (British), 1983. Came with assorted H.C.F. school products. Packaged in shallow window box with color artwork, several different assortments ....$10–$20
String Dispenser, Sigma, 1982. Ceramic, shaped like R2–D2. Lid comes off to insert string which is fed through hole in top ....$25–$40
Tape Dispenser, Butterfly Originals, 1983. Red plastic, standard size and shape, illustrated with Darth Vader figure and Jedi logo, came Blister packed on card with Jedi logo........$3–$6
Tape Dispenser, Sigma, 1982. Ceramic, in the shape of C–3PO seated with tape spool between his knees..$30–$45

Pens, Pencils, and Accessories

Erasers, Butterfly Originals, 1983. Colored figure erasers. Came blister packed on color artwork headers with Jedi logo
Admiral Ackbar, Baby Ewoks, Bib Fortuna, Darth Vader, Emperor's Royal Guard, Gammorrean Guard, Jabba the Hutt, Rebo Band (set of three), R2–D2, Wicket, Yoda ....
....$5–$10
Erasers, Butterfly Originals, 1983. Glow-in-the-dark, set of three, Darth head, C–3PO head, and Millennium Falcon. Came blister packed on header with Jedi logo. Per set............$5–$10
Eraser, Butterfly Originals, 1983. Small rectangular eraser with decal of Emperor's Guard on top ....$.75–$1
Erasers, H.C.F. (British), 1982. Character erasers, color artwork printed on flat die-cut eraser
....$2–$3
Erasers, H.C.F. (British), 1982, Record Erasers. Shaped like record albums, 3¾" diameter with Darth head and Jedi logo on label, packaged in plastic wrap with paper cover art of Jedi lightsaber logo or Darth and Luke, assorted colors. Price each ....$1–$2
Erasers, H.C.F. (British), 1982. Perfumed character erasers, came in illustrated clear plastic cases. Six different
Chewbacca (orange), Darth Vader (grape), Han Solo (apple), Luke Skywalker (mint), Princess Leia (strawberry), R2–D2 and C–3PO (raspberry)..$3–$5
Erasers, Helix (British), 1978. Carded character erasers. Price each.............................$3–$5
Pens, Butterfly Originals, 1983. White pens with drawings of characters in blue and Jedi logo in red. Blister packed two pens per card. Card has Emperor's Guard and Jedi logo. Per card
....$5–$10
Pens, Butterfly Originals, 1983. Felt tip, two per package. Blue and black or red and black with Jedi logos, blister packed on header with artwork of C–3PO. Per pack ....$5–$10
Pens, Helix (British), 1978. Colored felt tips, boxed sets. Two different sizes
Large (ten different)...$10–$15
Small (five different) ....$5–$10
Pen, Star Tours, Disney. Star Tours logo and stars on black nylon-tip-type with cap ......$1–$3
Pencils, H.C.F. (British), 1982, Tag-Top Pencils. Decorated with puffy flower-shaped tag. Four different
Han and Chewbacca, Luke and Leia, Darth Vader and Stormtroopers, R2–D2 and C–3PO..
....$2–$5
Pencils, Helix (British), 1978. Ten colored pencils, packaging pictures Stormtroopers. Per package ....$4–$8

Assorted erasers.

Butterfly Originals: Pencils, markers, and pens.

Pencils, Helix (British), 1978. With shaped tops. Four different.

C–3PO...$2–$3

Darth Vader..$2–$3

R2–D2..$2–$3

Stormtrooper..$2–$3

Pencil, Helix (British), 1978. Blue with "May the Force Be With You" in gold ....$1–$2

Pencil, Star Wars Fan Club, 1980. White and red with pictures of characters and Empire logo

....$1–$2

Pencils, Butterfly Originals, 1983. Packed in sets of four on header with picture of Darth Vader and Jedi logo. Per set

Darth Vader, C–3PO, Jedi logo..$2–$5

Pencils (Mechanical), Butterfly Originals, 1983, Pop-A-Point. Red plastic sparkle embossed with "May the Force Be With You" in gold. Came blister packed on header with picture of Darth Vader and Jedi logo. Two pencils and box of 22 points per package....................$5–$10

Pencil and Eraser Set, Butterfly Originals, 1983. Flat character eraser and plastic pencil sharpener blister packed together on Jedi header card ....$5–$10

Pencil Box, Helix (British), 1978. Contains pencils, eraser, and sharpener ....$15–$25

Pencil Cup, Sigma, 1982. Open ceramic container with Yoda relief on the front ....$25–$35

Pencil Heads, Butterfly Originals, 1983. Colored plastic, variously sold on pencils, separately or in sets. Four different.

Emperor's Guard, Darth Vader, C–3PO, Ewok ....$1–$3

Pencil Pouch, Butterfly Originals, 1983. Zippered plastic pouch with artwork of Luke, Darth Vader, and Jedi logo...$4–$10

Pencil Pouches, Helix (British), 1978. Zippered plastic. Eight different

Ben Kenobi, C–3PO, Darth Vader, Han, Luke, Leia, R2–D2, Stormtrooper..............$5–$10

Pencil Pouch, H.C.F. (British), 1983. Zippered plastic with artwork of Darth Vader, spaceships, and Jedi logo...$4–$10

Pencil Sharpener, Butterfly Originals, 1983. Round plastic with paper decal of TIE Fighter

....$2–$5

Pencil Sharpeners, Butterfly Originals, 1983. Colored plastic figures, came individualy blister packed on header with Jedi logo. Three different

Darth Vader, R2–D2, Yoda ....$5–$10

Pencil Sharpeners, H.C.F. (British), 1982. Domed with line drawing on top. Four different

Luke and Leia (blue), Han and Chewbacca (yellow), C–3PO and R2–D2 (red), Darth Vader and Stormtrooper (gray)...$4–$8

Pencil Sharpener, Helix (British), 1978. Shaped like the Death Star.........................$5–$10

Pencil Sharpener and Eraser Set, Butterfly Originals, 1983. Wicket the Ewok. Flat die-cut Ewok eraser and sharpener with Ewok decal, blister packed on color header with cartoon Ewok artwork ....$5–$10

Pencil Tins, Metal Box Co., 1980. Shallow, hinged rectangular tins with color photo covers and Empire logo on bottom. Four different

C–3PO and R2–D2, Chewbacca, Darth Vader, Yoda ....$10–$15

Pencil Tops, H.C.F. (British), 1"–2", color full-figure pencil decorations. Sold separately or in various sets. Two series

Series One

Chewbacca, DarthVader, Han Solo (Hoth Gear), Luke (Flight Suit), R2–D2, Yoda ....

....$2–$5

Series Two
Admiral Ackbar, Bib Fortuna, Darth Vader, Gammorrean Guard, Imperial Guard, Wicket.
....$2–$5
Pencil Tray, Sigma, 1982. White ceramic with C–3PO decoration on right side ....$20–$30

Stationery

Die-Cut Stationery, Drawing Board, 1977. Shaped like R2–D2, 18 sheets and 12 envelopes
per package ....$5–$10
Envelopes, Letraset (British), 1977. Pack of 12, illustrated in front corner and on reverse.......
....$5–$10
Foldover Notes, Drawing Board, 1977. No envelope neccessary, fold and mail, R2–D2 on
cover. 12 to a pack ....$5–$10
Lap Pack, Drawing Board, 1977. Ten printed sheets, ten plain sheets, and ten envelopes in
folder with Hildebrandt poster art and Star Wars logo on front ....$5–$10
Note Pads, Drawing Board, 1977. Two different, both have title at top with drawing of charac-
ter and Star Wars logo at bottom
Official Duty Roster (Darth Vader) ....$2–$5
Wookie Doodle Pad (Chewbacca) ....$2–$5
Notes (Boxed), Drawing Board, 1977. Ten fold-over note cards with envelopes, color artwork
covers, two different. Per box
Hildebrandt poster art ....$15–$20
R2–D2 and C–3PO ....$15–$20
Notes (Boxed), Drawing Board, 1977. 12 assorted fold-over note cards with envelopes. Four
each of three different designs: Chewbacca, C–3PO, and Darth Vader artwork. Per box ....
....$20–$25
Padded Stationery, Drawing Board, 1977. Pad of 25 sheets, Hildebrandt poster art on cover
and corners of sheets...$5–$8
Postcards, Drawing Board, 1977. C–3PO and R2–D2, 20 to a package.........................$4–$8
Postcards, Oral B, 1983. Dental check-up reminders
R2–D2/C–3PO, Ewoks, Heroes, Luke and Darth...$1–$2
Postcards, Star Tours, Disney
Large, 8″ × 10″
C–3PO, C–3PO and R2–D2, Luke, Han Solo, Two Stormtroopers ....$1–$3
Small, 4″ × 6″
Tatooine (artwork of Jabba's palace), Bespin (Cloud City), Star Tours (color artwork) ....
....$1–$2
Note: *See also "Greeting Cards" section.*

Stickers

Puffy Stickers, 1977. Three stickers per assortment card: Stormtrooper, Darth Vader, and
R2–D2...$3–$5
Puffy Stickers, Topps, 1980. Eight different color plastic 3–D character stickers packaged
with color header with Darth Vader head and Empire logo ....$1–$3
Puffy Stickers, Drawing Board, 1983. 3–D Perk-Up Stickers. Three different assortments
Ewoks and other characters, Heroes, Villains ....$1–$3
Puffy Stickers, Fun Products, 1983. 5″ × 8″, one sticker per pack
Klaatu...$1–$2
Ewoks...$1–$2
Puffy Stickers, Happymates, 1983. Two different sets of Return of the Jedi stickers. Per set
....$1–$3
Stickers, Drawing Board, 1980. Perk-Up Stickers. Three sheets per package, three designs
Bad guys, Good guys, Ewoks ....$1–$3
Stickers, Drawing Board, 1983. Perk-Up Stickers. Three sheets per package. Three different
sets: two character and one of vehicles. Per set..$1–$3
Stickers, 1987. 10th anniversary logo, 3″ × 5″ ....$1–$2
Reinforcements, Butterfly Originals, 1983. Foil stickers of characters and ships with punch-
out holes, 48 per package..$1–$3

Rubber Stamps

All Night Media, Inc., set of six in clear plastic case with color artwork of stamps .....$8–$12
Return of the Jedi, Adam Joseph, 1983. Color plastic silhouette of character or ship was handle to stamp. Came individually blister packed on Jedi header or in boxed counter display. Twelve different
  Admiral Ackbar, Biker Scout, C–3PO, Chewbacca, Darth Vader, Emperor's Royal Guard, Gammorrean Guard, Millennium Falcon, TIE Fighter, Wicket, X-Wing, Yoda ....$1–$3
Wicket the Ewok, Adam Joseph, 1983. Boy or girl Ewok is handle to set which includes three interchangeable stamps. Came blister packed on header card. Per set.............................$3–$5

SCRIPTS

Most of what was said in the "Star Trek Scripts" section applies to Star Wars scripts, except more so. First of all, Star Wars scripts are not as common. Star Trek has five movies and three (if you count the animated) television series to draw from. Possible Star Wars script material is just not that numerous. In addition, Lucasfilm is uncommonly vigilant in regards to their property. They dislike letting this kind of item get out to the public. As a result, anyone claiming to have an authentic script should be regarded with extreme suspicion. If you are sure the script is genuine, $500 for a movie script would be fair—less, of course, for an Ewok live-action movie or an episode (there were 13) from the radio drama. Less still should be expected for an Ewok or Droids animated episode.

TOYS AND CRAFTS

Many of the products in this section were manufactured in the United States by Kenner. In Europe, nearly identical toys to the Kenner ones were manufactured by various companies—Palitoy in Britain, Meccano in France, Clipper in Spain, and Harbert in Italy. Prices on these items tend to mirror their U.S. counterparts. In Japan, however, Takara, the primary Star Wars toy licensee, manufactured toys distinctly different from their U.S. counterparts. These will be listed separately.

Crafts

Like models, craft kits should be complete and in original packaging to have collectible value. A completed craft project is worth only a fraction of the prices given here.
Color N' Clean Machine, Craft Master (Fundimensions), 1980. Box decorated with color scenes and logo from Empire frames 50″ continuous roll of reusable line-drawn scenes to color. Kit comes with four crayons and wipe cloth ....$35–$45
Dip Dots, Kenner, 1977. Water color paint set. Book of 16 8½″ × 11″ scenes plus tray of eight paints and brush. Box shows color photo of child painting and Star Wars logo ....$25–$40
Figurine Painting Set, Craft Master (Fundimensions), 1980. Kit includes 5½″ plastic figurine, four different paints, and brush. Came blister packed on header card with photo of finished figurine and Empire logo, four different. Price each
  Leia, Luke on Tauntaun, Yoda, Han Solo..$25–$40
Figurine Painting Set, Craft Master, 1983. Return of the Jedi. Plastic figures, paints, and brush. Blister packed on header card. Glo-in-the-dark accents
  C-3PO/R2-D2, Admiral Ackbar, Wicket..$20–$35
Latch Hook Rug Kit, Lee Wards, 1980. Printed mesh backing and yarn. Six different
  C-3PO and R2-D2, Chewbacca, Darth Vader, R2-D2, Stormtrooper, Yoda ....$25–$40
Make and Bake It, Craft Master (Fundimensions), 1983. Suncatchers. Kit includes metal outline and colored plastic beads for making "stained glass" ornament, several different. Price each ....$10–$15

**Left: Assorted Star Wars toys
and crafts. Right: Dip Dots
craft kit.**

Paint-By-Number, Craft Master (Fundimensions), 1980. Glow-in-the-dark accents. Kit included one 8″ × 10″ scene plus supplies. Box art shows finished artwork and movie logo, four different. Price each
    Darth Vader, Han and Leia, Luke, Yoda ....$10–$20
Paint-By-Number, Craft Master (Fundimensions), 1983. Glow-in-the-dark accents. Kits similar to the above but with scenes from Return of the Jedi. Four different
    C-3PO and R2-D2, Jabba the Hutt, Lando and Boush, Sy Snootles ....$10–$20
Paint-By-Number, Craft Master (Fundimensions), 1980. "Classic Scenes" from The Empire Strikes Back. Set includes 10″ × 14″ scene plus 12 acrylic paints, brush, and instructions, two different. Price per set
    The Battle on Hoth...$15–$25
    The Chase Through the Asteroids ....$15–$25
Pen and Poster Set, Craft Master (Fundimensions), 1980. Two 17″ × 22″ posters and six pens
....$10–$20
Pen and Poster Set, Craft Master (Fundimensions), 1982. Two 11½″ × 18″ posters and eight crayons ....$10–$20
Playnts, Kenner, 1977. Set includes five different 16″ × 24″ posters to be painted, six different paints, two brushes, and color guide. Came packaged with paints blister packed on outside of color photo cover sheet ....$20–$35
Presto Magix, American Publishing, 1980. Fold-out poster with color artwork scene from Empire and transfer sheets. Came folded in plastic bag. Six different
    Asteroid storm, Beneath Cloud City, Dagobah bog planet, Deck of the Star Destroyer, Ice planet Hoth, Rebel base ....$3–$5
Presto Magix, American Publishing, 1983. Color artwork fold-out poster of Jedi scenes and transfer sheets
    Death Star, Ewok village, Jabba's throne room, Sarlaccs Pit.......................................$2–$4

Presto Magix, American Publishing, 1983. 16″ × 24″ fold-out color scene board plus six transfer sheets and transfer stick. Comes boxed, box shows color photo of scene and Jedi logo
   Jabba's throne room, Endor, Ewok village ....$15–$25
Stamp Collecting Kit, H.E. Harris, 1977. Kit includes stamp album, 24 Star War seals, 35 stamps, stamp hinges and magnifier. Comes boxed, color box art shows X-Wing, TIE Fighter, and Star Wars logo ....$15–$25
Transfer Set, Kenner, 1985. Wicket the Ewok boxed set ....$8–$12
Transfer Set, Letraset (British), 1978. Included scene plus sheet of rub-off transfers. Three different
   Destruction of Alderaan, Rebel base on Yavin, Tatooine ....$4–$8
Transfer Sets, Thomas Salter (British), 1983. Sets included sheet(s) of transfers and cardboard scene. Several sizes, larger sets were boxed
   Ewoks, small pack ....$4–$8
   Jabba the Hutt, small pack ....$4–$8
   Ewok village, large pack ....$6–$10
   Sarlacc Pit, large pack ....$6–$10
   Battle on Endor, small box ....$10–$15
   Jabba's throne room, small box ....$10–$15
   Ewok village, large box ....$15–$20
Water Color Paint Set, Fundimensions, 1983. Contains 8″ × 10″ Ewok cartoon, eight paints, brush, and instructions. Three different
   Ewok, Ewok village, Ewok flyer ....$15–$20

Die-Cast Toys

Die-Cast Vehicles, Kenner, 1978–80

This is one of the most popular and one of the fastest appreciating categories of Star Wars collectibles. Vehicles, which were not to scale with each other, were made of metal and plastic, from 4″ to 7″ in size, and always had some moving parts. They came packaged two ways. Smaller vehicles were blister packed on header cards. The four heavier ones (Star Destoyer, Y-Wing, Millennium Falcon, and TIE Bomber) were blister packed on cards that were then secured inside open 3″-deep frame boxes. Color artwork on both package styles showed craft in action. The first four vehicles produced in the series—Land Speeder, TIE Fighter, Darth Vader TIE Fighter, and X-Wing—displayed Star Wars logos on the package. All subsequent die-casts were Empire. Die-casts are one of the few Star Wars collectibles that are in as much demand by collectors out of the package as in. Prices given here are for packaged vehicles. Unpackaged vehicles are worth approximately 50% of these values.
Darth Vader TIE Fighter, pop-off side panels, removable figure of Darth Vader .....$50–$75
Landspeeder, rolls, Luke and C-3PO in cockpit, windshield is often missing from unpackaged vehicle ....$75–$125

X-Wing and rare TIE Bomber showing two types of die-cast packaging.

Takara (Japanese) die-cast metal toys.

Millennium Falcon, swiveling cannon and antennae dish, retractable landing gear ....
....$150–$250
Snowspeeder, canopy opens, cannon swivels, and landing gear retracts ....$75–$125
Slave I, retractable landing gear, cannon and flaps swivel ....$75–$125
Star Destroyer, sliding door on underside, compartment holds tiny removable rebel ship.......
....$150–$250
TIE Bomber, pop-off side panels, this toy was only test marketed, never generally released,
rare ....$1,000–$1,500
TIE Fighter, pop-off side panels, removable pilot ....$50–$75
Twin-Pod Cloud Car, retractable landing gear ....$75–$100
X-Wing, wings and canopy open, canopy is often missing from unpackaged vehicles.............
....$75–$100
Y-Wing, pop-off wing pods, swiveling cannon, and small red bomb that is dropped with re-
lease button ....$150–$250

Die-Cast Figures and Vehicles, Takara (Japan)

These are much more complicated toys than the Kenner die-cast series and tend to
have unexpected functions. C-3PO, for instance, shoots projectiles from his stom-
ach. Toys came packaged in boxes with color artwork of toy.
C-3PO...$200–$300
Darth Vader ....$200–$300
R2-D2 ....$200–$300
X-Wing..$200–$300

Takara Zetca: Die-Cast Miniatures

C-3PO..$75–$100
Landspeeder ....$75–$100
R2-D2 ....$75–$100
TIE Fighter ....$75–$100
X-Wing..$75–$100

Guns

Biker Scout Laser Pistol, Kenner, 1983. Dark gray plastic, approximately 9″ long, sight on
right side of pistol, Jedi logo on sight. Packaged in open frame box.............................$40–$75
Laser Pistol, Kenner, 1979–83. Black plastic, approximately 10″ long with sight above pistol.
Battery sound, movie logo sticker on side, packaged in open frame box. This toy was produced
throughout the movie trilogy with logos on the package and toy itself changing to display the
most recent movie. Earlier logos are slightly more valuable ....$50–$75

Three-position laser rifle (top), laser pistol, and Biker Scout laser pistol.

Three-Position Laser Rifle, Kenner, 1979. Black plastic, approximately 18″ long (with stock folded). Battery sound, movie logo sticker on side, stock would swing from shoulder position to front handgrip or fold flat against body of gun. Came packaged in open frame box displayed with stock fully extended..$100–$150
Electronic Laser Rifle, Kenner, 1980. Essentially the same toy as the Three-Position Laser Rifle but without the stock..$75–$100

Film Projectors, Kenner

1979, "Movie Viewer," blue plastic hand-held toy film projector, hand-cranked, Star Wars logo on side. Box had windows over crank and eye-piece so toy could be used inside box. Back of box shows child using toy. Came complete with film cassette (May the Force Be With You)
....$50–$75
Four different Star Wars cassettes were available for this toy. They are as follows:
Assault on Death Star, Battle in Hyperspace, Danger at the Cantina, Destroy Death Star.....
....$15–$20
1979, "Give-a-Show Projector," blue and red plastic toy film-strip projector. Star Wars logo on front, battery operated. Kit includes 16 film strips..$65–$100
1984, "Give-a-Show Projector," similar to other Kenner toy but with Ewoks logo and film strip ....$30–$50

Kites

Palitoy (British), 1978. Winged shape with X-Wing and TIE Fighter. Also used as a promotional item with KP Crisps, promotional version has "Star Wars" logo in addition to picture...
....$15–$20
Spectra Star, 1983. Color plastic kite and framing tubes, packaged in plastic bag picturing kite design and Jedi logo. Three different
Darth Vader, 55″ figure kite..$10–$15
Luke, 55″ figure kite..$10–$15
Star Wars, 42″ delta wing kite ....$10–$15
Spectra Star, 1983. Eight different character box kites. Price each............................$10–$15
Spectra Star, 1984. 64″ streamer kites
Darth Vader ....$10–$15
Darth and Luke ....$10–$15
Spectra Star, 1985. Two different based on cartoon series
Droids, 80″ streamer kite ....$15–$20
Ewoks on hang glider, 80″ Mylar octopus kite ....$15–$20

Lightsabers, Kenner

These were understandably very popular items during the time of the Star Wars saga. Because the simple application of a plastic tube to the end of a flashlight could produce a reasonable lightsaber facsimile, many unlicensed replicas were produced. These are essentially valueless as collectibles. For this reason only authorized lightsabers will be listed here.

1978, inflatable, vinyl "blade" attached to battery-operated light source, 35″ long. Came boxed with patch kit, color box photo showed Darth and Obi-Wan dueling ....$50–$75
1980–83, "The Force," black plastic handle with foil decals to produce detail. Rigid red or green plastic blade, produced howling sound when swung, no battery functions. Usually sold from store floor displays holding several lightsabers...$10–$20
1984, pop-out, black and silver plastic handle, red or green plastic retractable blade, approximately 17″ long when extended. Battery light, attached belt clip, Droids (animated) logo on handle. Came packaged in open tray with low header with Droids logo and photo of child with toy ....$100–$175

Micro Collection Toys, Kenner, 1982

Plastic playsets and ships designed to scale with a series of painted 1¼″ die-cast metal figures in stationary poses. Sets were comprised of several small modules with assorted manual functions which could be interconnected with other modules in the series, or the complete set could be purchased in the form of a "World." Modules and sets included figures. The short-lived Micro series apparently could not compete successfully with Kenner's own line of 3¾″ action figures and action figure toys. As a result, Micro playsets and especially ships are relatively scarce.

Bespin Control Room, breakaway window, remote lever and platform, comes with four die-cast figures ....$25–$35
Bespin Freeze Chamber, platform lowers figures into chamber, remote claw, escape hatch, four figures...$35–$50
Bespin Gantry, remote door, rotating platform, comes with four figures...................$25–$35
Bespin World, control room, freeze chamber, and gantry sets plus 16 figures..........$75–$100
Death Star Compactor, trash compactor, escape hatch, blast door plus eight figures ....
....$30–$40
Death Star Escape, bridge, exploding cannon, elevator and rope assembly, six figures...........
....$30–$40
Death Star World, Death Star Compactor and Death Star Escape sets plus 14 figures............
....$75–$100

Left: Hoth World. Right: The three smaller sets that make up Hoth World.

Hoth Generator Attack, exploding generator, scout walker, and six figures..............$25–$35
Hoth Ion Cannon, cannon, observation tower with blast doors, and eight figures .....$40–$50
Hoth Turret Defense, two exploding gun turrets and six figures ....$20–$30
Hoth Wampa Cave, cave and four figures...$15–$25
Hoth World, Hoth Generator Attack, Hoth Ion Cannon, and Hoth Wampa Cave sets plus 19 figures ....$100–$150
Millennium Falcon, top comes off to reveal compartments, includes six figures ...$125–$175
Imperial TIE Fighter, break-apart feature, one figure ....$50–$75
Rebel Armored Snowspeeder, break-apart feature, cockpit opens, and working harpoon gun, two figures ....$75–$100
X-Wing Fighter, break-apart feature, one figure..$50–$75

Play-Doh Sets, Kenner

Star Wars Action Set, 1977. Boxed set includes play mat, trim knife, X-Wing toy, three hinged molds, and three cans of Play-Doh. Color box photo shows children and kit ..$20–$30
Empire Strikes Back Action Set, 1980. Boxed set includes play mat, trim knife, snowspeeder toy, three hinged molds, and three cans of Play-Doh. Color box photo shows children and kit ....$15–$25
Empire Strikes Back Yoda Playset, 1982. Boxed set includes play mat, trim knife, X-Wing toy, three hinged molds, and three cans of Play-Doh. Color box photo shows kit ....$15–$25
Return of the Jedi, Jabba the Hutt Playset, 1983. Boxed set includes play mat, four half molds, rolling pin, skiff toy, and three cans of Play-Doh. Color box photo shows kit ....
....$10–$15
Ewoks Playset, 1985. Boxed set includes play mat, trim knife, Ewok cart toy, rolling pin, three open molds, and three cans of Play-Doh ....$10–$15

Plush Toys

Chewbacca, Regal (Canada)..$45–$60
Chewbacca, Kenner, 1977. 20″ tall, covered with brown artificial fur. Comes with bandolier containing four removable gray plastic rectangles ....$25–$35
R2-D2, Kenner, 1977. 10″ tall, white with silver and blue trim, moving legs and squeaker......
....$35–$50
Ewoks, Kenner, 1983. Three sizes, all covered with artificial fur in various shades of brown and gray. Adults all came with hoods, packaged in open cardboard trays
    Tall Adult, 18″, Zephee, comes with pouch in addition to hood ....$30–$40
    Regular Adult, 14″
        Wicket ....$20–$30
        Princess Kneesa ....$20–$30
        Paploo ....$30–$40
        Latara ....$30–$40
    Baby (Wokling), 8″
        Wiley..$10–$15

Plush Ewok, Wokling, R2–D2, and Chewbacca, all by Kenner.

Nippet..$10–$15
Mookiee ....$10–$15
Leeni ....$10–$15
Gwig...$15–$20
Malani..$15–$20
Note: *Unpackaged Ewoks can be identified by name tag sewn to seam.*
Ewoks, Disney. Sold as souvenirs at Star Tours and used as video promotions
  Large, 12″, light brown with green cowl ....$10–$15
  Small, 8″, dark brown with pink cowl ....$8–$12

Miscellaneous

Bop Bags, Kenner, 1977. Inflatable vinyl punching bags with likeness of Star Wars character
printed on each. Four different
  Chewbacca, 50″ tall ....$50–$75
  Darth Vader, 50″ tall ....$50–$75
  Jawa, 36″ tall..$50–$75
  R2-D2, 36″ tall..$50–$75
Gym Set, Gym-Dandy, 1983. Scout Walker Command Tower. Child's gym set includes
Speeder bike swinging ride with sound effects ....$900–$1,200
Frisbee, 1977, Collector Series. Drawing of character and Star Wars logo on silver
plastic frisbee ....$8–$12
Frisbee, H.H. & B., 1981. Color artwork of R2-D2, C-3PO, and Darth Vader with Empire
logo. Promotional for Coca-Cola and Burger King....................................$5–$10
Ice Skates, Brookfield Athletic Shoe, 1983
  Darth Vader and Imperial Guard...$50–$75
  Wicket ....$50–$75
Puppet, Regal (Canada). Chewbacca hand puppet ....$35–$50
Puppet, Kenner, 1981. Yoda, hollow soft plastic figure, 8½″ tall, came packaged in window
box with Empire logo ....$30–$40
Racing Set, Fundimensions, 1978. Star Wars Duel at Death Star Racing Set. Slotless race set
included X-Wing and Darth Vader TIE Fighter "cars," track, two controllers, lap counter,
power pack, and decorative backdrops. 19″ × 20″ box shows color artwork of cars in fore-
ground with Darth and Death Star behind ....$150–$200
Radio Controlled R2-D2, Kenner, 1978. Control unit with antennae directs battery-powered
toy, 8″ tall. Sound and light, color box photo shows toy with child in background and Star Wars
logo ....$75–$100
Radio Controlled R2-D2, Takara (Japan) ....$150–$200
Note: *See "Action Figures" section for other radio-controlled toys.*
Riding Speeder Bike, Kenner, 1983. Pedal-powered metal riding toy shaped like speeder-
bike, child size ....$500–$1,000

Speeder Bike. Pedal-powered riding toy.

Yoda the Jedi Master Toy, by Kenner, 5¼".

Roller Skates, Brookfield Athletic Shoe, 1983. Children's shoe skates with circular design on ankle showing character and Jedi logo. Star Wars logo on tongue and wheels. Color box art reflected design on skate.

Darth and Imperial Guard...$50–$75

Wicket..$50–$75

R2-D2 (Talking), Palitoy (British). Came boxed...$300–$400

R2-D2 (Walking), Canadian. Came blister packed on header card.............................$50–$75

R2-D2 (Wind-Up), Takara (Japan)...$30–$50

Sit n' Spin, Kenner Preschool, 1984. Toy consisted of turntable base that child sat on with handle in center. Decorated with Ewok artwork, color photo of toy on box. Ewok packaging........
....$40–$60

Telephone, Kenner Preschool, 1984. Ewok Talking Telephone. Plastic toy telephone shaped like Ewok, battery operated, approximately 9" tall. Box shows color photo of toy, Ewok packaging...$40–$70

Van Set, Kenner, 1978. Set consisted of two toy vans approximately 7" in length, 12 toy barrels, four pylons, and two T-sticks (which motivated vans). White van had artwork of heroes. Black van had artwork of Darth Vader. Color box art showed vans in action and had windows to view toys themselves ....$100–$150

Yoda the Jedi Master, Kenner, 1981. Fortune-telling toy, 5¼" tall plastic figure of Yoda has "window" in base to allow answers to questions to be read ....$35–$50

TRADING CARDS AND STICKERS

American Gum Cards, Topps

Star Wars

FIRST SERIES CARDS

Blue Borders, No. 1–66.

Complete Set..$25–$40

Single Cards..$.50–$1

    1 Luke Skywalker, **2** C-3PO and R2-D2, **3** The Little Droid, R2-D2, **4** Space pirate, Han Solo, **5** Princess Leia Organa, **6** Ben (Obi-Wan) Kenobi, **7** The villanious Darth Vader, **8** Grand Moff Tarkin, **9** Rebels defend their standard, **10** Princess Leia captured, **11** R2 is imprisoned by the Jawas, **12** The Droids are reunited, **13** A sale on Droid, **14** Luke checks out his new Droid, **15** R2-D2 is left behind, **16** Jawas of Tatooine, **17** Lord Vader threatens Princess Leia, **18** R2-D2 is missing, **19** Searching for the little Droid, **20** Hunted by the Sand people, **21** The Tusken Raiders, **22** Rescued by Ben Kenobi, **23** C-3PO is injured, **24** Stormtroopers seek the Droids, **25** Luke rushed to save his loved ones, **26** A horrified Luke sees his family killed, **27** Some repairs for C-3PO, **28** Luke agrees to join Ben Kenobi, **29** Stopped by Stormtroopers, **30** Han in the Millennium Falcon, **31** Sighting the Death Star, **32** Lord Vader's guard, **33** The Droids in the control room, **34** C-3PO diverts the guards, **35**

Assorted Star Wars cards and stickers.

Luke and Han as Stormtroopers, **36** Blast of the laser rifle, **37** Cornered in the labyrinth, **38** Luke and Han in the refuse room, **39** Steel walls close in our heroes, **40** Droids rescue their master, **41** Facing the deadly chasm, **42** Stormtroopers attack, **43** Luke prepares to swing across the chasm, **44** Han and Chewie shoot it out, **45** The Lightsaber, **46** A desperate moment for Ben, **47** Luke prepares for battle, **48** R2-D2 is loaded aboard, **49** The rebels monitor the raid, **50** Rebel leaders wonder about their fate, **51** C-3PO and Princess Leia, **52** Who will win the final space war?, **53** Battle in outer space, **54** The victors receive their reward, **55** Han, Chewie, and Luke, **56** A day of rejoicing, **57** Mark Hamill as Luke Skywalker, **58** Harrison Ford as Han Solo, **59** Alec Guinness as Ben Kenobi, **60** Peter Cushing as Grand Moff Tarkin, **61** Mark Hamill in control room, **62** Lord Vader's Stormtroopers, **63** May the Force be with you!, **64** Govenor of Imperial Outlands, **65** Carrie Fisher and Mark Hamill, **66** Amazing robot C-3PO

Wrapper..$2–$5
Display Box..$5–$10
Unopened Pack...$3–$5
Unopened Box ....$100–$150

FIRST SERIES STICKERS
No. 1–11.
Complete set ....$10–$20
Single sticker ....$1–$2
    1 Luke Skywalker, **2** Princess Leia Organa, **3** Han Solo, **4** Chewbacca, the Wookie, **5** C-3PO, **6** R2-D2, **7** Lord Darth Vader, **8** Grand Moff Tarkin, **9** Ben (Obi-Wan) Kenobi, **10** Tusken Raider, **11** X-Wing Fighter

SECOND SERIES CARDS
Red borders, No. 67–132.
Complete Set..$20–$30
Single Cards..$.50–$1

67 C-3PO, **68** The Millennium Falcon, **69** C-3PO's desert trek!, **70** Special mission for R2-D2!, **71** The incredible C-3PO!, **72** Ben Kenobi rescues Luke!, **73** The Droids wait for Luke!, **74** Luke Skywalker on Tatooine, **75** Darth Vader strangles a rebel!, **76** R2-D2 on the rebel, **77** Waiting in the control room, **78** Droids to the rescue!, **79** Preparing to board Solo's spaceship!, **80** "Where has R2-D2 gone?", **81** Weapons of the Death Star!, **82** A daring rescue!, **83** Aboard the Millennium Falcon, **84** Rebel pilot prepares for the raid!, **85** Luke on the Sand planet, **86** A mighty explosion!, **87** The Droids try to rescue Luke!, **88** Stormtroopers guard Solo's ship, **89** The imprisoned Princess Leia, **90** Honoring the victors!, **91** Solo and Chewie prepare to leave Luke, **92** Advance of the Tusken Raider, **93** Stormtroopers blast the rebels!, **94** Interrogated by Stormtroopers!, **95** Sighting R2-D2!, **96** The Droids on Tatooine, **97** Meeting at the cantina, **98** C-3PO, **99** Ben with the lightsaber!, **100** Our heroes at the spaceport, **101** The Wookie Chewbacca, **102** Rebels prepare for the big fight!, **103** Stormtroopers attack our heroes!, **104** Luke's uncle and aunt, **105** Imperial soldiers burn through the starship!, **106** A message from Princess Leia!, **107** The Tusken Raider, **108** Princess Leia observes the battle!, **109** Ben turns off the tractor beam, **110** C-3PO fools the guards!, **111** Chewie and Han Solo!, **112** Threatened by Sand people, **113** Ben hides from Imperial Stormtroopers!, **114** Planning to escape!, **115** Hiding in the Millennium Falcon!, **116** Honored for their heroism!, **117** Chewbacca poses as a prisoner!, **118** R2-D2 and C-3PO, **119** C-3PO, Ben, and Luke!, **120** Luke destroys an Imperial ship!, **121** Han Solo and Chewbacca, **122** The Millennium Falcon speeds through space!, **123** Solo blasts a Stormtrooper!, **124** C-3PO searches for R2-D2, **125** Luke in disguise!, **126** A quizzical C-3PO!, **127** The Rebel fleet, **128** Roar of the Wookies!, **129** "May the Force be with you!", **130** Pursued by the Jawas!, **131** Spectacular battle!, **132** Lord Vader and a soldier

Wrapper...$2–$4
Display Box...$4–$8
Unopened Pack...$3–$5
Unopened Box..$75–$125

SECOND SERIES STICKERS
No. 12–22.
Complete Set...$10–$20
Single Stickers ....$1–$2
    12 Han and Chewbacca, **13** Alec Guinness as Ben, **14** The Tusken Raider, **15** C-3PO, **16** Chewbacca, **17** Tusken Raider and Luke on Tatooine, **18** Hanger deck at rebel base, **19** Chewbacca at docking base 94, **20** R2-D2 and C-3PO, **21** The Millennium Falcon, **22** X-Wing and TIE Fighter near the Death Star

THIRD SERIES CARDS
Yellow borders, No. 133–198.
Complete Set...$15–$25
Single Cards..$.50–$1
    133 Ben and Luke help C-3PO to his feet, **134** Luke dreams of being a star pilot, **135** Cantina troubles!, **136** Danger from all sides!, **137** Luke attacked by a strange creature!, **138** On the track of the Droids, **139** Han Solo . . . hero or mercenary?, **140** "R2-D2, where are you?", **141** Some quick thinking by Luke, **142** Darth Vader inspects the throttled ship, **143** Droids on the Sand planet, **144** Harrison on the Sand planet, **145** Escape from the Death Star!, **146** Luke Skywalker's aunt preparing dinner, **147** Bargaining with the Jawas!, **148** The fearsome Stormtroopers, **149** The evil Grand Moff Tarkin, **150** Shoot-out at the chasm!, **151** Planning an escape!, **152** Spirited Princess Leia, **153** The fantastic Droid, C-3PO, **154** Princess Leia comforts Luke!, **155** The escape pod is jettisoned!, **156** R2-D2 is lifted aboard!, **157** "Learn about the Force, Luke!", **158** Rebel victory, **159** Luke Skywalker's home, **160** Destroying the world!, **161** Preparing for the raid!, **162** Han Solo cornered by Greedo!, **163** Caught in the tractor beam!, **164** Tusken Raiders capture Luke!, **165** Escaping from Stormtroopers!, **166** A close call for Luke and Princess Leia, **167** Surrounded by Lord Vader's soldiers!, **168** Hunting the fugitives, **169** Meeting at the Death Star!, **170** Luke and the Princess . . . trapped!, **171** "The walls are moving", **172** Droids in the escape pod, **173** The Stormtroopers, **174** Solo aims for trouble!, **175** A closer look at a "Jawa", **176** Luke Skywalker's dream, **177** Solo swings into action!, **178** The Star Warriors, **179** Stormtroopers search the spaceport!, **180** Princess Leia honors the victors!, **181** Peter Cushing as Grand Moff Tarkin, **182** Deadly blasters!, **183** Dave Prowse as Darth Vader, **184** Luke and his uncle, **185** Luke on Tatooine, **186** The Jawas, **187** C-3PO and friend, **188** Starship under fire!,

189 Mark Hamill as Luke, **190** Carrie Fisher as Princess Leia, **191** Life on the desert world, **192** Liberated Princess, **193** Luke's uncle buys C-3PO, **194** Stormtrooper attack!, **195** Alec Guinness as Ben Kenobi, **196** Lord Darth Vader, **197** Leia blasts a Stormtrooper!, **198** Luke decides to leave Tatooine!

Wrapper	$2–$4
Display Box	$4–$8
Unopened Pack	$3–$5
Unopened Box	$75–$125

THIRD SERIES STICKERS
No. 23–33.

Complete Set	$15–$25
Single Stickers	$1–$2

23 Darth Vader, **24** C-3PO and R2-D2, **25** Escape pod, **26** C-3PO, **27** Jawa, **28** Moff Tarkin, **29** Han Solo, **30** Stormtroopers, **31** Luke and Leia, **32** Y-Wing and X-Wings, **33** Han Solo with blaster

FOURTH SERIES CARDS
Green borders, No. 199–264.

Complete Set	$15–$25
Single Cards	$.50–$1

199 The Star Warriors aim for action, **200** C-3PO searches for his counterpart, **201** Raid at Mos Eisley!, **202** Inquiring about Obi-Wan Kenobi, **203** A band of Jawas, **204** Stalking the corridors of Death Star, **205** Desperate moments for our heroes!, **206** Searching for the missing Droid!, **207** C-3PO (Anthony Daniels), **208** Luke Skywalker on the desert planet, **209** The rebel troops, **210** Princess Leia blasts the enemy, **211** A proud moment for Han and Luke, **212** A Stormtrooper is blasted!, **213** Monitoring the battle, **214** Luke and Leia shortly before the raid, **215** Han bows out of the battle, **216** Han and Leia quarrel about the escape plan, **217** The Dark Lord of the Sith, **218** Luke Skywalker's home—destroyed!, **219** The swing to freedom!, **220** "I'm going to regret this!", **221** Princess Leia (Carrie Fisher), **222** "Evacuate? In our moment of triumph?", **223** Han Solo covers his friends, **224** Luke's secret yen for action!, **225** Aunt Beru Lars (Sgekagh Fraser), **226** Portrait of a Princess, **227** Instructing the rebel pilots, **228** R2-D2 is inspected by the Jawas, **229** Grand Moff Tarkin (Peter Cushing), **230** Guarding the Millennium Falcon, **231** Discussing the Death Star's future, **232** The Empire strikes back!, **233** Raiding the rebel starship, **234** Envisioning the rebel's destruction, **235** Luke Skywalker (Mark Hamill), **236** Readying the rebel fleet, **237** The deadly grip of Darth Vader, **238** Uncle Owen Lars (Phil Brown), **239** The young star warrior, **240** R2's desperate mission!, **241** The rebel fighter ships, **242** Death Star shootout!, **243** Rebels in the trench!, **244** Waiting at Mos Eisley, **245** Member of the Evil Empire, **246** Stormtroopers—tool of the Empire, **247** Soldier of evil!, **248** Luke suspects the worst about this family, **249** Ben Kenobi (Alec Guinness), **250** Luke and Ben on Tatooine, **251** An overjoyed Han Solo!, **252** The honored heroes!, **253** R2-D2 (Kenny Baker), **254** Darth Vader (David Prowse), **255** Luke poses with his weapon, **256** The marvelous Droid, C-3PO!, **257** A pair of Jawas, **258** Fighting impossible odds!, **259** Challenging the Evil Empire!, **260** Han Solo (Harrison Ford), **261** Fury of the Tusken Raider, **262** Creature of Tatooine, **263** The Courage of Luke Skywalker, **264** Star pilot Luke Skywalker

Wrapper	$2–$4
Display Box	$4–$8
Unopened Pack	$3–$5
Unopened Box	$75–$125

FOURTH SERIES STICKERS
No. 34–44.

Complete Set	$15–$25
Single Stickers	$1–$2

34 Han and Chewbacca, in fighting pose, **35** Han Solo holding gun, **36** Luke Skywalker in fighting gear, **37** C-3PO, **38** R2-D2, **39** Tusken Raider, **40** Darth Vader, **41** Jawas, **42** Luke Skywalker and gun, **43** Imperial Stormtrooper, **44** Princess Leia, by targeting board

FIFTH SERIES CARDS

Orange borders, No. 265–330.

Complete Set...$15–$25
Single Cards...$.50–$1

265 Anxious moments for the rebels, 266 C-3PO and Leia monitor the battle, 267 No-nonsense privateer Han Solo!, 268 Ben prepares to turn off the tractor beam, 269 Droids on the run!, 270 Luke Skywalker: farmboy-turned-warrior!, 271 "Do you think they'll melt us down, R2?", 272 Corridors of the Death Star, 273 "This is all your fault, R2!", 274 Droids trick the Stormtroopers, 275 Guarding the Millennium Falcon, 276 It's not wise to upset a Wookie!, 277 Bizarre inhabitants of the Cantina!, 278 A narrow escape!, 279 Awaiting the Imperial attack, 280 "Remember Luke, The Force will be with you", 281 A monstrous thirst!, 282 "Hurry up, Luke, we're gonna have company!", 283 The Cantina musicians, 284 Distracted by Solo's assault, 285 Spiffed-up for the awards ceremony, 286 Cantina deni-zens!, 287 Han and Chewie ready for action!, 288 Blasting the enemy!, 289 The rebel fight-ers take off!, 290 Chewie aims for danger!, 291 Lord Vader senses the Force, 292 The Stormtroopers assemble, 293 A friendly chat among alien friends!, 294 Droids make their way to the escape pod, 295 Han and the Rebel pilots, 296 R2-D2 is abducted by Jawas!, 297 Inside the Sandcrawler, 298 Chewie gets riled!, 299 Leia wishes Luke good luck!, 300 A crucial moment for Luke Skywalker, 301 Luke, the Star Warrior!, 302 3PO and R2, 303 Var-ious Droids collected by the Jawas, 304 The Jawas ready their new merchandise, 305 Direc-tor George Lucas and "Greedo", 306 Technicians ready C-3PO for the cameras, 307 A touch-up for Chewbacca, 308 Directing the Cantina creatures, 309 The birthday celebration for Sir Alec Guinness, 310 Filming the awards ceremony, 311 The model builders proudly display their work, 312 Using the "blue screen" process for X-Wings, 313 The birth of a Droid, 314 Shooting in Tunisia, 315 Inside the Millennium Falcon, 316 Photographing the miniature explosions, 317 Filming explosions of the Death Star, 318 "Make-up" for the Bantha, 319 Dave Prowse and Alec Guinness rehearse, 320 Flight of the Falcon, 321 George Lucas directs his counterpart "Luke", 322 Constructing the Star Destroyer, 323 Aboard the Millennium Falcon, 324 Chewie takes a breather between scenes, 325 The Princess gets the brush!, 326 Animating the "chessboard" creatures, 327 Filming the Sandcrawler, 328 X-Wings positioned for the cameras, 329 Sir Alec Guinness and George Lucas, 330 Filming Luke and C-3PO in Tunisia

Wrapper...$2–$4
Display Box...$4–$8
Unopened Pack...$3–$5
Unopened Box ....$75–$125

FIFTH SERIES STICKERS

No. 45–55.

Complete Set...$15–$25
Single Stickers...$1–$2

45 Luke Skywalker, in fighter helmet, 46 Chewbacca, with cross gun, 47 Droids, in Death Star control room, 48 Droids, in Sandcrawler, 49 Luke, in Millennium Falcon gun turret, 50 George Lucas and Greedo, 51 Anthony Daniels being put in C-3PO costume, 52 Jawas and Sandcrawler on Tatooine, 53 George Lucas preparing the Cantina scene, 54 Luke and Leia say farewell, 55 Putting on Chewbacca's mask

The Empire Strikes Back

FIRST SERIES CARDS

No. 1–132.

Complete Set...$20–$30
Single Cards...$.50–$1

2 Luke Skywalker, 3 Princess Leia, 4 Han Solo, 5 Chewbacca, 6 C-3PO, 7 R2-D2, 8 Lando Calrissian, 9 Yoda, 10 Darth Vader, 11 Boba Fett, 12 The Imperial Probot, 13 Planet of Ice, 14 "Where's Luke?", 15 Droids on patrol, 16 The hidden rebel base, 17 New rebel strategy, 18 General Rieekan, 19 Leia's plan, 20 Prey of the Wampa, 21 Examined: Luke's Tauntaun, 22 "But Sir, I Mmh.. Mffh..", 23 In search of Luke, 24 Frozen Death, 25 Skywalker's rescue, 26 Luke's fight for life, 27 Rejuvenation chamber, 28 Surgeon Droid, 29 R2's icy vigil, 30 Metal monster, 31 Zeroing in on Chewie!, 32 Han aims for action, 33 Destroying the Probot, 34 Death of Admiral Ozzel, 35 The freedom fighter, 36 Rebel defenses, 37 Armed against

the enemy, **38** Joined by Dack, **39** The sound of terror, **40** Suddenly . . . starfire!, **41?** Rattled by the enemy, **42** Might of the Imperial Forces, **43** The Snowwalkers, **44** Luke . . . Trapped!, **45** Escape from icy peril, **46** "Retreat! Retreat!", **47** Headquarters in shambles, **48** Solo's makeshift escape, **49** Invaded!, **50** Vader and the Snowtroopers, **51** Snowtroopers of the Empire, **52** Millennium Falcon: getaway ship!, **53** Emergency blast off!, **54** Battle of the Star Destroyer, **55** Fix-it man Han Solo!, **56** A sudden change of plan, **57** Misty world of Dagobah, **58** The creature called Yoda, **59** "Welcome, Young Luke!", **60** Journey through the swamp, **61** Yoda's house, **62** R2 peeking through, **63** The secret of Yoda, **64** The Princess lends a hand, **65** Repairing hyperdrive, **66** Star lovers, **67** "Pardon Me Sir, But . . . Ohhh!", **68** Mysterious and deadly chamber, **69** Attacked by Badlike creatures!, **70** "Use the Force, Luke!", **71** Raising Luke's X-Wing, **72** A need beyond reason, **73** A gathering of evils, **74** The bounty hunters, **75** IG-88 and Boba Fett, **76** Enter Lando Calrissian, **77** Warm welcome for an old buddy, **78** Coming pals, **79** "Greetings, Sweet Lady", **80** Calrissian's main man, **81** Pretty as a Princess, **82** "A Swarm of . . .?", **83** 3PO . . . blasted to bits!, **84** A pile of C-3PO!, **85** Escorted by Lando, **86** Dinner guests, **87** Host of horror, **88** Deflecting Solo's blasts, **89** Alas, poor 3PO!, **90** The ordeal, **91** The prize of Boba Fett, **92** His day of triumph, **93** The carbon-freezing chamber, **94** End of the Star Warriors?, **95** Pawn of the evil one, **96** "No! This can't be happening!", **97** The fate of Han Solo, **98** Boba's special delivery, **99** Observed by Luke, **100** Luke arrives, **101** Ready for action!, **102** The search for Vader, **103** "Where are you, Skywalker?", **104** Dark Lord of the Sith, **105** Weapon of light, **106** The confrontation, **107** Duel of the lightsabers, **108** Escape from their captors, **109** Lando . . . friend or foe?, **110** Leia takes control!, **111** Blasting the Stormtroopers!, **112** R2 to the rescue!, **113** Spectacular battle!, **114** "Embrace the Dark Side!", **115** "Hate me, Luke! Destroy me!", **116** Luke's last stand, **117** "Do you have a foot in my size?", **118** Probot, **119** Falcon on Hoth, **120** Snow Walkers, **121** The pursued, **122** Darth Vader, **123** Swamps of Dagobah, **124** Cloud City, **125** Lando's greeting, **126** 3PO's destruction, **127** Luke battling Darth, **128** The final stand, **129** Rescue, **130** Ion cannon, **131** Checklist, No. 1–66, **132** Checklist, No. 67–132

Wrapper..$1–$3
Display Box...$3–$6
Unopened Pack...$2–$4
Unopened Box ....$50–$100

FIRST SERIES STICKERS

Alphabet stickers, two letters per card, yellow background, No. 1–33.
Complete Set...$20–$30
Single Stickers ....$.50–$1

1 F, O, **2** R, I, **3** A, E, **4** B, X **5** U, I, **6** W, U, **7** M, N **8** C, D, **9** O, U, **10** H, E, **11** F, O, **12** Y, U, **13** A, K, **14** A, V, **15** E, S, **16** Q, L, **17** A, I, **18** I, O, **19** Z, T, **20** G, J, **21** E, I, **22** A, P, **23** Luke, Darth, Luke in Hoth Gear, **24** C-3PO, **25** Luke and Yoda, Luke and Tan-Tan, **26** Stormtrooper and Boba Fett, **27** Yoda and Luke, **28** Various aliens, **29** Luke, Leia, Han, and Chewbacca, **30** Full view of Boba Fett, **31** Full view of Stormtrooper and Bounty Hunter, **32** Lando Calrission, R2-D2, and C-3PO, **33** Darth Vader

SECOND SERIES CARDS

Blue borders, No. 133–264.
Complete Set...$15–$25
Single Cards...$.25–$.50

133 Introduction, **134** Millennium Falcon, **135** The executor, **136** Imperial Star Destroyer, **137** Twin-Pod Cloud Car, **138** Slave 1, **139** Rebel armored snowspeeder, **140** The avenger, **141** TIE Fighter, **142** Rebel transport, **143** TIE Bomber, **144** Preparing for battle, **145** Seeking the missing Luke, **146** The searcher, **147** Star pilot Luke Skywalker, **148** Luke's patrol, **149** Shelter on icy Hoth, **150** Imperial sky, **151** Tracking the Probot, **152** Han Solo, rescuer, **153** Medical treatment, **154** Worried Droids on Hoth, **155** Imperial assault!, **156** Narrow escape!, **157** Fighting against the Empire, **158** Roar of the Wookie, **159** Chewie's task, **160** Moments before the escape, **161** Last stages of the battle, **162** Gallant warrior, **163** "Raise those ships!", **164** The awesome one, **165** Vader and his Snowtroopers, **166** Takeover of rebel base, **167** The man called Han Solo, **168** The Falcon in repairs, **169** Skills of the star pilot, **170** "Sir . . . wait for me!", **171** Han's desperate plan, **172** An overworked Wookie?, **173** "Oh, hello there, Chewbacca!", **174** R2's bumpy landing, **175** Mysterious planet, **176** "Luke . . . in trouble?", **177** Working against time, **178** Han and the Princess, **179** Soldiers of the

Empire, **180** The Wookies at work, **181** Vader and a Bounty Hunter, **182** World of darkness, **183** Taking no chances!, **184** Farewell to Yoda and Dagobah, **185** Racing to the Falcon, **186** The ominous Vader, **187** The dark pursuer, **188** Young senator from Alderan, **189** Don't fool with Han Solo, **190** Kindred spirits, **191** Lobot's task, **192** A brave Princess, **193** Corridor of Bespin, **194** Lando's aide, Lobot, **195** "Get back quick . . . It's Vader!", **196** Held by the Stormtroopers, **197** Han's torment, **198** Lando's game, **199** Deadly device, **200** In Vader's clutches, **201** A tearful farewell, **202** Han faces his fate, **203** Into the carbon-freezing pit!, **204** An Ugnaught, **205** Tears of a Princess, **206** Suspended in carbon freeze, **207** Gruesome fate!, **208** Evil threatens!, **209** "This deal is getting worse!", **210** The captor, Boba Fett, **211** Fear on Cloud City, **212** A warrior drive, **213** Courage of Skywalker, **214** The pursuer, **215** Stalked by Vader!, **216** A Droid gone to pieces, **217** 3PO's free ride, **218** Stormtrooper take-over!, **219** Princess Leia under guard!, **220** Bounty Hunter, Boba Fett, **221** Lando covers their escape!, **222** Tumbling to an unknown fate, **223** On the verge of defeat, **224** Gifted per-former, **225** Actress Carrie Fisher, **226** Han Solo (Harrison Ford), **227** Anthony Daniels as C-3PO, **228** Our favorite protocol Droid, **229** R2-D2 (Kenny Baker), **230** "Mynocks out-side? Oh, my!", **231** Actor Billy Dee Williams, **232** Galaxy's most loyal Droids, **233** Dash-ing Han Solo, **234** The Force and the fury, **235** Yoda's squabble with R2-D2, **236** Blasted by Leia!, **237** The art of Levitation, **238** Snowswept Chewbacca, **239** Dreamworld . . . or trap?, **240** Swampland peril, **241** "Tried, have you?", **242** Encounter on Dagobah, **243** Captain Solo senses a trap, **244** A test for Luke, **245** R2-D2 on the misty bog, **246** Confronting the Dark Side, **247** Luke battles . . . himself?, **248** Blooming romance, **249** Chewie retaliated, **250** Stormtrooper battle, **251** Director Irvin Kershner, **252** Spiffing up a Wookie, **253** Film-ing of the Falcon, **254** Kershner directs Mark Hamill, **255** Shooting the exciting climax, **256** Filming Vader in his chamber, **257** Dagobah comes to life, **258** Building the Falcon, **259** Hoth rebel base sequence, **260** Filming the Explosion, **261** Spectacular swampland set, **262** Acting can be a dirty job!, **263** Checklist, No. 133–198, **264** Checklist, No. 199–264

Wrapper ....$1–$3
Display Box ....$3–$6
Unopened Pack ....$2–$4
Unopened Box ....$50–$100

SECOND SERIES STICKERS
Alphabet stickers, two letters per card, blue background, No. 34–66.
Complete Set ....$10–$20
Single Stickers ....$.25–$.50
34 F, O, **35** R, I, **36** A, E, **37** B, X, **38** U, I, **39** W, U, **40** M, N, **41** C, D, **42** O, U, **43** H, E, **44** E, O, **45** Y, U, **46** A, K, **47** A, V, **48** E, S, **49** Q, L, **50** A, I, **51** I, O, **52** Z, T, **53** G, J, **54** E, I, **55** A, P, **56** Darth Vader in gold outline, **57** Boba Fett, **58** Probot, **59** Luke Skywalker, **60** Princess Leia, **61** Han Solo, **62** Lando Calrissian, **63** Chewbacca, **64** R2-D2, **65** C-3PO, **66** Yoda

THIRD SERIES CARDS
Yellow borders, No. 266–352.
Complete Set ....$15–$25
Single Cards ....$.25–$.50
266 Han Solo, **267** Princess Leia, **268** Luke Skywalker, **269** C-3PO, **270** R2-D2, **271** Darth Vader, **272** Boba Fett, **273** Probot, **274** Dengar, **275** Bossk, **276** IG-88, **277** FX-7, **278** Chewbacca, **279** Lando Calrissian, **280** Stormtrooper, **281** Yoda, **282** Imperial ships ap-proaching!, **283** The courageous trench fighters!, **284** Too-Onebee, **285** Rebel protocol Droids, **286** Within the hidden base, **287** Calrissian of Bespin, **288** Testing the carbon-freezing process, **289** Flight of the X-Wing, **290** Dodging deadly laser blasts!, **291** The lov-ers part, **292** Canyons of death!, **293** Magnificent rebel starship, **294** Old friends . . . or foes?, **295** Power of the Empire, **296** 3PO in a jam!, **297** Swamp plane!, **298** A hasty retreat!, **299** Hostile world of Hoth, **300** Descent into danger!, **301** Luke . . . long overdue!, **302** To-ward the unknown, **303** In search of Han, **304** Luke's desperate decision, **305** Emerging from the pit, **306** Busy as a Wookie, **307** Portrait of an Ugnaught, **308** The wizard of Dagobah, **309** Emergency repairs!, **310** Han on the icy wasteland, **311** The walkers close in!, **312** Toward tomorrow, **313** In the path of danger!, **314** The X-Wing cockpit, **315** Hero of the rebellion, **316** Vader's private chamber, **317** Aboard the Executor, **318** The ominous one, **319** Lord Vader orders, **320** "He's still alive!", **321** Lando's warm reception, **322** The land-ing, **323** Their last kiss?, **324** Bounty hunter IG-88, **325** The icy plains of Hoth, **326** Luke

astride his Tauntaun, **327** Rebel snowspeeders zero in!, **328** Champions of freedom, **329** Inside the Falcon, **330** The training of a Jedi, **331** Yoda's instruction, **332** The Warrior and the Jedi Master, **333** Imperial Snow Walker attack!, **334** The asteroid chase, **335** Approaching planet Dagobah, **336** Power generators, **337** Beauty of Bespin, **338** Dreamlike city, **339** Luke's training, **340** Snow Walker terror, **341** Tauntaun, **342** Cloud City reactor shaft, **343** Yoda's home, **344** Escape from Bespin, **345** Deadly stompers, **346** Snow Walker model, **347** Of helmets and costumes, **348** Filming the Star Destroyer, **349** Millennium Falcon miniature, **350** Launching an X-Wing, **351** Model Star Destroyer, **352** Checklist, No. 265–352

Wrapper...$1–$3
Display Box...$3–$6
Unopened Pack..$2–$4
Unopened Box ....$50–$100

THIRD SERIES STICKERS

Alphabet stickers, two letters per card, green background, No. 67–88.

Complete Set...$10–$20
Single Stickers ....$.25–$.50

67 F, O, **68** R, I, **69** A, E, **70** B, X, **71** U, I, **72** W, U, **73** M, N, **74** C, D, **75** O, U, **76** H, E, **77** E, O, **78** Y, U, **79** A, K, **80** A, V, **81** E, S, **82** Q, L, **83** A, I, **84** I, O, **85** Z, T, **86** C, J, **87** E, I, **88** A, P

The Return of the Jedi

FIRST SERIES CARDS

No. 1–132.

Complete Set...$10–$20
Single Cards...$.25–$.50

1 Title card, **2** Luke Skywalker, **3** Darth Vader, **4** Han Solo, **5** Princess Leia Organa, **6** Lando Calrissian, **7** Chewbacca, **8** C-3PO and R2-D2, **9** The new Death Star, **10** The inspections, **11** Toward the Desert Palace, **12** Bib Fortuna, **13** Court of evil, **14** Jabba the Hutt, **15** Intergalactic gangster, **16** Salacious Crumb, **17** A message for Jabba the Hutt, **18** Dungeons of Jabba the Hutt, **19** Beddo and a Jawa, **20** Sy Snootles and the Rebo Band, **21** Droopy McCool, **22** Sy Snootles, **23** Watched by Boba Fett, **24** Boushh's captive, **25** The Bounty Hunter Boushh, **26** The villains confer, **27** Han Solo's plight, **28** The rescuer, **29** Decarbonized!, **30** Princess Leia to the rescue!, **31** Heroes in disguise, **32** The Princess enslaved, **33** Luke Skywalker arrives, **34** The young Jedi, **35** The court in chaos!, **36** The Rancor Pit, **37** Facing Jabba the Hutt, **38** The sail barge and the desert skiff, **39** Jabba the Hutt's new dancing girl, **40** On the sail barge, **41** A monstrous fate!, **42** The battle begins, **43** Lando Calrissian's fight for life, **44** Fury of the Jedi!, **45** Princess Leia strikes back!, **46** The demise of Jabba the Hutt, **47** Boba Fett's last stand, **48** The rescue, **49** Gammorrean Guard, **50** The deadly cannon, **51** The raging battle, **52** Princess Leia swings into action!, **53** Swing to safety, **54** On the Death Star, **55** Guards of the Emperor, **56** The deciders, **57** The Emperor, **58** Yoda, the Jedi Master, **59** A word with Ben (Obi-Wan) Kenobi, **60** The allies meet, **61** A new challenge, **62** Pondering the raid, **63** Mission: destroy the Death Star!, **64** Mon Mothma, **65** The friends depart, **66** Benevolent creature, **67** The plan begins, **68** Forest of Endor, **69** Droids on the move, **70** Blasting a speeder bike, **71** Approaching the Princess, **72** A new-found friend, **73** Princess Leia's smile, **74** Under attack!, **75** Imperial Scout peril!, **76** Entering the throne room, **77** The Skywalker factor, **78** Captured by the Ewoks, **79** The netted Droid, **80** All hail C-3PO!, **81** Royal treatment, **82** Sitting with royalty, **83** Levitated by Luke, **84** The Ewok leaders, **85** Logray and Chief Chirpa, **86** Help from Princess Leia, **87** Will Han Solo be dinner?, **88** The baby Ewok, **89** The forest creatures, **90** The Droid and the Ewok, **91** R2-D2 meets Wicket, **92** Unexpected allies, **93** Serious situation, **94** Luke Skywalker's destiny, **95** Quiet, C-3PO!, **96** Imperial Biker Scout, **97** Biker Scout and the battlefield, **98** Han Solo's approach, **99** The ultimate mission, **100** Ready for action!, **101** Ambushed by the Empire, **102** Observed by the Ewoks, **103** The courageous Ewoks, **104** Prisoners!, **105** Revising their plan, **106** AT-ST (All Terrain Scout Transport), **107** The forest fighters, **108** Break for freedom!, **109** R2-D2—Hit!, **110** Chewbacca triumphant!, **111** Ewoks to the rescue!, **112** Battle in the forest, **113** Stormtrooper attack!, **114** The victorious rebels, **115** Time out for love, **116** Facing the emperor, **117** Master of terror, **118** The Emperor's offer, **119** Battle of the Jedi, **120** Lightsaber battle!, **121** Darth Vader is down!, **122** The confrontation, **123** The Death Star raid, **124** Military leader Admiral Ackbar, **125** Within the Death Star, **126** Victory celebration!, **127** Congratulating Wedge, **128** The triumphant trio, **129** The heroic Droids, **130** Toward brighter tomorrows, **131** Checklist I, **132** Checklist II

Wrapper..$1–$2
Display Box...$2–$4
Unopened Pack..$2–$4
Unopened Box..$25–$50

FIRST SERIES STICKERS

No. 1–33.

Complete Set..$10–$20
Single Stickers...$.50–$1

1 Yoda, **2** Ewok, **3** Musician from Jabba's court, **4** Jabba the Hutt, **5** Alien from Jabba's court, **6** Admiral Ackbar, **7** Princess Leia dressed as Bounty Hunter, **8** Han Solo, **9** Princess Leia, **10** Luke Skywalker, **11** Han Solo, **12** C-3PO, **13** Chewbacca the Wookie, **14** Sy Snoodles, **15** Baby Ewok, **16** Lando Calrissian's co-pilot, **17** Lando Calrissian, **18** R2-D2, **19** Obi-Wan Kenobi (Ben), **20** Luke Skywalker on Jabba's ship, **21** Luke Skywalker, **22** Gammorrean Guard, **23** Salacious Crumb (Jabba's jester), **24** Treebo the Ewok, **25** Boba Fett on Tatooine, **26** Wicket the Ewok, **27** Jabba the Hut, **28** Lando dressed as one of Jabba's guards, **29** Max Rebbo, one of Jabba's musicians, **30** Princess Leia dresses in forest attire on Endor, **31** Princess Leia, **32** Han Solo, **33** Stormtrooper on Endor

SECOND SERIES CARDS

No. 133–221.

Complete Set..$10–$20
Single Cards..$.25–$.50

133 Title card, **134** Path to destiny, **135** Captured!, **136** The courageous Jedi, **137** The victors, **138** Wicket and Princess Leia, **139** The Emperor's arrival, **140** Sail barge battle!, **141** Luke Skywalker, the Jedi, **142** The approach of Wicket, **143** A close call!, **144** Above the Scarlacc Pit, **145** Admiral Ackbar's defenders, **146** R2-D2 on Endor, **147** Boba Fett attacks!, **148** Deadly plunge!, **149** Lando Calrissian's disguise, **150** Soldiers of the Empire, **151** A curious Ewok, **152** A pensive Luke Skywalker, **153** The captive Princess, **154** Luke Skywalker surrenders, **155** Thoughts of a Jedi, **156** The Jaws of death, **157** Princess Leia has the Force!, **158** Arrival of the Emperor, **159** Reunion on Endor, **160** Toward the Sarlacc Pit, **161** Sail barge creatures, **162** Friends of the Alliance!, **163** The dreaded rancor, **164** Face of terror, **165** Inside Jabba the Hutt's palace, **166** The Ewok village, **167** A collection of creatures, **168** Alert to danger!, **169** Walking the plank!, **170** A Gammorrean Guard emerges, **171** The Imperial Fleet, **172** Jabba the Hutt on the sail barge, **173** Escorted to the Ewok village, **174** A monstrous guest!, **175** Village of the Ewoks, **176** Aboard the sail barge, **177** Confronting their destiny, **178** "Where's Princess Leia?", **179** Horror from the Pit, **180** "Give in to your hate!", **181** Awaiting His Majesty, **182** A mother Ewok and child, **183** A concerned Princess Leia, **184** Lead singer by Snootles, **185** The arrival of Boushh, **186** Master of his child, **187** Star lovers, **188** Luke Skywalker . . . now a Jedi, **189** Battle of the Bunker!, **190** Portrait of Wicket, **191** Trapped by the Empire, **192** Their secret revealed, **193** Rethinking the plan, **194** Snagged by the Ewoks, **195** Han Solo's in trouble!, **196** Is Han Solo giving up?, **197** The Royal Droid, **198** Princess Leia intercedes, **199** Rescuing Han Solo, **200** Father versus son, **201** Luke Skywalker, Jedi Warrior, **202** The young Jedi Knight, **203** Han Solo is alive!, **204** Lando Calrissian undercover, **205** Horrendous creature, **206** Corridors of the Imperial Destroyer!, **207** Surrounded by Ewoks, **208** Gammorrean Guard profile, **209** Hulking Gammorrean Guard, **210** Guest of Jabba the Hutt, **211** A full-fledged Jedi!, **212** Bizarre alien creatures, **213** Headquarters frigate, **214** TIE Interceptor (¾ view), **215** The nearly completed Death Star, **216** Rebel cruiser, **217** TIE Interceptor (front view), **218** The Emperor's shuttle, **219** Portrait of Chewbacca, **220** Checklist

Wrapper..$1–$2
Display Box...$2–$4
Unopened Pack..$2–$4
Unopened Box..$25–$50

SECOND SERIES STICKERS

No. 34–55.

Complete Set..$10–$20
Single Stickers...$.50–$1

34 Darth Vader, 35 Luke Skywalker, 36 Han Solo, 37 Princess Leia, 38 C-3PO, 39 R2-D2, 40 Wicket the Ewok, 41 Admiral Ackbar of the rebel forces, 42 Chewbacca the Wookie, 43 The Emperor, 44 The Millennium Falcon, 45 R2-D2 and C-3PO at Jabba's fortress, 46 Han tied to a branch on Endor by the Ewoks, 47 Luke, Leia, and Jabba the Hutt in Jabba's throne room, 48 Lando Calrissian and his co-pilot in the Millennium Falcon 49 Princess Leia and Jabba the Hutt in Jabba's throne room, 50 Luke, Leia, Han, Chewbacca, and the Droids on Endor, 51 Leia shushing C-3PO, Chewbacca laughing in the background, 52 Darth Vader, 53 R2-D2 and Ewoks on Endor, 54 Han Solo at door of Stormtrooper bunker on Endor, 55 Salacious Crumb (Jabba's jester)

Note: *Topps also issued a 10″ square collector's album to hold stickers.*

Giant Photo Cards, Topps
Empire Strikes Back

5″ × 7″, No. 1–30, photos on the front with no lettering. Cards 1–15 have checklist with small photos for first half of set, cards 16–30 have checklist for second half of set.

Complete Set..$30–$50
Single Card...$1–$2

1 Darth Vader, 2 Lando Calrissian, 3 Chewbacca, 4 Princess Leia and Han Solo, 5 Luke Skywalker and Darth Vader, 6 Darth Vader and Lando Calrissian, 7 Han Solo and C-3PO, 8 Luke Skywalker and Yoda, 9 Inside the Millennium Falcon, 10 Chewbacca and Princess Leia, 11 Darth Vader interviews Bounty Hunters, 12 Yoda, 13 Luke rides his Tauntaun, 14 TIE Fighter and the Millennium Falcon, 15 The Imperial Snow Walkers, 16 Darth Vader, 17 Yoda, 18 Darth Vader's flagship, 19 Luke Skywalker rides his Tauntaun, 20 X-Wing and planet Dagobah, 21 Luke, Princess Leia, C-3PO, and R2-D2, 22 Snowspeeders battle the Imperial Snow Walkers, 23 Darth Vader, 24 Han Solo, 25 Stormtrooper, 26 Luke Skywalker, 27 Luke being trained by Yoda, 28 C-3PO, 29 Yoda, 30 Luke, Princess Leia, Han Solo, and Chewie prepare to defend themselves

Wrapper...$1–$2
Display Box..$1–$2
Unopened Pack..$2–$4
Unopened Box ....$50–$100

Foreign and Promotional
Star Wars

Culturama De Centro America, Costa Rica, small size with collector's album, set of 187....
....$35–$45
Dixie Cups, United States, back of box cutout photos, 5″ × 6″, set of eight ....$15–$25
General Mills Cereal, United States, 1977 series, one sticker in each box of cereal, set of 16
....$30–$50
General Mills Cereal, United States, 1978 series, one card per box, set of 18........$15–$25
Opeechee Chewing Gum, Canada, same as Topps series, with minor changes, information in French and Spanish, set of 264 ....$50–$100
Pacosa Dos International, Spain, small size with collector's album, set of 187........$35–$60
Panini, Italy, 1977, same as Topps with collector's album, set of 256 stickers............$50–$75
Streets Ice Cream, Ltd., Australia, shaped bottom, cutouts, set of 12 ....$20–$35
Tip Top Ice Confections, New Zealand, one sticker inside each wrapper of R2-D2 ice cream, set of 15..$20–$30
Topps Chewing Gum, England, same as series I and II, but whiter backs, set of 132 ....
....$30–$50
Topps Chewing Gum, Mexico, same as American series I except card information is in Spanish, set of 66 ....$20–$30
Topps Chewing Gum, United States, 1978, Star Wars sugar-free bubble gum, wrapper has picture of different characters, inside wrapper contains a movie photo pin-up, set of 56..........
....$100–$200
Wonder Bread, United States, 1977, 16 different, came one card to a loaf of bread ..$15–$20

Empire Strikes Back

Bibb Linen Co., United States, side of box cutouts, 5″ × 5″, set of six ....$8–$15
Burger King/Coca-Cola, 1980, The Empire Strikes Back and Star Wars, series 1—36 cards, attached by threes with perforations, photographs from the film, red lettering at base, no numbering, distributed to customers 12 years old and younger, 3½″ × 2½″. Set ....$10–$20
   Space Adventurer Han Solo, Raid on the Death Star!, R2-D2 and C-3PO, Luke disguised as a Stormtrooper!, Flight of the Millennium Falcon, Captured by the Jawas!, The wonderful Droid, R2-D2, Han Solo in action, Star pilots prepare for battle!, One of the Sand people, Stormtrooper attack, Jedi warrior Ben Kenobi, Cantina denizens!, Han and Chewie mean business!, Search for the Droids, Weird Cantina patrons!, Jawas of Tatooine, Princess Leia Organa, Yoda, the Jedi Master, Darth Vader and Boba Fett, Chase through the asteroids, Snowswept Chewbacca, Battle of the lightsabers!, The Bounty Hunters, Yoda on Dagobah, Pursued by the Empire, Luke astride his Tauntaun, The defenders of freedom!, Luke's training, The Imperial Stormtrooper, Droids inside the rebel base, Seduced by the Dark Side!, The dashing Han Solo, Luke instructed by Yoda
Dixie, United States, 1981, Empire Strikes Back story cards, four per box, set of 24...............
....$10–$25
Vanderhout, Dutch, 1980, album for cards, color cover shows C-3PO and Empire logo.........
....$3–$5
York, 1980, Canadian, set of six round picture cards ....$10–$15

Return of the Jedi

Kellogg's Star Wars Sticker/Trading (Jedi) Issue, distributed inside boxes of C-3PO Cereal, 1984. Peel-away sticker on top, trading card underneath. Pictures from Empire Strikes Back and Return of the Jedi. Set of ten ....$15–$30

Stickers	Cards
Luke	Luke with lightsaber
Han Solo	Group with Imperial Shuttle
R2-D2	R2-D2
C-3PO	C-3PO and R2-D2
C-3PO and R2-D2	C-3PO with Ewoks
Ewok	R2-D2 with Ewoks
Yoda	Luke and Yoda
Darth Vader	Darth, Lando, and Boba Fett
Chewbacca	Chewbacca with Boussh
Princess Leia	Leia, C-3PO, and Chewbacca

Panini 180 Cards, 1983, Italian market set ....$15–$25

INDEX